Contents

Preface

By studying the principles of horticulture, one is able to learn how and why plants grow and develop. In this way, horticulturists are better able to understand the responses of the plant to various conditions, and therefore to perform their function more efficiently. They are able to *manipulate* the plant so that they achieve their own particular requirements of maximum yield and/or quality at the correct time. The text therefore introduces **the plant** in its own right, and explains how a correct naming method is vital for distinguishing one plant from another. The internal structure of the plant is studied in relation to the functions performed in order that we can understand why the plant takes it particular form. The environment of a plant contains many variable factors, all of which have their effects, and some of which can dramatically modify growth and development. It is therefore important to distinguish the effects of these factors in order to have precise control of growth. The environment which surrounds the parts of the plant above the ground includes factors such as light, day-length, temperature, carbon dioxide and oxygen, and all of these must ideally be provided in the correct proportions to achieve the type of growth and development required. The growing medium is the means of providing nutrients, water, air and usually anchorage for the plants.

In the wild, a plant will interact with other plants, often to different species and other organisms to create a balanced community. Ecology is the study of this balance. In growing plants for our own ends we have created a new type of community which creates problems – problems of competition for the environmental factors between one plant and another of the same species, between the crop plant and a weed, or between the plant and a pest or disease organism. These latter two competitive aspects create the need for **crop protection**.

It is only by identification of these competitive organisms (weeds, pests and diseases) that the horticulturist may select the correct method of control. With the larger pests there is little problem of recognition, but the smaller insects, mites, nematodes, fungi and bacteria are invisible to the naked eye and, in this situation, the grower must rely on the **symptoms** produced (type of damage). For this reason, the pests are covered under major headings of the organism, whereas the diseases are described under symptoms. Symptoms (other than those caused by an organism) such as frost damage, herbicide damage and mineral deficiencies may be confused with pest or disease damage, and reference is made in the text to this problem. Weeds are broadly identified as perennial or annual problems. References at the end of each chapter encourage students to expand their knowledge of symptoms. In an understanding of crop protection, the **structure** and **life cycle** of the organism must be emphasized in order that specific measures, e.g. chemical control, may be used at the correct time and place to avoid complications such as phytotoxicity, resistant pest production or death of beneficial organisms. For this reason, each weed, pest and disease is described in such a way that **control** measures follow logically from an understanding of its biology. More detailed explanations of **specific** types of control, such as biological control, are contained in a separate chapter where concepts such as economic damage are discussed.

This book is not intended to be a reference source of weeds, pests and diseases; its aim is to show the *range* of these organisms in horticulture. References are given to texts which cover symptoms and life cycle stages of a wider range of organisms. Latin names of species are included in order that confusion about the varied common names may be avoided.

Growing media include soils and soil substitutes such as composts, aggregate culture and nutrient film technique. Usually the plant's water and mineral requirements are taken up from the growing medium by roots. Active roots need a supply of oxygen, and therefore the root environment must be managed to include aeration as well as to supply water and minerals. The growing medium must also provide anchorage and stability, to avoid soils that 'blow', trees that uproot in shallow soils or tall pot plants that topple in lightweight composts.

The components of the soil are described to enable satisfactory root environments to be produced and maintained where practicable. Soil conditions are modified by cultivations, irrigation, drainage and liming, while fertilizers are used to adjust the nutrient status to achieve the type of growth required.

The use of soil substitutes, and the management of plants grown in pots, troughs, peat bags and other containers where there is a restricted rooting zone, are also discussed in the final chapter.

In this, the fourth edition of the book the authors have continued to make changes to align the text with the significant syllabus changes to courses for which the book has been produced to support.

Revision has also been made in the light of recommendations from key users. This has lead to a substantial increase in the nature of the plant's immediate environment, its **microclimate**, its measurement and methods of modifying it. This is put in context by the inclusion of a full discussion of the **climate**, the underlying factors that drive the weather systems and the nature of local climates in the British Isles. There has been an expansion of the **genetics** section to accommodate the need for more details on dominance and dihybrid crosses along with an introduction to genetic modification (GM), and the associated crown gall, to reflect the interest in this topic in the industry. The changes in the classification system have been accommodated and the plant divisions revised without losing the familiar names of plant groups, such as monocotyledon, in the text. The plant science chapters have also been revised to accommodate requests for more detail on the principles underlying horticultural practices such as grafting, photosynthesis and the subject of growth. Concerns about **biodiversity** and the interest in plant conservation are addressed along with more detail on ecology and companion planting. More examples of plant adaptions have been provided and more emphasis has been given to the practical application of plant form in the amenity use of plants. The use of pesticides has been revised in the light of continued regulations about their use. More details have been included on the use of inert growing media such as **rockwool** with a substantial expansion on the use of water in protected culture.

For the first time there has been the use of **colour** to illustrate the text and the number of supporting diagrams has been increased. There has been a determination by the authors to further integrate topics across the whole span of the text and to provide further practical examples related to the growing of plants in all aspects of horticulture. The indexing and key word cross-referencing have been improved to help the reader integrate the subject areas and to pursue related topics without laborious searching.

The text of this new edition has been amended to support students studying for the National Certificate in Horticulture, National Diplomas in Horticulture and the RHS General Examination in Horticulture. The knowledge and understanding acquired from this textbook will be of value in preparation for Vocational Qualifications (NVQ and SVQ) assessments up to Level III. Furthermore, the content of the text will provide an excellent introductory text for those studying the RHS Advanced Certificate and Diploma modules, Higher National Diplomas and those without a strong science background embarking on Foundation Degrees. It is also intended to be a comprehensive source of information for the keen gardener, especially for those taking City and Guilds Certificate in Gardening modules.

Acknowledgements

We are indebted to the following people:

Marjorie Adams and Ann Taylor have shown tremendous patience, skill and fortitude in interpreting our script for typing and Richard Adams for technical support.

Gill Parks has developed and printed many of the photographs, and we are also grateful to John Parkin for the microscope photographs of plant structure.

Drs J. Bridge, D. Govier and S. Dowbiggin read the early drafts and provided valuable suggestions. Ms Marion Brown very kindly had read the proofs.

Thanks are also due to the following individuals, firms and organizations that provided photographs and tables:

Agricultural Lime Producers' Association.
Dr C.C. Doncaster, Rothamsted Experimental Station.
Dr P.R. Ellis, National Vegetable Research Station.
Mr P. Evans, Rothamsted Experimental Station.
Dr D. Govier, Rothamsted Experimental Station.
Dr M. Hollings, Glasshouse Crops Research Institute.
Mr Neale Holmes-Smith
Dr M.S. Ledieu, Glasshouse Crops Research Institute.

Ministry of Agriculture, Fisheries and Food.
Muntons Microplants Ltd, Stowmarket, Suffolk.
Shell Chemicals.
Soil Survey of England and Wales.
Mr Alex Taylor
Dr E. Thomas, Rothamsted Experimental Station.

Two figures illustrating weed biology and chemical weed control are reproduced after modification, with permission of Drs H.A. Roberts, R.J. Chancellor and J.M. Thurston and those illustrating the carbon and nitrogen cycles are adapted from diagrams devised by Dr E.G. Coker who also provided the photograph of the apple tree with exposed root system.

Thanks for help in revision are due to:

Christine Atkinson; Chris Bird, Sparsholt College; David Carey, Hadlow College; Tom Cole, Capel Manor; Stephen Dando, Brackenhurst College; Tom Deans, Reaseheath College; Josie Hutchinson, Brooksby College; Rita Lait, Harlow Carr; Andy Parrett, Yvonne Sharp, Oaklands College; John Sales; John Salter, Elmwood College; David Steed; Hilary Thomas, Capel Manor and John Truscott, de Montford University. Particular thanks are given to Bob Evans for his help in the preparation of the fourth edition.

1

Horticulture in Context

> *The many facets of horticulture have much in common, each being concerned with the growing of plants. Despite the wide range of the industry, embracing as it does activities from the preparation of a cricket square to the production of uniformly sized cucumbers, there are common principles which guide the successful management of the plants involved. This chapter puts the industry, the plant, the plant communities and ecology into perspective, and considers the aspects of conservation and organic growing and looks forward to the more detailed explanations of horticultural practice in the following chapters.*

Horticulture may be described as the practice of growing plants in a relatively intensive manner. This contrasts with agriculture, which, in most western European countries, relies on a high level of machinery use over an extensive area of land, consequently involving few people in the production process. However, the boundary between the two is far from clear, especially when considering large-scale *vegetable production*. Horticulture often involves the manipulation of plant material, e.g. by propagation (*see* Chapter 7), by changing the above-ground environment (*see* Chapter 2), or by changing the root environment (*see* Chapter 13). There is a fundamental difference between **production**

horticulture, whether producing plants themselves or plant products, and **service horticulture**, i.e. the development and upkeep of gardens and landscape for their amenity, cultural and recreational values. Increasingly, horticulture can be seen to be involved with social well-being and welfare through the impact of plants for human physical and mental health. It encompasses environmental protection and conservation through large- and small-scale landscape design and management. Where the tending of plants for leisure moves from being horticulture to **countryside management** is another moot point. In contrast, the change associated with replacing plants with alternative materials, as in the creation of artificial playing surfaces, tests what is meant by horticulture in a quite different way.

This book concerns itself with the principles underlying the growing of plants in the following sectors of horticulture:

- *Turf culture*, which includes decorative lawns and sports surfaces for football, cricket, golf, etc.
- *Landscaping, garden construction and maintenance* which involves the skills of construction together with the development of planted areas (**soft landscaping**). Closely associated with this sector is **grounds maintenance**, the maintenance of trees and woodlands (**arboriculture** and **tree surgery**), specialist features within the garden such as walls and patios (**hard landscaping**) and the use of water (**aquatic gardening**).

- *Interior landscaping* is the provision of semi-permanent plant arrangements inside conservatories, offices and many public buildings, and involves the skills of careful plant selection and maintenance.
- *Protected cropping* enables plant material to be supplied outside its normal availability, e.g. chrysanthemums all the year round, tomatoes to a high specification over an extended season, and cucumbers from an area where the climate is not otherwise suitable. Plant propagation, providing seedlings and cuttings, serves outdoor growing as well as the greenhouse industry. Protected culture, mainly using low or walk-in polythene tunnels, is increasingly import-ant in the production of vegetables, salads, bedding plants and flowers.
- *Nursery stock* is concerned with the production of soil-grown or container-grown shrubs and trees. Young stock of fruit may also be established by this sector for sale to the fruit growers: **soft fruit** (strawberries, etc.), **cane fruit** (raspberries, etc.) and **top fruit** (apples, pears, etc.).
- *Professional gardening* covers the growing of plants in gardens including both public and private gardens and may reflect many aspects of the areas of horticulture described. It often embraces both the decorative and productive aspects of horticulture.
- *Garden centres* provide plants for sale to the public, which involves handling plants, maintaining them and providing horticultural advice. A few have some production on site, but stock is usually bought in.

THE PLANT

There is a feature common to all the above aspects of horticulture: the grower or gardener benefits from knowing about the factors that may increase or decrease the plant's growth and development. The main aim of this book is to provide an understanding of how these factors contribute to the ideal performance of the plant in particular circumstances. In most cases this will mean optimum growth, as in the case of a salad crop such as lettuce

where a fast turnover of the crop with once over harvesting that grades out well. However, the aim may equally be restricted growth, as in the production of dwarf chrysanthemum pot plants or in the case of a lawn that would otherwise require frequent cutting. The main factors to be considered are summarized in Figure 1.1, which shows where in this book each is discussed.

It must be stressed that the incorrect functioning of any one factor may result in undesired plant performance. It should also be understood that factors such as the soil conditions, which affect the underground parts of the plant, are just as important as those such as light, which affect the aerial parts. The nature of soil is dealt with in Chapter 13. Increasingly, plants are grown in alternatives to soil such as composts and rockwool and these are reviewed in Chapter 17.

Weather generally plays an important part in horticulture. It is not surprising that those involved in growing plants have such a keen interest in weather forecasting in order to establish whether conditions are suitable to work in or because of the direct effect of temperature, water and light on the growth of plants. The climate is dealt with in Chapter 2, which also gives particular attention to the microclimate (the environment the plant actually experiences).

A single plant growing in isolation with no competition is as unusual in horticulture as it is in nature. However, specimen plants such as leeks, marrows and potatoes, lovingly reared by enthusiasts looking for prizes in local shows, grow to enormous sizes when freed from competition. In landscaping, specimen plants are placed away from the influence of others so that they not only stand out and act as a point of focus, but also can attain perfection of form. A pot plant such as a fuchsia is isolated in its container, but the influence of other plants, and the consequent effect on its growth, depend on spacing. Generally, plants are to be found in groups, or communities.

PLANT COMMUNITIES

Neighbouring plants can have a significant effect on each other since there is competition for factors

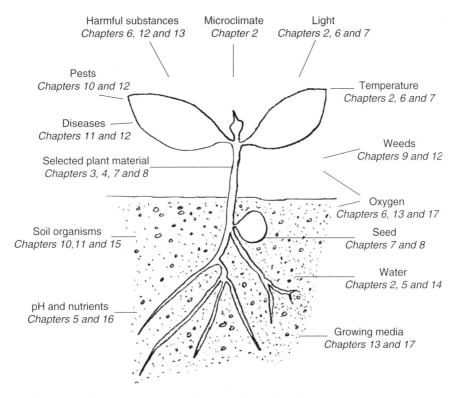

Harmful substances
Chapters 6, 12 and 13

Microclimate
Chapter 2

Light
Chapters 2, 6 and 7

Pests
Chapters 10 and 12

Diseases
Chapters 11 and 12

Selected plant material
Chapters 3, 4, 7 and 8

Soil organisms
Chapters 10, 11 and 15

pH and nutrients
Chapters 5 and 16

Temperature
Chapters 2, 6 and 7

Weeds
Chapters 9 and 12

Oxygen
Chapters 6, 13 and 17

Seed
Chapters 7 and 8

Water
Chapters 2, 5 and 14

Growing media
Chapters 13 and 17

Figure 1.1 *The requirements of the plant for the healthy growth and development.*

such as root space, nutrient supply and light. As in natural plant communities, some of the effects can be beneficial whilst others are detrimental to the achievement of horticultural objectives.

Single species communities

When a plant community is made up of one species it is referred to as a **monoculture**. On a football field there may be only ryegrass (*Lolium* species) with all plants closely spaced just a few millimetres apart. Each plant species, whether growing in the wild or in the garden, may be considered in terms of its own characteristic spacing distance (or plant density).

In a decorative border, the bedding plant *Alyssum* will be spaced at 15 cm intervals, whereas a *Pelargonium* plant may require 45 cm between plants. For decorative effect, the larger plants are normally placed towards the back of the border and at a wider spacing.

In a field of potatoes, the plant spacing will be closer within the row (40 cm) than between the rows (70 cm) so that suitable soil ridges can be produced to encourage tuber production, and machinery can pass unhindered along the row.

In nursery stock production, small trees are often planted in a square formation with a spacing ideal for the plant species, e.g. the conifer *Chamaecyparis* at 1.5 m. The recent trend in producing commercial top fruit, e.g. apples, is towards small trees (using dwarf rootstocks) in order to produce manageable plants with easily harvested fruit. This has resulted in spacing reduced from 6 to 4 m.

A correct plant-spacing distance is that most likely to provide the requirements shown in Figure 1.1 at their optimum level. Too much competition for soil space by the roots of adjacent plants, or for light by their leaves, would quickly lead to reduced growth. Three ways of overcoming this problem may be seen in the horticulturist's activities of transplanting seedlings from trays into pots, increasing the spacing of pot plants in greenhouses, and hoeing out a proportion of young vegetable seedlings from a densely sown row. An interesting horticultural practice, which reduces root competition, is the deep-bed system, in which a 1 m depth of well-structured and fertilized soil enables deep root penetration. However, growers often deliberately grow plants closer to restrict growth in order to produce the correct size and the desired uniformity as in the growing of carrots for the processing companies.

Whilst spacing is a vital aspect of plant growth, it should be realized that the grower might need to adjust the physical environment in one of many other specific ways in order to favour a chosen plant species. This may involve the selection of the correct light intensity; a rose, for example, whether in the garden, greenhouse or conservatory, will respond best to high-light levels, while a fern will grow better in low light.

Another factor may be the artificial alteration of day length, as in the use of 'black-outs' and cyclic lighting in the commercial production of chrysanthemums to induce flowering. Correct soil acidity (pH) is a vital aspect of good growing: heathers prefer high acidity, whilst saxifrages grow more actively in non-acid (alkaline) soils. Soil texture, e.g. on golf greens may need to be adjusted to a loamy sand type at the time of green preparation in order to reduce compaction and maintain drainage.

Each crop species has particular requirements, and it requires the skill of the horticulturist to bring all these together. In greenhouse production, sophisticated control equipment may monitor air and root-medium conditions every few minutes, in order to provide the ideal day and night requirements.

Competition between species

The subject of '**ecology**' deals with the interrelationship of plant (and animal) species and their environment. Below are described some of the ecological terms and concepts which most commonly apply to the natural environment, where human interference is minimal. It will be seen, however, that such concepts have relevance to horticulture, with its more controlled environment.

Habitat.   This term refers to the place where a plant or animal lives. For a water lily, its only habitat is a pond or a slow-moving river. In contrast, a species such as a blackberry may be found in more than one habitat, e.g. heathland, woodland and in hedges. The common rat, often associated with humans, is seen in various habitats (e.g. farms, sewers, hedgerows and food stores).

On a smaller scale, the term **microhabitat** is used to pinpoint a particular part of a plant or soil where a particular plant, or a small organism occurs. The glasshouse whitefly occupies the under-leaf microhabitat of a *Fuchsia* plant. The wilt fungus *Verticillium albo-atrum* lives in the xylem microhabitat of plants.

Niche.   Given the dynamic way that plants and animals grow in size and numbers, and compete against each other, it is not surprising to find that each species of plant or animal has an ideal location for its best growth and survival (this location is called its *niche*). The term 'niche' carries with it an idea of the specialization that a species may exhibit within a community of other plants and animals. A niche involves, for plants, such factors as temperature, light intensity, humidity, pH, nutrient levels, etc. For animals such as pests and their predators, there are also factors such as preferred food and chosen time of activity determining the niche.

The term is rather hard to apply in an exact way, since each species shows a certain tolerance of the factors mentioned above, but it is useful in emphasizing specialization within a habitat. The biologist, Gause, showed that no two species can exist together if they occupy the same niche. One species will, sooner or later, start to dominate.

For the horticulturalist, here is the important concept that for each species planted in the ground, there is an ideal combination of factors to be considered if the plant is to grow well. Although this concept is an important one, it should not be taken to an extreme. Most plants tolerate a range of conditions, but the closer the grower gets to the ideal, the more likely they are to establish a healthy plant.

Biome. This term refers to a wider grouping of organisms than that of a habitat. As with the term habitat, the term biome is biological in emphasis, concentrating on the species present. This is in contrast to the wider ecosystem concept described below. Commonly recognized biomes would be 'temperate woodland', 'tropical rainforest', 'desert', 'alpine' and 'steppe'. About 35 types of biomes are recognized worldwide, the classification being based largely on climate; on whether they are land based or water based; on geology and soil; and on altitude above sea level. Each example of a biome will have within it many habitats. Different biomes may be characterized by markedly different potential for annual growth. For example, a square metre of temperate-forest biome may produce about 10 times the growth of an alpine biome.

Ecosystem. This term brings emphasis to both the community of living organisms and to their non-living environment. Examples of ecosystems are a wood, a meadow, a chalk hillside, a shoreline and a pond. Implicit within this term (unlike the terms habitat, niche and biome) is the idea of a whole integrated system, involving both the living (biotic) plant and animal species, and the non-living (abiotic) units such as soil and climate, all reacting together within the ecosystem. Ecosystems can be described in terms of their **energy flow**, showing how much light is stored (or lost) within the system as plant products such as starch (in the plant) or as organic matter (in the soil). Also, the several other systems such as carbon, nitrogen and sulphur cycles (*see* pages 186–8), and water conservation (*see* page 182) may also be presented as features of the ecosystem in question.

Succession. Communities of plants and animals change with time. The species composition will change as will the number of individuals within each species. This process of change is known as 'succession'. Two types of succession are recognized. The first one, known as **primary succession** is seen in a situation of uncolonized ground. Sand dunes, disused quarries and landslide locations are

good examples. This process runs in parallel with the formation of soils (*see* page 152). It can be seen that plant and animal species from outside the new habitat will be the ones involved in colonization.

The second (and more common example in Britain) is **secondary succession**, where a bare habitat is formed after vegetation has been burnt, or chopped down, or covered over with a flood silt deposit. In this situation, there will often be plant seeds and animals which survive under the barren surface to begin colonization again, by bringing top soil to the surface, or at least some of its associated beneficial bacteria and other micro-organisms.

The first species to establish are aptly called the 'pioneer community'. In felled woodland, these may well be mosses, lichens, ferns and fungi. In contrast, a drained pond will probably have *Sphagnum* moss, reeds and rushes, more at home in this wetter habitat.

The second succession stage will see plants such as grasses, foxgloves and willow herb taking over in the ex-woodland area. Grasses and sedges are the most common examples seen in the drained pond. Such early colonizing species are sometimes referred to as **opportunistic**. They often have similar characteristics to horticultural weeds (*see* page 88), viz. extended seed germination period, rapid plant establishment, short time to maturity and considerable seed production. They quickly cover over the previously bare ground.

The third succession stage involves larger plants, which, over a period of about 5 years, gradually reduce the opportunists' dominance. Honeysuckle, elder, and bramble are often species that appear in ex-woodland, whilst willows and alder occupy a similar position in the drained pond. The term **competitive** is applied to such species.

The fourth stage introduces tree species that have the potential to achieve considerable heights. It may well happen that both the ex-woodland and the drained pond situation end up with the same tree species such as birch, oak and beech. These are described as **climax** species, and will dominate the habitat for a long time so long as it remains undisturbed, by natural or human forces. Within the climax community, there often remain some specimens of the preceding succession stages, but they are now held in check by the ever-larger trees.

This short discussion of succession has emphasized the plant members of the community. As succession progresses along the four stages described, there is usually an increase in **biodiversity**, i.e. increase in numbers of plant species. It should also be borne in mind that, for every plant species there will be several animal species dependent on it for food, and thus succession brings biodiversity in the plant, animal, fungal and bacterial realms.

Succession to the climax stage is often quite rapid, occurring within 20 years from the occurrence of the bare habitat. Once established, a climax community of plants and animals in a natural habitat will usually remain quite stable for many years.

Food chains

At any one stage along the succession sequence in a habitat, there will be a particular combination of living things (organisms) associated with the plant **community**. In a crop situation, e.g. strawberries, the crop plant itself is the main source of energy for the other organisms, and is referred to, along with any weeds present, as the **primary producer** in that habitat. Any pest (e.g. aphid) or disease (e.g. mildew) feeding on the strawberries is termed a **primary consumer**, whilst a ladybird eating the aphid is called a **secondary consumer**. A habitat may include also tertiary, quaternary consumers, etc. Any combination of species such as the above is referred to as a **food chain** and each stage within a food chain is called a *trophic level*: e.g.

strawberry → aphids → ladybird

In the pond habitat, a comparable food chain would be

green algae → Daphnia crustacean → minnow fish

Within any plant community, there will be comparable food chains to the one described above. It is normally observed that in a monoculture such as strawberry, there will be a relatively short period of time (up to 5 years) for a complex food chain to develop. However, in a long-term stable habitat such as oak woodland or a mature garden-growing perennial, there will be many plant (primary producer) species, allowing many food chains to occur. Furthermore, primary consumer species, e.g. caterpillars and pigeons, may be eating from several different plant types, whilst secondary consumers such as predatory beetles and tits will be devouring a range of primary consumers on several plant species. In this way, a more complex, interconnected community is developed, called a **food web**. An interesting feature of succession is that, as time passes, the habitat acquires a greater diversity of species, and more complex food webs, including the important rotting organisms such as fungi which break down ageing and fallen trees. Effective countryside management particularly utilizes these food webs, and succession principles when striking a balance between the production of species diversity and the maintenance of an acceptably orderly managed area.

Decomposers

At this point, the whole group of organisms involved in the recycling of dead organic matter (called **decomposers** or **detritovores**) should be mentioned in relation to the food-web concept. The organic matter (*see* also Chapter 15) derived from dead plants and animals of all kinds is digested by a succession of species: large animals by crows, large trees by bracket fungi, small insects by ants, roots and fallen leaves by earthworms, mammal and bird faeces by dung beetles, etc. Subsequently, progressively small organic particles are consumed by millipedes, springtails, mites, nematodes, fungi and bacteria to eventually create the organic molecules of humus that are so vital a source of nutrients, and a means of soil stability in most plant-growth situations. It can thus be seen that although decomposers do not normally link directly to the food web; they are often eaten by secondary consumers. They also are extremely important in supplying inorganic nutrients to the primary producer plant community.

Sustainable development

From the content of preceding paragraphs, it can be seen that the provision of as extensive a system of varied habitats, each with its complex food web, in as many locations as possible, is increasingly being considered desirable in a nation's environment provision. In this way, a wide variety of species numbers (**biodiversity**) is maintained, habitats are more attractive and species of potential use to mankind are preserved. In addition, a society that bequeaths its natural habitats and ecosystems to future generations in an acceptably varied, useful and pleasant condition, is contributing to the **sustainable development** of that nation.

Biomass

At any one time in a habitat, the amount of living plant and animal tissue (**biomass**) can be measured or estimated. In production horticulture, it is clearly desirable to have as close to 100 per cent of this biomass in the form of the primary producer (crop), with as little primary consumer (pest or disease) as possible present. On the other hand, in a natural woodland habitat, the primary producer would represent approximately 85 per cent of the biomass, the primary consumer 3 per cent, the secondary consumer 0.1 per cent and the decomposers 12 per cent. This weight relationship between different trophic levels in a habitat (particularly the first three) is often summarized in graphical form as the 'pyramid of species'.

A further concept relevant to the plant–animal relationships relates to energy. The process of photosynthesis enables the plant to retain, as chemical energy, approximately 1 per cent of the sun's radiant energy falling on the particular leaf's surface. As the plant is consumed by primary consumers, approximately 90 per cent of the leaf energy is lost from the biomass, either by respiration in the primary consumer, by heat radiation from the primary consumer's body or as dead organic matter excreted by the primary consumer. This

organic matter, when incorporated in the soil, remains usefully within the habitat.

The relative levels in a habitat of its total biomass as against its total organic matter are an important feature. This balance can be markedly affected by *physical factors* such as soil type, by *climatic factors* such as temperature, rainfall and humidity, and can also be affected by the management system operating in that habitat (or ecosystem). For example, a temperate woodland on 'heavy' soil with 750 mm annual rainfall will maintain a relatively large soil organic matter content, permitting good nutrient retention, good water retention and resisting soil erosion even under extreme weather conditions. For these reasons, the habitat is seen to be relatively stable. On the other hand, a tropical forest on a 'light' soil with 3000 mm rainfall will have a much smaller soil organic matter reserve, with most of its carbon compounds being used in the living plants and animal tissues. As a consequence, nutrient and moisture retention and resistance to soil erosion are usually low; serious habitat loss can result when wind damage or human interference occurs. For temperate horticulturists, the main lesson to keep in mind is that high levels of soil organic matter are usually highly desirable, especially in sandy soils that readily lose organic matter.

Garden considerations

When contemplating the distribution of our favourite species in the garden (ranging from tiny annuals to huge trees), a thought may be given to their position in the succession process back in the natural habitat of their country of origin. Some will be species commonly seen to colonize bare habitats. Most garden species will fall into the middle stages of succession. A few, whether they be trees, climbers or low-light-requirement annuals or perennials will be species of the climax succession.

The garden border contains plant species, which compete aggressively in their native habitat. The artificial interplanting of species from different parts of the world (the situation found in almost all gardens), may give rise to unexpected results as this competition continues year after year. Such experiences are part of the joys, and the heartaches of gardening.

Companion planting

An increasingly common practice in some areas of horticulture (usually in small-scale situations) is the deliberate establishment of two or more plant species in close proximity with the intention of deriving some cultural benefit from their association. Such a situation may seem at first sight to encourage competition rather than mutual benefit. Many supporters of companion planting reply that plant and animal species, in the natural world show more evidence of mutual cooperation than of competition.

Some experimental results have given support to the practice, but most evidence remains anecdotal. It should be stated, however, that whilst most commercial producers in western Europe grow blocks of a single species, in many other parts of the world two or three different species are interplanted as a regular practice.

Several biological mechanisms are quoted in support of companion planting:

- *Nitrogen fixation*. Legumes such as beans convert atmospheric nitrogen to useful plant nitrogenous substances (*see* page 188) by means of *Rhizobium* bacteria in their root nodules. Beans interplanted with maize are claimed to improve maize's growth by increasing its nitrogen uptake.
- *Pest suppression*. Some plant species are claimed to deter pests and diseases. Some examples are listed. Onions, sage and rosemary release chemicals that mask the carrot crop's odour thus deterring the most serious pest, carrot fly from infesting the carrot crop. African marigolds (*Tagetes*) deter glasshouse whitefly and soil-borne nematodes by means of the chemical, thiophene. Wormwood (*Artemisia*) releases methyl jasmonate as vapour that reduces caterpillar feeding, and stimulates plants to resist diseases such as rusts. Chives and garlic reduce aphid attacks.

- *Beneficial habitats*. Some plant species present a useful refuge for beneficial insects (*see* page 139), such as ladybirds, lacewings and hoverflies. In this way, companion planting may preserve a sufficient level of these predators and parasites to effectively counter pest infestations. The following examples may be given: carrots attract lacewings; yarrow (*Achillea*), ladybirds; goldenrod (*Solidago*), small parasitic wasps; poached-egg plant (*Limnanthes*) attracts hover flies. In addition, some plant species can be considered as traps for important pests. Aphids are attracted to nasturtiums, flea beetles to radishes thus keeping the pests away from a plant such as cabbage.
- *Spacial aspects*. A pest or disease, specific to a plant species will spread more slowly if the distance between individual plants is increased. Companion planting achieves this goal. For example, potatoes interplanted with cabbages will be less likely to suffer from potato blight disease. The cabbages similarly would be less likely to be attacked by aphid.

ORGANISMS OCCURRING ON PLANT SURFACES

A further aspect of species interaction can be seen at the microscopic level in the soil and on the aerial parts of plants. The plant surfaces of leaves, stems and roots present an environment for beneficial and for damaging organisms. The latter group are described in Chapter 11.

Research has indicated the complex microbial composition of plant surfaces and their importance to successful plant growth. The term **rhizosphere** is used to describe the environment for bacteria, fungi, mites and nematodes situated around the root, whilst the comparable term **phyllosphere** applies to the environment on the leaf and stem.

Rhizosphere

The term 'rhizosphere' refers to the environment closely adjacent to roots. It is relatively stable compared to the leaf environment, particularly in terms of temperature and humidity. The components of this zone (soil mineral particles, water, gases, organic matter and micro-organisms) interact to influence root activity. The area of root near the tip produces numerous root hairs, which are important for absorption of water and nutrients. In the area behind this tip zone, however, there is often a complex association of micro-organisms whose contribution to root activity may be equal to that of the root hairs. The most striking members of this community are the fungi that develop close associations with the root tissues, often invading the root, but not damaging it. These fungi are known as **mycorrhizae**. The tiny strands spread out into the surrounding soil and act as an additional absorption system for the plant.

Most plant families have been shown to utilize mycorrhizae. In some plant families, e.g. Rosaceae, there is a well-developed network of tiny fungal strands (*see* Hyphae, page 122) inside the roots, whereas in others, such as the Ericaceae (heathers), the hyphae develop in masses outside but very close to the root surface. Some mycorrhizae belong to the group of fungi that produces toadstools (the Basidiomycota group). The toadstool species are often quite specific to the plant on which they have an association. For example, the fly agaric (*Amanita regalis*), the red toadstool well known in fairy tales, is a mycorrhizal fungus found mainly on spruce roots.

Mycorrhizae have been shown in many species to have important roles in absorbing water and nutrients such as phosphate and nitrate. Phosphate is the least mobile major nutrient in the soil, and the plant must 'reach out' to find it (*see* page 203). Mycorrhizae help plants to do this. An extreme case is the heather (*Erica*) genus which is often found growing in acidic soils, where phosphate is insoluble, where root growth is limited, and where there are very few bacteria involved in the breakdown of organic matter. Under these conditions, there is a special need for mycorrhizae. Whilst the mycorrhizae are responsible for assisting the root's function, there is a reciprocal process whereby the plant, in return, provides the fungus with sugars and other organic substances favourable for its growth. This plant–fungus association is a good example of symbiosis (*see* page 186).

The use of sterile, compost-based growing media for propagation may deny the young plants a source of mycorrhizal fungi. Consequently, specially prepared cultures of these fungi are sometimes introduced into growing media to stimulate plant growth, e.g in the production of young conifers. The particular requirements of the mycorrhizae have to be met where they are important for the plants success, e.g. many orchids are grown in translucent pots in order to provide for the light requirement of the species of fungus concerned.

Phyllosphere

Phyllosphere bacteria on the leaf may be 'casual' or 'resident'. Casual species, e.g. *Bacillus* mainly arrive from soil, roots and water, and are more common on the leaves close to the ground. These species are capable of rapid increase under favourable conditions, but then may decline. Resident species, e.g. *Pseudomonas*, may be weakly parasitic on plants, but more commonly persist (often for considerable periods) without causing damage, and on a wide variety of plants.

There is increasing evidence that phyllosphere bacteria may reduce the infection of diseases such as powdery mildews, *Botrytis* diseases on lettuce and onion, and turfgrass diseases. Practical disease control strategies by phyllosphere organisms have not been developed, but there remains the general principle that a healthy, well-nourished plant will be more likely to have organisms on the leaf surface available to reduce fungal infection.

CONSERVATION

The ecological aspects of horticulture have been highlighted in recent years by the **conservation** movement. One aim is to promote the growing of crops and maintaining of wildlife areas in such a way that the natural diversity of wild species of both plants and animals is maintained alongside crop production, with a minimum input of fertilizers and pesticides. Major public concern has focused on the effects of intensive production (monoculture) and the indiscriminate use by horticulturists and farmers of pesticides and quick-release fertilizers.

An example of wildlife conservation is the conversion of an area of regularly mown and 'weed-killed' grass into a wild flower meadow, providing an attractive display during several months of the year. The conversion of productive land into wild flower meadow requires lowered soil fertility (in order to favour wild species establishment and competition), a choice of grass seed species with low opportunistic properties, and a mixture of selected wild flower seed. The maintenance of the wild flower meadow may involve harvesting the area in July, having allowed time for natural flower seed dispersal. After a few years, butterflies and other insects become established as part of the wild flower habitat.

The horticulturist has three notable aspects of conservation to consider. Firstly, there must be no wilful abuse of the environment in horticultural practice. Nitrogen fertilizer used in excess has been shown, especially in porous soil areas, to be washed into streams, since the soil has little ability to hold on to this nutrient (*see* page 202). The presence of nitrogen in watercourses encourages abnormal multiplication of micro-organisms (mainly algae). On decaying, these remove oxygen sources needed by other stream life; particularly fish (a process called 'eutrophication').

Secondly, another aspect of good practice increasingly expected of horticulturists is the intelligent use of pesticides. This involves a selection of those materials least toxic to man and beneficial animals, and particularly excludes those materials that increase in concentration along a food chain. Lessons are still being learned from the widespread use of dichlorodiphenyltrichloroethane (DDT) in the 1950s. Three of DDT's properties should be noted. Firstly, it is long lived (residual) in the soil. Secondly, it is absorbed in the bodies of most organisms with which it comes into contact, being retained in the fatty storage tissues. Thirdly, it increases in concentration approximately 10 times as it passes to the next member of the food chain. As a consequence of its chemical properties, DDT was seen to achieve high concentrations in the bodies of secondary (and tertiary) consumers, such as hawks, influencing the reproductive rate and hence causing a rapid decline in their numbers in the 1960s. This experience rang alarm bells for society in general, and DDT was eventually banned in most of Europe.

The irresponsible action of allowing pesticide spray to drift onto adjacent crops, woodland or rivers has decreased considerably in recent years. This has in part been due to the Food and Environment Protection Act (FEPA) 1985, which has helped raise the horticulturist's awareness of conservation.

A third aspect of conservation to consider is the deliberate selection of trees, features and areas which promote a wider range of appropriate species in a controlled manner. A golf course manager may set aside special areas with wild flowers adjacent to the fairway, preserve wet areas and plant native trees. Planting bush species such as hawthorn, field maple and spindle together in a hedgerow provides variety and supports a mixed population of insects for cultural control of pests. Tit and bat boxes in private gardens, an increasingly common sight, provide attractive homes for species that help in pest control. Continuous hedgerows will provide safe passage for mammals. Strips of grassland maintained around the edges of fields form a habitat for small mammal species as food for predatory birds such as owls. Gardeners can select plants for the deliberate encouragement of desirable species (nettles and *Buddleia* for butterflies; *Rugosa* roses and *Cotoneaster* for winter feeding of seed-eating birds; poached-egg plants for hoverflies).

It is emphasized that the **development and maintenance of conservation areas require continuous management and consistent effort to maintain the desired balance of species and required appearance of the area**. As with gardens and orchards, any lapse in attention will result in **invasion by unwanted weeds and trees**.

In a wider sense, the conservation movement is addressing itself to the loss of certain habitats and the consequent disappearance of endangered species such as orchids from their native areas. Horticulturists are involved indirectly because some of the peat used in growing media is taken from lowland bogs much valued for their rich variety of vegetation. Considerable efforts have been made to find alternatives to peat in horticulture (*see* page 213) and protect the wetland habits of the British Isles.

Conservationists also draw attention to the thoughtless neglect and eradication of wild-ancestor strains of present-day crops; the gene-bank on which future plant breeders can draw for further improvement of plant species. There is also concern about the extinction of plants especially those on the margins of deserts that are particularly vulnerable if global warming leads to reduced water supplies. *In situ* conservation mainly applies to wild species related to crop plants and involves the creation of natural reserves to protect habitats such as wild apple orchards and there is particular interest in preserving species with different ecological adaptions. *Ex situ* conservation includes whole plant collections in botanic gardens, arboreta, pineta and gene-banks where seeds, vegetative materials and tissue cultures are maintained. The botanic gardens are coordinated by the Botanic Gardens Conservation International (BGCI), which is based at Kew Gardens, London, and are primarily concerned with the conservation of wild species.

Large national collections include the **National Fruit Collection** at Brogdale, Kent (administered by Wye College) and the Horticultural Research International at Wellesbourne, Birmingham, holds vegetables. The **Henry Doubleday Heritage Seed Scheme** conserves old varieties of vegetables which were once commercially available but which have been dropped from the National List (and so become illegal to sell). They encourage the exchange of seeds. **The National Council for the Conservation of Plants and Gardens** (NCCPG) was set up by the Royal Horticultural Society at Wisley in 1978 and is an excellent example of professionals and amateurs working together to conserve stocks of extinction-threatened garden plants, to ensure the availability of a wider range of plants and to stimulate scientific, taxonomic, horticultural,

historical and artistic studies of garden plants. There are over 600 collections of ornamental plants encompassing 400 genera and some 5000 plants. A third of these are maintained in private gardens but many are held in publicly funded institutions such as colleges, e.g. *Sarcococca* at Capel Manor College in North London, *Escallonia* at the Duchy College in Cornwall, *Penstemon* and *Philadelphus* at Pershore College and *Papaver orientale* at the Scottish Agricultural College, Auchincruive. Rare plants are identified and classified as 'pink sheet' plants.

ORGANIC GROWING

The **organic movement** broadly believes that crops and ornamental plants should be produced with as little disturbance as possible to the balance of microscopic and larger organisms present in the soil, and also in the above-soil zone. This stance can be seen as closely allied to the conservation position, but with the difference that the emphasis here is on the balance of micro-organisms. Organic growers maintain soil fertility by the incorporation of animal manures, or green manure crops such as grass–clover leys. The claim is made that crops receive a steady, balanced release of nutrients through their roots; in a soil where earthworm activity recycles organic matter deep down, the resulting deep root penetration allows an effective uptake of water and nutrient reserves.

The use of most **pesticides** and **quick-release fertilizers** is said to be the main cause of species imbalance, and formal approval for licensed organic production may require soil to have been free from these two groups of chemicals for at least 2 years. Control of pests and diseases is achieved by a combination of resistant cultivars and 'safe' pesticides derived from plant extracts, by careful rotation of plant species, and by the use of naturally occurring predators and parasites. Weeds are controlled by mechanical and heat-producing weed-controlling equipment, and by the use of mulches. The balanced **nutrition** of the crop is said to induce greater resistance to pests and diseases, and the taste of organically grown food is claimed to be superior to that of conventionally grown produce.

The organic production of food and non-edible crops at present represents about 5 per cent of the European market. The European Community Regulations (1991) on the 'organic production of agricultural products' specify the substances that may be used as 'plant-protection products, detergents, fertilizers or soil conditioners' (*see* pages 148 and 194). 'Conventional horticulture' is, thus, still by far the major method of production and this is reflected in this book. However, it should be realized that much of the subsistence cropping and animal production in the Third World could be considered 'organic'.

FURTHER READING

Allaby, M. *Concise Oxford Dictionary of Botany* (Oxford University Press, 1992).

Ayres, A. *Gardening without Chemicals* (Which/ Hodder & Stoughton, 1990).

Baines, C. and Smart, J. *A Guide to Habitat Creation* (Packard Publishing, 1991).

Blake, F. *Organic Farming and Growing* (Crowood Press, 1987).

Carson, R. *Silent Spring* (Hamish Hamilton, 1962).

Carr, S. and Bell, M. *Practical Conservation* (Open University/Nature Conservation Council, 1991).

Caplan, B. *Complete Manual of Organic Gardening* (Headline Publishing, 1992).

Dowdeswell, W.H. *Ecology Principles and Practice* (Heinemann Educational Books, 1984).

Innis, D.Q. *Intercropping and the Scientific Basis of Traditional Agriculture* (Intermediate Technology Publications, 1997).

Lampkin, N. *Organic Farming* (Farming Press, 1990).

Lisansky, S.G., Robinson, A.P. and Coombs, J. *Green Growers Guide* (CPL Scientific Ltd, 1991).

Mannion, A.M. and Bowlby (Editors). *Environmental Issues in the 1990s* (John Wiley & Sons, 1992).

Tait, J. *et al. Practical Conservation* (Open University, 1988).

2

Climate and Microclimate

Sunlight, temperature, rainfall, humidity, frost and wind affect plant growth directly by affecting its physiology or indirectly through influencing working conditions. In general, growers either seek to modify conditions to enable them to grow the plants of their choice, or select plants that will grow in a given location.

This chapter explains how weather systems are created and outlines the climate of the British Isles including the nature of the growing season. This is contrasted with some of the main types of climate from which plants have been collected. Factors such as altitude, topography and proximity to large bodies of water that modify the general climate to produce the local climates are described. The microclimate that the plant actually experiences is described and methods of modifying conditions are discussed.

The chapter ends by looking at the measurement of temperature, humidity, rainfall, wind and sunshine and how the automation of environmental control in protected cropping is achieved.

THE SUN'S ENERGY

The energy that drives our weather systems comes from the sun in the form of **solar radiation**. The sun radiates waves of **electro-magnetic energy** and high-energy particles into space. This type of energy can pass through a vacuum and through gases. The **Earth intercepts the radiation energy** and, as these energy waves pass through the atmosphere, they are absorbed, scattered and reflected by gases, air molecules, small particles and cloud masses (*see* Figure 2.1).

About a quarter of the total radiation entering the atmosphere reaches the Earth's surface directly. Another 18 per cent arrives indirectly after being scattered (diffused). The surface is warmed as the molecules of rock, soil and water at the surface become excited by the incoming radiation; the energy in the electro-magnetic waves is converted to heat energy as the surface material absorbs the radiation. A reasonable estimate of energy can be calculated from the relationship between radiation and sunshine levels. The amounts received in the British Isles are shown in Figure 2.2, where the differences between winter and summer are illustrated.

However, the nature of the surface has a significant effect on the proportion of the incoming radiation that is absorbed. The sea can absorb over 90 per cent of radiation when the sun is overhead, whereas for land it is generally between 60 and 90 per cent. Across the Earth darker areas tend to absorb more energy than lighter ones; dark soils warm up more quickly than light ones; afforested areas more than lighter, bare areas with grass in between. Where the surface is white (ice or snow) nearly all the radiation is reflected.

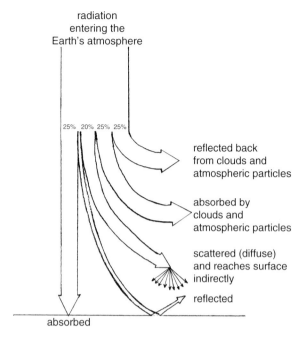

radiation
entering the
Earth's atmosphere

25% 20% 25% 25%

reflected back
from clouds and
atmospheric particles

absorbed by
clouds and
atmospheric particles

scattered (diffuse)
and reaches surface
indirectly

reflected

absorbed

Figure 2.1 *Radiation energy reaching the Earth's surface showing the proportions that are reflected back and absorbed as it passes through the atmosphere and that which reaches plants indirectly. About 5 per cent of the radiation strikes the Earth's surface but is reflected back (this is considerably more if the surface is light coloured, e.g. snow, and as the angle of incidence is increased).*

Effect of latitude

Over the Earth's surface some areas become warmed more than others because of the differences in the quantity of radiation absorbed. Most energy is received around the Equator where the sun is directly overhead and the radiation hits the surface at a right angle. In higher latitudes, such as the UK, more of the radiation is lost as it travels further through the atmosphere. Furthermore the energy waves strike the ground at an acute angle leading to a high proportion being reflected before affecting the molecules at the surface (*see* Figure 2.3).

As a consequence of the above, more energy is received than lost over the span of a year in the region on either side of the Equator between the Tropic of Capricorn and Tropic of Cancer. In contrast, to the north and south of these areas more energy radiates out into space, which would lead to all parts of this region becoming very cold. However, air and water (making up the Earth's atmosphere and oceans) are able to redistribute the heat.

Movement of heat and weather systems

Heat energy moves from warmer areas (i.e. those at a higher temperature) into cooler areas (i.e. those at a lower temperature), and there are three types of energy movement involved. **Radiation** energy moves efficiently through air (or a vacuum), but not through water or solids. Heat is transferred from the Earth's surface to the lower layers by **conduction**. As soil surfaces warm up in the spring, temperatures in the lower layers lag behind, but this is reversed in the autumn as the surface cools and heat is conducted upwards from the warmer lower layers. At about 1m down the soil temperature tends to be the same all the year round (about 10°C in lowland Britain).

Heat generated at the Earth's surface is also available for redistribution into the atmosphere. However, air is a poor conductor of heat (which explains its usefulness in materials used for insulation such as polystyrene foam, glass fibre and wool). This means that, initially, only the air immediately in contact with the warmed surface gains energy. Although the warming of the air layers above would occur only very slowly by conduction, it is the process of **convection** that warms the atmosphere above. As fluids are warmed they expand, take up more room and become lighter. Warmed air at the surface becomes less dense than that above, so air begins to circulate with the lighter air rising and the cooler denser air falling to take its place; just as like a convector heater warming up a room. This circulation of air is referred to as **wind**.

In contrast, the water in seas and lakes is warmed at the surface making it less dense which tends to keep it near the surface. The lower layers gain heat very slowly by conduction and generally

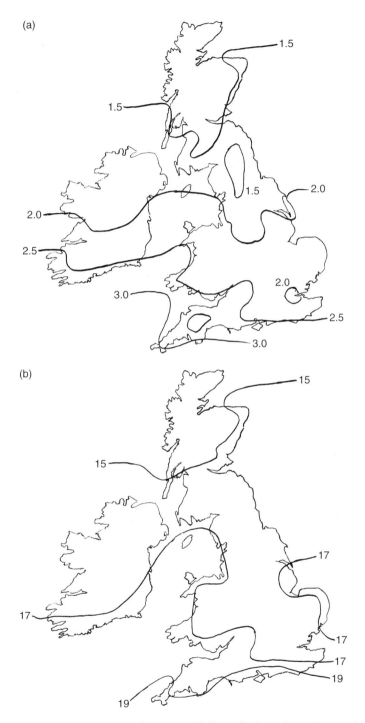

Figure 2.2 *Radiation received in the British Isles; mean daily radiation given in megajoules per metre square: (a) January and (b) July.*

depend on gaining heat from the surface by turbulence. Large-scale water **currents** are created by the effect of tides and the winds blowing over them.

On a global scale, the differences in temperature at the Earth's surface lead to our major **weather**

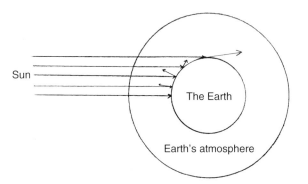

Figure 2.3 *Effect of angle of incidence on heating at the Earth's surface. A higher proportion of the incoming radiation is reflected as the angle of incidence increases. Note also that a higher proportion of the incoming radiation is absorbed or reflected back as it travels longer through the atmosphere in the higher latitudes.*

systems. Convection currents occur across the world in response to the position of the hotter and colder areas and the influence of the Earth's spin (the Coriolis Effect). These global air movements, known as the trade winds, set in motion the sea currents, which follow the same path but are modified as they are deflected by the continental land masses (*see* Figure 2.4).

WEATHER AND CLIMATE

Weather is the manifestation of the state of the atmosphere. Plant growth and horticultural operations are affected by weather; the influence of rain and sunshine is very familiar, but other factors such as frost, wind and humidity have important effects. It is not surprising that growers usually have a keen interest in the weather and often seek to modify its effect on their plants. Whilst most people depend on the public weather forecasting, some growers are prepared to pay for extra information and others believe in making their own forecasts, especially if their locality tends to have different weather from

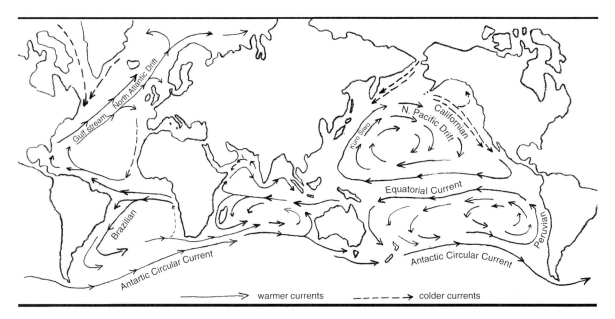

Figure 2.4 *Global sea and wind movements. Warmer and colder water currents set in motion by the wind circulation around the world.*

the rest of the forecast area. Weather forecasting is well covered in literature and only its component parts are considered here.

Climate can be thought of as a description of the weather experienced by an area over a long period of time. More accurately, it is the long-term state of the atmosphere. Usually the descriptions apply to large areas dominated by atmospheric systems (global, countrywide or regional) but local climate reflects the influence of the topography (hills and valleys), altitude and large bodies of water (lakes and seas).

Climate of the British Isles

The British Isles has a **maritime** climate, which is characterized by mild winters and relatively cool summers, that is a consequence of its proximity to the sea. This is because water has a much larger **heat capacity** than materials making up the land. As a consequence, it takes more heat energy to raise the temperature of water by 1°C, and there is more heat energy to give up when the water cools by 1°C when compared with rock and soil. Consequently, bodies of water warm up and cool down more slowly than adjoining land. The nearby sea thus prevents coastal areas becoming as cold in the winter as inland areas and also helps maintain temperatures well in the autumn.

In contrast, inland areas on the great land masses at the same latitude have a more extreme climate with very cold winters and hot summers: the

features of a **continental climate**. Whereas most of the British Isles lowland is normally above freezing for most of the winter, average mid-winter temperatures for Moscow and Hudson Bay (both continental climate situations) are nearer −15°C.

The **North Atlantic Drift**, the ocean current flowing from the Gulf of Mexico towards Norway, dominates the climate of the British Isles (*see* Figure 2.4). The effect of the warm water, and the prevailing south-westerly winds blowing over it, is particularly influential in the winter. It creates mild conditions compared with places in similar latitudes, such as Labrador and the Russian coast well to the north of Vladivostock, which are frozen in the winter.

The mixing of this warm moist air stream and the cold air masses over the rest of the Atlantic leads to the formation of a succession of **depressions**. These regularly pass over the British Isles bringing the characteristic unsettled weather with clouds and rain where cold air meets the moist warm air in the slowly swirling air mass. Furthermore, the moist air is also cooled as it is forced to rise over the hills to the west of the islands giving rise to **orographic rain**. In both instances clouds form when the dew point is reached (*see* page 25). This results in much higher rainfall levels in the west and north compared with the south and east of the British Isles. In contrast, a **rain shadow** is created on the opposite side of the hills because, once the air has lost water vapour and falls to lower, warmer levels, there is less likelihood of the dew point being reached again (*see* Figure 2.5). Depressions are also associated with windier weather.

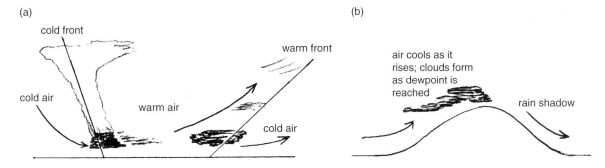

Figure 2.5 *Cloud formation and rainfall caused by (a) fronts and (b) higher ground (orographic rain). Note: warm air caused to rise over cold air or higher ground forms cloud when the air reaches the dew point of the air mass.*

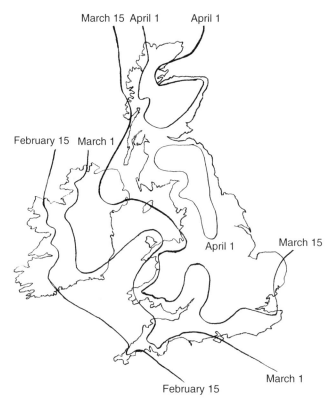

Figure 2.6 *Beginning of spring in the British Isles (average dates when soil reaches 6°C).*

The sequence of depressions (low pressure areas) is displaced from time to time by the development of **high-pressure areas** (anti-cyclones). These usually bring periods of settled drier weather. In the summer, these are associated with hotter weather with air drawn in from the hot European land mass or north Africa. In the winter, clear cold weather occurs as air is drawn in from the very cold, dry continental land mass. In the spring, these anti-cyclones often lead to radiation **frosts**, which are damaging to young plants and top fruit blossom.

The growing season

The outdoor growing season is considered to be the time when temperatures are high enough for plant growth. Temperate plants usually start growing when the daily mean temperatures are above

6°C. Spring in the south-west of the British Isles usually begins in March, but there is nearly a 2-months difference between its start in this area and the north-east (*see* Figure 2.6).

In contrast, as temperatures drop below 6°C the growing season draws to a close. This occurs in the autumn, but in the south-west of England and the west of Ireland this does not occur until December, and on the coast in those areas there can be 365 growing days per year. Within the general picture, there are variations of growth periods related to altitude, aspect, frost pockets, proximity of heat stores, shelter and shade: the so-called local climates and microclimates (*see* page 22). However, for most of mainland UK, the potential growing season spans between 8 and 9 months. Examples are given in Table 2.1.

Although this length of growing period will be a straightforward guide to grass growing days and

Table 2.1 Length of growing season in the British Isles

Area	Length of growing* season (days)	Time of year	
		Start	Finish
South-west Ireland	320	February 15	January 7
Cornwall	320	February 15	January 7
Isle of Wight	300	March 1	January 1
Anglesey	275	March 1	December 15
South Wales	270	March 15	December 15
East Lancashire	270	March 15	December 1
East Kent	265	March 15	November 28
North Ireland	265	March 15	November 28
Lincolnshire	255	March 21	November 25
Warwickshire	250	March 21	November 22
West Scotland	250	March 21	November 20
East Scotland	240	March 28	November 15
North-east Scotland	235	April 1	November 10

*Length of season is given for lower land in the area; reduce by 15 days for each 100 m rise into the hills (approximately 5 days per 100 ft).

the corresponding need for mowing, many other plants will stop growing as they complete their life cycle well before low temperatures affect them. Furthermore, there are plants whose growing season is defined differently. For example, most plants introduced from tropical or sub-tropical areas do not start growing until a mean daily temperature of 10°C is experienced. More significantly they are restricted by their intolerance of cold, so for many their outdoor season runs from the **last frost** of spring to the **first frost** of autumn.

Proximity to the sea not only increases the length of the growing season but also it reduces its intensity, i.e. the extent to which temperatures exceed the minimum for growth. Although inland areas have a shorter season they become much warmer more quickly before cooling down more rapidly in the autumn. The differences in intensity can be expressed in terms of **accumulated temperature units (ATUs)**.

ATUs are an attempt to relate plant growth and development to temperature and to the duration of each temperature. There is an assumption that the rate of plant growth and development increases with temperature. This is successful over the normal range of temperatures that affect most crops. On the basis that most temperate plants begin growing at temperatures above 6°C, the simplest method accredits each day with the number of degrees above the baseline of 6°C and accumulates them (note that negative values are not included). A second method calculates ATUs from weather records on a monthly rather than daily basis. Examples are given in Table 2.2. This method provides a basis for comparing the growing potential of different areas (*see* Table 2.3 and Figure 2.7).

Methods such as these can be used to predict likely harvest dates from different sowing dates. Growers may also use such information to calculate the required sowing date that will achieve a desired harvest date. In the production of crops for the freezing industry, it has been possible to smooth out the supply to the factory by this method. For example, a steady supply of peas over 6 weeks can be organized by using the local weather statistics to calculate when a range of early to late varieties of peas (i.e. with different harvest ATUs) should be sown.

More accurate methods, such as the **Ontario Units**, use day and night temperatures in the calculation. These have been used to study the

Table 2.2 Examples of ATUs calculated on (a) a daily basis and (b) monthly basis

Date	Average temperature (°C)	Temperature units (day-degrees)	ATUs (day-degrees)
(a)			
March 1	6	$1 \times 0 = 0$	0
March 2	7	$1 \times 1 = 1$	$0 + 1 = 1$
March 3	7	$1 \times 1 = 1$	$1 + 1 = 2$
March 4	5	$1 \times 0 = 0$	$2 + 0 = 2$
March 5	8	$1 \times 2 = 2$	$2 + 2 = 4$
March 6	7	$1 \times 1 = 1$	$4 + 1 = 5$
March 7	8	$1 \times 2 = 2$	$5 + 2 = 7$
(b)			
February	5	$28 \times 0 = 0$	0
March	7	$31 \times 1 = 31$	31
April	8	$30 \times 2 = 60$	91
May	11	$31 \times 5 = 155$	246
June	13	$30 \times 7 = 210$	456
July	14	$31 \times 8 = 248$	704

Table 2.3 AHUs for different places in Europe

Location	AHUs		
	May to June	July to September	Total
Edinburgh	300	700	1000
Glasgow	250	650	900
Belfast	300	700	1000
Manchester	425	875	1300
Norwich	430	950	1380
Birmingham	450	900	1350
Amsterdam	480	980	1460
Swansea	450	900	1350
London	470	950	1420
Littlehampton	450	950	1400
Channel Isles	480	970	1450
Paris	550	1100	1650
Bordeaux	600	1200	1800
Marseilles	800	1500	2300

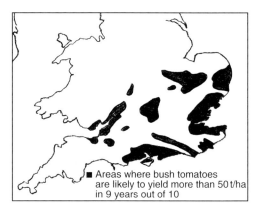

■ Areas where bush tomatoes are likely to yield more than 50 t/ha in 9 years out of 10

Figure 2.7 *Use of Ontario Units to determine the likely success of bush tomato crops.*

growth of tropical crops such as sunflowers, tomatoes and sweetcorn grown in a temperate area. Using this approach the extent to which bush tomatoes could be grown in southern England for an expected yield of 50 t/ha in 9 years out of 10 could be mapped (*see* Figure 2.7).

The accumulated heat unit (AHU) concept can also be used to estimate greenhouse-heating requirements by measuring the extent to which the outside temperature falls below a base or control temperature, called 'degrees of cold'. In January, a greenhouse maintained at 18°C at Littlehampton

Table 2.4 A summary of some of the world climates

Climatic region	Temperature			Rainfall	
	Range	Winter	Summer	Distribution	Total
Temperate					
Maritime	Narrow	Mild	Warm	Even	Moderate
Continental	Wide	Very cold	Very warm	Summer maximum	Moderate
Mediterranean	Moderate	Mild	Hot	Winter maximum	Moderate
Sub-tropical	Moderate	Mild*	Hot	Summer maximum	High
Tropical maritime	Narrow	Warm**	Hot	Even	Moderate
Equatorial	Narrow	Hot**	Hot	Even	High

*Frosts uncommon, **no frosts.

on the coast in Sussex accumulates, on average, 420 cold-degrees C compared with 430 for the same structure inland at Kew, near London. For a hectare of glass this difference of 10 cold-degrees C is the equivalent of burning an extra 5000 l of oil. This provides a useful means of assessing possible horticultural sites when other data such as solar heating and wind speed are all brought together. Other methods based on this concept enable growers to calculate when different varieties of rhubarb will start growing and the energy requirements for chill stores and refrigeration units.

World climates

In addition to **maritime** and **continental** climates already mentioned, there are many others including the **Mediterranean** climate (as found in southern parts of Europe, California, South Africa, Australia and central Chile) that is typified by hot, dry summers and mild winters. The characteristics of a range of the world climate types are given in Table 2.4. Plants native to these other areas can present a challenge for those wishing to grow them in the British Isles. To some extent plants are tolerant, but care must be taken when dealing with the plant's degree of hardiness (its ability to withstand all the features in the climate to which it is exposed). Plant species that originated in **sub-tropical** areas (such as south-east China and USA) tend to be vulnerable

to frosts and those from **tropical** and **equatorial** regions are most commonly associated with growing under complete protection such as in conservatories and hothouses.

LOCAL CLIMATE

Most people will be aware that even their regional weather forecast does not do justice to the whole of the area. The local climate reflects the influence of the topography (hills and valleys), altitude and lakes and seas that modifies the general influence of the atmospheric conditions.

Coastal areas are subject to the moderating influence of the body of water (*see* page 17). Water has a large heat capacity compared with other materials and this modifies the temperature of the surroundings.

Altitude. The climate of the area is affected by altitude: there is a fall in temperature with increase in height above sea level of nearly 1°C for each 100 m. The frequency of snow is an obvious manifestation of the effect. In the south-west of England, there are typically only 5 days of snow falling at sea level each year, whereas there are 8 days at 300 m. At higher altitudes the effect is more dramatic; in Scotland there are nearly 35 days per year at sea level, 38 days at 300 m but 60 days at 600 m.

The colder conditions at higher altitudes have a direct effect on the growing season. On the south-west coast of England, there are nearly 365 growing days per year but this decreases by 9 days for each 30 m above sea level. In northern England and Scotland there are only about 250 growing days which are reduced by 5 days per 30 m rise, i.e. to just 200 days at 300 m (1000 ft) above sea level in northern England.

Topography. The presence of slopes modifies climate by its aspect and its effect on air drainage. **Aspect** is the combination of the slope and the direction that it faces. North-facing slopes offer plants less sunlight than a south-facing one. This is dramatically illustrated when observing the snow on opposite sides of an east–west valley (or roofs in a street) when the north-facing sides are left white long after the snow has melted on the other side (*see* Plate 14); much more radiation is intercepted by the surface on the south-facing slope. Closer examination reveals considerable differences in the growth of the plants in these situations and it is quite likely that different species grow better in one situation compared with the other. Plants on such slopes experience not only different levels of light and heat but also different water regimes; south-facing slopes can be less favourable for some plants because they are too dry.

Air drainage. Cold air tends to fall, because it is denser than warm air, and collects at the bottom of slopes such as in valleys. **Frost pockets** occur where cold air collects; plants in such areas are more likely to experience frosts than those in similar land around them. This is why orchards, where blossom is vulnerable to frost damage, are established on the slopes away from the valley floor. Cold air can also collect in hollows on the way down slopes. It can also develop as a result of barriers such as walls and solid fences placed across the slope (*see* Figure 2.8). Permeable barriers such as trees making up shelterbelts are less of a problem as the cold air is able to leak through. Frost susceptible plants grown where there is good **air drainage** may well experience a considerably longer growing season. Gardens on slopes can be modified to advantage by having a low-permeable hedge above (a woodland is even better) and a very permeable one on the lower boundary.

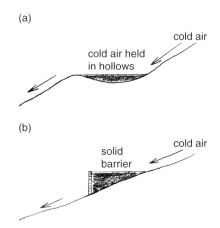

Figure 2.8 *The creation of frost pockets: (a) natural hollows on the sides of valleys and (b) effect of solid barriers preventing the drainage of cold air.*

MICROCLIMATES

The features of the immediate surroundings of the plant can further modify the local climate to create the precise conditions experienced by the plant. This is known as its **microclimate**. The significant factors that affect plants include nearness to a body of water or other heat stores, shelter or exposure, shade, altitude, aspect and air drainage. The modifications for improvement, such as barriers reducing the effect of wind, or worse, such as barriers causing frost pockets, can be natural or artificial. The microclimate can vary over very small distances. Gardeners will be familiar with the differences across their garden from the cool, shady areas to the hot, sunny positions and the implications this has in terms of the choice of plants and their management.

Growers improve the microclimate of plants when they establish windbreaks, darken the soil, wrap tender plants in straw, etc. More elaborate attempts involve the use of fleece, cold frames, cloches, polytunnels, greenhouses and conservatories. Automatically controlled, fully equipped greenhouses with irrigation, heating, ventilation fans, supplementary lighting and carbon dioxide are extreme examples of an attempt to create the ideal microclimate for plants.

(a)

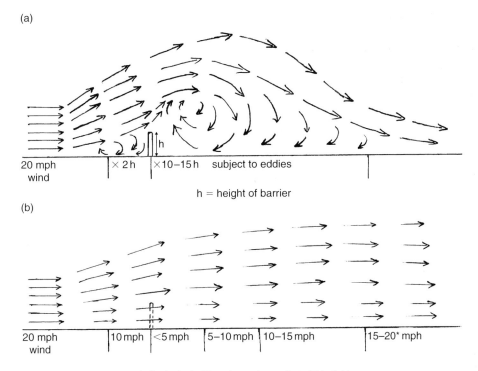

20 mph
wind
× 2 h   ×10–15 h   subject to eddies

h = height of barrier

(b)

20 mph
wind
10 mph   <5 mph   5–10 mph   10–15 mph   15–20* mph

*effect of wind break can be up to ×40 height

Figure 2.9 *The effect of windbreaks: (a) solid barriers tend to create eddies to windward and, more extensively, to lee-ward and (b) a permeable barrier tends to filter the air and reduce its speed without setting up eddies.*

Heat stores are materials such as water (*see* heat capacity, page 17) and brickwork, which collect heat energy and then release it to the immediate environment that would otherwise experience more severe drops in temperature. Gardeners can make good use of brick walls to extend the growing season and to grow plants that would otherwise be vulnerable to low temperatures. Water can also be used to prevent frost damage when sprayed onto fruit trees. It protects the blossom because of its **latent heat**: the energy that has to be removed from the water at 0°C to turn it to ice. This effect is considerable, and until the water on the surface has frozen, the plant tissues below are protected from freezing.

Shelter that reduces the effect of wind comes in many different forms. Plants that are grown in groups, or stands, experience different conditions from those that stand alone. As well as the self-sheltering from the effect of wind, the grouped plants also tend to retain a moister atmosphere, which can be an advantage but can also create conditions conducive to pest and disease attack. Walls, fences, hedges and the introduction of shelterbelts also moderate winds but there are some important differences in the effect they have. The reduction in flow downwind depends on the height of the barrier but there is a smaller but significant effect on the windward side (*see* Figure 2.9). The diagram also shows how turbulence can be created in the lee of the barrier, which can lead to plants being damaged by down forces. Solid materials such as brick and wooden fences create the most turbulence. In contrast, hedges and meshes filter the wind; the best effect coming from those with equal gap to solid presented to the wind. However, the introduction of a shelterbelt can bring problems if it holds back cold air to create a frost pocket (*see* page 22).

Shade reduces the radiation that the plant and its surroundings receive. This tends to produce a cooler, moister environment in which some species thrive (*see* Ecology, page 4). This should be taken into account when selecting plants for different positions outside in gardens. The grower will deliberately introduce shading on propagation units or on greenhouses in summer to prevent plants being exposed to high temperatures and to reduce water losses.

Plant selection. The horticulturist is always confronted with choices; plants can be selected to fit the microclimate or attempts can be made to change the microclimate to suit the plant that is desired.

Forecasting. Not only is there an interest in weather forecasting in order to plan operations such as cultivations, planting, frost protection, etc. but also for predicting pest and disease attacks, many of which are linked to factors such as temperature and humidity. Examples of outbreaks and methods of predicting them, such as **Critical Periods** that are used to predict potato blight, are to be found on page 124.

MEASUREMENT

The range of instruments in an agro-meteorological weather station are used to measure precipitation, temperature, wind and humidity. The measurements are normally made at 09.00 Greenwich Mean Time (GMT) each day. Most of the instruments are housed in a characteristic Stevenson's Screen although there are usually other instruments on the designated ground or mounted on poles nearby (*see* Plate 15).

Temperature

The normal method of measuring the **air temperature** uses a vertically mounted mercury-in-glass thermometer that is able to read to the nearest 0.1°C. In order to obtain an accurate result, thermometers used must be protected from direct radiation, i.e. the readings must be made 'in the shade'.

In meteorological stations, they are held in the **Stevenson's Screen** (*see* Plates 15 and 16), which is designed to ensure that accurate results are obtained at a standard distance from the ground. The screen's most obvious feature is the slatted sides, which ensure that the sun does not shine directly onto the instruments (*see* Radiation, page 13) whilst allowing the free flow of air around the instruments. The whole screen is painted white to reflect radiation that, along with its insulated top and base, keeps the conditions inside similar to that of the surrounding air. In controlled environments such as glasshouses the environment is monitored by instruments held in an **aspirated screen**, which draws air across the instruments to give a more accurate indication of the surrounding conditions.

The dry bulb thermometer is paired with a wet bulb thermometer that has, around its bulb, a muslin bag kept wet with distilled water. In combination, they are used to determine the **humidity** (*see* page 25). Robust mercury-in-glass thermometers set in sleeves are also used to determine soil temperatures; temperatures both at the soil surface and at 300 mm depth are usually recorded in agro-meterological stations. The highest and lowest temperatures over the day (and night) are recorded on the **Max–Min (maximum and minimum) thermometers** (*see* Plate 16) mounted horizontally on the floor of the screen. The maximum thermometer is a mercury-in-glass design, but with a constriction in the narrow tube near the bulb that contains the mercury. This allows the mercury to expand as it warms up, but when temperatures fall the mercury cannot pass back into the bulb and so the highest temperature achieved can be read off ('today's high'). Shaking the contents back into the bulb resets it. The minimum thermometer contains alcohol. This expands as it warms but as it contracts to the lowest temperature ('tonight's low') a thin marker is pulled down by the retreating liquid. As it is lightly sprung, the marker is left behind whenever the temperature rises. Using a magnet, or tilting, to bring the marker back to the surface of the liquid in the tube can reset the thermometer. In addition to the screen reading, there is another lowest-temperature thermometer placed at ground

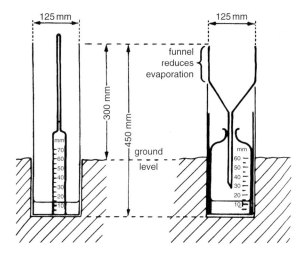

Figure 2.10 *Rain gauges: a simple rain gauge consists of a straight-sided can in which the depth of water accumulated each day can be measured with a dipstick. An improved design incorporates a funnel, to reduce evaporation, and a calibrated collection bottle. A rain gauge should be set firmly in the soil away from overhanging trees, etc. and the rim should be 300 mm above ground to prevent water flowing or bouncing in from surrounding ground.*

level giving 'over bare soil' and 'grass' temperatures (*see* Plate 15).

Precipitation

The term precipitation covers all the ways in which water reaches the ground as rain, snow and hail. It is usually measured with a **rain gauge** (*see* Figure 2.10).

Simple rain gauges are based on straight-sided cans set in the ground with a dipstick used to determine the depth of water collected. Accurate readings to provide daily totals are achieved with a design that maximizes collection, but minimizes evaporation losses by intercepting the precipitation water in a funnel. This leads to a tapered measuring glass calibrated to 0.1 mm. These gauges are positioned away from anything that affects the local airflow, e.g. buildings, trees and shrubs. They are set in the ground but with the rim above it to prevent water running in from the surroundings.

Recording rain gauges are available which also give more details of the pattern of rainfall within the 24 h periods. The 'tipping bucket' type has two open containers on a see-saw mechanism so arranged that as one bucket is filled, it tips and this is recorded on a continuous chart; meanwhile the other bucket is moved into position to continue collection.

Humidity

Humidity is the amount of water vapour in the atmosphere, i.e. the quantity of water held in the air. It increases as the air is heated because warm air is able to hold more water, as water vapour. Saturated air at 0°C can hold 3 g of water per kilogram of air, whereas it can hold 7 g at 10°C, 14 g at 20°C and 26 g at 30°C. The maximum figure for each temperature is known as its saturation point or **dew point** and if such air is cooled further, then water vapour condenses out to liquid water. One kilogram of saturated air at 20°C would give up 7 g of water as its temperature falls to 10°C. Indoors, this is seen as 'condensation' on the coolest surfaces in the vicinity; outdoors it happens when warm air mixes with cold air. Droplets of water form as clouds, fog and mist; dew forms on cool surfaces near the ground. If the air is holding less than the maximum amount of water it has **drying capacity**, i.e. it can take up water from its surroundings.

One of the most commonly used measurements of humidity is **relative humidity** (**RH**) which is **the ratio, expressed as a percentage, of the actual quantity of water vapour contained in a sample of air to the amount it could contain if saturated at the dry bulb temperature.** This is usually estimated by using the wet and dry bulb temperatures (*see* above) in conjunction with hygrometric tables. If the absolute humidity for air at 20°C (on the dry bulb) is found to be 14 g/kg this compares with the maximum of 14 g that can be held when such air is saturated. Therefore, the RH is 100 per cent. It can be seen that RH falls to 25 per cent when the wet bulb depression shows only 3.5 g of water is present. This means that its drying capacity has increased (it can now take up 10.5 g of water before it becomes saturated).

An example of working out the RH from wet and dry bulb measurements is given in Table 2.5.

The **whirling hygrometer** is the most accurate portable instrument used for taking air measurements (*see* Plate 17). The wet and dry bulb thermometers are mounted such that they can be rotated

Table 2.5 Calculation of RH from wet and dry bulb measurements

	Example			
	1	2	3	4
Dry bulb reading (A) (°C)	25	25	25	10
Wet bulb reading (°C)	21	19.5	18	6.5
Depression of the wet bulb (B) (°C)	4	5.5	7	3.5
RH (%)*	**70**	**60**	**50**	**60**

*Found from tables supplied with the hygrometer by reading along the dry bulb reading row (A) then find where the column intersects the depression of the wet bulb figure (B).

around a shaft held in the hand rather like a football rattle. The humidity is again calculated using hygrometric tables after the full depression of the wet bulb temperature has been found. **Hygrometers** made out of hair, which lengthens as the humidity increases, are also used to indicate humidity levels. These can be connected to a pen that traces the changes on a revolving drum carrying a hygrogram chart. Other hygrometers are based on the moisture absorbing properties of different materials including the low technology 'bunch of seaweed' comparable to Humidity on page 25.

Wind

Wind speed is measured with an **anemometer**, which is made up of three hemispherical cups on a vertical shaft ideally set 10 m above the ground (*see* Plate 15). The wind puts a greater pressure on the inside of the concave surface than on the

Table 2.6 The Beaufort Scale

Force	Description for use on land	Equivalent wind speed	
		m/s	Approximate miles/h
0	**Calm**: smoke rises vertically	0	0–1
1	**Light air**: wind direction seen by smoke drift rather than by wind vanes	2	1–3
2	**Light breeze**: wind felt on face, vane moves, leaves rustle	5	4–7
3	**Gentle breeze**: light flags lift, leaves and small twigs move	9	8–12
4	**Moderate breeze**: small branches move, dust and loose paper move	13	13–18
5	**Fresh breeze**: small leafy trees sway, crested wavelets on lakes	19	19–24
6	**Strong breeze**: large branches sway, umbrellas difficult to use	24	25–31
7	**Near gale**: whole trees move, difficult to walk against	30	32–38
8	**Gale**: small twigs break off, impedes all walking	37	39–46
9	**Strong gale**: slight structural damage	44	47–55
10	**Storm**: trees uprooted, considerable structural damage	52	55–63

convex one so that the shaft is spun round; the rotation is displayed on a dial usually calibrated in knots (nautical miles per hour) or metres per second. An older and still much used visual method is the **Beaufort Scale**; originally based on observations made at sea, it is used to indicate the wind forces at sea or on land (*see* Table 2.6).

Wind direction is indicated with a wind vane, which is often combined with an anemometer. Decorative wind vanes are a familiar sight, but the standard meteorological design comprises a pointer with a streamlined vertical plate on one end mounted so that it can rotate freely. The arrow shape points into the wind and the movements over a minute or so are averaged. The direction the wind is **coming from** is recorded as the number of degrees read clockwise from true north, i.e. a westerly wind is given as 270, south-easterly as 135 and a northerly one as 360 (000 is used for recording no wind).

Light

The units used when measuring the intensity of all wavelengths are watts per square metre (W/m^2), whereas lux (lumens/m^2) are used when only light in the photosynthetic range is being measured. More usually in horticulture, the **light integral** is used. The light sensors used for this measure the light received over a period of time and expressed as gram calories per square centimetre (gcals/cm^2) or megajoules per square metre (MJ/m^2). These are used to calculate the irrigation need of plants in protected culture.

The usual method of measuring **sunlight** at a metrological station is the Campbell–Stokes Sunshine Recorder, a glass sphere that focuses the sun's rays onto a sensitive card; the burnt trail indicates the periods of bright sunshine. Another approach is to use a **solarimeter**, which converts the incoming solar radiation to heat and then to electrical energy that can be displayed on a dial.

Automation

Increasingly, instrumentation is automated and, in protected culture, linked to computers programmed to maintain the desired environment by adjusting the ventilation and boiler settings. To achieve this, the computer is informed by external instruments measuring wind speed, air temperature and humidity, and internally by those measuring CO_2 levels, ventilation settings, heating pipe temperature, air temperature and humidity.

FURTHER READING

Bakker, J.C. *Greenhouse Climate Control – An Integrated Approach* (Wageningen Press, 1995).

Barry, R. *et al. Atmosphere, Weather and Climate*, 6th edition (Routledge, 1992).

Kamp, P.G.H. and Timmerman, G.J. *Computerised Environmental Control in Greenhouses* (IPC Plant, 1996).

Reynolds, R. *Guide to Weather* (Philips, 2000).

Taylor, J. *Weather in the Garden* (John Murray, 1996).

3

Classification and Naming

The pressures of evolution have produced widely varying plant types, found in differing habitats, and distinguished by characteristic structures and modes of life. An orderly system of classification seeks to ensure that the horticulturist, plant scientist and naturalist can identify and name any plant, animal, fungus or bacteria without ambiguity. A detailed procedure for naming organisms is therefore essential and is outlined with examples from the plant kingdom. Features of plants that are used in identification are discussed.

PRINCIPLES OF CLASSIFICATION

Any **classification** system involves the grouping of organisms or objects using characteristics common to members within the group. The organisms constituting the plant kingdom are distinguishable from animals in having sedentary growth, cellulose cell walls and polyploidy (*see* Chapter 8). They are able to change energy from one form, light, into another, organic molecules (autotrophic nutrition; *see* Photosynthesis, page 53). Animals, amongst other things, have no cell walls and rely on eating ready-made organic molecules (heterotrophic nutrition).

Terms that are used in classification are:

- **taxonomy**, which deals with the principles on which a classification is based,

- **systematics**, which identifies the groups to be used in the classification,
- **nomenclature**, which deals with naming.

Various systems have been devised throughout history, but a seventeenth-century Swedish botanist, **Linnaeus**, laid the basis for much subsequent work in the classification of plants, animals and also minerals. The original divisions of the plant kingdom were the main groupings of organisms according to their place in evolutionary history. Simple single-celled organisms from aquatic environments evolved to more complex descendants, multicellular plants with diverse structures, which were able to survive in a terrestrial habitat and develop sophisticated reproduction mechanisms.

The world of living organisms is currently divided into five kingdoms including Plantae (plants), Animalia (animals) and fungi. Less familiar are the two other categories Prokaryotae (bacteria) and the Protoctista (all other organisms that are not in the other kingdoms including algae and protozoa). In order to produce a universally acceptable system, the International Code of Botanical Nomenclature (ICBN) was formulated, which includes both non-cultivated plants and details specific to cultivated plants.

KINGDOM PLANTAE (PLANTS)

Plant **divisions** (the names ending in -phyta) are further subdivided into **class** (ending -psida), **order** (ending -ales), **family** (ending -aceae), **genus** and **species**. Species is the basic unit of classification, and is defined as **a group of individuals with the greatest mutual resemblance, which are able to breed amongst themselves**. A number of species with basic similarities constitute a genus (plural genera), a number of genera, a family and a number of families, an order (*see* example given in Table 3.1).

Divisions of the plant kingdom

The division of the plant kingdom is given in Table 3.2.

Mosses and liverworts. Over 25 000 plant species which do not have a vascular system (*see* page 42) are included in the divisions Bryophyta and Hepatophyta. They have distinctive vegetative and sexual reproductive structures, the latter producing spores that require damp conditions for survival. Many from both divisions are pioneer plants that play an important part in the early stages of soil formation. The low spreading carpets of vegetation also present a weed problem on the surface of compost in container-grown plants, on capillary benches, and around glazing bars on greenhouse roofs.

Ferns and horsetails, in the division Pteridophyta and Equisetophyta, have identifiable leaf, stem and root organs, but produce spores rather than seeds from the sexual reproduction process. Many species of ferns, e.g. maidenhair fern (*Adiantum cuniatum*), and some tropical horsetails, are grown for decorative purposes, but the common horsetail (*Equisetum arvense*), and bracken (*Pteris aquilina*) that spread by underground rhizomes, are difficult weeds to control.

Seed-producing plants (Superdivision: spermatophyta) contain the most highly evolved and structurally complex plants. There are species adapted to most habitats and extremes of environment. Sexual reproduction produces a seed, which is a small, embryo plant contained within a protective layer.

Conifers (Coniferophyta) are a large division of many hundred species that include the pines (Order: Pinales) and yews (Order: Taxales). Characteristically they produce 'naked' seeds, usually in cones, the female organ. They show some primitive features, and often display structural adaptations to reduce water loss (*see* Figure 5.3). There are very many important conifers. Some are major sources of wood or wood pulp, but within horticulture many are valued because of their interesting plant habits, and foliage shape and colours. For example, the Cupressaceae includes fast-growing species, which can be used as windbreaks, and small, slow-growing types very useful for rock gardens. The yews are a highly poisonous group of plants that includes the common yew (*Taxus baccata*) used in ornamental hedges and mazes. The division Ginkgophyta is represented by a single surviving species, the maidenhair tree (*Ginkgo biloba*), which has an unusual slit-leaf shape, and distinctive bright yellow colour in autumn.

Table 3.1 Classification. The lettuce cultivar 'Little Gem' used to illustrate the hierarchy of the classification up to kingdom

Kingdom	**Plantae**	**Plants**
Sub-kingdom	Tracheobionta	Vascular plants
Superdivision	Spermatophyta	Seed plants
Division	**Magnoliophyta**	**Flowering plants**
Class	**Magnoliopsida**	**Dicotyledons**
Subclass	Asteridae	
Order	**Asterales**	
Family	**Asteraceae**	**Aster family**
Genus	*Lactuca*	**Lettuce**
Species	*L. sativa*	**Garden lettuce**
Cultivar	*L. sativa* 'Little Gem'	

Table 3.2 Divisions of the plant kingdom

	Divisions	Common name
	Bryophyta	Mosses
	Hepatophyta	Liverworts
Vascular plants	Equisetophyta	Horsetails
	Pteridophyta	Ferns
Seed plants	Coniferophyta	Conifers
	Ginkgophyta	Ginkgo
	Magnoliophyta	Flowering plants

Flowering plants (Division: Magnoliophyta) have a flower structure for sexual reproduction producing seeds protected by fruits. This characteristic structure is used as the basis of their classification. There are estimated to be some 25 000 species, occupying a very wide range of habitats. Many in the division are important to horticulture, both as crop plants and weeds. This division is split into two main classes the Liliopsida formerly the Monocotyledonae and generally known as the **monocotyledons** and the Magnoliopsida, the **dicotyledons**.

Monocotyledons include some important horticultural families, e.g. Arecaceae, the palms; Musaceae, the bananas; Cyperaceae, the sedges; Juncaceae, the rushes; Poaceae (formerly Graminae), the grasses; Iridaceae, the irises; Liliaceae, the lilies and the Orchidaceae, the orchids.

Dicotyledons has many more families significant to horticulture, including Magnoliaceae, the magnolias; Caprifoliaceae, the honeysuckles; Cactaceae, the cactuses; Malvaceae, the mallows; Ranunculaceae, the buttercups; Theaceae, the teas; Lauraceae, the laurels; Betulaceae, the birches, Fagaceae, the beeches; Solanaceae, the potatoes and tomato; Nymphaeaceae, the water lilies and Crassulaceae, the stonecrops. Four of the biggest and most economically important families in this class have had a change of name. Fabaceae (formerly the Leguminosae), the pea and bean family, have five-petalled asymmetric or **zygomorphic** (having only one plane of symmetry) flowers, which develop into long pods (legumes) containing starchy seeds. The characteristic upturned umbrella-shaped flower head or **umbel** is found in the Apiaceae (formerly the Umbelliferae), the carrot family, and bears small white five-petalled flowers, which are wind pollinated. Asteraceae (formerly Compositae), the members have a characteristic flower head with many small florets making up the composite, regular (or **actinomorphic**) structure, e.g. chrysanthemum, groundsel. Members of the Brassicaceae (formerly Cruciferae) are characterized by their four-petalled flower and contain the genus *Brassica* with a number of important crop plants such as cabbage, cauliflowers, swedes, brussels sprouts as well as the wallflower (*Cheiranthus cheiri*). Most of the brassicas have a **biennial** growth habit producing vegetative growth in the first season, and flowers in the second, usually in response to a cold stimulus (*see* vernalization). A number of weed species are found in this family, including shepherd's purse (*Capsella bursapastoris*), which is an **annual**. Many important genera, e.g. apples (*Malus*), pear (*Pyrus*) and rose (*Rosa*), are found within the Rosaceae family, which generally produces succulent fruit from a flower with five petals and often many male and female organs. Many species within this family display a **perennial**-growth habit (*see* Table 3.3).

NAMING OF CULTIVATED PLANTS

The binomial system

The name given to a plant species is very important. It is the key to identification in the field or garden, and also an international form of identity, which can lead to much information from books and the Internet. The common names, which we use for plants, such as potato and lettuce, are, of course, acceptable in English, but are not universally used. **Linnaeus**, a Swedish biologist in the eighteenth century, formulated a system that he claimed should identify an individual plant type, by means of the composed **genus** name, followed by the **species** name. For example, the chrysanthemum used for cut flowers is *Chrysanthemum* genus and *morifolium* species; note that the genus name begins with a capital letter, while the species has a small letter. Other examples are *Ilex aquifolium* (holly), *Magnolia stellata* (star-magnolia) and *Ribes sanguineum* (redcurrant).

The genus and species names must be written in *italics*, or underlined where this is not possible, to indicate that they are internationally accepted terms. However, these two words may not encompass all possible variations, since a species can give rise to a number of naturally occurring **varieties** with distinctive characteristics. In addition, cultivation, selection and breeding have produced variation in species referred to as cultivated varieties or **cultivars**. The two terms, variety and cultivar, are exactly equivalent, but the botanical variety name is referred to in Latin, beginning with a small letter, while the cultivar is given a name often relating to the plant breeder who produced it. There is no other significant difference in the use of the two terms, and therefore either is acceptable. However, the term cultivar will be used throughout this text. A cultivar name should be written in inverted commas and begin with a capital letter, after the binomial name or, when applicable, the common name. Examples include *Prunus padus* 'Grandiflora', tomato 'Ailsa Craig', apple 'Bramley's Seedling'. If a cultivar name has more than one acceptable alternative, they are said to be synonyms (sometimes written syn.).

Hybrids

When **cross pollination** occurs between two plants, hybridization results, and the offspring usually bear the characteristics distinct from either parent. Hybridization can occur between different cultivars within a species, sometimes resulting in a new and distinctive cultivar (*see* Chapter 8), or between two species, resulting in an **interspecific hybrid**, e.g. *Prunus* × *yedoensis* and *Erica* × *darleyensis*. A much rarer hybridization between two different genera results in an **intergeneric hybrid**, e.g. ×*Cupressocyparis leylandii* and ×*Fatshedera lizei*. The names of the resulting hybrid types include elements from the names of the parents, connected or preceded by a multiplication sign (×). A chimaera, consisting of tissue from two distinct parents, is indicated by a 'plus' sign, e.g. +*Laburnocystisus adamii*, the result of a graft.

Identifying plants

A **flora** is a text written for the identification of flowering plant species. Some floras use only pictures to classify plants. More detailed texts use a more systematic approach where reference is made to a **key** of features that, by elimination, will lead to the name of a plant. Species are described

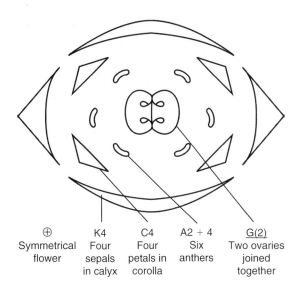

$\oplus$	K4	C4	A2 + 4	G(2)
Symmetrical flower	Four sepals in calyx	Four petals in corolla	Six anthers	Two ovaries joined together

Figure 3.1 *Floral diagram for wallflower.*

in terms of their flowers, inflorescences, stems, leaves and fruit. This description will often include details of shape, size and colour of these plant parts.

Flowers. The number and arrangement of flower parts are the most important features for classification and is a primary feature in plant identification. It can be described in shorthand using a floral formula or a floral diagram (*see* Figure 3.1). For example, the floral formula, with the interpretation, for wallflower (*Cheiranthus cheiri*), a member of the Cruciferae family is given.

Other examples of floral formulae include:

Sweet pea (Leguminosae)	·|·	K(5) C5	A(9) + 1	G1
Buttercup (Ranunculaceae)	$\oplus$	K5 C5	A	G
Dead nettle (Labiatae)	·|·	K(5) C(5)A4		G(2)
Daisy (Asteraceae)	$\oplus$	K C(5)A(5)		G(2)

The way that **flowers** are arranged on the plant is also distinctive in different families: raceme, corymb, umbel and capitulum (*see* Figure 3.2).

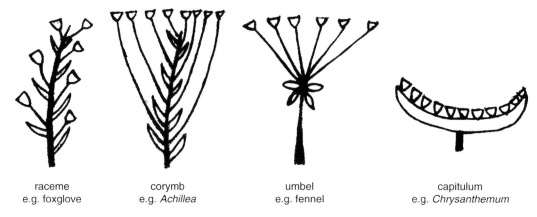

raceme	corymb	umbel	capitulum
e.g. foxglove	e.g. *Achillea*	e.g. fennel	e.g. *Chrysanthemum*

Figure 3.2 *Flower forms. Four examples of inflorescence – the arrangement of flowers on the stem.*

Leaf form (*see* Figure 3.3) is a useful indicator when attempting to identify a plant and descriptions often include specific terms; a few are described below but many more are used in flora. **Simple** leaves have a continuous leaf blade, e.g. linear, lanceolate, ovate, obovate, orbicular and oval. The **margins** of leaves can be described: entire, sinuous, serrate and crenate. The arrangement of the leaf **veins** also characterizes the plant: reticulate, parallel, pinnate and palmate. **Compound** leaves, such as compound palmate and compound pinnate, have separate leaflets each with an individual base on one leaf stalk (*see* page 57 for leaf structure), but the axillary bud is at the base of the main leaf stalk.

Most horticulturists yearn for stability in the naming of plants. Changes in names confuse many people who do not have access to up-to-date literature. On the other hand, the reasons for change are justifiable. New scientific findings may have shown that a genus or species belongs to a different section of a plant family, and that a new name is the correct way of acknowledging this fact. Alternatively, a plant introduced from abroad, maybe many years ago, may have mistakenly been given the incorrect name, along with all the cultivars derived from it.

Evidence from biochemistry, microscopy and deoxyribonucleic acid (DNA) analysis is proving increasingly important in adding to the more conventional plant structural evidence for plant naming. There may be differing views whether a genus or species should be 'split' into smaller units, or several species be 'lumped' into an existing species or genus, or left unchanged. It would seem likely that changes in plant names would continue to be a fact of horticultural life.

There has been a massive increase in communication across the world, especially as a result of the Internet. The level of information about plant names has improved. The ICBN has laid down an international system. Within Britain, the Royal Horticultural Society (RHS) has an advisory panel to help resolve problems in this area. An invaluable reference document 'Index Kewensis' is maintained by Kew Gardens listing the first publication of the name for each plant species not having specific horticultural importance. Cultivated species are listed in the 'RHS Plant Finder', which also indicates where they can be sourced.

Geographical origins of plants

Gardens and horticultural units, from the tropics to more temperate climates, contain an astonishing variety of plant species from the different continents. Below is a brief selection of well-known plants, grown in Britain, illustrating this diversity of origins. It is salutary, when considering these far-flung places, to reflect on the sophisticated

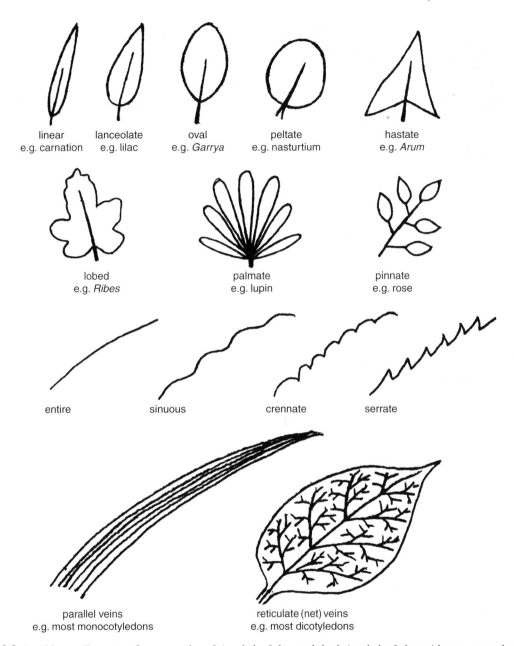

linear
e.g. carnation

lanceolate
e.g. lilac

oval
e.g. *Garrya*

peltate
e.g. nasturtium

hastate
e.g. *Arum*

lobed
e.g. *Ribes*

palmate
e.g. lupin

pinnate
e.g. rose

entire

sinuous

crennate

serrate

parallel veins
e.g. most monocotyledons

reticulate (net) veins
e.g. most dicotyledons

Figure 3.3 *Leaf forms. From top: five examples of simple leaf shapes; lobed simple leaf alongside two examples of compound leaves (with leaflets on petiole); four descriptors of leaf margins; the commonest forms of vein pattern.*

cultures, with skills in plant breeding and a passion for horticulture over the centuries that have taken wild plants and transformed them into the wonders that we now see in our gardens:

- **Far East** (China and Japan): cherry, cucumber, peach, walnut, *Clematis*, *Forsythia*, hollyhock, *Azalea*, rose;
- **India and South-East Asia**: mustard, radish;

Table 3.3 Some commonly used terms that describe the life cycles, size and survival strategies of plants

	Description	Examples
Life cycles		
Ephemeral	A plant that has several life cycles in a growing season and can increase in numbers rapidly.	Groundsel (*Senecio vulgaris*)
Annual	A plant that completes its life cycle within a growing season.	Poached-egg flower (*Limnanthes douglasii*)
Biennial	A plant with a life cycle that spans two growing seasons.	Foxglove (*Digitalis purpurea*)
Perennial	A plant living through several growing seasons.	
Herbaceous perennial	A perennial that loses its stems and foliage at the end of the growing season.	Michaelmas daisy (*Aster* spp.) and hop (*Humulus lupulus*)
Woody plants		
Woody perennial	A perennial that maintains live woody stem growth at the end of the growing season.	Bush fruit, shrubs, trees, climbers (e.g. grape)
Shrub	A woody perennial plant having side branches emerging from near ground level. Up to 5 m tall.	Lilac (*Syringa vulgaris*)
Tree	A large woody perennial unbranched for some distance above ground. Usually more than 5 m.	Horse chestnut (*Aesculus hippocastanum*)
Deciduous	A plant that sheds all its leaves at once.	Mock orange (*Philadelphus delavayi*)
Evergreen	A plant retaining leaves in all seasons.	Aucuba (*Aucuba japonica*)
Hardiness		
Very hardy	A plant able to survive −18°C.	*Kerria japonica*
Moderately hardy	A plant able to survive −15°C.	*Camellia japonica*
Semi-hardy	A plant able to survive −6°C.	*Pittosporum crassifolium*
Tender	A plant not hardy below −1°C.	*Pelargonium cvs*

- **Australasia**: *Acacia, Helichrysum, Hebe*;
- **Africa**: *Phaseolus*, pea, African violet, *Strelitzia, Freesia, Gladiolus, Impatiens, Pelargonium, Plumbago*;
- **Mediterranean**: asparagus, celery, lettuce, onion, parsnip, rhubarb, carnation, hyacinth, *Antirrhinum*, sweet pea;
- **Middle East and Central Asia**: apple, carrot, garlic, grape, leek, pear, spinach;
- **Northern Europe**: cabbage, *Campanula*, *Crocus*, forget-me-not, foxglove, pansy, *Primula*, rose, wallflower;
- **North America**: *Aquilegia, Ceonothus*, lupin, *Aster, Penstemon, Phlox*, sunflower;
- **Central and South America**: *Capsicum*, maize,

potato, tomato, *Fuchsia*, nasturtium, *Petunia, Verbena*.

Further classifications of plants

Plants can be grouped into other useful categories. A classification based on their life cycle (ephemerals, annuals, biennials and perennials) has long been used by growers who also distinguish between the different woody plants such as trees and shrubs. Growers distinguish between those plants that are able to withstand a frost (hardy) and those that cannot (tender); plants can be grouped according to their degree of hardiness. Table 3.3 brings together these useful terms, provides some definitions and gives some plant examples.

KINGDOM FUNGI

Some *fungi* are single celled (such as yeasts), but others are multicellular such as the moulds and the more familiar mushrooms and toadstools. Most are made up of a **mycelium**, which is a mass of thread-like filaments (**hyphae**). Their cell walls are made of chitin. Their energy and supply of organic molecules are obtained from other organisms (heterotrophic nutrition). They achieve this by secreting digestive enzymes onto their food source and absorbing the soluble products. They obtain their food directly from other living organisms, possibly causing disease (*see* Chapter 11), or from dead organic matter, so contributing to its breakdown in the soil (*see* Chapter 15).

Fungi are classified into three divisions:

- **Zygomycota** (mitosporic fungi) have simple asexual and sexual spore forms. Damping off, downy mildew and potato blight belong to this group.
- **Ascomycota** have chitin cell walls, and show, throughout the group, a wide variety of asexual spore forms. The sexual spores are consistently formed within small sacs (asci), numbers of which may themselves be embedded within flask-shaped structures (perithecia), just visible to the naked eye. Black spot of rose, apple canker, powdery mildew and Dutch elm disease belong to this group.
- **Basidiomycota** have chitin cell walls, and may produce, within one fungal species (e.g. cereal rust), as many as five different spore forms, involving more than one plant host. The fungi within this group bear sexual spores (basidiospores) from a microscopic club-shaped structure (basidium). Carnation rust, honey fungus and silver leaf diseases belong to this group.

An artificially derived fourth grouping of fungi is included in the classification of fungi. The **Deuteromycota** include species of fungi that only very rarely produce a sexual spore stage. As with plants, the sexual structures of fungi form the most reliable basis for classification. But, here, the main basis for naming is the asexual spore and mycelium structure. Grey mould (*Botrytis*), *Fusarium* patch of turf and *Rhizoctonia* rot are placed within this group.

KINGDOM ANIMALIA (ANIMALS)

The **animal** kingdom includes a very large number of species that have a significant influence on horticulture mainly as pests (*see* Chapter 10) or as contributors to the recycling of organic matter (*see* Chapter 15).

Some of the most familiar animals are in the phylum **Chordata** that includes mammals, birds, fish, reptiles and amphibians. Mammal pest species include moles (*see* page 99), rabbits (*see* page 97), deer, rats and mice. Bird pest species are numerous including pigeons and bullfinches, but there are very many that are beneficial in that they feed on harmful organisms such as tits that eat greenfly. Less familiar are important members of the phylum **Nematoda** (the roundworms) that includes a very large number of plant-disease-causing organisms including stem and bulb eelworm (*see* page 118), root knot eelworms (*see* page 119), chrysanthemum eelworm and potato root eelworm (*see* page 117). Phylum **Arthropoda** are the most numerous animals on Earth and includes insects, centipedes, millipedes and spiders; many of these are dealt with in the chapter on plant pests (Chapter 10), but it should be noted that there are many that are beneficial, e.g. honey bees (*see* page 77) and centipedes, which are carnivorous and many live on insect species that are harmful. Phylum **Annelida** (the segmented worms) includes earthworms, which are generally considered to be useful organisms especially when they are helping to decompose organic matter (*see* page 185) or when improving soils structure (*see* page 165), but some species cause problems in fine turf when they produce worm casts. Phylum **Mollusca** is best known for the major pests slugs and snails (*see* page 100).

KINGDOM PROKARYOTAE (MONERA)

Bacteria, the sole members of this kingdom, are single-celled organisms sometimes arranged in chains or groups (colonial). They are autotrophic (can produce their own energy supply and organic molecules); some photosynthesize (*see* page 53) but others are able to make organic molecules using the energy released from chemical reactions usually involving simple inorganic compounds. They have great importance to horticulture by their beneficial activities in the soil (*see* page 185), and as causative organisms of plant diseases (*see* page 129).

KINGDOM PROTOCTISTA (PROTISTA)

The **algae**, comprising some 18 000 species, are true plants, since they use chlorophyll to photosynthesize (*see* Chapter 6). The division Chlorophyta (green algae) contains single-celled organisms that require water for reproduction and can present problems when blocking irrigation lines and clogging water tanks. Marine algal species in Phaeophyta (brown algae) and Rhodophyta (red algae) are multicellular, and have leaf-like structures. They include the seaweeds, which accumulate mineral nutrients, and are therefore a useful source of compound fertilizer as a liquid feed. (The blue-green algae, which can cause problems in water because they produce unsightly blooms but are also toxic, have been renamed Cyanobacteria and placed in Kingdom Prokaryotae.)

Lichen classification is complex since each lichen consists of both fungal and algal parts. Both organisms are mutually beneficial or symbiotic. The significance of lichens to horticulture is not great. Of the 15 000 species, one species is considered a food delicacy in Japan. However, lichens growing on tree bark or walls are very sensitive to atmospheric pollution, particularly to the sulphur dioxide content of the air. Different lichen species can withstand varying levels of sulphur dioxide, and a survey of lichen species can be used to indicate levels of atmospheric pollution in a particular area. Many contribute to the weathering of rock in the initial stages of soil formation (*see* page 152). Lichens are also used as a natural dye, and can form an important part of the diet of some deer.

VIRUSES

Viruses are not included in any of the kingdoms. They are visible only under an electron microscope, and do not have a cellular structure, but consist of nucleic acid surrounded by an outer protein coat (a capsid). They do not have cytoplasm, organelles and internal membranes found in the cells of living organisms (*see* page 40). They cannot grow, move or reproduce without access to the cells of a host cell, so they are not included in the classification of living things. Viruses survive by invading the cells of other organisms, modifying their behaviour and often causing disease: e.g. arabis mosaic, chrysanthemum stunt, cucumber mosaic, leaf mosaic, plum pox, reversion, tomato mosaic and tulip break (*see* pages 131–4).

FURTHER READING

Allaby, M. *Concise Oxford Dictionary of Botany* (Oxford University Press, 1992).

Ayres, A. *Gardening without Chemicals* (Which/Hodder & Stoughton, 1990).

Baines, C. and Smart, J. *A Guide to Habitat Creation* (Packard Publishing, 1991).

Brown, L.V. *Applied Principles of Horticulture*, 2nd edition (Butterworth-Heinemann, 2002).

Carson, R. *Silent Spring* (Hamish Hamilton, 1962).

Caplin, B. *Complete Manual of Organic Gardening* (Headline Publishing, 1992).

Dowdeswell, W.H. *Ecology, Principles and Practice* (Heinemann Educational Books, 1984).

Ingram, D.S. *et al.* (Editors) *Science and the Garden* (Blackwell Science Ltd., 2002).

Lampkin, N. *Organic Farming* (Farming Press, 1990).

Mannion, A.M. *et al.* (Editors). *Environmental Issues in the 1990s* (John Wiley & Sons, 1992).

Tait, J. *et al. Practical Conservation* (Open University, 1998).

4

Plant Organization

The main interest of many of those growing plants is the nature of the plant's external appearance, its form or morphology. This chapter begins by describing the external features and discusses ways in which plants are used in gardens and landscapes.

A multicellular organism such as the plant, which carries out many complex processes involved in its growth and development, requires a complex organization to carry out its functions. To be efficient, the plant's structural unit must be subdivided so that a particular area in the plant, i.e. an organ, carries out each major function. The individual units of the plant, the cells, are grouped together into tissues of similar cell types, and each tissue contributes to the activities of the whole organ. These structures and the nature of plant growth are explored and explained in the context of the stem.

PLANT FORM

Most plant species at first sight appear very similar, since all four organs, the **root, stem, leaf and flower**, are present in approximately the same form and have the same major functions. The generalized plant form for a dicotyledonous and a monocotyledonous plant can be seen in Figure 4.1.

In most species the functions of the **root system** are to take up water and minerals from the growing medium and to anchor the plant in the growing medium. Two types of root system are produced; a **taproot** is a single large root which usually maintains a direction of growth in response to gravity (*see* geotropism) with many small lateral roots growing from it, e.g. in chrysanthemums, brassicas and dock. In contrast, a **fibrous root** system consists of many roots growing out from the base of the stem, as in grasses and groundsel (*see* page 47 for root structure).

The **leaf**, consisting of the leaf blade (**lamina**) and stalk (**petiole**), carries out photosynthesis, its shape and arrangement on the stem depending on the water and light energy supply in the species' habitat (*see* page 57 for leaf structure).

The **stem's** function is physically to support the leaves and the flowers, and to transport water, minerals and food between roots, leaves and flowers (*see* page 41 for stem structure). The leaf joins the stem at the **node** and has in its angle (axil) with the stem an **axillary bud**, which may grow out to produce a lateral shoot. The distance between one node and the next is termed the **internode**.

Sexual reproduction is carried out in the flower, and therefore its appearance depends principally on the agents of pollination (*see* page 76 for general flower structure).

Adaptation to plant organs have enabled plants to compete and survive in their habitat. Plants adapted to dry areas (**xerophytes**) such as cacti

(a)   (b)

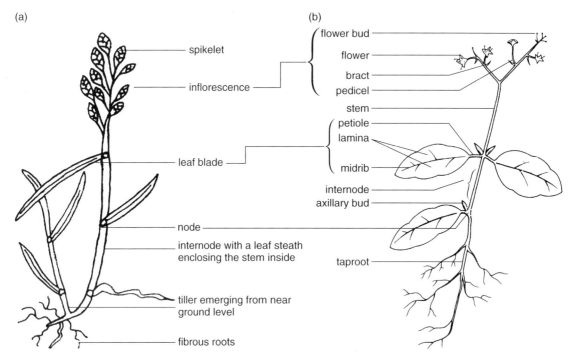

Figure 4.1 *Generalized plant form: (a) monocotyledon and (b) dicotyledon.*

have leaves reduced to protective **spines** and stems capable of photosynthesis (*see* Plate 4). **Thorns**, which are modified branches growing from axillary buds, also have a protective function, e.g. hawthorn (*Crataegus*). **Prickles** are specialized outgrowths of the stem epidermis, which not only protect but also assist the plant in scrambling over other vegetation, as in wild roses (*see* Plate 13).

Several species possess leaves modified specifically for climbing in the form of **tendrils**, as in many members of the Leguminosae family; and Clematis climb by means of a sensitive, elongated leaf stalk, which twist round their support. In runner beans and honeysuckle (*Lonicera*), twining stems wind around other uprights for support. Others are able to climb with the help of adventitious roots such as ivies and virginia creeper (*Parthenocissus*). **Epiphytes** are physically attached to aerial parts of other plants for support: they absorb and sometimes store water in aerial roots, as in some orchids.

To survive an environment with very low nutrient levels, such as the sphagnum peat moor (*see* page 190), some plants have evolved methods of trapping insects and utilize the soluble products of their decomposed prey. These **insectivorous** plants include the native sundew (*Drosera*) and butterwort (*Pinguicula* spp.), which trap their prey with sticky glands on their leaves. Pitcher plants (*Sarracenia* spp.) have leaves that form containers into which insects are able to enter but are prevented from escaping by slippery surfaces or barriers of stiff hairs. The venus flytrap (*Dionaea muscipula*) has leaves that are hinged so that they can snap shut on their prey when it alights on one of the trigger hairs.

Plants found growing in coastal areas have adaptations that allow them to withstand high salt levels, e.g. salt glands as found in the cord grass (*Spartina* spp.) or *succulent* tissues in 'scurvy grass' (*Cochlearia*), both inhabitants of coastal areas.

Other modifications in plants are dealt with elsewhere. This includes the use of stems and roots as food and water storage organs (*see* vegetative propagation).

Plant form in design

Plant form, as individual plants or in groups, is the main interest for many in horticulture who use plants in the garden or landscape. Contrasts in plant shapes and sizes can be combined to please the eye of the observer.

The dominant plant within a garden feature is usually a tree or shrub chosen for its **special** striking appearance. In a large feature, it may be a *Betula pendula* (silver birch) tree growing up to 20 m in height with a graceful form, striking white bark and golden autumn colour. In a smaller feature, *Euphorbia characias* provides a very special effect with its 1 m high evergreen foliage, and springtime yellow blooms. Such plants can form a focal point in a garden or landscape.

Spaced around these special plants, there may be included species providing a visually supportive **background or skeletal** form to the decorative feature. *Garrya elliptica*, a 4 m shrub with elliptical, wavy edged evergreen leaves and mid-winter catkins fits naturally into this category against a larger special plant. At 2.5 m, the evergreen shrub *Choisya ternata* (Mexican orange blossom) bearing fragrant white flowers in spring is a popular background species in decorative borders. *Jasminum nudifolium* (winter jasmine) is an example of a climber fulfilling this role. Such framework plants not only provide a suitable background, but also can provide continuity or unity through the garden or landscape and ensure interest all the year round.

Fitting further into the mosaic of plantings are the numerous examples of **decorative** species, exhibiting particular aspects of general structure or flowering, and often having a deciduous growth. An example is the 0.3 m tall *Cytisus* × *kewensis* (broom) with its downy arching stems and profuse creamy-white spring flowers. A contrasting example

is the 2 m clump-forming grass species, *Cortadieria selloana*, producing narrow leaves and feathery late summer flowering panicles. Climbing species from the *Rosa* and *Clematis* genera also fit into the decorative category. Garden designers are also able to call on a very wide range of leaf forms to create textural or architectural interest in the border (*see* Plate 2).

A host of deciduous **pretty** herbaceous and evergreen perennials is available for filling the decorative feature, fitting around the above-mentioned three categories. *Delphiniums* (up to 2 m), *Lupins* (up to 1.5 m), *Asters* (up to 1.5 m), *Sedums* (up to 0.5 m) and *Alchemillas* (up to 0.5 m) are five examples illustrating a range of heights.

Finally, **infill** species either as bulbs (e.g. *Tulipa*, *Narcissus*, or *Lilium*), perennials (e.g. *Saxifraga* or *Campanula*) or annuals (e.g. *Nicotiana* or *Begonia*) may be placed within the feature, sometimes for a relatively short period whilst other perennials are growing towards full size. They are also used in colourful bedding displays.

Plant size and growth rate

It is important for anyone planning a garden that they recognize the eventual size (both in terms of height and of width) of trees, shrubs and perennials. This vital information is quite often ignored or forgotten at the time of purchase. The impressive *Ginkgo* (Maidenhair tree) really can grow up to 30 m in height (at least twice the height of a normal house) and is, therefore, not the plant to put in a small bed. Similarly, × *Cupressocyparis leylandii* (Leyland cypress), seemingly so useful in rapidly creating a fine hedge, can also grow up to 30 m, and reach 5 m in width, to the consternation of even the most neighbourly of neighbours.

The eventual size of a plant is recorded in plant encyclopaedias, which should be carefully scrutinized for this vital statistic. It may also be wise to contact a specialist nursery which deals with this important aspect on a day-to-day basis, and will give advise to potential buyers. It should be remembered that the eventual size of a tree or shrub may vary considerably in different parts of the country, and may be affected within a garden by factors such as aspect, soil, shade and wind.

Attention should also be given to the rate at which a plant grows; *Taxus* (yew) or *Magnolia stellata* (star magnolia) are two notable examples of slow growing species.

THE ANATOMY OF THE PLANT

A close examination of the internal structure (anatomy) of the plant with a microscope will reveal how it is made up of different tissues. Each **tissue** is a collection of specialized cells carrying out one function such as xylem conducting water. An **organ** is made up of a group of tissues carrying out a specific function such as a leaf producing sugars for the plant. In the following section, the anatomy of the stem is illustrated and there is a comparable discussion of root and leaf structures in the next two chapters.

The cell

Without the use of a microscope, the horticulturist will not be able to see cells, since they are very small (about a twentieth of a millimetre in size). They are very complex and scientific studies continued to discover more of the organization displayed in this fundamental unit.

A simple, unspecialized cell of parenchyma (*see* Figure 4.2) consists of a cellulose cell wall, and contents (**protoplasm**) enclosed in a **cell membrane**, which is selective for the passage of materials in and out of the cell. The cellulose in the cell wall is laid down in a mesh pattern, which allows for stretching as the cell expands. Within the mesh framework are many apertures that, in active cells such as parenchyma, allow for strands of cytoplasm (called **plasmodesmata**) connecting between adjacent cells. These strands carry nutrients and hormones between cells, and are able to control the speed at which this movement takes place. When a plant wilts, its cells become smaller, but the plasmodesmata normally retain their links with adjacent cells. In the situation of 'permanent wilting' (*see* page 174) or plasmolysis (*see* page 47), there is a breakage of these strands, and the plant is not able to recover.

Suspended in the jelly-like cytoplasm are small structures (organelles) each enclosed within a membrane and having specialized functions within the cell. In all tissues, the cell walls of adjoining cells are held together by calcium pectate (a glue-like substance which is an important setting ingredient in 'jam-making'). Some types of cell (e.g. xylem vessels) do not remain biochemically active, but die in order to achieve their usefulness. Here, the first wall of cellulose becomes thickened by additional cellulose layers and lignin, which is a strong, impervious substance.

The cell is made up of two parts, the nucleus and the cytoplasm. The nucleus coordinates the chemistry of the cell. The long chromosome strands that fill the **nucleus** (*see* also page 80) are made up of the complex chemical deoxyribosenucleic acid, usually known as DNA. In addition to its ability to produce more of itself for the process of cell division, DNA is also constantly manufacturing smaller but similar ribosenucleic acid (RNA) units, which are able to pass through the nucleus membrane and attach themselves to other organelles. In this way, the nucleus is able to transmit instructions for the assembling, or destruction, of important chemicals within the cell.

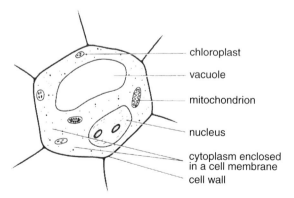

Figure 4.2 *An unspecialized plant cell showing the organelles responsible for the life processes.*

There are six main types of organelle in the cytoplasm. The first, the **vacuole** is a sac containing dilute sugar, nutrients and waste products. It may occupy the major volume of a cell, and its main functions are storage and maintaining cell shape. The **ribosomes** make proteins from amino acids. Enzymes, which speed up chemical processes, are made up of protein. The **Golgi apparatus** is involved in modifying and storing chemicals being made in the cell before they are transported where they are required. **Mitochondria** release energy, in a controlled way, by the process of respiration, to be used by the other organelles. The energy is transferred via a chemical called adenosine triphosphate (ATP). The meristem areas of the stem, root and flower have cells with the highest number of mitochondria in order to help the rapid cell division and growth in these areas. **Plastids** such as the chloroplasts are involved in the production of sugar by the process of photosynthesis,

and in the short-term storage of condensed sugar (in the form of starch). Lastly, the **endoplasmic reticulum** is a complex mesh of membranes that enables transport of chemicals within the cell, and links with the plasmodesmata at the cell surface. Ribosomes are commonly located on the endoplasmic reticulum. The whole of the living matter of a cell, nucleus and cytoplasm, is collectively called **protoplasm**.

TISSUES OF THE STEM

Dicotyledonous stem

The internal structure of a dicotyledonous plant, as viewed in cross-section, is shown in Figure 4.3. Three terms, epidermis, cortex and pith, are used to broadly describe the distribution of tissues across the stem. The **epidermis** is present as an

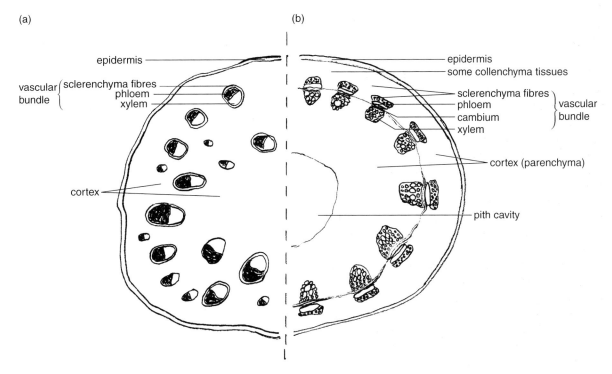

Figure 4.3 *Cross-sections of (a) monocotyledonous stem showing scattered vascular bundles with associated support tissue and (b) dicotyledonous stem showing a ring of vascular bundles.*

outer protective layer of the stem, leaves and roots. It consists of a single layer of cells; a small proportion of them are modified to allow gases to pass through an otherwise impermeable layer (*see* stomata). The second general term, **cortex**, describes the zone of tissues found inside the epidermis and reaching inwards to the the inner edge of the vascular bundles. A third term, **pith**, refers to the central zone of the stem, which is mainly made up of parenchyma cells.

Collenchyma and **sclerenchyma cells** are usually found to the inside of the epidermis and are responsible for **support** in the young plant. Both tissues have cells with specially thickened walls. When a cell is first formed it has a wall composed mainly of **cellulose** fibres. In collenchyma cells the amount of cellulose is increased to provide extra strength, but otherwise the cells remain relatively unspecialized. In sclerenchyma cells, the thickness of the wall is increased by the addition of a substance called **lignin**, which is tough and causes the living contents of the cell to disappear. These cells, which are long and tapering and interlock for additional strength, consist only of cell walls.

The cortex of the stem contains a number of tissues. Many are made up of unspecialized cells such as **parenchyma**. In these tissues, the cells are thin walled and maintained in an approximately spherical shape by osmotic pressure (*see* page 47). The mass of parenchyma cells (surrounding the other tissues) combine to maintain plant shape. Lack of water results in the partial collapse of the parenchyma cells, which is seen as wilting. Parenchyma cells also carry out other functions, when required. Many of these cells contain chlorophyll (giving the stems their green colour) and so are able to photosynthesize. They release energy, by respiration, for use in the surrounding tissues. In some plants such as the potato they are also capable of acting as food stores (the potato tuber which stores starch). They are also able to undergo cell division, a useful property when a plant has been damaged. This property has practical significance when plant parts such as cuttings are being propagated, since new cells can be created by the parenchyma to heal wounds and initiate root development.

Contained in the cortex are **vascular bundles**, so named because they contain two vascular tissues that are responsible for transport. The first, **xylem**, contains long, wide, open-ended cells with very thick lignified walls, able to withstand the high pressures of water with dissolved minerals which they carry. The second vascular tissue, **phloem**, consists again of long, tube-like cells, and is responsible for the transport of food manufactured in the leaves carried to the roots, stems or flowers (*see* translocation). The phloem tubes, in contrast to xylem, have fairly soft cellulose cell walls. The end walls are only partially broken down to leave sieve-like structures (sieve plates) at intervals along the phloem tubes. Alongside every phloem tube cell, there is a small companion cell, which regulates the flow of liquids down the sieve tube. The phloem is seen on either side of the xylem in the marrow stem, but is found to the outside of the xylem in most other species. Phloem is penetrated by the stylets of feeding aphids (*see* Chapter 10).

Also contained within the vascular bundles is the **cambium** tissue, which contains actively dividing cells producing more xylem and phloem tissues as the stem grows.

Monocotyledonous stem

This has the same functions as those of a dicotyledon; therefore the cell types and tissues are similar. However, the arrangement of the tissues does differ because increase in diameter by **secondary growth** does not take place. The stem relies on extensive sclerenchyma tissue for support that, in the maize stem shown in Figure 4.3, is found as a sheath around each of the scattered vascular bundles. Monocotyledonous stem structures are seen at their most complex in the palm family. From the outside, the trunk would appear to be made of wood, but an internal investigation shows that the stem is a mass of sclerified vascular bundles. The absence of secondary growth in the vascular bundles makes the presence of cambium tissue unnecessary.

STEM GROWTH

Growth of stems is initiated in the **apical**, or terminal, **bud** at the end of the stem (the apex). Deep inside the apical bud lies a tiny mass of small, delicate jelly-like cells, each with a conspicuous nucleus but no cell vacuole. This mass is the **apical meristem** (*see* Figure 4.4). Here, cells divide frequently to produce four kinds of meristematic tissues. The first, at the very tip, continues as meristem cells. The second (protoderm) near the outside develops into the epidermis. The third (procambium) becomes the vascular bundles. The fourth (ground meristem) turns into the parenchyma, collenchyma and sclerenchyma tissues of the cortex and pith. In addition to its role in tissue formation, the apical meristem also gives rise to small leaves (bud scales) that collectively protect the meristem. These scales and the meristem together form the **bud**. It should be noted that any damage to the sensitive meristem region by aphids, fungi, bacteria or herbicides would result in distorted growth. A fairly common example of such a distortion is **fasciation**, a condition that resembles a number of stems fused together. Buds located lower down the stem, in the angle of the leaf (the axil), are called **axillary buds**, and these often give rise to side branches.

In some plant families, e.g. the Graminae, the meristem remains at the base of the leaves, which are therefore protected against some herbicides, e.g. 2,4-D (*see* Chapter 9). This also means that grasses re-grow from their base after animals have grazed them. The new blades of grass grow from meristems between the old leaf and the stem. This means grasses can be **mown** which enables us to create lawns. The process of cutting back the grass also leads it to sending up several shoots instead of just one. This process of **tillering** helps thicken up the turf sward to make it such a useful surface for sport as well as decoration. Mowing kills the dicotyledonous plants that have their stems cutoff at the base and lose their meristems. However, many species are successful lawn weeds by growing in prostrate form; the foreshortened stem (very short internodes) creates a **rosette** of leaves

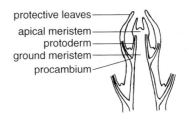

Figure 4.4 *The tip of a dicotyledonous stem showing the four meristematic areas.*

that helps to conserve water, shades out surrounding plants and the growing point stays below the cutting height of the mower.

Elongation of the plant stem takes place in two stages. Firstly, cell division, described above, contributes a little. The second phase is cell **expansion**, which occurs at the base of the meristem. Here, the tiny unspecialized meristem cells begin to take in water and nutrients to form a cell vacuole. As a result, each cell elongates, and the stem rapidly grows. In the expansion zone, other developments begin to occur. Most importantly, the cells begin to create their cell walls, and the connections between cells (plasmodesmata). The exact shape and chemical composition of the wall is different for each type of tissue cell, since it has a particular function to perform. This whole process of cell maturation is referred to as '**cell differentiation**'.

As the stem length increases, so the width also increases to support the bigger plant and supply the greater amount of water and minerals required. This process in dicotyledons is called **secondary growth** (*see* Figure 4.5). Additional phloem and xylem are produced on either side of the cambium tissue, which now forms a complete ring. As these tissues increase towards the centre of the stem, so the circumference of the stem must also increase. Therefore a secondary ring of cambium (cork cambium) is formed, just to the inside of the epidermis, the cells of which divide to produce a layer of corky cells on the outside of the stem. This layer will increase with the growth of the tissue inside the stem, and will prevent loss of water if cracks should occur. As more secondary growth takes place, so more phloem and xylem tissues are

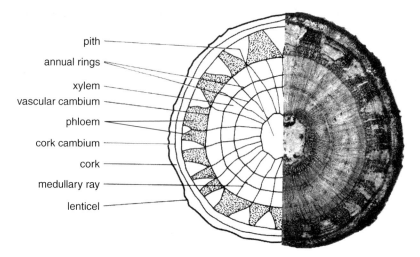

pith
annual rings
xylem
vascular cambium
phloem
cork cambium
cork
medullary ray
lenticel

Figure 4.5 *Cross-section of woody stem of lime (Tilia europea) showing large central woody area and development of bark to the outside.*

produced but the phloem tubes, being soft, are squashed as the more numerous and very hard xylem vessels occupy more and more of the cross-section of the stem. Eventually, the majority of the stem consists of secondary xylem that forms the **wood**.

The central region of xylem sometimes becomes darkly stained with gums and resins (**heartwood**) and performs the long-term function of support for a heavy trunk or branch. The outer xylem, the **sapwood**, is still functional in transporting water and nutrients, and is often lighter in colour. The xylem tissue produced in the spring has larger diameter vessels than autumn-produced xylem, due to the greater volume of water that must be transported; a distinct ring is therefore produced where the two types of tissue meet. As these rings will be formed each season, their number can indicate the age of the branch or trunk; they are called **annual rings**. The phloem tissue is pushed against the cork layers by the increasing volume of xylem so that a woody stem appears to have two distinct layers, the wood in the centre and the **bark** on the outside.

If **bark** is removed, the phloem also will be lost, leaving the vascular cambium exposed. The stem's food transport system from leaves to the roots is

thus removed and, if a trunk is completely **ringed** (or 'girdled'), the plant will die. Rabbits or deer in an orchard may cause this sort of damage. 'Partial ringing', i.e. removing the bark from almost the whole of the circumference can achieve a deliberate reduction in growth rate of vigorous tree fruit cultivars and woody ornamental species. Initially, the **bark** is smooth and shiny but with age it thickens and the outer layers accumulate chemicals (including suberin) that make it an effective protection against water loss and pest attack. This part of the bark (called **cork**) starts to peel or flake off. This is replaced from below and the cork gradually takes on its characteristic colours and textures. Many trees such as silver birch, London plane, *Prunus serrula, Acer davidii* and many pines and rhododendrons have attractive bark and are particularly valued for winter interest (*see* Plate 13).

Since the division of cells in the cambium produces secondary growth, it is important that when **grafting** a **scion** (the material to be grafted) to a **stock**, the vascular cambium tissues of both components be positioned as close to each other as possible. The success of a graft depends very much on the rapid **callus** growth derived from the cambium, from which new cambial cells form and subsequently from which the new xylem and phloem vessels form to complete the union. The two parts then grow as one to carry out the functions of the plant stem.

A further feature of a woody stem is the mass of lines radiating outwards from the centre, most obvious in the xylem tissues. These are **medullary rays**, consisting of parenchyma tissue linking up with small areas on the bark where the corky cells are less tightly packed together (**lenticels**). These allow air to move into the stem and across the stem from cell to cell in the medullary rays. The oxygen in the air is needed for the process of **respiration**, but the openings can be a means of entry of some diseases, e.g. fireblight. Other external features of woody stems include the **leaf scars**, which mark the point of attachment of leaves fallen at the end of a growing season, and can be a point of entry of fungal spores such as apple canker.

Secondary thickening is found not only in trees and shrubs, but also in many herbaceous perennials and annuals that have woody stem. However, trees and shrubs do exhibit this feature to the greatest extent.

Note that **trees** are large woody plants that have a main stem with branches appearing some distance above ground level. **Shrubs** are smaller, usually less than 3 m in height, but with branches developing at or near ground level to give a bushy appearance to the plant.

FURTHER READING

Bowes, B.G. *A Colour Atlas of Plant Structure* (Manson Publishing, 1996).

Brown, L.V. *Applied Principles of Horticulture*, 2nd edition (Butterworth-Heinemann, 2002).

Clegg, C.J. and Cox, G. *Anatomy and Activities of Plants* (John Murray, 1978).

Cutler, D.F. *Applied Plant Anatomy* (Longman, 1978).

Ingram, D.S. *et al.* (editors). *Science and the Garden* (Blackwell Science Ltd, 2002).

Lewes, D. *Plants and Nitrogen – New Studies in Biology* (Edward Arnold, 1986).

Mauseth, J.P. *Botany – An Introduction to Plant Biology* (Saunders, 1998).

5

Water and Minerals in the Plant

Water is the major constituent of any living organism and the maintenance of a plant with optimum water content is a very important part of plant growth and development (see Soil Water, Chapter 14). Probably more plants die from lack of water than from any other cause. Minerals are also raw materials essential to growth, and are supplied through the root system.

WATER

Functions of water

The plant consists of about 95 per cent water, which is the main constituent of **protoplasm** or living matter. When the plant cell is full of water, or **turgid**, the pressure of water enclosed within a membrane or vacuole acts as a means of support for the cell and therefore the whole plant, so that when a plant loses more water than it is taking up, the cells collapse and the plant may wilt. Aquatic plants are supported largely by external water and have very little specialized support tissue. In order to survive, any organism must carry out complex chemical reactions, which are explained, and their horticultural application described, in Chapters 6 and 7. Raw materials for chemical reactions must be transported and brought into contact with each other by a suitable medium; water is an excellent solvent. One of the most important processes in the plant is photosynthesis, and a small amount of water is used up as a raw material in this process.

MOVEMENT OF WATER

Water moves into the plant through the roots, the stem and into the leaves, and is lost to the atmosphere. By the process of **diffusion, molecules of a gas or liquid move from an area of high concentration to an area where there is a relatively lower concentration of the diffusing substance.** Thus, water vapour moves through the **stomata** (*see* page 57) from an area of high concentration inside the leaf into the air immediately surrounding the leaf where there is a lower relative humidity. The pathway of water movement through the plant falls into three distinct stages: water uptake, movement up the stem and transpiration loss from the leaves.

Water uptake

The movement of water into the roots is by a special type of diffusion called **osmosis**. Soil water enters root cells through the **cell wall** and **membrane**. The cell wall is permeable to both soil water and the dissolved inorganic minerals, but the cell membrane, although permeable to water, allows only the smallest molecules to pass through, somewhat like a sieve, and is therefore described as a **partially permeable membrane**.

The minerals move into the cells by a process that requires energy to 'push' the molecules into the cell, and a greater concentration of minerals is usually maintained inside the cell compared with that in the soil water. This means that, by osmosis, water will move from the soil into the cell where there is relatively less water, as there are more inorganic salts and sugars. The greater the difference in concentration of inorganic salts either side of the cell membrane, the greater the **osmotic pressure** and the faster the water moves into the root cells, also affected by increased temperature. **Osmosis** can therefore be defined **as the movement of water from an area of low salt concentration to an area of relatively higher salt concentration, through a partially permeable membrane**. If there is a build-up of salts in the soil, either over a period of time or, e.g. where too much fertilizer is added, water may move out of the roots by osmosis, and the cells are then described as **plasmolysed**. Cells that lose water this way can recover their water content if the conditions are rectified quickly, but it can lead to permanent damage to the cell interconnections (*see* page 40). Such situations can be avoided by correct dosage of fertilizer and by monitoring of conductivity levels in greenhouse soils and nutrient film technique (NFT) systems (*see* Chapter 17).

Root structure (*see* Figure 5.1).   The function of the root system is to take up water and mineral nutrients from the growing medium and to anchor the plant in that medium. Its major function involves making contact with the water in the growing medium. To achieve this it must have as a large surface area as possible. The root surface near to the tip where growth occurs (cell division in the meristem, *see* page 43) is protected by the **root cap**. The root zone behind the root tip has tiny projections called **root hairs** reaching numbers of 200–400/mm^2, which greatly increase the surface area in this region (*see* Figure 5.2). Plants grown in hydroculture, e.g. NFT (page 218), produce considerably fewer root hairs. The loss of root hairs during transplanting can check plant

growth considerably, and the hairs can be points of entry of diseases such as club root (*see* Chapter 11). The layer with the root hairs, the **epidermis**, is comparable with the epidermis of the stem (*see* stem structure); it is a single layer of cells which has a protective as well as an absorptive function.

Inside the epidermis is the parenchymatous **cortex** layer. The main function of this tissue is respiration to produce energy for growth of the root and for the absorption of mineral nutrients. The cortex can also be used for the storage of food where the root is an overwintering organ (*see* page 68). The

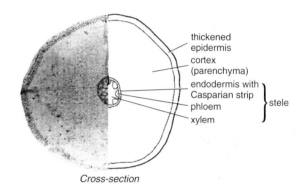

Cross-section

Figure 5.1 *Cross section of lily root showing thickened outer region, large area of cortex and central vascular region enclosed in a single-celled endodermis.*

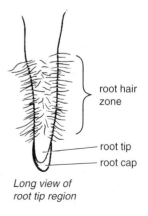

Long view of root tip region

Figure 5.2 *Root tip showing the tip protected by root cap and the root hair zone.*

cortex is often quite extensive and water must move across it in order to reach the transporting tissue that is in the centre of the root. This central region, called the **stele**, is separated from the cortex by a single layer of cells, the **endodermis**, which has the function of controlling the passage of water into the stele. A waxy strip forming part of the cell wall of many of the endodermal cells (the Casparian strip) prevents water from moving into the cell by all except the cells outside it, called **passage cells**. In this way, the volume of water passing into the stele is restricted. If such control did not occur, more water could move into the transport system than can be lost through the leaves. In some conditions, such as in high air humidity (*see* page 25), more water moves into the leaves than is being lost to the air, and the more delicate cell walls in the leaf may burst. This condition is known as **oedema**, and commonly occurs in *Pelargonium* as dark green patches becoming brown, and also weak-celled plants such as lettuce, when it is known as **tipburn**, because the margins of the leaves in particular will appear scorched. **Guttation** may occur when liquid water is forced onto the leaf surface.

Water passes through the endodermis to the **xylem** tissue, which transports the water and dissolved minerals up to the stem and leaves. The arrangement of the xylem tissue varies between species, but often appears in transverse section as a star with varying numbers of 'arms'. **Phloem** tissue is responsible for transporting carbohydrates from the leaves as a food supply for the production of energy in the cortex.

A distinct area in the root inside the endodermis, the **pericycle**, supports cell division and produces lateral roots, which push through to the main root surface from deep within the structure.

Roots age and become thickened with waxy substances, and the uptake rate of water becomes restricted.

Movement of water up the stem

Three factors contribute to water movement. **Osmotic forces**, previously described, push water up the stem to a height of about 30 cm. This effect, called **root pressure**, can provide a large proportion of the plant's water needs in smaller annual species. A second effect is the **capillary action** (attraction of the water molecules for the sides of the xylem vessels), which may lift water a few centimetres, but is not considered a significant factor in water movement. The third factor, **transpiration pull**, is the major process that moves soil water to all parts of the plant.

Transpiration

Transpiration is the loss of water vapour from the leaves of the plant. Any plant takes up a lot of water through its roots; e.g. a tree can take up about 1000 litres (about 200 gallons) a day. Approximately 98 per cent of the water taken up moves through the plant and is lost by transpiration; only about 2 per cent is retained as part of the plant's structure, and a yet smaller amount is used up in photosynthesis.

The seemingly extravagant loss through leaves is due to the unavoidably large pores in the leaf surface (**stomata**) essential for carbon dioxide diffusion (*see* Figure 6.1). Two other points, however, should be considered here. Water vapour diffuses outwards through the leaf stomata more quickly than carbon dioxide (to be used for photosynthesis)

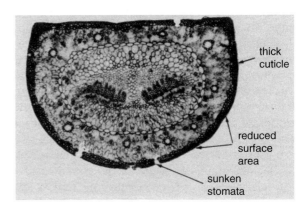

thick cuticle

reduced surface area

sunken stomata

Figure 5.3 *Cross-section of pine* (Pinus) *leaf showing some adaptations to reduce excessive water loss.*

entering. However, the plant is able to partially close the stomata to reduce water loss without causing a carbon dioxide deficiency in the leaf. Secondly, the diffusion rate of water vapour through the stomata leads to a leaf cooling effect enabling the leaf to function whilst being exposed to high levels of radiation. A remarkable aspect of transpiration is that water can be pulled ('sucked') such a long way to the tops of tall trees. Engineers have long known that columns of water break when they are more than about 10 m long; and yet even tall trees such as the giant redwoods pull water up a 100 m from ground level. This apparent ability to flout the laws of nature is probably due to the small size of the xylem vessels, which greatly reduce the possibility of the water columns collapsing. A further impressive aspect of the plant structure is seen in the extreme ramifications of the xylem system in the veins of the leaf. This fine network ensures that water moves by transpiration pull right up to the spongy mesophyll spaces in the leaf (*see* page 57), and avoids any water movement through living cells, which would slow down the process many thousand times.

The potential for the entry of other factors, e.g. fungi, is also due partly to the existence of the stomata. If the air surrounding the leaf becomes very humid, then the **diffusion** of water vapour will be much reduced and the rate of transpiration will decrease. Application of water to greenhouse paths during the summer, **damping down**, increases relative humidity and reduces transpiration rate. If the air surrounding the leaf is moving, humidity of air around the leaf is low, so that transpiration is maintained. Windbreaks, e.g. some woody species, reduce the risk of desiccation of crops. Ambient temperatures affect the rate at which liquid water in the leaf evaporates and thus determines the transpiration rate. The plant is able to control its transpiration rate because the **cuticle** (a waxy waterproof layer) protects most of its surface and the stomata are able to close up as the cells in the leaf start to lose their turgor (*see* leaf structure, page 57). The stomatal pore is bordered by two sausage-shaped guard cells, which have thick cell walls near to the pore. When the guard cells are

fully turgid, the pressure of water on the thinner walls causes the cells to buckle and the pore to open. If the plant begins to lose more water, the guard cells lose their turgidity and the stomata close to prevent any further water loss. Stomata also respond to light and dark, respectively, by opening and closing. The mechanism of this action is not fully understood. The very quick response of the chloroplast-containing guard cells is unlikely to be due to cell turgor induced by photosynthesis. Stomata also close if carbon dioxide concentration in the air rises above optimum levels.

A close relationship exists between the daily fluctuation in the rate of transpiration and the variation in solar radiation. This is used to assess the amount of water being lost from cuttings in mist units (*see* misting); a light-sensitive cell automatically switches on the misting. In artificial conditions, e.g. in a florist shop, transpiration rate can be reduced by providing a cool, humid and shaded environment.

Plasmolysed leaf cells can occur if highly concentrated sprays cause water to leave the cells and result in scorching (*see* page 47).

The evaporation of water from the cells of the leaf means that in order for the leaf to remain turgid, which is important for efficient photosynthesis, the water lost must be replaced by water in the xylem. Pressure is created in the xylem by the loss from an otherwise closed system and water moves up the petiole of the leaf and stem of the plant by suction (*see* **transpiration pull**). If the water in the xylem column is broken, e.g. when a stem of a flower is cut, air moves into the xylem and may restrict the further movement of water when the cut flower is placed in water. However, once the column is restored water enters by the cut surface at a faster rate than if the plant was intact with a root system.

Anti-transpirants are plastic substances which, when sprayed onto the leaves, will create a temporary barrier to water loss over the whole leaf surface, including the stomata. These substances are useful to protect a plant during a critical period in its cultivation; e.g. conifers can be treated while they are moved to another site.

Structural adaptations to the leaf occur in some species to enable them to withstand low water supplies with a reduced surface area, a very thick cuticle and sunken guard cells protected below the leaf surface Figure 5.3. Compare this cross section with that of a more typical leaf shown in Figure 6.1. In extreme cases, e.g. cacti, the leaf is reduced to a spine, and the stem takes over the function of photosynthesis and is also capable of water storage, as in the stonecrop (*Sedum*). Other adaptations are described on page 58.

MINERALS

Essential minerals are those inorganic substances necessary for the plant to grow and develop normally. They can be conveniently divided into two groups. The **major nutrients (macronutrients)** are required in relatively large quantities whereas the **micronutrients (trace elements)** are needed in relatively small quantities, usually measured in parts per million (ppm), and within a narrow concentration range to avoid deficiency or toxicity. The list of essential nutrients is given in Table 5.1.

Non-essential minerals, such as sodium and chlorine, have important functions in some plants but are not constantly required for plant growth and development.

Table 5.1 Nutrient requirements of plants

Macronutrients (major nutrients)	
N	Nitrogen
P	Phosphate
K	Potassium
Mg	Magnesium
Ca	Calcium
S	Sulphur
Micronutrients (trace elements)	
Fe	Iron
Bo	Boron
Mn	Manganese
Cu	Copper
Zn	Zinc
Mo	Molybdenum

Functions and deficiency symptoms of minerals in the plant

Many essential minerals have very specific functions in the plant cell processes. When in short supply (**deficient**) the plant shows certain characteristic symptoms, but these symptoms tend to indicate an extreme deficiency. To ensure optimal mineral supplies, growing media analysis (*see* Chapter 16) or plant tissue analysis can be used to forecast low nutrient levels, which can then be suitably increased.

Nitrogen is a constituent of **proteins**, nucleic acids and chlorophyll and, as such, is a major requirement for plant growth. Its compounds comprise about 50 per cent of the dry matter of protoplasm, the living substance of plant cells. Deficiency causes slow, spindly growth in all plants and yellowing of the leaves (chlorosis) due to lack of chlorophyll. Stems may be red or purple due to the formation of other pigments. The high mobility of nitrogen in the plant to the younger, active leaves leads to the old leaves showing the symptoms first.

Phosphorus is important in the production of nucleic acid and the formation of adenosine triphosphate (ATP) (*see* page 41). Large amounts are therefore concentrated in the meristem. Organic phosphates, so vital for the plant's respiration, are also required in active organs such as roots and fruit, while the seed must store adequate levels for germination. Phosphorus supplies at the seedling stage are critical; the growing root has a high requirement and the plant's ability to establish itself depends on the roots being able to tap into supplies in the soil before the reserves in the seed are used up (*see* 202). Deficiency symptoms are not very distinctive. Poor establishment of seedlings results from a general reduction in growth of stem and root systems. Sometimes a general darkening of the leaves in dicotyledonous plants leads to brown leaf patches, while a reddish tinge is seen in monocotyledons. In cucumbers grown in deficient peat composts or NFT, characteristic stunting and development of small young leaves lead to brown spotting on older leaves.

Potassium. Although present in relatively large amounts in plant cells, this mineral does not have any clear function in the formation of important cell products. It exists as a cation and acts as an osmotic regulator, e.g. in guard cells (*see* osmosis, page 47), and is involved in resistance to chilling injury, drought and disease.

Deficiency results in brown, scorched patches on leaf tips and margins, especially on older leaves, due to the high mobility of potassium towards growing points. Leaves may develop a bronzed appearance and roll inwards and downwards (*see* Plate 9).

Magnesium is a constituent of chlorophyll. It is also involved in the activation of some enzymes and in the movement of phosphorus in the plant. Deficiency symptoms appear initially in older leaves because magnesium is mobile in the plant. A characteristic interveinal chlorosis appears, which subsequently become reddened and eventually necrotic (dead) areas develop (*see* Plate 10).

Calcium is a major constituent of plant cell walls as calcium pectate, which binds the cells together. It also influences the activity of meristems especially in root tips. Calcium is not mobile in the plant so the deficiency symptoms tend to appear in the younger tissues first. It causes weakened cell walls, resulting in inward curling, pale young leaves and sometimes death of the growing point. Specific disorders include 'topple' in tulips, when the flower head cannot be supported by the top of the stem, 'blossom end rot' in tomato fruit, and 'bitter pit' in apple fruit.

Sulphur is a vital component of many proteins that includes many important enzymes. It is also involved in the synthesis of chlorophyll. Consequently a deficiency produces a chlorosis that, due to the relative immobility of sulphur in the plant, is shown in younger leaves first.

Iron and manganese are involved in the synthesis of chlorophyll; although they do not form part of the molecule they are components of some enzymes required in its synthesis. Deficiencies of both minerals result in leaf chlorosis. The immobility of iron causes the younger leaves to show interveinal chlorosis first. In extreme cases, the growing area turns white.

Boron affects various processes, such as the translocation of sugars and the synthesis of gibberellic acid in some seeds (*see* dormancy, page 63). Deficiency causes a breakdown and disorganization of tissues, leading to early death of the growing point. Characteristic disorders include 'brown heart' of turnips, and 'hollow stem' in brassicas. The leaves may become misshapen, and stems may break. Flowering is often suppressed, while malformed fruit are produced, e.g. 'corky core' in apples and 'cracked fruit' of peaches.

Copper is a component of a number of enzymes. Deficiency in many species results in dark green leaves, which become twisted and may prematurely wither.

Zinc, also involved in enzymes, produces characteristic deficiency symptoms associated with the poor development of leaves, e.g. 'little leaf' in citrus and peach, and 'rosette leaf' in apples.

Molybdenum assists the uptake of nitrogen, and although required in very much smaller quantities, its deficiency can result in reduced plant nitrogen levels. In tomatoes and lettuce, deficiency of molybdenum can lead to chlorosis in older leaves, followed by death of cells between the veins (interveinal necrosis) and leaf margins. Tissue browning and infolding of the leaves may occur. In brassicas, the 'whiptail' leaf symptom involves a dominant midrib and loss of leaf lamina.

Mineral uptake

Minerals are absorbed in water by the root system, which obtains its supply from the growing medium (*see* Chapter 17). The plants take up only water-soluble material. Therefore all supplies of nutrients including fertilizers and manures must be in the form of **ions** (charged particles). The movement of the elements in the form of **ions** occurs in the direction of root cells containing a higher mineral concentration than the soil, i.e. **against a concentration gradient**. The passage in the water medium across the root cortex is by simple diffusion, but transport across the endodermis requires a supply of energy from the root cortex.

Figure 5.4 *Apple (Cox on M1) excavated at 16 years to reveal distribution of roots. Note the vigorous main root system near the surface with some penetrating deeply (courtesy of Dr E.G. Coker).*

The process is therefore related to temperature and oxygen supply (*see* respiration, page 59).

Nutrients are taken up predominantly by the extensive network of fine roots that grow in the top layers of the soil (*see* Figure 5.4). Damage to the roots near the soil surface by cultivations should be avoided because it can significantly reduce the plant's ability to extract nutrients. It is recommended that care should be taken to ensure that trees and shrubs are planted so their roots are not buried too deeply and many advocate that the horizontally growing roots should be set virtually at the surface to give the best conditions for establishment.

The surface thickening that occurs in the ageing root does not significantly reduce the absorption ability of most minerals, e.g. potassium and phosphate, but calcium is found to be principally taken up by the young roots.

FURTHER READING

Bowes, B.G. *A Colour Atlas of Plant Structure* (Manson, 1996).

Brown, L.V. *Applied Principles of Horticulture*, 2nd edition (Butterworth-Heinemann, 2002).

Capon, B. *Botany for Gardeners* (Timber Press, 1990).

Clegg, C.J. and Cox, G. *Anatomy and Activities of Plants* (John Murray, 1978).

Ingram, D.S. *et al.* (Editors) *Science and the Garden* (Blackwell Science Ltd., 2002).

MAFF. *Diagnosis of Mineral Disorders in Plants*, Vol. 1 *Principles* (HMSO, 1984), Vol. 2 *Vegetables* (HMSO, 1984), Vol. 3 *Glasshouse Crops* (HMSO, 1987).

Mauseth, J.P. *Botany – An Introduction to Plant Biology* (Saunders, 1998).

Scott Russell, R. *Plant Root Systems: Their Function and Interaction with the Soil* (McGraw-Hill, 1982).

Sutcliffe, J. *Plants and Water* (Edward Arnold, 1971).

Sutcliffe, J.F. and Baker, D.A. *Plant and Mineral Salts* (Edward Arnold, 1976).

6

Plant Growth

In any horticultural situation, growers are concerned with controlling and even manipulating plant growth. They must provide for the plants the optimum conditions to produce the most efficient growth rate and the end-product required. Therefore the processes that result in growth are explored in order that the most suitable or economic growth can be achieved. Photosynthesis is probably the single most important process in plant growth. Respiration is the process by which the food matter produced by photosynthesis is converted into energy usable for growth of the plant. Photosynthesis and respiration make these processes possible and the balance between these results in growth. It must be emphasized that growth involves the plant in hundreds of chemical processes, occurring in the different organs and tissues throughout the plant.

Growth is a difficult term to define because it really encompasses the totality of all the processes that takes place during the life of an organism. However, it is useful to distinguish between the processes which result in an increase in size and weight, and those processes which cause the changes in the plant during its life cycle, which can usefully be called development, described in Chapter 7.

PHOTOSYNTHESIS

Photosynthesis is the process in the chloroplasts of the leaf and stem cells by which a green plant manufactures food in the form of high energy carbohydrates such as sugars and starch, using light as energy. All living organisms require organic matter as food to build up their structure and to provide chemical energy to fuel their activities. Whilst photosynthesis is the crucial process, it should be remembered that a multitude of other processes is occurring all over the plant. Proteins are being produced, many of which are enzymes necessary to speed up chemical reactions in the leaf, the stem, the root, and later in the flower and fruit. The complex carbohydrate, cellulose is being built up as cell walls of almost every cell. Nucleoprotcins are being provided in meristematic areas to enable cell division. These are three examples of the many, to show that growth involves much more than just photosynthesis and respiration.

All the complex organic compounds, based on carbon, must be produced from the simple raw materials, water and carbon dioxide. Many organisms are unable to manufacture their own food, and must therefore feed on already manufactured organic matter such as plants or animals. As large animals predate on smaller animals, which themselves feed on plants, all organisms depend directly or indirectly on photosynthesis occurring in the plant as the basis of a **food web** or chain.

Table 6.1   Two ways to represent the chemistry involved in photosynthesis

(a) *Written in a conventional way, the process can be expressed in the following way:*

$$\text{Carbon dioxide} + \text{water} + \text{light} \rightarrow \text{glucose} + \text{oxygen}$$
(when in the presence of chlorophyll)

(b) *Written in the form of a chemical equation, which represents molecular happenings at the, sub-microscopic level; the above sentence becomes:*

$$6CO_2 \text{ molecules} + 6H_2O \text{ molecules} + \text{light} \rightarrow 1C_6H_{12}O_6 \text{ molecule} + 6O_2 \text{ molecules}$$
(when in the presence of chlorophyll)

A summary of the process of photosynthesis is given in Table 6.1 as a word formula and as a chemical equation. This apparently simple equation represents, in reality, two different stages in the production of glucose. The first, the 'light reaction', occurs during daylight, and splits water into hydrogen and oxygen. The second, the 'dark reaction' occurring at night, takes the hydrogen and joins it to carbon dioxide to make glucose.

Most plant species follow a 'C-3' process of photosynthesis where the intermediate chemical compound contains three-carbon atoms (C-3) before producing the six-carbon glucose molecule (C-6). Many C-3 plants are not able to increase their rate of photosynthesis under conditions of very high light levels.

In contrast, a 'C-4' process is seen in many tropical families, including the maize family, where plants, which use an intermediate compound containing four-carbon atoms (C-4), are able to continue to respond to very high levels of light, thus increasing their productivity.

A third process, called 'crassulacean acid metabolism' (**CAM**), was first discovered in the stonecrop family. Here, the intermediate chemical is a different four-carbon compound, malic acid. This third process has more recently been found in several other succulent plant families (including cacti), all of which need to survive conditions of drought. Such plants need to keep their stomata closed during the heat of the day, but this prevents the entry of carbon dioxide. During the night, carbon dioxide is absorbed and stored as malic acid, ready for conversion to glucose, the next day. CAM plants do not normally grow very fast because they are not able to store large quantities of this malic acid, and thus their potential for glucose production is limited.

Requirements for photosynthesis

Carbon dioxide
In order that a plant may build up organic compounds such as sugars, it must have a supply of carbon which is readily available. **Carbon dioxide** is present in the air in concentrations of 330 ppm (parts per million) or 0.03 per cent, and can diffuse into the leaf through the stomata, as described in Chapter 5. Carbon dioxide gas moves 10 000 times faster than it would in solution through the roots. The amount of carbon dioxide in the air immediately surrounding the plant can fall when planting is very dense, or when plants have been photosynthesizing rapidly, especially in an unventilated greenhouse.

This reduction will slow down the rate of photosynthesis, but a grower may supply additional carbon dioxide inside a greenhouse or polythene tunnel to **enrich** the atmosphere up to about three times the normal concentration, or an optimum of 1000 ppm (0.1 per cent) in lettuce. Such practices will produce a corresponding increase in growth, provided other factors are available to the plant. If any one of these is in short supply, then the process will be slowed down. This principle, called the **law of limiting factors**, states that the factor in least supply will limit the rate of the process, and applies to other non-photosynthetic processes in the plant. It would be wasteful, therefore, to increase the carbon dioxide concentration artificially, e.g. by burning propane gas, or releasing pure carbon dioxide gas, if other factors were not proportionally increased.

Light

Light is a factor required in order that photosynthesis can occur. In any series of chemical reactions where one substance combines with another to form a larger compound, energy is needed to fuel the reactions. Energy for photosynthesis is provided by light from the sun or from artificial lamps. As with carbon dioxide, the amount of light energy present is important in determining the rate of photosynthesis – simply, the more light or greater **illuminance** (intensity) absorbed by the plant, the more photosynthesis can take place. Light energy is measured in joules per square metre, but for practical purposes the light for plant growth is measured according to the light falling on a given area, i.e. lumens per square metre (lux). Radiant energy (**irradiance**) is a less useful method of measurement because it includes a significant quantity of energy from wavelengths that do not contribute to photosynthesis. However, photosynthetically active radiation (**PAR**) is the most useful method as it is the energy that can be used for photosynthesis (units = W/m^2). Whilst the measurement of illuminance is a very useful tool for the grower, it is difficult to state the plant's precise requirements, as variation occurs with species, age, temperature, carbon dioxide levels, nutrient supply and health of the plant.

However, it is possible to suggest approximate limits within which photosynthesis will take place; a minimum intensity of about 500–1000 lux enables the plant's photosynthesis rate to keep pace with **respiration**, and thus maintain itself. The maximum amount of light many plants can usefully absorb is approximately 30 000 lux, while good growth in many plants will occur at 10 000–15 000 lux. Plant species adapted to shade conditions, however, e.g. *Ficus benjamina*, require only 1000 lux. Other shade-tolerant plants include *Taxus* spp., *Mahonia* and *Hedera*. In summer, light intensity can reach 50 000–90 000 lux and is therefore not limiting, but in winter months, between November and February, the low natural light intensity of about 3000–8000 lux is the limiting factor for plants actively growing in a heated greenhouse or polythene tunnel. Care must be taken to maintain clean glass or polythene, and to avoid condensation that restricts light transmission. Intensity can be increased by using artificial lighting, which can also extend the length of day, which is short during the winter, by **supplementary lighting**. This method is used for plants such as lettuce, bedding plants and brassica seedlings.

Total replacement lighting. Growing rooms which receive no natural sunlight at all use controlled temperatures, humidities and carbon dioxide levels, as well as light. Young plants which can be grown in a relatively small area, and which are capable of responding well to good growing conditions in terms of growth rate, are often raised in a growing room.

The type of lamp. Lamps are chosen for increasing intensity, and therefore more photosynthesis. All such lamps must have a relatively high efficiency of conversion of electricity to light, and only the **gas discharge** lamps are able to do this. Light is produced when an electric arc is formed across the gas filament enclosed under pressure inside an inner tube. Light, like other forms of energy, e.g. heat, X-rays and radio waves, travels in the form of waves, and the distance between one wave peak and the next is termed as the wavelength. Light wavelengths are measured in nanometres (nm); 1 nm = one thousandth of a micrometre. Visible light wavelengths vary from 800 nm (red light – in the long wavelength area) to 350 nm (blue light – in the short wavelength area), and a combination of different wavelengths (colours) appears as white light. Each type of lamp produces a characteristic wavelength range and, just as different coloured substances absorb and reflect varying colours of light, so a plant absorbs and reflects specific wavelengths of light.

Since the photosynthetic green pigment chlorophyll absorbs mainly red and blue light and reflects more of the yellow and green part of the spectrum, it is important that the lamps used produce a balanced wavelength spectrum to include as high a proportion of those colours as possible, in order that the plant makes most efficient use of the light provided. The gas included in a lamp determines its light characteristics. The two most commonly used gases for horticultural lighting are mercury vapour, producing a green blue light with no red, and sodium, producing yellow light. This limited spectrum may be modified by the inclusion of fluorescent materials in the inner tube, which allow the tube to re-emit wavelengths more useful to the plant emitted by the gas and re-emit the energy as a shorter wavelength. Thus, modified mercury lamps produce the desirable red light missing from the basic emission.

Low-pressure mercury-filled tubes produce diffuse light and, when suitably grouped in banks, provide uniform light close to plants. These are especially useful in a growing room, provided that they produce a broad spectrum of light as is seen in the 'full spectrum fluorescent tubes'. Gas enclosed at **high pressure** in a second inner tube produces a small, high intensity source of light. These small lamps do not greatly obstruct natural light entering a greenhouse and, while producing valuable uniform supplementary illumination at a distance, cause no leaf scorch. Probably the most useful lamp for supplementary lighting in a greenhouse is a high-pressure sodium lamp, which produces a high intensity of light, and is relatively efficient (27 per cent).

Carbon dioxide **enrichment** should be matched to artificial lighting in order to produce the greatest growth rate and most efficient use of both factors.

Temperature

The complex chemical reactions, which occur during the formation of carbohydrates from water and carbon dioxide requires the presence of chemicals called **enzymes** to accelerate the rate of reactions. Without these enzymes, only little chemical activity would occur. Enzyme activity in living things increases with temperature from $0°C$ to $36°C$, and ceases at $40°C$. This pattern is mirrored by the effect of air temperature on the rate of photosynthesis. But here, the optimum temperature varies with plant species from $25°C$ to $36°C$ as optimum. It should be borne in mind that at very low light levels, the increase in photosynthetic rate with increased temperature is only limited. This means that any input of heating into the growing situation

during cold weather will be largely wasted if the light levels are low.

Integrated environmental control in a greenhouse is a form of computerized system developed to maintain near-optimum levels of the main environmental factors (light, temperature and carbon dioxide) necessary for plant growth. It achieves this by frequent monitoring of the greenhouse using carefully positioned sensors. Such a system is able to avoid the low temperature/light interaction described above. The beneficial effects to plant growth of lower night temperatures compared with day are well known in many species, e.g. tomato. The explanation is inconclusive, but the accumulation of sugars during the night appears to be greater, suggesting a relationship between photosynthesis and respiration rates. Such responses are shown to be related to temperature regimes experienced in the areas of origin of the species.

Temperature adaptations.   Adaptation to extremes in temperature can be found in a number of species; e.g. resistance to high temperatures above $40°C$ in **thermophiles**; resistance to **chilling injury** is brought about by lowering the freezing point of cell constituents. Both depend on the stage of development of the plant, e.g. a seed is relatively resistant, but the hypocotyl of a young seedling is particularly vulnerable. Resistance to chilling injury is imparted by the cell membrane, which can also allow the accumulation of substances to prevent freezing of the cell contents. **Hardening off** of plants by gradual exposure to cold temperatures can develop a change in the cell membrane as in bedding plants and peas. Examples of plant hardiness are found in Table 3.3.

Water

Water is required in the photosynthesis reaction but this represents only a very small proportion of the total water taken up by the plant (*see* transpiration). Water supply through the xylem is essential to maintain leaf turgidity and retain fully open stomata for carbon dioxide movement into the leaf. In a situation where a leaf contains only 90 per cent of its optimum water content, stomatal closure will prevent carbon dioxide entry to such an extent that there may be as much as 50 per cent reduction in photosynthesis. A visibly wilting plant will not be photosynthesizing at all.

Minerals

Minerals are required by the leaf to produce the **chlorophyll** pigment that absorbs most of the light energy for photosynthesis. Production of chlorophyll must be continuous, since it loses its efficiency quickly. A plant deficient in iron, or magnesium especially, turns yellow (**chlorotic**) and loses much of its photosynthetic ability. **Variegation** similarly results in a slower growth rate.

The leaf

The leaf is the main organ for photosynthesis in the plant, and its cells are organized in a way that provides maximum efficiency. The upper epidermis is transparent enough to allow the transmission of light into the lower-leaf tissues. The sausage-shaped palisade-mesophyll cells are packed together, pointing downwards, under the upper epidermis. The sub-cellular **chloroplasts** within them carry out the photosynthesis process. The absorption of light by chlorophyll occurs at one site and the energy is transferred to a second site within the chloroplast where it is used to build up carbohydrates, usually in the form of insoluble starch. The spongy mesophyll, below the palisade mesophyll, has a loose structure with many air spaces. These spaces allow for the two-way diffusion of gases. The carbon dioxide from the air is able to reach the palisade mesophyll; and oxygen, the waste product from photosynthesis, leaves the leaf. The numerous **stomata** on the lower-leaf surface are the openings to the outside by which this gas movement occurs. The numerous small vascular bundles (veins) within the leaf structure contain the xylem vessels that provide the water for the photosynthesis reaction. The phloem cells are similarly present in the vascular bundles, for the removal of sugar to other plant parts. Figure 6.1 shows the structure of the leaf and its relevance to the process of photosynthesis. A newly expanded leaf is most efficient in the absorption of light, and this ability reduces with age.

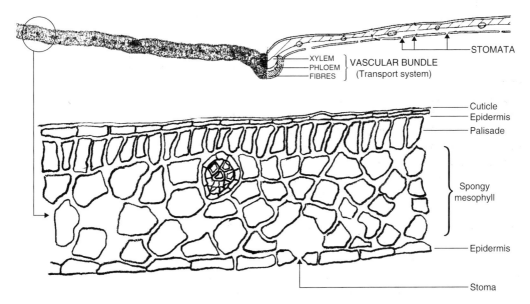

Figure 6.1 *Cross-section of privet* (Ligustrum) *leaf showing features for efficient photosynthesis. Inset shows the tissues making up the leaf blade in more detail.*

Movement of sugar

The product of photosynthesis in most plants is starch (some plants produce sugars only), which is stored temporarily in the chloroplast or moved in the phloem to be more permanently stored in the seed, the stem cortex or root, where specialized storage organs such as **rhizomes** and **tubers** may occur. The movement or **translocation** of materials around the plant in the phloem and xylem is a complex operation, and does not have a full scientific explanation. The phloem is principally responsible for the transport of the products of photosynthesis as soluble sugars, usually sucrose, which move under pressure to areas of need, such as roots, flowers or storage organs. Each phloem sieve-tube cell has a smaller companion cell that has a high metabolic rate. Energy is thus made available to the protoplasm at the end of each sieve plate, which is able to 'pump' dilute sugar solutions around the plant. The flow can be interrupted by the presence of disease organisms such as club root.

Leaf adaptations

Whilst remaining essentially the organ of photosynthesis and transpiration, the leaf takes on other functions in some species. The most notable of these is the climbing function. Tendrils are slender extensions of the leaf, and are of three types. In *Clematis* spp., the leaf petiole curls round the stems of other plants or garden structures in order to support the climber. In sweet pea (*Lathyrus odoratus*), the plant holds on with tendrils modified from the end-leaflets of the compound leaf. In the monocotyledonous climber (*Smilax china*), the support is provided by modified stipules (found at the base of the petiole). In cleavers (*Galium aparine*), both the leaf and stipules, borne in a whorl, have prickles that allow the weed to sprawl over other plant species.

Buds and bulbs are composed mainly of leaf tissue. In the former, the leaves (called scales) are reduced in size, hard and brown rather than green. They tightly overlap each other, giving protection to the delicate meristematic tissues inside the

bud. In a bulb, the succulent, light-coloured scale leaves contain all the nutrients and moisture necessary for the bulbs emergence. The scales are packed densely together around the terminal bud, minimizing the risk that might be caused by extremes of climate, or by pests such as eelworms or mice.

In the houseplant, *Bryophyllum daigremontianum*, the succulent leaf bears adventitious buds that are able to develop into young plantlets (*see* also page 69).

Leaf form

The novice gardener may easily overlook the importance that the shape, texture, venation, colour and size of leaves can contribute to the general appearance of a garden, as they focus more on the floral side of things. Flowers are the most striking feature, but they are often short lived. It should be emphasized that the dominant theme in most gardens is the foliage and not the flowers (*see* Plates 1, 2 and 5). The possibilities for contrast are almost endless when these five leaf aspects are considered.

In Chapter 3 (*see* page 33) the range of leaf forms is described. Consider leaf shape first. The large linear leaves of *Phormium tenax* (New Zealand Flax) are a well-known striking example. In contrast are the large palmate leaves of *Gunnera manicata*. On a smaller scale, the shade-loving *Hostas*, with their lanceolate leaves, mix well with the pinnate-leaved *Dryopteris filix-mas* (male fern).

Secondly, leaf texture is also important. Most species have quite smooth textured leaves. Notably different are *Verbascum olympicum*, *Stachys byzantina* (lamb's tongue) and the alpine *Leontopodium alpinum* (edelweiss) which all are woolly in texture. Glossy-leaved species such as *Ilex aquifolium* (holly) and *Pieris japonica* provide a striking appearance.

Thirdly, the plant kingdom exhibits a wide variety of leaf colour tones (*see* Plate 5). The conifer *Juniperus chinensis* (Chinese juniper), shrubs of the *Ceanothus* genus and *Helleborus viridus* (Christmas rose) are examples of dark-leaved plants. Notable examples of plants with light-coloured leaves are the tree *Robinia pseudoacacia* (false acacia), the climber *Humulus lupulinus* 'Aureus' (common hop) and the creeping herbaceous perennial *Lysimachia nummularia* 'Aurea' (Creeping Jenny). Plants with unusually coloured foliage may also be briefly mentioned: the small tree *Prunus* 'Shirofugen' (bronze-red), the sub-shrub *Senecio maritima* (silver-grey) and the shade perennial *Ajuga reptans* 'Atropurpurea' (bronze-purple).

Variegation (the presence of both yellow and green areas on the leaf) gives a novel appearance to the plant (*see* Plate 8). Example species are *Aucuba japonica* (Laurel), *Euonymus fortunei* and *Glechoma hederacea* (ground ivy). Fourthly, in autumn, the leaves of several tree, shrub and climber species change from green to a striking orange-red colour. *Acer japonicum* (Japanese maple), *Euonymus alatus* (Winged spindle) and *Parthenocissus tricuspidata* (Boston ivy) are examples.

Pollution

Gases in the air, which are usually products of industrial processes or burning fuels, can cause damage to plants, often resulting in scorching symptoms of the leaves. Fluoride can accumulate in composts and be present in tap water, so causing marginal and tip scorch in leaves of susceptible species such as *Dracaena* and *Gladiolus*. Sulphur dioxide and carbon dioxide may be produced by faulty heat exchangers in glasshouse burners, especially those using paraffin. Scorch damage over the whole leaf is preceded by a reddish discoloration.

RESPIRATION

Respiration is the process by which sugars and related substances are broken down to yield energy, the end-products being carbon dioxide and water. In order that growth can occur, the food must be broken down in a controlled manner to release energy for the production of useful structural substances such as cellulose, the main constituent of plant cell walls, and proteins for enzymes. This energy is used also to fuel cell division and the many chemical reactions that occur in the cell.

The energy requirement within the plant varies, and reproductive organs can respire at twice the rate of the leaves. Also, in apical meristems, the processes of cell division and cell differentiation require high inputs of energy. In order that the breakdown is complete, oxygen is required in the process of aerobic respiration. A summary of the process is given in Table 6.2.

It would appear, at first sight, that respiration is the reverse of photosynthesis (*see* page 54). This supposition is correct in the sense that photosynthesis creates glucose as an energy-saving strategy, and respiration breaks down glucose as an energy-releasing mechanism. It is also correct in the sense that the simple equations representing the two processes are mirror images of each other.

It should, however, be emphasized that the two processes have two notable differences. The first is that respiration in plants (as in animals) occurs in all living cells of all tissues at all times (in leaves, stems, flowers, roots and fruits). Photosynthesis occurs predominantly in the palisade-mesophyll tissue of leaves. Secondly, respiration takes place

Table 6.2 A summary of the process of aerobic respiration

(a) *Written in a conventional way, the process can be expressed in the following way:*

Glucose + oxygen → carbon dioxide + water + energy
(in the mitochondria of the cell)

(b) *Written in the form of a chemical equation, which represents molecular happenings at the sub-microscopic level; the above sentence becomes:*

$1C_6H_{12}O_6$ molecule + $6O_2$ molecules → $6CO_2$ molecules + $6H_2O$ molecules + energy
(in the mitochondria of the cell)

---

in the torpedo-shaped organelles of the cell called mitochondria. Photosynthesis occurs in the oval-shaped chloroplasts. Details of biochemistry, beyond the scope of this book, would reveal how different these processes are, in spite of their superficial similarities. In the absence of oxygen, inefficient **anaerobic** respiration takes place and incomplete breakdown of the carbohydrates produces alcohol as a waste product, with energy still trapped in the molecule. If a plant or plant organ such as root is supplied with low oxygen concentrations in a waterlogged or compacted soil, the consequent alcohol production may prove toxic enough to cause root death. Over-watering, especially of pot plants, leads to this damage and encourages damping-off fungi.

Storage of plants

The actively growing plant is supplied with the necessary factors for photosynthesis and respiration to take place. Roots, leaves or flower stems removed from the plant for sale or planting will cease to photosynthesize, though respiration continues. Carbohydrates and other storage products, such as proteins and fats, continue to be broken down to release energy, but the plant reserves are depleted and dry weight reduced. A reduction in the respiration rate should therefore be considered for stored plant material, whether the period of storage is a few days, e.g. tomatoes and cut flowers, or several months, e.g. apples. Attention to the following factors may achieve this aim.

Temperature.   The enzymes involved in respiration become progressively less active with a reduction in temperatures from 36°C (optimum) to 0°C. Therefore, a cold store employing temperatures between 0°C and 10°C is commonly used for the storage of materials such as cut flowers, e.g. roses; fruit, e.g. apples; vegetables, e.g. onions; and cuttings, e.g. chrysanthemums, which root more readily later. Long-term storage of seeds in **gene banks** (*see* Chapter 8) uses liquid nitrogen at −20°C.

Oxygen and carbon dioxide.   Respiration requires oxygen in sufficient concentration; if oxygen concentration is reduced, the rate of respiration will decrease. Conversely, carbon dioxide is a product of the process and, as with many processes, a build-up of a product will cause the rate of the process to decrease. A controlled environment store for long-term storage, e.g. of top fruit, is maintained at 0–5°C according to cultivar, and is fed with inert nitrogen gas to exclude oxygen. Carbon dioxide is increased by up to 10 per cent for some apple cultivars.

Water loss.   Loss of water may quickly desiccate and kill stored material, such as cuttings. Seeds also must not be allowed to lose so much water that they become non-viable, but too humid an environment may encourage premature germination with equal loss of viability.

FURTHER READING

Attridge, T.H. *Light and Plant Responses* (Edward Arnold, 1991).

Bickford, E.D. *et al. Lighting for Plant Growth* (Kent State University Press, 1973).

Bleasdale, J.K.A. *Plant Physiology in Relation to Horticulture* (Macmillan, 1983).

Bowes, B.G. *A Colour Atlas of Plant Structure* (Manson, 1996).

Brown, L.V. *Applied Principles of Horticulture*, 2nd edition (Butterworth-Heinemann, 2002).

Capon, B. *Botany for Gardeners* (Timber Press, 1990).

Grow Electric Handbook No. 2. *Lighting in Greenhouses*, Part 1 (Electricity Council, 1974).

Hopkins, W.G. *Introduction to Plant Physiology* (Wiley and Sons, 1995).

Ingram, D.S. *et al.* (editors). *Science and the Garden* (Blackwell Science Ltd, 2002).

MAFF. *Carbon Dioxide Enrichment for Lettuce, HPG51* (HMSO, 1978).

Moorby, J. *Transport Systems in Plants* (Longman, 1981).

Sutcliffe, J. *Plants and Temperature* (Edward Arnold, 1977).

Thompson, A.K. *Postharvest Technology of Fruit and Vegetables.* (Blackwell Science Ltd, 1996).

7

Plant Development

The life cycle of the flowering plant contains a number of identifiable stages, each with a distinct significance to horticulture. The seed is the means by which a new generation begins, usually resulting in great variation in the plants produced. This is followed by the sensitive seedling, vulnerable to diseases, pest attack and physiological disorders, but highly responsive to good growing conditions. The vegetative stage may be manipulated to the required size and shape or used for propagation. The flowering stage is often the desired objective, while the formation of fruit may be an important horticultural aim, whether in an edible form or as the precursor of seeds.

The characteristics of the plant are under genetic control (*see* Chapter 8). **However, the development of the plant, from one stage of the life cycle to the next, takes place in response to a number of stimuli, many of which are changes in factors occurring in the plant's environment.**

The plant's most reliable indicator of season, especially in temperate regions, is the daylength, which shortens and lengthens with the time of year. Annual temperature fluctuations are a valuable, if less precise, indicator of seasonal occurrence. The plant responds to these environmental factors by breaking seed or bud dormancy in spring, by

flowering at appropriate seasons and by the dropping (**abscission**) of leaves in autumn.

PLANT HORMONES

In order that the genetic potential of a plant can be stimulated by factors of the environment, it must possess a system that, having perceived the stimulus, is able to activate the response. Such control is achieved by chemicals produced by the plant. These chemicals are the plant hormones. The concentration of hormone may vary according to the stage of plant development. Equally important, the balance of hormones and their relative concentrations will determine, to a large extent, the kind of response required. The concentration of these chemicals, required to cause an effect on plant development, is extremely low (measured in parts per million). The chemicals are all relatively simple in structure and can be moved around the plant quite easily. The plant's development is best achieved when the hormone is at the optimal concentration. Any decrease or increase in concentration away from the optimum level at the site of activity may result in delayed development or distorted growth.

There are five main types of plant hormones:

- **Auxin (indoleacetic acid)** is primarily produced in the dividing cells of the apical and leaf meristems. Its role in the plant is varied. It induces decreased cell division and increased cell elongation in the tip of the stem, inhibits growth of side shoots, promotes secondary growth in vascular tissues, inhibits leaf fall, promotes fruit development whilst inhibiting fruit drop and stimulates cell differentiation in wounded tissue.

- **Gibberellin** is produced in young leaves, seed embryos and root tips. It is involved in stem elongation, increased cell division and initiating seed germination.
- **Cytokinin** is produced in dividing cells of root tips, seeds and fruits. It is involved in stimulating cell division in meristems, promoting side-bud growth on stems, delaying leaf ageing and stimulating fruit development. It may travel in the transpiration stream from root to leaf.
- **Abscisic acid** and **ethylene** contribute to the precision achieved by the three above-described hormones. Abscisic acid is produced in ageing leaves, and in stems, fruits and seeds. It induces dormancy in buds, halts cell elongation in roots, promotes leaf fall and fruit fall, and promotes closure of stomata in drought conditions. Ethylene (ethene) is produced in all plant parts, but has its greatest effect in promoting the ripening of fruits.

The horticulturist is able to both modify the plant environment and also utilize synthetic chemicals similar in action to those produced by the plant, called **plant growth regulators**, to manipulate the growth and development of the plant. The relevance of these applications will be discussed at each stage of development.

The **life cycle of plants** is described and includes several of the vast number of variations on the basic pattern. One of the most obvious differences is the length of the life cycle and the terms 'ephemeral', 'annual', 'biennial', 'perennial', 'shrub' and 'tree' are described in Table 3.3 along with other differences which are usefully adopted by growers.

THE SEED

The seed, resulting from sexual reproduction, creates a new generation of plants that bear characteristics of both parents. The plant must survive often through conditions that would be damaging to a growing vegetative organism. The seed is a means of protecting against extreme conditions of temperature and moisture, and is thus the **overwintering stage**. The seed structure may be specialized for wind dispersal, e.g. members of the Asteraceae family, including groundsel, dandelion and thistle, that have parachutes, as does *Clematis* (Ranunculaceae). Many woody species such as lime (*Tilia*), ash (*Fraxinus*) and sycamore (*Acer*) produce winged fruit. Other seedpods are explosive, e.g. balsam and hairy bittercress. Organisms such as birds and mammals distribute hooked fruits such as goosegrass and burdock, succulent types (e.g. tomato, blackberry and elderberry) or those that are filled with protein (e.g. dock). Dispersal mechanisms are summarized in Table 7.1.

Seed structure

The basic seed structure is shown in Figure 7.1. In order to survive, the seed must contain a small immature plant (**embryo**) protected by a seed coat or **testa**, which is formed from the outer layers of the ovule after **fertilization**. A weakness in the testa, the **micropyle**, marks the point of entry of the pollen tube prior to fertilization, and the **hilum** is the point of attachment to the fruit. The embryo consists of a **radicle**, which will develop into the primary root of the seedling and a **plumule**, which develops into the shoot system, the two being joined by a region called the **hypocotyl**. A single seed leaf (**cotyledon**) will be found in monocotyledons, while two are present as part of the embryo of dicotyledons. The cotyledons may occupy a large part of the seed, e.g. in beans, to act as the food store for the embryo.

In some species, e.g. grasses and Ricinus (castor oil plant), the food of the seed is found in a different tissue from the cotyledons. This tissue is called **endosperm** and is derived from the fusion of extra cell nuclei, at the same time as fertilization. Plant food is usually stored as the carbohydrate, starch, formed from sugars as the seed matures, e.g. in

Table 7.1 Fruits and the dispersal of seeds

Fruits

True fruits (formed from the ovary wall after fertilization)

Succulent (indehiscent)	Drupes	Cherry, plum
		Blackberry (collection of drupes)
	Berries	Gooseberry, marrow, banana
Dry indehiscent	Schizocarps	
	Samara	Sycamore
	Lomentum	Trefoil
	Cremocarb	Hogweed
	Carcerulus	Hollyhocks
	Achenes (nuts)	Acorn, rose, strawberry
Dry dehiscent	Capsules	Poppy, violet, campanula
	Siliquas	Wallflowers, stocks
	Siliculas	Shepherd's purse, honesty
	Legumes	Pea, bean, lupin,
	Follicles	Delphinium, monkshood

False fruits (formed from parts other than, or as well as, the ovary wall)

From inflorescence	Pineapple, mulberry
From receptable	Apple

Seed dispersal

Method of seed dispersal	Type of fruit	Examples
Animals	Succulent	Elderberry, blackberry – eaten by birds
		Mistletoe, yew – stick to beaks
	Hooked	Burdock, goosegrass – catch on fur
Wind	Winged	Ash, sycamore, lime, elm
	Parachutes	Dandelion, clematis, thistles
	Censer (dry capsules)	Poppy, campion, antirrhinum
Explosion	Pods	Peas, lupins, gorse, vetches, geranium

peas and beans. Other seeds, such as sunflowers, contain high proportions of fats and oils, and proteins are often present in varying proportions. The seed is also a rich store of nutrients such as phosphorus (*see* page 202) that it requires when it germinates as a seedling.

Seed dormancy

As soon as the embryo begins to grow out of the seed, i.e. **germinates**, the plant is vulnerable to damage from cold or drought. Therefore, the seed must have a mechanism to prevent germination when poor growing conditions prevail. **Dormancy** is a period during which very little activity occurs in the seed, other than a very slow rate of respiration. Seeds will not germinate until dormancy is broken.

A **thick testa** prevents water and oxygen, essential in germination, from entering the seed. Gradual breakdown of the testa, occurring through bacterial action or freezing and thawing, eventually permits germination following unsuitable conditions. The passing of fruit through the digestive system of an animal such as a bird may promote germination, e.g. in tomato, cotoneaster and holly. Many

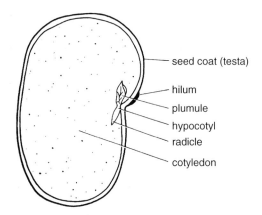

seed coat (testa)

hilum

plumule

hypocotyl

radicle

cotyledon

Figure 7.1 *Long section of a broad bean seed showing the structure of seed coat and embryo essential for germination.*

species, e.g. fat hen, produce seed with variable dormancy periods, to spread germination time over a number of growing seasons. Spring soil cultivations can break the seed coat and induce germination of weed seeds (*see* page 88). This structural dormancy, in horticultural crops, may present germination problems in plants such as rose rootstock species and *Acacia*. Physical methods using sandpaper or chemical treatment with sulphuric acid (collectively known as **scarification**) can break down the seed coat and therefore the dormancy mechanism.

Chemical inhibitors may occur in the seed to prevent the germination process. **Abscisic acid** at high concentrations helps maintain dormancy while, as dormancy breaks, progressively lower levels occur, with a simultaneous increase in concentrations of growth promotors such as gibberellic acid and cytokinins. Inhibitory chemicals located just below the testa may be washed out by soaking in water.

Cold temperatures cause similar breaks of dormancy in other species (**stratification**), the exact temperature requirement varying with the period of exposure and the plant species. Many alpine plants require a 4°C stratification temperature while other species, e.g. *Ailanthus, Thuja*, ash, and many other trees and shrubs, require both moisture and the chilling treatment. The chemical balance inside the seed may be changed in favour of germination by treatment with chemicals such as gibberellic acid and potassium nitrate.

An **undeveloped embryo** in a seed is incapable of germinating until time has elapsed after the seed is removed from the parent plant, i.e. the **after ripening** period has occurred, as in the tomato and many tropical species such as palms. Some seeds such as *Acacia* are recorded to have a dormancy of more than a 100 years.

Seed germination

Seed germination is the emergence of the radicle through the testa, usually at the micropyle. There are a number of essential germination requirements in order that successful seedling emergence occurs.

A **viable seed** has the potential for germination given the required external conditions. Its viability, therefore, indicates the activity of the seed's internal organs, i.e. whether the seed is 'alive' or not. Most seeds remain viable until the next growing season, a period of about 8 months, but many can remain dormant for a number of years until conditions are favourable for germination. In general, viability of a batch of seed diminishes with time, its maximum viability period depending largely on the species. For example, celery seed quickly loses viability after the first season, but wheat has been reported to germinate after scores of years. The germination potential of any seed batch will depend on the storage conditions of the seed, which should be cool and dry, slowing down respiration, and maintaining the internal status of the seed. These conditions are achieved in commercial seed stores by means of sensitive control equipment. Packaging of seed for sale takes account of these requirements and often includes a waterproof lining of the packet, which maintains a constant water content in the seeds. The main requirements for the successful germination of most seed are as follows.

Water supply to the seed is the first environmental requirement for germination. The water content of the seed may fall to 10 per cent during storage, but must be restored to about 70 per cent to enable full chemical activity. Water initially is absorbed into the structure of the testa in a way similar to a sponge taking up water into its air space, i.e. by **imbibition**. This softens the testa and moistens the cell walls of the seed in order that the next stages can proceed. The cells of the seed take up water by **osmosis** often assuming twice the size of the dry seed. The water provides a suitable medium for the activity of enzymes in the process of respiration. A continuous water supply is now required if germination is to proceed at a consistent rate, but the growing medium, whether it is outdoor soil or compost in a seed tray, must not be waterlogged, because **oxygen** essential for aerobic respiration would be withheld from the growing embryo. In the absence of oxygen, **anaerobic respiration** occurs and eventually causes death of the germinating seed, or suspended germination, i.e. **induced dormancy**.

Temperature is a very important germination requirement, and is usually specific to a given species or even cultivar. It acts by fundamentally influencing the activity of the enzymes involved in the biochemical processes of respiration, which occurs between 0°C and 40°C. However, species adapted to specialized environments respond to a narrow range of germination temperatures. For example, cucumbers require a minimum temperature of 15°C and tomatoes 10°C. On the other hand, lettuce germination may be inhibited by temperatures higher than 30°C, and in some cultivars, at 25°C, a period of induced dormancy occurs. Some species, such as mustard, will germinate in temperatures just above freezing and up to 40°C, provided they are not allowed to dry out.

Light is a factor that may influence germination in some species, but most species are indifferent. Seeds of *Rhododendron*, *Veronica* and *Phlox* are inhibited in its germination by exposure to light, while that of celery, lettuce, most grasses, conifers and many herbaceous flowering plants is slowed down when light is excluded. This should be taken into account when the covering material for a seedbed is considered (*see* tilth). The colour (wavelength) of light involved may be critical in the particular response created. Far red light (720 nm), occurring between red light and infra-red light and invisible to the human eye, is found to inhibit germination in some seeds, e.g. birch, while red light

(660 nm) promotes it. A canopy of tall deciduous plants filters out red light for photosynthesis. Seeds of species growing under this canopy receive mainly far red light, and are prevented from germinating. When the leaves fall in autumn, these seeds will germinate both in response to the now available red light and to the low winter temperatures.

The Seeds Acts

In the UK the Seeds Acts control the quality of seed to be used by growers. A seed producer must satisfy the minimum requirements for species of vegetables and forest tree seed by subjecting a seed batch to a government testing procedure. A sample of the seed is subjected to standardized ideal germination conditions, to find the proportion that is viable (**germination percentage**). The germination and emergence under less ideal field conditions (**field emergence**) where tilth and disease factors are variable may be much lower than germination percentage.

The sample is also tested for **quality** which provides information, available to the purchaser of the seed, covering trueness to type; i.e. whether the characteristics of the plants are consistent with those of the named cultivar; the percentage of non-seed material, such as dust; the percentage of weed seeds, particularly those of a poisonous nature (*see* **Weeds Act**, Chapter 12). The precise regulations for sampling and testing, and requirements for specific species, have changed slightly since the 1920 Act, the 1964 Act (which also included the details of plant varieties) and entry of Britain into the European Community (EC). Some control under EC regulations is made of the provenance of forestry seed, as the geographical location of its source is important in relation to a number of factors, including response to drought, cold, dormancy, habit, and pest and disease susceptibility.

THE SEEDLING

Within the seed is a food store that provides the means to produce energy for germination. Once the food store has been exhausted, the seedling must rapidly become independent in its food supply and begin to photosynthesize. It must therefore **respond to stimuli in its environment to establish the direction of growth**. Such a response is termed as **tropism**, and is very important in the early survival of the seedling (*see* Figure 7.2).

Geotropism is a directional growth response to gravity. The emergence of the radicle from the testa is followed by growth of the root system, which must quickly take up water and minerals in order that the shoot system may develop. A seed germinating near the surface of a growing medium must not put out roots that grow onto the surface and dry out, but the roots must grow downwards to tap water supplies. Conversely, the plumule must grow away from the pull of gravity in order that the leaves develop in the light.

Etiolation is the type of growth which the shoot produces as it moves through the soil in response to gravity. The developing shoot is delicate and vulnerable to physical damage, and therefore often the growing tip is protected by being bent into plumular hook. The stem grows quickly, is supported by the structure of the soil and therefore is very thin and spindly, stimulated by friction in the soil which causes release of ethylene. The leaves are undeveloped, as they do not begin to function until they move into the light. Mature plants that are grown in dark conditions also appear etiolated.

Seedling development

The emergence of the plumule above the growing medium is usually the first occasion that the seedling is subjected to light. This stimulus inhibits the extension growth of the stem so that it becomes thicker and stronger, but the seedling is still very susceptible to attack from pests and damping-off diseases. The leaves unfold and become green in response to light, which enables the seedling to photosynthesize and so supports it. The first leaves to develop, the cotyledons, derive from the seed and may emerge from the testa while still in the soil, as in peach and broad bean (**hypogeal** germination), or be carried with the testa into the air, where the cotyledons then expand (**epigeal** germination), e.g. in tomatoes and cherry.

Phototropism occurs in order that the shoot grows towards a light source that provides the energy for photosynthesis. A bend takes place in the stem just below the tip as cells in the stem away from the light grow larger than those near to the light source. A greater concentration of auxin in the shaded part of the stem causes the extended growth (Figure 7.2). Roots display a negative phototropic response, growing away from light when exposed at the surface of the growing medium, e.g. on a steep bank. The growth away from light may supersede the root's geotropic response, and will cause the roots to grow back into the growing medium.

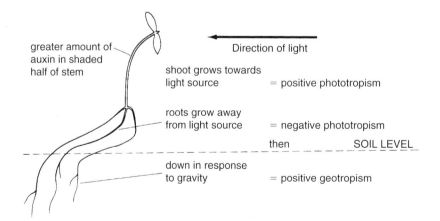

greater amount of auxin in shaded half of stem

Direction of light

shoot grows towards light source   = positive phototropism

roots grow away from light source   = negative phototropism

then   SOIL LEVEL

down in response to gravity   = positive geotropism

Figure 7.2 *Geotropism and phototropism shown as mechanisms assisting the survival of a seedling.*

Hydrotropism is the growing of roots towards a source of water. The explanation of this tropism has not been found, but it can be shown to occur.

The **cotyledons** that emerge from the testa contribute to the growth of the seedling in photosynthesis, but the **true leaves** of the plant, which often have a different appearance to the cotyledon, very quickly unfold.

Conditions for early plant growth

Many plant species are propagated in glasshouses. A few principles are described here to help ensure success. Seed trays should be thoroughly cleaned to prevent the occurrence of diseases such as 'damping off' (*see* page 127). Fresh growing medium should be used for these tiny plants that have little resistance to disease. Compost low in soluble fertilizer is less likely to scorch young plants. Compost should be firmed down in containers to provide closer contact with the developing root system.

With very small seed, there is a danger that too many seeds are sown together, with the result that the seedlings intertwine and are hard to separate. This problem can often be avoided by diluting batches of very small seed in some fine sand before sowing. Small seed samples need to be sown on the surface of the compost, and then covered with only a fine sprinkling of compost. In this way, their limited food reserves are not overtaxed as they struggle through the compost to reach the light.

Water quality is important with young plants. Mains water is recommended, as it will be free from diseases. Water butts and reservoirs need particular scrutiny to avoid this problem. Water that has been left to reach ambient temperature of the glasshouse is less likely to harm seedlings. The compost in seed trays should be kept permanently moist (but not waterlogged), as seedling roots easily dry out. Glass or plastic covers placed over seed trays will help prevent moisture loss, and these can be removed when root establishment has occurred and when seedlings are pushing against the covers.

As soon as seedlings have expanded their cotyledon leaves, they should be carefully transferred ('pricked off') from the seed tray and placed in another tray filled with compost having higher levels of fertility. The seedlings are spaced at approximately 2.5 cm intervals, thus providing a root volume for increased growth. Later, plants will be transferred to pots ('potted on') to allow for further growth.

Plants growing in glasshouses are tender. The cuticle covering leaves and stems is very thin. Growth is rapid and the stem's mechanical strength is likely to be dependent on tissues such as collenchyma and parenchyma rather than the sturdier xylem vessels (*see* page 42). When a plant is transferred from a glasshouse to cooler, windier outside conditions (e.g. in spring), it may become stressed, lose leaves and stop growing. It is advisable to 'harden off' plants before this stressful exposure. Reducing heat and increasing ventilation in the glasshouse are two ways of achieving this aim. Traditionally, plants were moved out into cold frames to gradually expose them to the conditions into which they are to be planted. Moving plants out during the day, and back inside overnight, for a number of weeks, is another strategy.

THE VEGETATIVE PLANT

The role of the vegetative stage in the life cycle of the plant is to grow rapidly and establish the individual in competition with others. It must therefore photosynthesize effectively and be capable of responding to good growing conditions. Growing rooms with near-ideal conditions of light, temperature and carbon dioxide utilize this capacity that will reduce with the ageing of the plant (*see* Chapter 6).

Juvenility

The early growth stage of the plant, the **juvenile** growth, is characterized by certain physical appearances and activities that are different from those found in the later stages or in **adult** growth. Often leaf shapes vary; e.g. the juvenile ivy leaf is three lobed while the adult leaf is more oval, as shown in Plate 8. The habit of the plant is also different; the juvenile stem of ivy tends to grow horizontally and is vegetative in nature, while the adult growth is vertical and bears flowers. Other examples are common in conifer species where the complete appearance of the plant is altered by the change in leaf form, e.g. *Chamaecyparis fletcheri* and many *Juniperus* species such as *J. chinensis*. In the genera *Chamaecyparis* and *Thuja*, the juvenile condition can be achieved permanently by repeated vegetative propagation producing a plant called a **retinospore**, which is used as decorative feature.

Leaf retention is also a characteristic of juvenility. It can be significant in species such as beech (*see* Plate 7), where the phenomenon is exaggerated, where the trees can be pruned back to the vegetative growth. This can create additional protection in **windbreaks** although the barrier created tends to be too solid to provide the ideal wind protection (*see* page 23).

The **juvenile stage is a period after germination that is capable of rapid vegetative growth and is unlikely to flower**. Many species that require an environmental change to stimulate flower initiation, such as the Brassicas that require a cold period, will not respond to the stimulus until the juvenile period is over; about 11 weeks in Brussels sprouts.

The adult stage essential for sexual reproduction is less useful for vegetative propagation than the responsive juvenile growth, a condition probably due to the hormonal balance in the tissues. Plate 8 shows the spontaneous production of adventitious roots on the ivy stem. Adult growth should be removed from **stock plants** to leave the more successful juvenile growth for cutting.

Vegetative propagation

Although the life cycle of most plants leads to sexual reproduction, **all plants have the potential to reproduce asexually or by vegetative propagation, when pieces of the parent plant are removed and develop into a wholly independent plant**. All living cells contain a nucleus with a complete set of genetical information (*see* genetic code, Chapter 8), with the potential to become any specialized cell type. Only part of the total information is brought into operation at any one time and position in the plant.

If parts of the plant are removed, then cells lose their orientation in the whole plant and are able to produce organs in positions not found in the usual organization. These are described as **adventitious** and can, for example, be roots on a stem cutting, buds on a piece of root, or roots and buds on a piece of leaf used for vegetative propagation. Many plant species use the ability for vegetative propagation in their normal pattern of development, in order to increase the number of individuals of the species in the population. The production of these vegetative **propagules**, as with the production of seed, is often the means by which the plant survives adverse conditions (*see* overwintering), acting as a food store which will provide for the renewed growth when it begins. The stored energy in the swollen taproots of dock and dandelion enables these plants to compete more effectively with seedlings of other weed and crop species, which would also apply to roots of *Gypsophila paniculata*, carrots and beetroot.

Stems are telescoped in the form of a **corm** in freesia and cyclamen, or swollen into a **tuber** in potato, or a horizontally growing underground **rhizome** in iris and couch grass. Leaves expanded with food may form a large bud or **offset** found in lilies. A **bulb**, as seen in daffodils, tulips and onions, is largely composed of succulent white leaves enveloping the much reduced stem, found at the base of the bulb (Figure 7.3).

Other natural means of propagation include lateral stems, which grow horizontally on the soil surface to produce nodal, adventitious roots and subsequently plantlets, e.g. **runners** or **stolons** of strawberries and yarrow. The adventitious nature of stems is exploited when they are deliberately bent to touch the ground, or enclosed in compost, in the method known as **layering**, used in carnations, some apple rootstocks, many deciduous shrubs such as *Forsythia*, and pot plants such as *Ficus* and *Dieffenbachia*. The roots of species, especially in

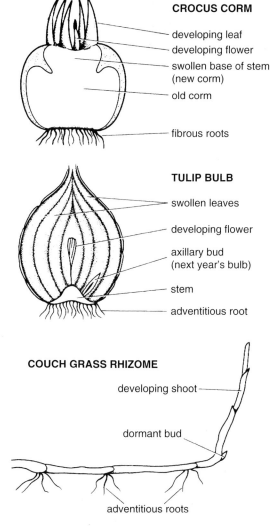

CROCUS CORM

- developing leaf
- developing flower
- swollen base of stem (new corm)
- old corm
- fibrous roots

TULIP BULB

- swollen leaves
- developing flower
- axillary bud (next year's bulb)
- stem
- adventitious root

COUCH GRASS RHIZOME

- developing shoot
- dormant bud
- adventitious roots

Figure 7.3 *Structure of organs responsible for overwintering and vegetative propagation.*

plant. This group of plants, or **clone**, strictly speaking, is an extension of the parent plant, and therefore all have the same genetical characteristics. The horticulturist is able to reproduce a cultivar, by this means, in which all the resulting plants exhibit consistent characteristics. Seed production is likely to result in variation of characteristics. Even in vegetatively propagated cultivars, changes can occur (*see* mutations), and differing clonal characteristics within the same cultivar can be distinguished in some conifer species, e.g. the leaf colour and plant habit of × *Cupressocyparis leylandii*. Seeds produced without fertilization (i.e. by **apomixis**) found in Rosaceae and Graminae present a special case of natural clonal propagation.

Artificial methods of propagation

The artificial methods of vegetative propagation encompass most organs of the plant. Cuttings are parts of plants that have been carefully cut away from the parent plant, and which are then used to produce a new plant. Many species can be propagated in this way. Different methods may be necessary for different species. Only healthy parent plants should be used. Hygienic use of knives, compost and containers is strongly recommended. Cuttings are normally taken from parts of the plant exhibiting juvenile growth. Below is a brief description of the most common methods used for cuttings.

Stem cuttings can be taken from stems that have attained different stages of maturity. **Hardwood cuttings** are from pieces of dormant woody stem containing a number of buds, which grow out into shoots when dormancy is broken in spring. The base of the cutting is cut cleanly to expose the cambium tissue from which the adventitious roots will grow (e.g. in rose rootstocks, *Forsythia* and many deciduous ornamental shrubs). In *Hydrangea* and currant the stems show evidence of preformed adventitious roots (root initials), which aid the process of root establishment. Hardwood cuttings are normally taken in late autumn (they are 15–25 cm in length), and are often placed with half their length immersed in a growing medium

the Rosaceae family, are able to produce underground adventitious buds that grow into aerial stems or **suckers**, e.g. pears and raspberries. By all these methods of runners, layering and suckers, the newly developing plant (**propagule**) will subsequently become detached from the parent plant by the disintegration of the connecting stem or root.

These natural methods are used in horticulture to produce number of plants from a single parent containing half compost and half sand. A 12 months period is often necessary before the cuttings can be lifted.

Semi-ripe cuttings are taken from stems, which are just becoming woody. They are normally taken from mid-summer to early autumn. Most cuttings of this kind are 5–10 cm long. Rooting in a sand/compost mixture may be achieved in cold frames or, more quickly, in a heated structure at about 18°C. *Eleagnus* (oleaster) will root only if heat is provided. Many shrub and tree species, e.g. holly and conifers, are propagated as 'heeled' cuttings. Here, the semi-ripe cutting is taken in such a way that a 1 cm sliver of last year's wood (the **heel**) is still attached. The heel cambium facilitates root formation and, hence, easier establishment of cuttings.

Stems without a woody nature are used for the propagation of species such as of *Fuchsia, Pelargonium* and *Chrysanthemum*. These are called **softwood cuttings**, and they are most often taken in late spring and early summer. The area of leaf on these cuttings should be kept to a minimum to reduce water loss. Misting (which is spraying the plants with fine droplets of water to increase humidity and reduce temperature) can further reduce this risk by slowing down the transpiration rate.

Automatic misting employs a switch attached to a sensitive device used for assessing the evaporation rate from the leaves. The cool conditions favouring the survival of the aerial parts of the cutting, however, do not encourage the division of cells in the cambium area of the root initials. Therefore, the temperature in the rooting medium may be increased with electric cables producing **bottom heat**. These special conditions for the encouragement of the success of cuttings are provided in propagation benches in a greenhouse.

Leaf cuttings are also susceptible to wilting before the essential roots have been formed, and will benefit from mist, provided the wet conditions do not encourage rotting of the plant material. Leaves of species such as *Begonia, Streptocarpus* and *Sansevieria* are divided into pieces from which small plantlets are initiated, while leaves plus petioles are used for *Saintpaulia* propagation. Nursery stock species, e.g. *Camellia* and *Rhododendron*, require a complete leaf and associated axillary bud in a leaf-bud cutting.

Root cuttings may be an option when other methods are not seen to succeed. This method is used for species such as *Phlox paniculata* and *Anchusa azurea* (*alkanet*). Roots about a centimetre in thickness are taken in winter and cut into 5 cm lengths. They are inserted vertically into a sand/compost mixture in most species but thinner-rooted species such as *Phlox* are placed horizontally. It is important that root cuttings are not, inadvertently, placed upside-down, as this will prevent establishment.

Tissue culture

Tissue culture is a method used for vegetative propagation, employing a small piece of plant tissue, the explant, grown in a sterile artificial medium that supplies all vitamins, mineral and organic nutrients. The medium and explant are enclosed in a sterile jar or tube and subjected to precisely controlled environmental conditions (Figures 7.4 and 7.5). This method has advantages over conventional propagation techniques, since large numbers of propagules can be produced from one original plant. This method has particular value with rare or novel plants. An added advantage is the reduced time taken for bulking up plant stocks. Some species that traditionally propagate only by seed, e.g. orchids and asparagus, can now be grown by tissue culture. One of the problems of conventional vegetative propagation is that diseases and pests are passed onto the propagules.

Stock plants grown at high temperatures are able to greatly reduce levels of disease (particularly virus) in their growing tips. Following this heat treatment, a **meristem tip** can be dissected out of the stem and grown in a tissue culture medium, to produce stock that is free from disease (e.g. chrysanthemum stunt viroid, *see* Chapter 11). This method of propagation is now used for species including *Begonia, Alstroemeria, Figus, Malus, Pelargonium*, Boston fern (*Nephrolepsis exaltata*), roses and many others.

Figure 7.4 *Tissue cultures of Sorghum bicolour showing: (a) early growth of callus tissue and (b) later plantlet production.*

Figure 7.5 *Plantlets growing in tubs under tissue culture conditions in a commercial laboratory.*

In all the methods described, **cell division** (*see* mitosis) must be stimulated in order to produce the new tissues and organs. The correct balance of hormones produced by the cells triggers this **initiation**. Auxins are found to stimulate the initiation of adventitious roots of cuttings. In the propagation of cuttings, the bases may be dipped in powder or liquid formulations of auxin-like chemicals such as naphthalene acetic acid to achieve this result. The number of roots is increased and production time reduced. The precise concentration of chemical in the cells is critical in producing the desired growth response. A large amount of hormone can bring about an inhibition of growth rather than promotion. For this reason, manufacturers of **hormone powders** and dips produce several distinct formulations with differing hormone concentrations, relevant to the hardwood, the semi-ripe and the softwood cutting situations. Also different organs respond to different concentration ranges; e.g. the amount of auxin needed to increase stem growth would inhibit the production of roots. The same principle applies to another group of chemicals important in cell division, the cytokinins, which can be applied to leaf cuttings to increase the incidence of plantlet formation.

Both auxin and cytokinin must be included in a tissue culture medium, at concentrations appropriate to the species and the type of growth required. The subsequent weaning of plantlets from their protected environment in tissue culture conditions requires care and usually conditions of high relative humidity, shade and warmth.

Grafting

Grafting involves the union of a **scion** (portion of stem) with a **rootstock** (root system) taken from another plant (*see* also page 44). Grafted plants are commonly used in top fruit, grapes, roses and amenity shrubs with novel shapes and colours. Rootstocks resistant to soil-borne pests and disease are sometimes used when the desired cultivars would succumb if grown on their own roots, e.g. grapevines, tomatoes and cucumbers grown in border soils. Grafting is not usually attempted in monocotyledons, as they do not produce continuous areas of secondary cambium tissue, suitable for successful graft-unions.

In top fruit, grafting is used for several reasons. A grafted plant will establish more quickly than a seedling. Plants derived from seedlings will show different (usually inferior) qualities of fruiting compared with their commercially useful parent plants, so a means of vegetative propagation is advantageous; the cultivars are, therefore, clones derived from one original parent. Another reason for grafting is to control the size of the tree through the choice of **dwarfing rootstock**. The M27 apple rootstock causes the grafted scion cultivar to be dwarfed. Reduced levels of auxin and cytokinin in the rootstock possibly bring this about.

There are numerous grafting methods that have been developed for particular plant species. Several principles common to all methods can be briefly mentioned. Firstly, the scion and stock should be genetically very similar. Secondly, the scion and stock will need to have been carefully cut so that their cambial components are able to come in contact. In this way, there will be a higher likelihood of **callus growth** (resulting from cambial contact), which quickly leads to graft establishment. Thirdly, the graft union should be sealed with grafting tape to maintain the graft contact, to prevent drying out and to keep out disease organisms such as *Botrytis*. Fourthly, the buds on the stem taken as scion material should, ideally, be dormant (leafy material would quickly dry out). The rootstock should be starting active growth, and thus bring water, minerals and nutrients to the graft area.

More details of common methods of grafting such as 'whip and tongue', 'approach graft' and 'bud graft' are available in specialist textbooks.

Apical dominance

After the germination of the seed, the plumule establishes a direction of growth partly due to the geotropic and phototropic forces acting on it. Often the terminal bud of the main stem sustains the major growth pattern, while the axillary buds are inhibited in growth to a degree that depends on the species.

In tomatoes and chrysanthemums, the lateral shoots have the potential to grow out, but are inhibited by a high concentration of auxin, which accumulates in these buds. The source of the chemical is the terminal bud, which maintains the inhibition. In commercial chrysanthemum production, the removal of the main shoot (**stopping**) is a common practice. It takes away the auxin supply to the axillary buds, which are then able to grow out to create a larger, more balanced inflorescence. Conversely, the practice of **disbudding** in chrysanthemums and carnations takes out the axillary buds to allow the terminal bud to develop into a bigger bloom that benefits from the greater food availability.

Pruning

Parts of plants can be **pruned** (removed) to reduce the competition within the plant for the available resources. In this way, the plant is encouraged to grow, flower or fruit in a way the horticulturist requires. A reduction in the number of flower buds of, for example, chrysanthemum will cause the remaining buds to develop into larger flowers; a reduction in fruiting buds of apple trees will produce bigger apples, and the reduction in branches of soft fruit and ornamental shrubs will allow the plants to grow stronger when planted densely. Pruning will also affect the shape of the plant, as meristems previously inhibited by apical dominance will begin to develop. The success of such pruning depends very much on the skill of the operator, as a good knowledge of the species habit is required.

A few general principles apply to most **pruning** situations:

- **Young** plants should be trained in a way that will reflect the eventual shape of the more mature plant (formative pruning). For example, a young apple tree (called a 'maiden') can be pruned to have one dominant 'leader' shoot, which will give rise to taller, more slender shape. Alternative pruning strategies will lead to quite different plant shapes. Pruning back all branches in the first few years forms a bush apple. A cordon is a plant in which there is a leader shoot, often trained at 45° to the ground, and where all side shoots are pruned back to one or two buds. Cordon fruit bushes are usually grown against walls or fences. Similarly, fans and espalier forms can be developed.

- The **pruning cut** should be made just above a bud that points in the required direction (usually to the outside of the plant). In this way, the plant is less likely to acquire too dense growth in its centre.
- **Pruning should remove any shoots that are crossing**, as they will lead to dense growth. Some plants such as roses and gooseberries are made less susceptible to disease attack by the creation of an open centre to produce a more buoyant (less humid) atmosphere.
- **Weak shoots should be pruned the hardest** where growth within the plant is uneven, and strong shoots pruned less, since pruning causes a stimulation of growth.
- **Species that flower on the previous year's growth** of wood (e.g. *Forsythia*) should be pruned soon after flowering has stopped. Conversely, species that flower later in the year on the present year's wood, e.g. *Buddleia davidii*, should be pruned the following spring.

Root pruning was used to restrict over-vigorous cultivars, especially in fruit species, but this technique has been largely superseded by the use of dwarfing rootstock grafted onto commercially grown scions. Root pruning is still seen, however, in the growing of Bonsai plants.

Pruning is largely concerned with creating the shape of a plant, and controlling apical dominance. But the removal of dead, damaged and diseased parts is also an important aspect.

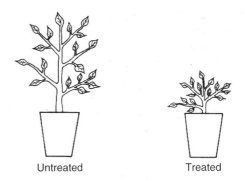

Untreated   Treated

Figure 7.6 *Chemical growth retardant is incorporated into compost used for pot plants such as chrysanthemum.*

Growth retardation

Stem extension growth is controlled by auxins produced by the plant, and also by gibberellins that can dramatically increase stem length, especially when externally applied. Growth retardation may be desirable, especially in the production of compact pot plants from species that would normally have long stems, e.g. chrysanthemums, tulips and *Azaleas*. Therefore, artificial chemicals such as daminozide or phosfon (Figure 7.6), which inhibit the action of the growth promoting hormones, can retard the development of the main stem, and also stimulate the growth of side shoots to produce a more bushy, compact plant. Flower production may be inhibited, but this can be countered by the application of flower stimulating chemicals.

THE FLOWERING PLANT

The progression from a vegetative to a flowering plant involves profound physical and chemical changes. The stem apex displays a more complex appearance under the microscope as flower initiation occurs, and is followed, usually irreversibly, by the development of a flower. The stimulus for this change may simply be genetically derived, but often an environmental stimulus is required which links flowering to an appropriate season.

Photoperiodism

Photoperiodism is a daylength-stimulated response involved in the initiation of flowers (and also in bud and seed dormancy, and in leaf abscission). Of these the flower initiation process is probably the most important for manipulation by the horticulturist. Repeated daily exposure to light for a given period of time (**critical period**), the length of which depends on the species, will bring about flower initiation, provided the light periods are separated by an appropriate period of darkness. Some species are adapted to flower after exposure to daylengths shorter than a critical period. These are **short day plants**, and this adaptation will ensure that they produce flowers at the most favourable time for successful seed production and survival, which for them is towards the autumn. *Chrysanthemum morifolium, Poinsettia,* and *Kalanchoe* species must have short days, followed by relatively long nights in order that flower buds are produced.

Long day plants which require a daylength longer than a critical period include hostas, *Campanula carpatica, Nigella damascena,* radish and carnation. Although this latter species will flower under any photoperiodic conditions, flowers are produced more readily when treated with long days. Many species previously considered to be non-responsive or **day neutral**, e.g. *Begonia elatior* and tomato, have been shown to respond in some degree to a lighting period, especially in combin-ation with temperature.

Light is absorbed in the photoperiodic response by a blue pigment called **phytochrome** (not present in sufficient amounts to contribute colour to the plant). The switching mechanism between the plant's vegetative growth and its need to initiate flowering, is controlled by phytochrome. The mechanism is a little complex. It involves a rapid reaction of a few seconds to produce 'activated phytochrome' under the influence of red light. Red light represents a considerable proportion of the emission of tungsten filament bulbs, which are used in glasshouses for flower initiation. There is a similar but much slower reversal from 'activated phytochrome' back to phytochrome which occurs

in total darkness. A rapid reversal of this reaction from 'activated phytochrome' back to phytochrome occurs when far red light is the dominant wavelength. Far red is just outside the visible spectrum (*see* example below).

Artificial control of lighting for flowering

Plants such as greenhouse chrysanthemums can be artificially induced to flower even though the natural daylength conditions are not suitable. The photoperiod can be extended by artificial lighting, or shortened by blacking out the daylight. The relatively low light intensity of approximately 100–150 lux, needed to stimulate a response, is adequately provided by incandescent tungsten filament lamps placed above the crop, while blackout can be provided using black polythene (*see* Figure 7.7).

Night breaks. In a short day plant such as chrysanthemum, the night period must be relatively long in order to bring about a flowering response. If a period of artificial lighting divides the night into two periods, i.e. a **night break**, then the flowering response does not occur. This practice is used to maintain vegetative growth in order to produce a full-length stem when a natural short day would flower before this had been achieved.

Cyclic lighting. For chrysanthemums, the red light effect results in 'activated phytochrome', which in turn results in flower initiation. Too long a period of darkness (15 min for chrysanthemums) results in a return to phytochrome, and this prevents flower initiation. Growers, therefore, use a strategy called **cyclic lighting** in which a repeated pattern is maintained: 15 min of light is followed by 15 min of darkness. In this way, the plant responds as if there was continuous daylight, and the resulting 'activated phytochrome' initiates flowering.

The development of **night-break lighting** (preventing flowering in immature plants) and **cyclic lighting** (enabling flowering during the 'unnatural' times of the year) has resulted in the 'all-year-round' (AYR or YR) chrysanthemum production.

Figure 7.7 *Chrysanthemum blooms with lighting and blackout for daylength control.*

Flower initiation

Flower initiation can be stimulated largely by photoperiodic or temperature changes, or a complex interaction between temperature and daylength.

Cold temperatures experienced during the winter bring about flower initiation (i.e. **vernalization**) in many biennial species such as *Brassica*, lettuce, red beet, *Lunaria* and onion. The period for the response depends on the exact temperature, as with budbreak and seed dormancy (*see* stratification). The optimum temperature for many of these responses is about 4°C. Hormones are involved in causing the flower apex to be produced. The balance of auxins, gibberellins and cytokinins is important, but some species respond to artificial treatment of one type of chemical; e.g. the daylength requirement for chrysanthemum plants can be partly replaced by gibberellic acid sprays.

The plant detects daylength in its leaves. The exact nature of the chemical link between leaf and flower has been the subject of much speculation. In spite of name such as 'florigen' and 'floral stimulus' being given to the hypothetical substance, research has not yet provided a definitive answer to this question. Some scientists consider that a mixture of auxin, gibberrelin and cytokinin moves from the leaf to initiate flowering.

Flower structure

The flower structure is shown in Figure 7.8. The flower is initially protected inside a flower bud by the **calyx** or ring of **sepals**, which are often green and can therefore photosynthesize. The development of the flower parts requires large energy expenditure by the plant, and therefore vegetative activities decrease. The **corolla** or ring of **petals** may be small and insignificant in **wind-pollinated flowers**, e.g. grasses, or large and colourful in **insect-pollinated species**. The colours and size of petals can be improved in cultivated plants by breeding, and may also involve the multiplication of the petals or **petalody**, when fewer male organs are produced.

The flowers of many species have both male and female organs (**hermaphrodite**), but some have separate male and female flowers (**monoecious**), e.g. *Cucurbita*, walnut, birch (*Betula*), whereas others produce male and female flowers on different plants (**dioecious**), e.g. holly, willows, *Skimmia japonica* and *Ginkgo biloba*.

Each male **stamen** bears an anther that produces and discharges the **pollen grains**. The female organ is positioned in the centre of the flower and

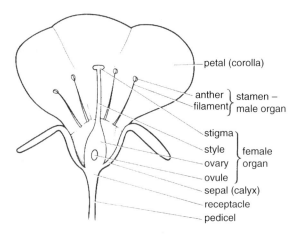

Figure 7.8 *Cross-section of a flower showing the structures involved in the function of sexual reproduction.*

consists of an **ovary** containing one or more **ovules** (egg cells). The **style** leads from the ovary to a stigma at its top where pollen is captured. The flower parts are positioned on the **receptacle**, which is at the tip of the **pedicel** (flower stalk). Associated with the flower head or **inflorescence** are leaf-like structures called **bracts**, which can sometimes assume the function of insect attraction, e.g. in *Poinsettia*.

Extended flower life

The flower opens to expose the organs for sexual reproduction. The life of the flower is limited to the time needed for pollination and fertilization, but it is often commercially desirable to extend the life of a cut flower or flowering pot plant. In cut flowers, water uptake must be maintained and dissolved nutrients for opening the flower bud are termed as an **opening solution**.

Vase life can be extended by the addition of sterilants and sugar to the water. A **sterilant**, e.g. silver nitrate, in the water can reduce the risk of blockage of xylem by bacterial or fungal growth. **Ethylene** has a considerable effect on flower development, and can bring about premature death (**senescence**) of the flower after it begins to open.

Cut flowers should therefore never be stored near to fruit, e.g. apples or bananas that produce ethylene. Some chemicals, such as sodium thiosulphate, reduce the production of ethylene in carnations and therefore extend their life.

Pollination and fertilization

The function of the flower is to bring about sexual reproduction, which is the production of offspring following the fusion of male and female nuclei. The male and female nuclei are contained within the pollen grain and ovule respectively, and **pollination is the transference of the pollen from the anther to the stigma**. The source of pollen may be the same flower in **self-pollination** or a different flower in **cross-pollination**, although for practical plant breeding purposes cross-pollination should include different plants. Cross-pollination ensures that variation is introduced into new generations of offspring. Natural agents of cross-pollination are mainly wind and insects.

Wind-pollinated flowers are usually small, green, lacking nectar and unscented, but produce large amounts of pollen, e.g. the grasses and catkins on trees such as *Salix* (willow), *Betula* (birch), *Corylus* (hazel), *Fagus* (beech), *Quercus* (oak), etc. They also tend to have proportionally large stigma that protrude from the flower to maximize the chances of intercepting pollen grains in the air. The Gymnosperma (conifers) also produces pollen from the small male cones.

Insect-pollinated flowers produce odours, have brightly coloured petals to attract insects and produce nectar to feed them. The insects such as bees and flies then collect pollen on their bodies and carry it to other flowers.

Plant breeders may use houseflies, enclosed in a glasshouse, to carry out pollination, or mechanical transference of pollen, which may be achieved by hand using brushes. Some floral mechanisms, e.g. snapdragon and clover, physically prevent non-pollinating species by allowing only heavy bees to enter the flower. Others trap pollinators for a period of time to give the best chance of successful fertilization, e.g. *Arum* lily. Certain *Primula* spp. have stigma and stamens of differing lengths to ensure cross-pollination.

The pollen grain on arrival at the stigma absorbs sugar and moisture from the stigma's surface and then produces a **pollen tube**. The male nuclei are carried in the pollen tube, which grows down inside the style and into the ovary wall. After entering the ovule, male and female nuclei fuse together in **fertilization**, resulting in the **zygote**, which divides and differentiates to become the embryo of the seed. The seed **endosperm** may be produced by more nuclear fusion, and the **testa** of the seed forms from the outer layers of the ovule. The ovary develops into a protective **fruit**.

Bees in pollination

The well-known social insect, the **honey bee** (*Apis mellifera*), is helpful to horticulturists. The female worker collects pollen and nectar in special pockets (honey baskets) on its hind legs. This is a supply of food for the hive and, in collecting it, the bee transfers pollen from plant to plant. Several crops, e.g. apple and pear, do not set fruit when self-pollinated. Thus, this insect provides a useful function to the fruit grower. In large areas of fruit production the number of resident hives is insufficient to provide effective pollination, and in cool, damp or windy springs, the flying periods of the bees are reduced. It may therefore be advantageous for the grower to introduce beehives into the orchards during the blossom time, as an insurance against bad weather. One hive is normally adequate to serve 0.5 ha of fruit. Blocks of four hives placed in the centre of a 2 ha area require foraging bees to travel a maximum distance of 140 m. In addition to honey bees, wild species, e.g. the potter flower bee (*Anthophora retusa*) and red-tailed bumble-bee (*Bombus lapidarius*), increase fruit set, but their numbers are not really high enough to dispense with the honey bee. The pollination of tomatoes in greenhouses is commonly achieved by small in-house populations of a bumble-bee species (*Bombus terrestris*).

All species of bee are killed by broad spectrum insecticides, e.g. deltamethrin, and it is important that spraying of such chemicals be restricted to early morning or evening during the blossom time period when hives have been introduced.

Colour in flowers

The use of different flower colours in the garden has been the subject of much discussion in Britain over the last 300 years. Many books have been written on the subject, and authorities on the subject will disagree about what combination of plants creates an impressive border. Some combinations are mentioned here, and Plate 1 illustrates one example of the harmony created by blue flowers placed next to yellow ones. Other combinations such as blue and white, e.g. *Ceanothus* 'Blue Mound' and *Clematis montana*; yellow and red, e.g. *Euphorbia polychroma* and *Geum rivale*; yellow and white, e.g. *Verbascum nigrum* and *Tanacetum parthenium*; purple and pale yellow, e.g. *Salvia* × *superba* and *Achillea* 'lucky break'; and red and lavender, e.g. *Rosa gallica* and *Clematis integrifolia*.

Removal of dead flowers

The removal of dead flowers, an activity called **dead heading**, is an effective way to help to maintain the appearance of a garden border. Examples of species needing this procedure are seen in bedding plants which flower over several months, e.g. African marigold (*Tagetes erecta*); in herbaceous perennials, e.g. *Delphinium* and *Lupin*; in small shrubs, e.g. *Penstemon fruticosus*; and in climbers, e.g. sweet pea and *Rosa* 'Pink Perpetue'. As flowers age, they begin to use up a considerable amount of the plant's energy in the production of fruits. Also, hormones produced by the fruit inhibit flower development. With species such as those mentioned above, the maturation of fruits will considerably reduce the plant's ability to continue producing flowers. The act of dead heading, therefore, will greatly improve subsequent flowering.

An added bonus is that plants that have been dead headed may continue to flower many weeks longer than those allowed to retain their dead flowers.

Many species such as wax begonia (*Begonia* × *semperflorens cultorum*) and busy lizzie (*Impatiens wallerana*) used as bedding plants have been specially bred as F1 hybrids (*see* page 84) where, in this case, flowers do not produce fruits containing viable seed. In such cases, there is not such a great need to dead head, but this activity will help prevent unsightly rotting brown petals from spoiling the appearance of foliage and newly produced flowers.

THE FRUITING PLANT

The development of the fruit involves either the expansion of the ovary into a juicy **succulent** structure, or the tissues becoming hard and **dry**, both providing protection and/or dispersal of the seeds. The succulent fruits are often eaten by animals, which help seed dispersal, and may also bring about chemical changes to break dormancy mechanisms (*see* page 63). Some fruits (described as being **dehiscent**) release their seeds into the air. They do this either by an explosive method as seen in the brooms and poppies, or by tiny feathery parachutes, seen in willow herb and groundsel. Dry fruits may rot away gradually to release their seeds by an **indehiscent** action. Different adaptations of fruit, many of which are of economic importance, and the methods by which seeds are dispersed are summarized in Table 7.1

Fruit set

The process of pollination, in most species, stimulates fruit set. The hormones, in particular gibberellins, carried in the pollen, trigger the production of auxin in the ovary, which causes the cells to develop. In species such as cucumber, the naturally high content of auxin enables fruit production without prior fertilization, i.e. **parthenocarpy**, a useful phenomenon when the object of the crop is the production of seedless fruit. Such activity can be simulated in other species, especially when poor conditions of light and temperature have caused poor fruit set in species such as tomato and peppers. Here, the flowers are sprayed with an auxin-like chemical, but the quality of fruit is usually inferior. Pears can be sprayed with a solution of gibberellic acid to replace the need for pollination. Fruit ripening occurs as a result of hormonal changes and involves a change in the sugar content in tomatoes, i.e. at the crucial stage called **climacteric**. After this point, fruit will continue to ripen and also respire after removal from the plant. Ethylene is released by ripening fruit, which contributes to deterioration in store. Early ripening can be brought about by a spray of a chemical, e.g. ethephon, which stimulates the release of ethylene by the plant, e.g. in the tomato.

THE AGEING PLANT

At the end of an annual plant's life, or the growing season of perennial plants, a number of changes take place. The changes in colour associated with autumn are due to pigments that develop in the leaves and stems and are revealed as the chlorophyll (green) is broken down and absorbed by the plant.

Pigments are substances that are capable of absorbing light; they also reflect certain wavelengths of light, which determine the colour of the pigment. In the actively growing plant, chlorophyll, which reflects mainly green light, is produced in considerable amounts, and therefore the plant, especially the leaves, appears predominantly green. Other pigments are present; e.g. the carotenoids (yellow) and xanthophylls (red), but usually the quantities are so small as to be masked by the chlorophyll. In some species, e.g. copper beech (*Fagus sylvatica*), other pigments predominate, masking chlorophyll. These pigments also occur in many species of deciduous plants at the end of the growing season, when chlorophyll synthesis ceases prior to the abscission of the leaves. Many colours are displayed in the leaves at this time in species such as *Acer platanoides*, turning gold and red, *Prunus cerasifera* 'pissardii' with light purple leaves, European larch with yellow leaves, virginia creeper (*Parthenocissus* and *Vitus* spp.) with red leaves, beech with brown leaves, *Cotoneaster* and *Pyracantha* with coloured berries and *Cornus* species, which have coloured stems. These are used in **autumn colour** displays at a time when fewer flowering plants are seen outdoors.

In deciduous woody species, the leaves drop in the process of **abscission**, which may be triggered by shortening of the daylength. In order to reduce risk of water loss from the remaining leaf scar, a corky layer is formed before the leaf falls. Auxin production in the leaf is reduced, and this stimulates the formation of the abscission layer, and abscisic acid is involved in the process. Auxin sprays can be used to achieve a premature leaf fall in nursery stock plants thus enabling the early lifting of bare-root plants. Ethylene inhibits the action of auxin, and can therefore also cause premature leaf fall, e.g. in *Hydrangea* prior to cold treatment for flower initiation.

FURTHER READING

Attridge, T.H. *Light and Plant Responses* (Edward Arnold, 1991).

Bleasdale, J.K.A. *Plant Physiology in Relation to Horticulture* (Macmillan, 1983).

Capon, B. *Botany for Gardeners* (Timber Press, 1990).

Donnely, D.J. and Vidaver, W.E. *Glossary of Plant Tissue Culture* (Cassell, 1995).

Electricity Council. Grow Electric Handbook No. 2 *Lighting in Greenhouses*, Part 2, 1974.

Gardner, R.J. *The Grafter's Handbook* (Cassell, 1993).

Hart, J.W. *Plant Tropisms and Other Growth Movements* (Unwin Hyman, 1990).

Hartman, H.T. *et al. Plant Propagation, Principles and Practice* (Prentice-Hall, 1990).

Hattatt, L. *Gardening with Colour* (Parragon, 1999).

Leopold, A.C. *Plant Growth and Development*, 2nd edition (McGraw-Hill, 1977).

Machin, B. *Year-round Chrysanthemums* (Grower Publications, 1983).

MAFF. *Quality in Seeds*, Advisory Leaflet 247.

MAFF. *Guide to the Seed Regulations* (HMSO, 1979).

Stanley, J. and Toogood, A. *The Modern Nurseryman* (Faber, 1981).

Wareing, P.F. and Phillips, I.D.J. *The Control of Growth and Differentiation in Plants* (Pergamon, 1981).

8

Genetics and Plant Breeding

Ever since growers selected seed for their next crop, they have influenced the genetic make-up and therefore the potential of succeeding crops. A basic understanding of plant breeding principles enables the grower to understand the potential and limits of plant cultivars and therefore make more realistic requests to the plant breeder. Plant breeding now supplies a wide range of plant types to meet growers' specific needs. The plant breeder's skill relies on his knowledge of genetics to manipulate inheritable characters, and the ability to recognize and select the desirable characters when they occur.

Plant breeding uses the basic principle that fundamental characteristics of a species are passed on from one generation to the next (heredity). However, sexual reproduction may produce different characteristics in the offspring (**variation**). A plant breeder relies on the principles of heredity to retain desirable characteristics in a breeding programme, and new characteristics are introduced in several ways to produce new cultivars.

In order to understand the principles of plant breeding, the genetic make-up of the plant must first be studied.

THE CELL

Every living plant cell contains a nucleus which controls every activity occurring in the cell (*see* page 40). Within the nucleus is the chemical deoxyribose nucleic acid (DNA), a very large molecule made up of thousands of atoms. The DNA contains hundreds of sub-units (nucleotides), each of which contains a chemically active zone called a 'base'. There are four different bases: guanine, cytosine, thymine and adenine. The sequence of these bases is the method by which genetic information is stored in the nucleus, and also the means by which information is transmitted from the nucleus to other cell organelles (this mechanism is called the **genetic code**). A change in the base sequencing of a plant's code will lead to it developing new characteristics. These very long molecules of DNA are called **chromosomes**.

Each species of plant has a specific number of chromosomes. The cells of tomato (*Lycopersicum esculentum*) contain 24 chromosomes, the cells of *Pinus* and *Abies* species 24 and onions 16 (human beings have 46). Each chromosome contains a succession of units, called **genes**, containing many base units. Each gene usually is the code for a single characteristic. Scientists have been able to relate the many gene locations to plant characteristics. Microscopic observation of cells during cell division reveals two similar sets of chromosomes, e.g. in tomatoes, 12 different pairs. This condition is termed as **diploid**. A gene for a particular characteristic, such as flower colour, has a precise location on one chromosome, on the same location of the paired chromosome (an homologous pair). For each characteristic, therefore, there are at least two alleles (gene alternatives), one on each chromosome in the homologous pair, which provides genetic information for that characteristic.

Cell division

When a plant grows, the cell number increases in the growing points of the stems and roots, the division of one cell producing two new ones. Genetic information in the nucleus must be reproduced exactly in the new cells to maintain the plant's characteristics. The process of **mitosis** achieves this. **Each chromosome in the parent cell produces a duplicate of itself producing sufficient material for the two new daughter cells.** A delicate, spindle-shaped structure ensures the separation of chromosomes, one complete set into each of the new cells. A dividing cell wall forms across the old cell to complete the division.

Sexual reproduction involves the fusion of genetic material contained in the sex cells from both parents (*see* fertilization). Half of the chromosomes in the cells of an offspring are therefore inherited from the male parent, and half from the female. To ensure that the offspring chromosome number equals that of the parents, contents of the nuclei of male and female sex cells (*see* pollen and ovule) must be halved. The cell division process (**meiosis**), occurring in the anthers and ovaries, produces the nuclei of the sex cells (**gametes**). It ensures the separation of each chromosome from its partner so that each sex cell contains only one complete set of chromosomes. This condition is termed as **haploid**.

INHERITANCE OF CHARACTERISTICS

Genetic information is passed from parent to offspring when material from male and female parent comes together by fusion of the sex cells. Genes from each parent can, in combination, produce a mixture of the parents' characteristics in the offspring; e.g. a gene for red flowers inherited from the male parent, combined with a gene for white flowers from the female parent, could produce pink-flowered offspring. If one of the genes, however, completely dominated the other, e.g. if the red gene inherited from the male parent was **dominant** over the white female gene, all offspring would produce red flowers (*see* Figure 8.1).

The **recessive** white gene will still be present as part of the genetic make-up of the offspring cells and can be passed on to the next generation. If it then combines at fertilization with another white gene, the offspring will be white-flowered offspring.

The example given considers the inheritance of one pair of genes by a single offspring (**monohybrid cross**). However, many sex cells are produced from one flower in the form of pollen grains and ovules, which fuse to form many seeds of the next generation. The plant breeder must know the genetic composition of the whole population of offspring.

Consider now the same example of flower colour. If a red-flowered plant, containing two genes for red (described as **pure**), is crossed with a pure white-flowered plant, the red-flowered plant supplies pollen as the male parent, and the white-flowered plant produces seed as the female parent. As both parents are pure, the male parent can produce only one type of sex cell, containing the 'red' version (**allele**) of the gene, and the female parent only the white (**allele**). Since all pollen grains will carry 'red' genes and all ovules 'white', then in the absence of dominance, the only possible combination for the first generation or **F1** yields pink offspring, each containing an allele for red and an allele for white (i.e. **impure**). Figure 8.2 illustrates this inheritance by using letters to describe genes, **R** to represent a red gene, and r to represent a white gene. The **genotype** (the inner genetic make-up of a cell) can be represented by using letters, e.g. Rr. The outward appearance resulting from the genotype's action (e.g. red, pink or white flower) is called the **phenotype**.

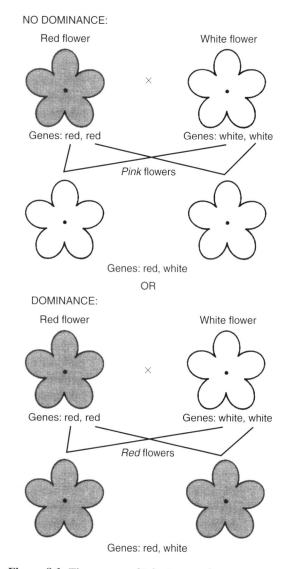

Figure 8.1 *The pattern of inheritance of genes.*

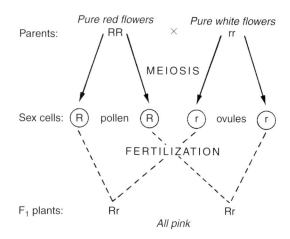

Figure 8.2 *Simple inheritance: production of the F1 generation.*

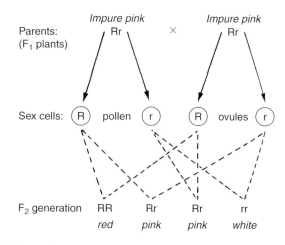

Figure 8.3 *Simple inheritance: production of the F2 generation.*

If the plants from the F1 generation were used as parents and crossed (or perhaps self-pollinated), then the results in the second or **F2** generation would be as shown in Figure 8.3, i.e. 25 per cent of the population, therefore, would have the phenotype of red flowers, 50 per cent pink flowers and 25 per cent white flowers (a ratio of 1:2:1). The plant breeder by analysing the ratios of each colour would therefore be able to calculate which colour genes were present in the parents, and whether the 'colour' was pure.

More usually, one of the alleles at the gene site exhibits **dominance** and the other is **recessive**. When offspring inherit both alleles, there is no intermediate phenotype; only the dominant gene expresses itself. It was the monk Gregor Mendel working in a monastery in what is now Brno in the Czech Republic, in the middle of the eighteenth century who laid the foundations of genetics with his breeding experiments. He used peas and worked with **single characteristics** including the height of the plant. He found that in the second or F2 generation they were either tall or short; there were no middle-sized phenotypes. They were found to be in the ratio of three tall to one short plant. Similarly, he crossed pure (homozygous) round pea parents (RR) with pure (homozygous) wrinkled pea parents (rr). Crossing the two pure parents (RR × rr) the genotype of the first generation or F1 follows the pattern as shown in Figure 8.2, but all the plants produced round peas, i.e. the round pea allele was dominant in peas. When the second or F2 generation was produced the genotype followed the pattern shown in Figure 8.3, but there were three round pea to every one wrinkled pea type. Both RR and Rr genotypes produced the same phenotype; only a double recessive (rr) produced plants with wrinkled peas. He went on to look at other simple 'single gene characteristics' including seed colour (yellow dominant and green recessive) and flower colour (purple dominant and white recessive). In all these cases he found that the ratio of phenotypes in the second or F2 generation was 3:1. By observation he established the **Principle of Segregation**; the phenotype is determined by the pair of alleles in the genotype and only one allele of the gene pair can be present in a single gamete (i.e. passed on by a parent).

Mendel then went on to investigate the crossing of plants that differed in **two contrasting characters**. The results of crossing tall purple-flowered peas with short white-flowered ones were to produce all tall purple-flowered peas, they all had the same genotype (TtPp) and the same phenotype. The F2 generation produced from these parents is illustrated in Figure 8.4, where the combinations are shown in a Punnet Square (or 'checkerboard' – a useful way of showing the genotypes produced in a crossing). Note that each gene has behaved independently; there are 12 tall to four short (ratio 3:1) and 12 purple to four white-flowered plants (3:1). This illustrates Mendel's **Principle of Independent Assortment**; the alleles of (unlinked) genes behave independently at meiosis. The cross involving

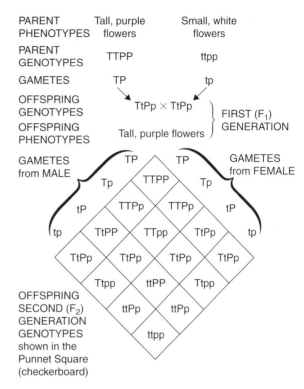

Figure 8.4 *Punnet square showing a dihybrid cross.*

two independent (unlinked, i.e. not on the same chromosome) genes produces combinations of phenotypes in the ratio 9:3:3:1. For the cross TtPp × TtPp, the genotypes produced are shown in Figure 8.4 and the phenotypes are as follows:

9 Tall, purple-flowered plants
  1 TTPP
  2 TTPp
  2 TtPP
  4 TtPp
3 Tall, white-flowered plants
  2 TTpp
  1 Ttpp
3 Short, purple-flowered plants
  2 ttPP
  1 ttPp
1 Short, white-flowered plants
  1 ttpp

Not all genes act independently, as some are linked by being on the same chromosome and will usually appear together. The number of grouped genes is equal to the number of chromosome pairs for the species (seven for peas).

F1 HYBRIDS

The importance of F1 hybrids to the grower is that, given a uniform environment, plants of the same cultivar that are F1 hybrids **will produce a uniform crop because they are all genetically identical** (Figure 8.2). Crops grown from F1 hybrid seed such as cabbage, Brussels sprouts and carrots can be harvested at one time and they have similar characteristics of yield; flower crops will have uniformity of colour and flower size.

Plants derived from crossing parent types with different characteristics display **hybrid vigour**, and generally respond well to good growing conditions. The desirable characteristics of the two parents, such as disease resistance, good plant habit, high yield and good fruit or flower quality, may be incorporated along with established characteristics of successful commercial cultivars by means of the F1 hybrid breeding programme. F1 hybrid seed production first requires suitable parent stock, which must be pure for all characteristics. In this way, genetically identical offspring are produced, as described in Figure 8.2. The production of pure parent plants involves repeated self-pollination (**selfing**) and selection, over eight to twelve generations, resulting in suitable **inbred parent lines**. During this and other self-pollination programmes vigour is lost but, of course, is restored by hybridization.

The parent lines must now be cross-pollinated to produce the F1 hybrid seed. It is essential to avoid self-pollination at this stage, therefore one of the lines is designated the male parent to supply pollen. The anthers in the flowers of the other line, the female parent, are removed, or treated to prevent the production of viable pollen. The growing area must be isolated to exclude foreign pollen, and seed is collected only from the female parent. This seed is expensive compared with other commercial seed, due to the complex programme requiring intensive labour. Seed collected from the commercial F1 hybrid crop represents the F2, and will produce plants with very diverse characteristics (Figure 8.3). It is clear, therefore, that seed from an F1 should not be saved for sowing, if uniform characteristics need to be retained. Some F2 seed, however, is produced in flowering plants such as geraniums and fuchsias, where variable colour and habit are required.

OTHER BREEDING PROGRAMMES

In addition to F1 hybrid breeding, where specific improvements are achieved, plant breeders may wish to bring about more general improvements to existing cultivars, or introduce characteristics such as disease resistance. Programmes are required for crops which self-pollinate (**inbreeders**), or those which cross-pollinate (**outbreeders**), and three of these strategies are described.

Pedigree breeding is the method for plant breeding most widely used by both amateurs and professionals. Two plants with different desirable characteristics are crossed to produce an F1 population. These are selfed and the offspring with useful characteristics is selected for further selfing to produce a line of plants. After repeated selfing and selection, the characteristics of the new lines are compared with existing cultivars and assessed for improvements. Further field trials will determine a new type's suitability for submission and potential registration as a new cultivar. If a plant breeder wishes to produce a strain adapted to particular conditions, such as hardiness, exposure of plants of a selected cultivar to the desired conditions will eliminate unsuitable plants, thus allowing the hardy plants to set seed. Repetition of this process gradually adapts the whole population, while other characteristics, such as earliness, may be selected by harvesting seed early.

Disease resistance (*see* Chapter 12), a genetic characteristic, enables the plant to combat fungal attack. The disease organism may itself develop a corresponding genetical capacity to overcome the plant's resistance by mutation. The introduction of disease resistance into existing cultivars requires a **backcross breeding** programme, involving a commercial cultivar lacking resistance, crossed with a wild plant which exhibits resistance. For example, a lettuce cultivar may lack resistance to downy mildew (*Bremia lactucae*), or a tomato cultivar lack tomato mosaic virus resistance. This commercial cultivar is crossed with a resistant wild plant to produce an F1, then an F2. From this F2, plants having both the characteristics of the commercial cultivar and also disease resistance are selected. The process continues with backcrossing of these selected plants with the original commercial parent to produce an F1, from which an F2 is produced. More commercial characteristics may be incorporated by further backcrossing and selection over a number of generations, until all the characteristics of the commercial cultivar are restored, but with the additional disease resistance.

POLYPLOIDS

Polyploids are plants with cells containing more than the diploid number of chromosomes; e.g. a triploid has three times the haploid number, a tetraploid four times and the polyploid series continues in many species up to octaploid (eight times haploid). An increase in size of cells, with a resultant increase in roots, fruit and flower size of many species of chrysanthemums, fuchsias, strawberries, turnips and grasses, is the result of polyploidy. There is a limit to the number of chromosomes that a species can contain within its nucleus.

Polyploidy occurs when duplication of chromosomes (*see* mitosis) fails to result in mitotic cell division. The multiplication of a polyploid cell within a meristem may form a complete polyploid shoot that, after flowering, may produce polyploid seed. The crossing of a tetraploid and a diploid gives rise to a triploid. Polyploid plants are often infertile, especially **triploids**, with an odd number of chromosomes which are unable to pair up during meiosis. A number of apple cultivars, such as Bramley's seedling and Crispin, are triploid and require

pollinator cultivars for the supply of viable pollen. Polyploidy can occur spontaneously, and has led to many variant types in wild plant populations. It can be artificially induced by the use of a mitosis inhibitor, colchicine.

MUTATIONS

Changes in the content or arrangement of the chromosomes cause changes in the characteristics of the individual. Very drastic alterations result in malformed and useless plants, while slight rearrangements may provide a horticulturally desirable change in flower colour or plant habit, as shown in chrysanthemums, dahlias or *Streptocarpus*. Mutation breeding has produced these variations using irradiation treatments with X-rays, gamma rays or mutagenic chemicals. Spontaneous mutations regularly occur in cells but, as in polyploids, the mutation only becomes significant in the plant when the mutated cell is part of a meristem.

A shoot with a different colour flower or leaf may arise in a group of plants, and is termed a **sport**. When a plant consists of two or more genetically distinct tissues, it is called a **chimaera**, often resulting in variegation of the leaves, e.g. *Acer* and *Pelargonium*. These conditions are maintained only by vegetative propagation, which encourages cell division in both tissue types. All mutations are inherited by a succeeding generation in the ways previously described, which enables new characteristics and potential new cultivars to be produced in just one generation.

RECOMBINANT DNA TECHNOLOGY

For the plant breeder it has historically been difficult to predict whether the progeny from a breeding programme would show the desired characteristics. The term **recombinant DNA technology** refers to the modern methods of breeding that enable novel sources of DNA to be integrated with greater certainty into a plant's existing genotype. Two new techniques have appeared in the last few years that have enabled this major shift in breeding practice.

The first technique is **marker-assisted breeding**. Breeders are now able to analyse chromosome material and establish what DNA sequence is present on the chromosome. Some plant characters such as disease resistance are hard to evaluate in newly bred plants, as it may be difficult to achieve infection under test conditions. Since the breeders are now able to recognize the chromosome DNA sequence for plant resistance, they can apply this knowledge by analysing newly bred plants for this desirable character. Whilst resistance to a disease may be complex, involving several genes acting together, the marker-assisted technique has proved a powerful form of assistance in this area.

The second technique is **genetic modification** (now known as GM), or genetic engineering. By this method, genes derived from other plant species can be incorporated into the species in question. The commonest technique involves the bacterium *Agrobacterium tumifasciens*. This organism (*see* page 130) causes crown gall disease on plants such as apple. The bacterium contains a circular piece of DNA (plasmid) that on entering plant cells can integrate its DNA into that of the infected plant cell. Breeders are able to develop strains of *A. tumifasciens* in large numbers. The new strains contain, in their plastids, a desirable gene taken from other variants of the same plant species, or taken from other sources. Wounded test plants can then be infected and the chosen gene begins to multiply by integrating itself into the cells of the plant. Tissues developing around the point of infection can then be used for propagation of the new genetically modified cultivar. Confirmation of successful genetic change can be achieved most easily when the newly introduced gene is linked in the bacterial plasmid with a marker gene. Two common kinds of marker have been used; resistance to an antibiotic and resistance to a herbicide. In this way, the breeder is able to test whether incorporation of a desirable new character has been successful by exposing it to the antibiotic or herbicide concerned.

There seems little doubt that major advances in the quantity and quality of horticultural crops could follow GM methods of breeding. However, the breeders have not been able to allay fears from the public that such methods may result in an insidious deterioration of food quality, or pose a threat to the environment.

THE PLANT VARIETIES AND SEEDS ACT, 1964

This Act protects the rights of producers of new cultivars. The registration of a new cultivar is acceptable only when its characteristics are shown to be significantly different from any existing type. Successful registration enables the plant breeder to control the licence for the cultivar's propagation, whether by seed or vegetative methods. Separate schemes operate for the individual genera of horticultural and agricultural crops, but all breeding activities may benefit from the 1964 Act.

GENE BANKS

As new specialized cultivars are produced and grown, using highly controlled cultivation methods, old cultivars and wild sources of variation, which could be useful in future breeding programmes, are being lost. There is much interest in gene **conservation**. A **gene bank** provides a means of storing the seed of many cultivars and species at very low temperatures, while some plant material is maintained in tissue culture conditions (*see* page 11).

FURTHER READING

George, R.A.T. *Vegetable Seed Production* (Longman, 1999).

Have, D.J. van der. *Plant Breeding Perspectives* (Centre for Agricultural Publishing and Documentation, Wageningen, 1979).

Ingram, D.S. *et al.* (Editors). *Science and the Garden* (Blackwell Science Ltd, 2002).

North, C. *Plant Breeding and Genetics in Horticulture* (Macmillan, 1979).

Simmonds, N.W. *Principles of Crop Improvement* (Longman, 1979).

Watts, L. *Flower and Vegetable Breeding* (Grower Books, 1980).

9

Weeds

> *Most plants, whether wild or cultivated, grow in competition with other organisms such as pests, diseases and other plants. Any competitive unwanted plant is termed as a weed. This chapter indicates the growing situations where weeds become problems, the means of weed identification, the specific biological features of weeds that make them important and the relevant control measures used against them. Detailed principles of control are described in Chapter 12.*

DAMAGE

A weed is a plant of any kind that is growing in the wrong place: groundsel smothering lettuce, moss covering a lawn, last year's potatoes emerging in a plot of cabbage, rose suckers spoiling a herbaceous border. Damage caused by weeds may be categorized into seven main areas:

1 **Competition** between the weed and the plant for water, nutrients and light may prove favourable to the weed if it is able to establish itself quickly. The plants are therefore deprived of their major requirement and poor growth results. The extent of this competition is largely unpredictable, varying with climatic factors such as temperature and rainfall, soil factors such as soil type and cultural factors such as cultivation method, plant spacing and quality of weed control in previous seasons. Large numbers of weed seed may be introduced into a plot in poor quality composts or farmyard manure. The uncontrolled proliferation of weeds will inevitably produce serious plant losses.

2 **Seed quality** is lowered by weed seed, e.g. fat hen contamination in batches of seed, e.g. carrots.

3 **Machinery**, e.g. mowing machines and harvesting equipment may be fouled by weeds, such as knotgrass, that have stringy stems.

4 **Poisonous plants**: Ragwort, sorrel and buttercups are eaten by farm animals when more desirable food is scarce. Poisonous fruits, e.g. black nightshade, may contaminate mechanically harvested crops such as peas for freezing.

5 **Pests and diseases** are commonly harboured on weeds. Chickweed supports whitefly, red spider mite and cucumber mosaic virus in greenhouses. Sowthistles are commonly attacked by chrysanthemum leaf miner. Groundsel is everywhere infected by a rust which attacks cinerarias. Charlock may support high levels of club root, a serious disease of brassica crops. Fat hen and docks allow early infestations of black bean aphid to build up. Speedwells may be infested with stem and bulb nematodes.

6 **Drainage** (*see* Chapter 14) depends on a free flow of water along ditches. Dense growth of chickweed may seriously reduce this flow and increase waterlogging of horticultural land.

7 **Tidiness** is essential in a well-maintained garden. The amenity horticulturist may consider that any plant spoiling the appearance of plants in pots, borders, paths or lawns should be removed, even though the garden plants themselves are not affected.

IDENTIFICATION

As with any problem in horticulture, recognition and identification are essential before any control measures can be attempted. The weed seedling causes little damage to a crop and is relatively easy to control. Identification of this stage is therefore important and, with a little practice, the gardener or grower may learn to recognize the important weeds using such features as shape, colour and hairiness of the cotyledons and first true leaves (*see* Figure 9.1).

Early recognition of a weed species may be crucial for control. The ivy-leaved speedwell is susceptible to the foliage-applied herbicides only at the cotyledon to three-leaf stages, and attempted control against the more mature weed will give poor results.

Within any crop or bedding display, a range of different weed species will be observed. Changes in the weed flora may occur because of environmental factors such as reduced pH; because of new crops that may encourage different weeds to develop; or because repeated use of one herbicide selectively encourages certain weeds, e.g. groundsel in lettuce crops or annual meadow grass in turf. Horticulturists must watch carefully for these changes so that their chemical control may be adjusted.

The mature weeds may be identified using an illustrated flora, which shows details of leaf and flower characters.

Weed biology

The range of weed species includes algae, mosses, liverworts, ferns (bracken) and flowering plants. These species display one or more special features of their life cycle which enable them to compete as **successful** weeds against the crop and cause problems for the horticulturist.

Many weeds, e.g. groundsel, produce seeds that germinate more quickly than crop seeds and thus emerge from the soil to crowd out the developing plants. Seeds of species such as charlock, annual meadow grass and groundsel germinate throughout the year, while others such as orache appear in spring and cleavers in autumn. Carefully timed cultivations or herbicidal control is effective against this growth stage.

The soil conditions may favour certain weeds. Sheep's sorrel prefers acid conditions, while mosses are found in badly drained soils. Knapweed competes well in dry soils, while common sorrel survives well on phosphate-deficient land. Yorkshire fog grass invades poorly fertilized turf, while nettle and chickweed favour highly fertile soils.

The growth habit of the weed may influence its success. Chickweed and slender speedwell produce prostrate stems bearing numerous leaves that prevent light reaching emergent plant seedlings, while groundsel and fat hen have an upright habit that competes less for light in the early period. Weeds such as bindweed, cleavers and nightshades are able to grow alongside woody plants, such as cane fruit and border shrubs, making control difficult.

Different weeds propagate in different ways. Chickweed completing several life cycles per year (*see* **ephemeral**, Table 3.3), and black nightshade completing one (**annual**), both produce seed in order to continue the species. Annual seed production may be high in certain species. A scentless mayweed plant may produce 300 000 seeds, fat hen 70 000 and groundsel 1000. A **dormancy** period is seen in many weed species, groundsel being an exception. Seed germination commonly continues over a period of 4 or 5 years after seed dispersal, presenting the grower with a continual problem.

Some of the most difficult perennial weeds to control rely on **vegetative propagation** for their long-term survival in soils. Bracken and couch grass survive and spread by means of underground stems (rhizomes). Field bindweed and creeping thistle,

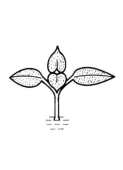

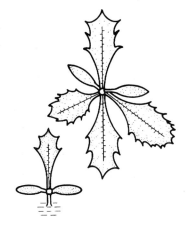

Chickweed (×1.5)
Bright green. Cotyledons have a light coloured tip and a prominent mid-vein. True leaves have long hairs on their petioles

Groundsel (×1.5)
Cotyledons are narrow and purple underneath. True leaves have step-like teeth

Large Field Speedwell (×1.5)
Cotyledons like the 'spade' on playing cards. True leaves hairy, notched and opposite

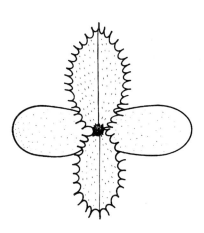

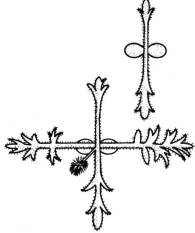

Creeping Thistle (×1.5)
Cotyledons large and fleshy. True leaves have prickly margins

Yarrow (×1.5)
Small broad cotyledons. True leaves hairy and with pointed lateral lobes

Broad-leaved Dock (×1.5)
Cotyledons narrow. First leaves often crimson, rounded with small lobes at the bottom

Figure 9.1 *Seedlings of common weeds. Notice the difference between cotyledons and true leaves. (Reproduced by permission of Blackwell Scientific Publications).*

on the other hand, produce creeping roots that, in the latter species, may grow 6 m in 1 year. Docks, dandelions and plantains develop swollen taproots, while horsetails survive the winter by means of underground tubers. The large quantities of food stored in vegetative organs enable these species to emerge quickly from the soil in spring, often from considerable depths if the soil has been ploughed in. The fragmentation of underground rhizomes and creeping roots by cultivation machinery enables these species to increase in disturbed soils. Weeds with swollen roots provide the greatest problems to the horticulturist in long-term crops such as soft fruit and turf because **foliage-acting** and residual herbicides may have little effect.

Fragmentation of above-ground parts may be important. A lawnmower used on turf containing the slender speedwell weed cuts and spreads the delicate stems that, under damp conditions, establish on other parts of the lawn.

Control measures are regularly necessary in most crop and amenity situations. Greenhouse production suffers much less from weed problems because composts and border soils are regularly sterilized.

Below are described important annual and perennial weeds. Specific descriptions of identification, damage, biology and control measures are given for each weed species.

Detailed discussion of weed control measures (legislative, cultural and chemical) is presented in Chapter 12.

ANNUAL WEEDS

While there are at least 50 successful annual weed species in horticulture, this book can cover only a few examples that illustrate the main points of life cycles and control. Three species, chickweed, groundsel and speedwell, are described below to demonstrate some features of their biology that make them successful weeds.

Chickweed (*Stellaria media*)

This species is found in many horticultural situations as a weed of flowerbeds, vegetables, soft fruit and greenhouse plantings. It has a wide distribution throughout Britain, grows on land up to altitudes of 700 m, and is most often seen on rich, heavy soils.

The seedling cotyledons are pointed with a light coloured tip, while its true leaves have hairy petioles (*see* Figure 9.1). The adult plant has a characteristic lush appearance (*see* Figure 9.2) and grows in a prostrate manner over the surface of the soil; in some cases it covers an area of 0.1 m², its leafy stems crowding out young plants as it increases in

Figure 9.2 *Chickweed: note the opposite leaves and small white flowers.*

size. Small white, five-petalled flowers are produced throughout the year, the flowering response being indifferent to daylength. The flowers are self-fertile. An average of 2500 disc-like seeds (1 mm in diameter) may result from the oblong fruit capsules produced by one plant.

Since the first seed may be dispersed within 6 weeks of the plant germinating, and the plant continues to produce seed for several months, it can be seen just how prolific the species is. The seeds are normally released as the fruit capsule opens during dry weather; they survive digestion by animals and birds and may thus be dispersed over large distances. Irrigation water may carry them into channels and ditches. The large numbers of seed (up to 14 million/ha) are most commonly

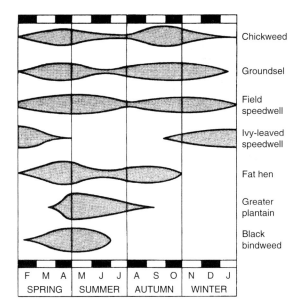

Figure 9.3 *Annual and perennial weeds: periods of seed germination. Note that chickweed, groundsel and field speedwell seeds germinate throughout the year. Many other species are more limited. (Reproduced by permission of Blackwell Scientific Publications.)*

found in the top 7 cm of the soil where, under conditions of light, fluctuating temperatures and nitrate ions, they may overcome the **dormancy** mechanism and germinate to form the seedling. Many seeds, however, survive up to the second, third and occasionally fourth years. Figure 9.3 shows that germination can occur at any time of the year, with April and September as peak periods.

Chickweed is an **alternate host** for many aphid transmitted viruses (e.g. cucumber mosaic), and the stem and bulb nematode.

Control of this weed is best achieved by a combination of methods. Partial sterilization of soil in greenhouses is effective, while hoeing in the spring and autumn periods prevents the developing seedling from flowering. The weed may be killed by **pre-emergent contact** sprays, e.g. paraquat applied before a crop emerges; by **soil-applied** root-acting herbicides, e.g. propachlor; or by **foliage-acting** herbicides applied in specific crop situations, e.g. linuron in potatoes. The weed in greenhouses

may, with care, be controlled by carefully directed sprays of contact herbicides, e.g. pentanochlor.

Groundsel (*Senecio vulgaris*)

This is a very common and important weed, found in many countries, particularly on heavy soil. It grows on both rich and poor soils up to almost 600 m in altitude.

The seedling cotyledons are narrow, purple underneath, and the true leaves have step-like teeth (Figure 9.1). The adult plant has an upright habit, and produces as many as 26 yellow, small-petalled flower heads; flowering occurs in *all* seasons of the year. About 45 column-shaped seeds, 2 mm in length, and densely packed in the fruit head, bear a mass of fine hairs which, when released in dry weather, carry the individual seeds along on air currents for many metres, while in wet weather the seeds become **sticky** and may be carried on the feet of animals, including humans. The seeds survive digestion by birds, and thus can be transported in this way. As can be seen in Figure 9.3, the seeds may germinate at any time of the year, with early May and September as peak periods. Since there may be more than three generations of groundsel per year (the autumn generation surviving the winter), and each generation may give rise to a thousand seeds, it is clear why groundsel is one of the most successful colonizers of cultivated ground. Its role as a symptomless carrier of the wilt fungus *Verticillium* increases its importance in certain crops, e.g. hops.

A combination of control methods may be necessary for successful control. Hoeing or alternative cultivation, particularly in spring and autumn, prevents developing seedlings from flowering, but uprooted flowering groundsel plants do produce viable seed. **Contact** herbicides, e.g. paraquat, may be sprayed to control the weed on paths or in fallow soil. **Soil-acting** chemicals, e.g. propachlor on brassicas, kill off the germinating seedling. An established groundsel population, especially in a crop such as lettuce, a fellow member of the Compositae family, requires careful choice of herbicide to avoid damage to the crop.

Speedwells (*Veronica persica and V. filiformis*)

The first species, the large field speedwell, is an important weed in vegetable production, while the second species, the slender or round-leaved speedwell, is no longer considered a pleasant rock garden plant but has become a serious turf problem.

The seedling cotyledons are spade shaped, while the true leaves are opposite, notched and hairy (*see* Figure 9.1) in both species. The adult plants have erect, hairy stems, and rather similar broadtoothed leaves.

V. persica produces up to 300 bright blue flowers, 1 cm wide, per plant. The flowers are self-fertile and occur throughout the year, but mainly between February and November. The adult plant produces an average of 2000 light brown boat-shaped seeds (2 mm across), which fall to the ground and may be dispersed by ants; the rather large seeds travel as contaminants of crop seeds. The seeds of this species germinate below soil level all year round, but most commonly from March to May (*see* Figure 9.3), the winter period being necessary to break **dormancy**. Seeds may remain viable for more than 2 years.

V. filiformis produces **self-sterile** purplish-blue flowers between March and May, and spreads by means of prostrate stems which root at their nodes to invade fine and coarse turf, especially in damp areas. Segments of this weed cut by lawnmowers easily root and further disperse the species. Seeds are not important in its spread.

Control of *V. persica* is best achieved by a combination of methods. Hoeing or alternative cultivation, particularly in spring, prevents developing seedlings from growing to mature plants and producing their many seeds. **Contact** herbicides, e.g. paraquat, may be sprayed to control the weed on paths or in fallow soils. **Soil-acting** chemicals, e.g. chlorpropham on onions, kill off the germinating weed seedling, while **contact** chemicals, e.g. clopyralid, may be sprayed onto a young onion crop to control emerging seedlings.

The slender speedwell (*V. filiformis*) represents a different problem for control. While preventative control on turf seedbed with a **contact** chemical,

e.g. paraquat, allows the turf to establish undisturbed, use of a more **selective** contact chemical, e.g. chlorthal dimethyl, is necessary to prevent chemical damage to established grass. Regular close mowing and spiking of turf removes the high humidity necessary for this weed's establishment and development.

PERENNIAL WEEDS

Four species, creeping thistle, couch, yarrow and broad-leaved dock are described below to demonstrate the major features of their biology (particularly perennating organs) that make them successful weeds. The flowering period of these weeds is mainly between June and October (*see* Figure 9.4), but the main problem for growers is the ability of these plants to survive and reproduce vegetatively.

Creeping thistle (*Cirsium arvense*)

This species is a common weed in grassland and perennial crops, e.g. apples, where it forms dense clumps of foliage.

The seedling cotyledons are broad and smooth, the true leaves spiky (*see* Figure 9.1). It is readily recognizable by its dark green spiny foliage growing

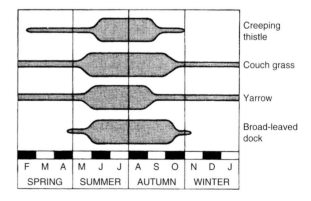

Figure 9.4 *Perennial weeds: periods of flowering. Most flowers and seeds are produced between June and October. Annual weeds commonly flower throughout the year. However the slender speedwell flowers only between March and May.*

up to a metre in height. It is found in all areas, even at altitudes of 750 m, and on saline soil. The species is **dioecious**, the male producing spherical and the female slightly elongated purple flower heads from July to September. Only when the two sexes of plants are within about 100 m of each other does fertilization occurs in sufficient quantities to produce large numbers of brown, shiny fruit, 4 mm long. These are wind-borne by a parachute of long hairs. The seeds may germinate beneath the soil surface in the same year as their production, or in the following spring, particularly when soil temperatures reach 20°C. The resulting seedlings develop a **taproot** which commonly reaches 3 m down into the soil. **Lateral roots**, growing out horizontally about 0.3 m below the soil surface, may penetrate 6 m in one season, and along their length are produced **adventitious buds** that, each spring, grow up as stems. Under permanent grassland, the roots may remain dormant for many years. Soil disturbance, such as ploughing, breaks up the roots and may result in a worse thistle problem unless drought or frost coincides with this activity.

Control of the seedling stage of this weed is not normally considered worthwhile. The main strategy must be to prevent the development of the perennial root system. Cutting down plants at the flower bud stage when sugars are being transferred from the roots upwards is said to achieve this objective. **Translocated** chemicals, e.g. MCPA, are commonly used on grassland, the spray chemical moving from the leaves to the perennial roots, particularly when applied in autumn at a time when sugars are similarly moving down the plant. In broad-leaved perennial crops, e.g. raspberries, **soil-acting** herbicides, e.g. bromacil, may be applied in late winter before crop bud burst, to suppress the emergence of established plants. Deep ploughing is often successful in newly cultivated land.

Couch grass (*Agropyron repens*)

This grass, sometimes called 'twitch', is a widely distributed and important weed found at altitudes up to 500 m.

The dull-green plant is often confused, in the vegetative stage, with the creeping bent (*Agrostis stolonifera*). However, the small 'ears' at the leaf base characterize couch. The plant may reach a metre in height and often grows in tufts. Flowering heads produced from May to October resemble **perennial ryegrass**, but the flat flower spikelets are positioned at right angles to the main stem in couch. Seeds (9 mm long) are produced only after cross-fertilization between different strains of the species, and the importance of the seed stage, therefore, varies from field to field. Couch seeds may be carried in cereal seed stocks over long distances, and may survive deep in the soil for up to 10 years. From May to October, stimulated by high light intensity, the overwintered plants produce horizontal **rhizomes** (*see* Figure 7.3) just under the soil; these white rhizomes may grow 16 cm per year in heavy soils, 32 cm in sandy soils. They bear scale leaves on nodes that, under **apical dominance**, remain suppressed until the rhizome is cut by ploughing. In the autumn, rhizomes attached to the mother plant grow above ground to produce new plants that survive the winter. The rapid growth and extensive root system of this species provide severe competition for light, water and nutrients in any infested crop.

Control is achieved by a combination of methods. In fallow soil **deep ploughing**, especially in heavy land, exposes the rhizomes to drying. Further control by **rotavating** the weed when it reaches the one or two leaf stage disturbs the plant at its weakest point, and repeated rotavating will eventually cut up couch rhizomes to such an extent that no further nodes are available for its propagation.

Translocated herbicides, e.g. glyphosate sprayed onto couch in fallow soils during active vegetative growth, kill most of the underground rhizomes. In established fruit and conifers, control is achieved in the dormant winter or early spring seasons by a translocated chemical, e.g. dalapon, which, if applied to a full weed cover, has a maximum effect without causing root damage to the trees. Soil intended for vegetable production, e.g. carrots and potatoes, may be sprayed with a chemical such as dalapon to control couch so long as a 7 weeks period is

Figure 9.5 *Couch grass: note the underground rhizome.*

observed between application and planting. Control by **contact** herbicides, e.g. paraquat, may be successful in exhausting couch rhizome reserves if applied repeatedly (Figure 9.5).

Yarrow (*Achillea millifolium*)

This strongly scented perennial, with its spreading flowering head (*see* Figure 9.6), is a common hedgerow plant found on most soils at altitudes up to 1200 m. Its persistence, together with its resistance to herbicides and drought in grassland, makes it a serious turf weed.

The seedling leaves are hairy, and elongated with sharp teeth (*see* Figure 9.1). The mature plant has dissected pinnate leaves produced throughout the

Figure 9.6 *Yarrow: note the divided leaves and branching inflorescence.*

year on wiry, woolly stems, which commonly reach 45 cm in height, and which from May to September produce flat-topped white to pink flower heads. An annual production of about 3000 small, flat fruits per plant is dispersed by birds. The seeds germinate on arrival at the soil surface. When not in flower, this species produces stolons along the ground (up to 20 cm long per year), and in autumn rooting from the nodes occurs.

Control of this weed may prove difficult. Routine scarification of turf does not easily remove the roots. Repeated sprays of **translocated** chemical mixtures, e.g. 2,4-D plus mecoprop, reach the roots to give some control.

Figure 9.7 *Broad-leaved dock. Note the large shiny leaves.*

Broad-leaved dock (*Rumex obtusifolius*)

The seedling cotyledons are narrow, the true leaves large, broad and crimson coloured (*see* Figure 9.1). This is a common weed of arable land, grassland and fallow soil. The mature plant is readily identified by its long (up to 25 cm) shiny green leaves (*see* Figure 9.7), known to many as an antidote to 'nettle rash'. The plant may grow 1 m tall, producing a conspicuous branched inflorescence of small green flowers from June to October. The numerous plate-like fruits (3 mm long) may fall to the ground or be dispersed by seed-eating birds such as finches, by cattle, and in batches of seed stocks. The seed represents an important stage in this perennial weed's life cycle, surviving many years in the soil, and most commonly germinating in spring. Like most *Rumex* spp., the seedling develops a stout, branched taproot, which may penetrate the soil down to 1 m in the mature plant, but most commonly reaches 25 cm. Segments of the taproot, chopped by cultivation implements, are capable of producing new plants.

High levels of seed production, a tough taproot, and a resistance to most herbicides, thus present a problem in the control of this weed. Attempts to exhaust the root system by repeated ploughing and rotavating have proved useful. Young seedlings are easily controlled by **translocated** chemicals, e.g. 2,4-D, but the mature plant is resistant to all but a few **translocated** chemicals, e.g. asulam, which may be used on grassland, soft fruit, top fruit and amenity areas, during periods of active vegetative weed growth when the chemical is moved most rapidly towards the roots.

Mixed weed populations

In the field, a wide variety of both annual and perennial weeds may occur together. The growers must recognize the most important weeds in their holding or garden, so that a decision on the **precise** use of chemical control with the correct herbicide is achieved. Particular care is required to match the **concentration** of the herbicide or herbicide mixtures to the weed species present. Also, the grower must be aware that continued use of one chemical may induce a change in weed species, some of which may be tolerant to that chemical.

MOSSES AND LIVERWORTS

These primitive plants may become weeds in wet growing conditions. The small cushion-forming moss (*Bryum* spp.) grows on **sand capillary** benches, and thin, acid turf that has been closely mown. Feathery moss (*Hypnum* spp.) is common on less closely mown, unscarified turf. A third type (*Polytrichum* spp.), erect and with a rosette of leaves, is found in dry acid conditions around golf greens.

Liverworts (*Pellia* spp.) are recognized by their flat (thallus) leaves growing on the surface of pot plant compost.

These organisms increase only when the soil and compost surface is excessively wet, or when nutrients are so low as to limit plant growth. **Cultural** methods such as improved drainage, aeration, liming, application of fertilizer and removal of shade usually achieve good results in turf. Control with **contact** scorching chemicals, e.g. alkaline ferrous sulphate, may give temporary results. Moss on sand benches becomes less of a problem if the sand is regularly washed.

FURTHER READING

ADAS. *Colour Atlas of Weed Seedlings* (Wolfe Science, 1987).

Hance, R.J. and Holly, K. *Weed Control Handbook*, Vol. 1 *Principles* (Blackwell Scientific Publications, 1990).

Hill, A.H. *The Biology of Weeds* (Edward Arnold, 1977).

Hope, F. *Turf Culture: A Manual for Groundsmen* (Cassell, 1990).

The UK Pesticide Guide (British Crop Protection Council, 2003).

Weed Guide (Hoechst Schering, 1997).

10

Horticultural Pests

This chapter looks at the pests that reduce growth in horticultural crops. In the case of the mammal and birds, which are relatively large and mobile, emphasis is placed on the control directed against individuals. With smaller invertebrate pests, such as slugs, insects, mites and nematodes, the range of life cycles is described to explain the kinds of damage caused and the particular strategy for control against the target population. A more general description of control measures is given in Chapter 12.

MAMMAL AND BIRD PESTS

The rabbit (*Oryctolagus cuniculus*)

The rabbit is common in most countries of central and southern Europe. It came to Britain around the eleventh century with the Normans, and became an established pest in the nineteenth century.

The rabbit may consume 0.5 kg of plant food per day. Young turf and cereal crops are the worst affected, particularly winter varieties that, in the seedling stage, may be almost completely destroyed. Rabbits may move from cereal crops to horticultural holdings. Stems of top fruit may be **ring barked** by rabbits, particularly in early spring when other food is scarce. Vegetables and recently planted garden-border plants are a common target for the pest, and fine turf on golf courses may be damaged, thus allowing lawn weeds, e.g. yarrow, to become established.

The rabbit's high reproductive ability enables it to maintain high populations even when continued control methods are in operation. The doe, weighing about 1 kg, can reproduce within a year of its birth, and may have three to five litters of three to six young ones in 1 year, commonly in the months of February–July. The young are blind and naked at birth, but emerge from the underground 'maternal' nest after only a few weeks to find their own food. Large burrow systems (**warrens**), penetrating as deep as 3 m in sandy soils, may contain as many as a 100 rabbits. Escape or **bolt** holes running off from the main burrow system allow the rabbit to escape from predators.

Control of rabbits is, by law, the responsibility of the land owner. **Preventative** measures are the most effective. **Wire fencing**, with the base 30 cm **underground** and facing outwards, represents an effective barrier to the pest, while thick plastic sheet **guards** are commonly coiled round the base of exposed young trees. Repellant chemicals, e.g. aluminium ammonium sulphate, may be sprayed on bedding displays and young trees.

Shotguns, small spring traps placed in the rabbit hole, winter ferreting or **long nets** placed at the corner of a field to catch herded rabbits are methods used as **curative** control. **Gassing**, however, is the most effective method. Crystals of powdered cyanide are introduced (only by trained operators) into the holes of warrens by means of long-handled spoons or by power operated machines. On contact with moisture hydrocyanic acid is released as a gas and, in well-blocked warrens, the rabbits are quickly killed. Care is required in the storage and use of powdered cyanide, where an **antidote**, amyl nitrite, should be readily available. **Myxamatosis**, a flea-borne virus disease of the rabbit, causing a swollen head and eyes, was introduced into Britain in 1953, and within a few years greatly reduced the rabbit population. The development of weaker virus strains, and the increase in rabbit resistance, has combined to reduce this disease's effectiveness in control, although its importance in any one area is constantly fluctuating.

The brown rat (*Rattus norvegicus*)

The brown rat, also called the common rat, is well known by its dark-brown colour, blunt nose, short ears and long, scaly tail. Its diet is varied; it will eat **seeds**, **succulent** stems, bulbs and tubers, and may grind its teeth down to size by the unlikely act of gnawing at plastic **piping** and electric cables. A rat's average annual food intake may reach 50 kg, a large amount for an animal weighing only about 300 g. This species has considerable reproductive powers. The female may begin to breed at 8 weeks of age, producing an average of six litters of six young ones per year. Its unpopular image is further increased by its habit of fouling the food it eats, and by the lethal human bacterium causing **Weil's disease**, which it transmits through its urine.

Control is best achieved by a preliminary survey of rat numbers in buildings and fields of the horticultural holding, and by the identification of the 'rat-runs' along which the animals travel. Baits containing a mixture of **anticoagulant** poison and food material such as oatmeal are placed near the runs, inside a container that, while attracting the rat, prevents access by children and pets. Drainage tiles or oil drums drilled with a small rat-sized hole often serve this purpose. The poison, e.g. difenacoum, takes about 3 days to kill the rat and, since the other individuals do not associate their comrade's death with the chemical, the whole family may be controlled. The bait should be placed wherever there are signs of rat activity, and repeated applications every 3 days for a period of 3 weeks should be effective.

Strains of rat resistant to some anticoagulants are commonly found in some areas, and a range of chemicals may need to be tried before successful control is achieved. The poison, when not in use, should be safely stored away from children and pets. Dead rats should be burnt to avoid poisoning of other animals.

Sonic devices are sometimes used to disturb the animal and provide a round-the-clock deterrent.

The grey squirrel (*Sciurus carolinensis*)

This attractive-looking, 45 cm long creature was introduced into Britain in the late nineteenth century, at a time when the red squirrel population was suffering from disease. The grey squirrel became dominant in most areas, with the red squirrel in pockets such as the Isle of Wight.

The horticultural damage caused by grey squirrels varies with each season. In spring, germinating bulbs may be eaten, and the **bark** of many tree species stripped off (*see* ring barking, page 44). In summer, pears, plums and peas may suffer. Autumn provides a large wild food source, although apples and potatoes may be damaged. In winter, little damage is done. Fields next to wooded areas are clearly prone to squirrel damage.

Squirrels most commonly produce two litters of three young ones from March to June, in twig platforms high in the trees; the female may become pregnant at an early age (6 months). As the squirrels have few natural enemies, and this species lives high above ground, control is difficult.

During the months of April–July, when most damage is seen, **cage traps** containing desirable food, e.g. maize seed, reduce the squirrel population to less damaging levels. **Spring traps** placed in natural or artificial tunnels achieve rapid results at this time of year if placed where the squirrel moves.

Poisoned bait containing a formulation of antico-agulant chemical, e.g. warfarin, when placed in a well-designed ground-level hopper (one hopper per 3 ha) may achieve successful squirrel control without seriously lowering other small wild mammal numbers. In winter and early spring, the destruction of squirrel nests (or **dreys**) by means of long poles may achieve some success.

The mole (*Talpa europea*)

The mole is found in all parts of the British Isles except Ireland. This dark-grey, 15 cm long mammal, weighing about 90 g, uses its shovel-shaped feet to create an underground system 5–20 cm deep and up to 0.25 ha in extent. The tunnel contents are excavated into mole hills. The resulting **root disturbance** to grassland and other crops causes wilting, and may result in serious losses.

In its dark environment, the solitary mole moves, actively searching for earthworms, slugs, millipedes and insects. About 5 h of activity is followed by about 3 h of rest. Only in spring do males and females meet. In June, one litter of two to seven young ones are born in a grass-lined underground nest, often located underneath a dense thicket. Young moles often move above ground, reach maturity at about 4 months, and live for about 4 years.

Natural **predators** of the mole include tawny owls, weasels and foxes.

The main control methods are **trapping** and **poison baiting**, usually carried out between October and April, when tunnelling is closer to the surface. Pincer or half barrel traps are placed in fresh tunnels and sprung without greatly changing the tunnel diameter. The soil must be replaced so that the mole sees no light from its position in the tunnel. The mole enters the trap, is caught and starves to death. In serious mole infestations, **strychnine salts** are mixed with earthworms at the rate of 2 g per 100 worms, and single worms carefully inserted into inhabited tunnels at the rate of 25 worms per hectare. Ministry of Agriculture authority is required before purchasing strychnine, a highly dangerous chemical, which must be stored with care.

Deer

Deer may become pests in land adjoining woodland where they hide. Muntjac and roe deer **ring-bark** (*see* page 44) trees and eat succulent crops. High fences and regular shooting may be used in their control.

The wood-pigeon (*Columba palumbus*)

This attractive, 40 cm long, blue-grey pigeon with white underwing bars is known to horticulturists as a serious pest on most outdoor edible crops. In **spring**, seeds and seedlings of crops such as brassicas, beans and germinating turf may be systematically eaten. In **summer**, cereals and clover receive its attention; in **autumn**, tree fruits may be taken in large quantities, while in **winter**, cereals and brassicas are often seriously attacked, the latter when snowfall prevents the consumption of other food. The wood-pigeon is invariably attracted to **high protein** foods such as seeds when they are available.

Wood-pigeons lay several clutches of two eggs per year from March to September. The August/September clutches show highest survival. The eggs, laid on a nest of twigs situated deep inside the tree, hatch after about 18 days, and the young ones remain in the nest for 20–30 days. Predators such as jays and magpies eat many eggs, but the main population control factor is the availability of food in winter. Numbers in the British Isles are boosted a little by migrating Scandinavian pigeons in April, but the large majority of this species is resident and non-migratory.

The wood-pigeon spends much of its time feeding on wild plants, and only a small proportion of its time on crops. Control of the whole population, therefore, seems both costly and impracticable. Protection of particular fields is achieved by **scaring** devices which include scarecrows, bangers (firecrackers or gas guns) or rotating orange and black vanes, which disturb the pigeon. Changing the **type** and **location** of the device every few days helps prevent the pigeon from becoming indifferent. The use of the **shotgun** from hidden positions such as hides and ditches, particularly when artificial pigeons (decoys) are placed in the field, is an important additional method of scaring birds and thus protecting the crop.

The bullfinch (*Pyrrhula pyrrhula*)

This delightful, 14 cm long bird is characterized by its sturdy appearance and broad bill. The male has a rose-red breast, blue-grey back and black head-cap. The female has a less striking pink breast and yellowish-brown back.

From April to September the bird progressively feeds on seeds of wild plants, e.g. chickweed, buttercup, dock, fat hen and blackberry. From September to April, the species forms small flocks that, in addition to feeding on buds and seeds of wild species, e.g. docks, willow, oak and hawthorn, turn their attention to **buds** of soft and top fruit. Gooseberries are attacked from November to January, apples from February to April and blackcurrants from March to April. The birds are shy, preferring to forage on the edges of orchards but, as winter advances, become bolder, moving towards the more central trees and bushes. The birds nip buds out at the rate of about 30 per minute, eating the central meristem tissues. Leaf, flower and fruit development may thus be seriously reduced, and since in some plums and gooseberries there is no regeneration of fruiting points, damage may be seen several years after attack.

The bullfinch produces a platform nest of twigs in birch or hazel trees, and between May and September lays two to three clutches of four to five pale blue eggs, with purple-brown streaks, and can thus quickly re-establish numbers reduced by lack of food or human attempts at control.

Fine mesh netting, cotton or synthetic thread draped over trees, or bitter chemicals, e.g. ziram sprayed at the time of expected attack, are used to some extent to prevent bullfinch attack. Most success is achieved by catching birds (usually immature individuals) in specially designed **traps**, which are closed when the bird lands on a perch to eat seeds. Trapping may be started as early as

September. Large-scale re-invasion by the birds in the same season is unlikely, as they are territorial, rarely moving more than 2 miles throughout their lives. Bullfinch control is permitted only in scheduled areas of wide-scale fruit production, e.g. Kent.

INVERTEBRATE PESTS

Slugs

These animals belong to the phylum Mollusca, a group including the octopus and whelk, and the slug's close relatives, the **snails**, which cause a little damage to plants in greenhouses and private gardens. Slugs move slowly by means of an undulating foot, the slime trails from which may indicate the slug's presence. Unlike the snail, their lack of shell permits movement through the soil in search of their food source, seedlings, roots, tubers and bulbs. The slug feeds by means of a file-like tongue (**radula**), which cuts through plant tissue held by the soft mouth, and scoops out cavities in the affected plants (*see* Figure 10.1). In moist, warm weather it may cause above-ground damage to leaves of plants such as border plants, establishing turf, lettuce and brussels sprouts. Slugs are **hermaphrodite** (bearing in their bodies both male and female organs), mate in spring and summer, and lay clusters of up to 50 round, white eggs in rotting vegetation, the warmth from which protects this sensitive stage during cold periods.

Slugs range in size from the black keeled slug (*Milax*), 3 cm long, to the garden slug (*Arion*) which reaches 10 cm in length. The mottled-carnivorous slug (*Testacella*) is occasionally found feeding on earthworms. Horticultural areas commonly support populations of 50 000 slugs per hectare.

Many non-chemical forms of control have been used, ranging from baits of grapefruit skins and stale beer to soot sprinkled around larger plants. The most effective methods, however, involve the two chemicals **metaldehyde**, which dries the slug out, and **methiocarb**, which acts as a stomach poison. The chemicals are most commonly used as small-coloured **pellets** (which include attractants

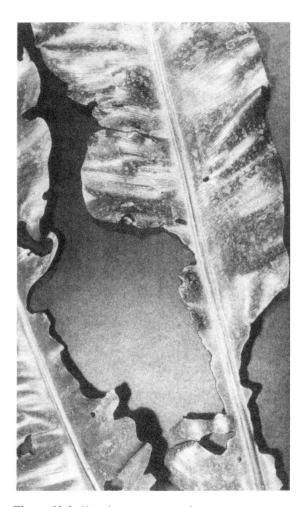

Figure 10.1 *Slug damage on pot plant.*

such as bran and sugar), but metaldehyde may also be applied as a drench. Some growers estimate the slug population using small heaps of pellets covered with a tile or flat stone (to prevent bird poisoning) before deciding on general control. Overuse of slug pellets in gardens has recently been claimed as a major contribution to the decline of the mistle- and song-thrush numbers.

INSECTS

Belonging to the large group **Arthropoda, which include also the woodlice, mites, millipedes** (*see* Table 10.1) and **symphilids**, the **insects** are horticulturally the most important arthropod group, both as pests, and also as beneficial soil animals.

Structure and biology

The body of the adult insect is made up of segments, and is divided into three main parts: the head, thorax and abdomen (*see* Figure 10.2).

The **head** bears three pairs of moving mouthparts. The first, the **mandibles** in insects (such as in caterpillars and beetles) have a biting action (*see* Figure 10.3). The second and third pairs, the **maxillae** and **labia** in these insects help in pushing food into the mouth. In the aphids, the mandibles and maxillae are fused to form a delicate tubular stylet, which sucks up liquids from the plant phloem tissues. Insects remain aware of their environment by means of compound eyes which are sensitive to movement (of predators) and to colour (of flowers). Their antennae may have a touching- and smelling function.

The **thorax** bears three pairs of legs, and in most insects two pairs of wings.

The **abdomen** bears breathing holes (spiracles) along its length, which lead to a respiratory system of tracheae. The blood is colourless, circulates digested food and has no respiratory function. The digestive system, in addition to its food absorbing role, removes waste cell products from the body by means of fine, hair-like growths (malpighian tubules) located near the end of the gut.

Since the animal has an **external** skeleton made of tough chitin, it must shed and replace its 'skin' (**cuticle**, *see* Figure 10.2) periodically by a process called **ecdysis**, in order to increase in size. An insect may develop from egg to adult in one of two ways. In the first group, typified by the aphids, thrips and earwigs, the egg hatches to form a first stage, or instar, called a **nymph**, which resembles the adult in all but size, wing development and possession of sexual organs. Successive nymph instars more closely resemble the adult. Two to seven **instars** (growth stages) occur before the adult emerges (*see* Figure 10.4).

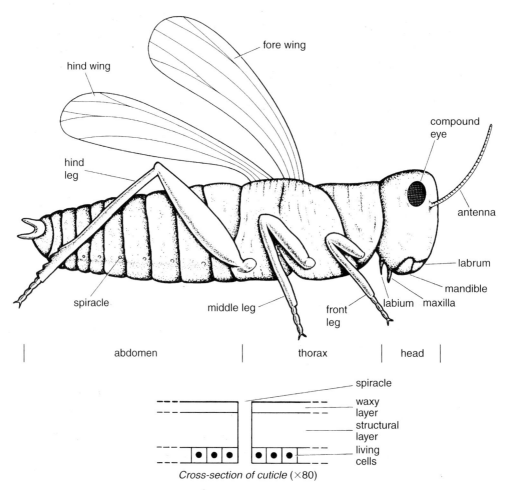

Figure 10.2 *External appearance of an insect. Note the mouthparts, spiracles and cuticle, the three main entry points for insecticides.*

In contrast, other groups of insects including the moths, butterflies, flies and beetles undergo a complete metamorphosis (complete changes of form); the egg hatches to form a first instar, called a **larva** which usually differs greatly in shape from the adult, e.g. the larva (caterpillar) of the cabbage white bears little resemblance to the adult butterfly. Some other damaging larval stages are shown in Figure 10.5 and these can be compared with the often more familiar adult stage. The great change (**metamorphosis**) necessary to achieve this transformation occurs inside the **pupa** stage (*see* Figure 10.4).

The method of overwintering differs between insect groups. The aphids survive mainly as the eggs, while most moths, butterflies and flies survive as the pupa (chrysalis).

The speed of increase of insects varies greatly between groups. Aphids may take as little as 20 days to complete a life cycle in summer, often resulting in vast numbers in the period June–September. On the other hand, the wireworm, the larva of the click beetle, usually takes 4 years to complete its life cycle.

Insect groups are classified into their appropriate order (Table 10.1) according to their general

Plate 1 *Flower border showing the use of flower colour. The light blue of* Brunnera macrophylla *harmonises with the darker blue* Anchusa azurea *and, in the background, the yellow-flowered* Asphodeline lutea.

Plate 2 *Contrasts in leaf shape and form: the linear leaves of Hemerocallis* lilioasphodelus *contrast with the palmate lobed leaves of* Rodgersia podophylla *and, in the background, the pinnate leaves of the fern* Osmunda regalis.

Plate 3 *Protective adaptions. Leaf prickles of holly (left): thorns of* Pyracantha *(left centre): stem prickles of rose (right centre): and thorns of* Eleagnus. *Note also the variegated leaves of the holly and* Eleagnus.

Plate 4 *Spines of cactus.*

Plate 5 *Foliage colour and contrast: The white foliage of* Cornus contraversa *'Variegata', and yellow foliage of the* Chaemaecyparis *'Nana Aurea' contrast with the dark-purple leaved tree (*Fagus sylvatica *Atropurpurea Group).*

Plate 6 *Blackspot of rose.*

Plate 7 *Juvenility. Leaf retention in the lower juvenile branches of beech tree and beech hedging; compare with the bare older branches.*

Plate 8 *Juvenility. The juvenile growth of ivy (left) showing adventititous roots on the stem and the lobed leaves compared with the adult leaf shape (right). Note also the variegated leaf pattern.*

Plate 9 *Potassium deficiency symptoms.*

Plate 10 *Magnesium deficiency symptoms.*

Plate 11 *Chrysanthemum powdery mildew.*

Plate 12 *Rose powdery mildew.*

Plate 13 *(a–g) Barks: decorative patterns and colours exhibited in a range of trees; (h) Apple canker; (i) Armillaria. Honey fungus rhizomorphs (bootlaces) on infected wood. Inset – a clump of characteristic honey-coloured toadstools on an infected trunk.*

Plate 14 *Effect of aspect; note the difference between the north-facing slope (right) with snow still lying after it has melted on the south-facing slope (left).*

Plate 15 *Agrometerological station showing rain gauge (left), Stevenson's screen (centre) and anemometer (right).*

Plates 16 *Stevenson's screen showing Max Min Thermometer (base) and Wet and Dry Thermometer (centre).*

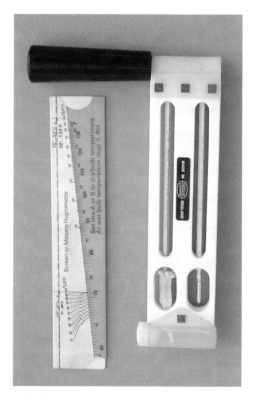

Plate 17 *Whirling hygrometer with calculator.*

Plate 18 *NFT lettuce with close up showing gullies and nutrient solution delivery.*

Plate 19 *Rocks. Granite: pink (left); silver (top); sandstone (right), shade (bottom).*

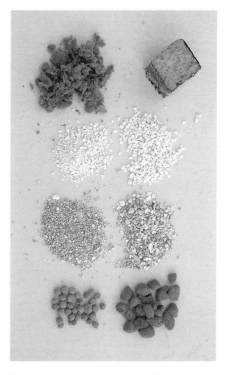

Plate 20 *Growing media. Top to bottom: rockwood, perlite, vermiculite, Leca.*

Plate 21 *Soil capping.*

(a)   (b)   (c)   (d)

Plate 22 *Soil types (a) Podsol; (b) Gley; (c) Brown earth; (d) Rendzina.*

Plate 23 *Soil prism. Note rusty mottle.*

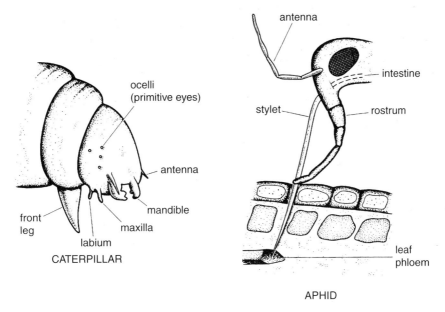

Figure 10.3 *Mouthparts of the caterpillar and aphid. Note the different methods of obtaining nutrients. The aphid selectively sucks up dilute sugar solution from the phloem tissue.*

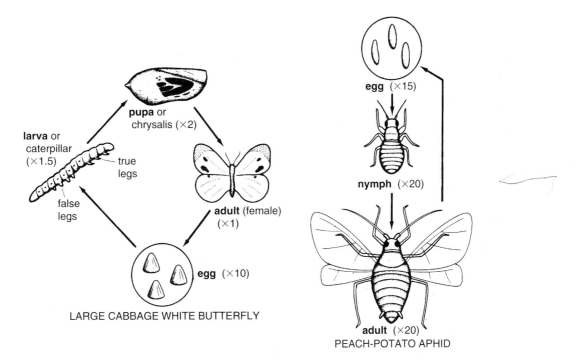

Figure 10.4 *Life cycle stages of a butterfly and an aphid pest. Note that all four stages of the butterfly's life cycle are very different in appearance. The nymph and adult of the aphid are similar.*

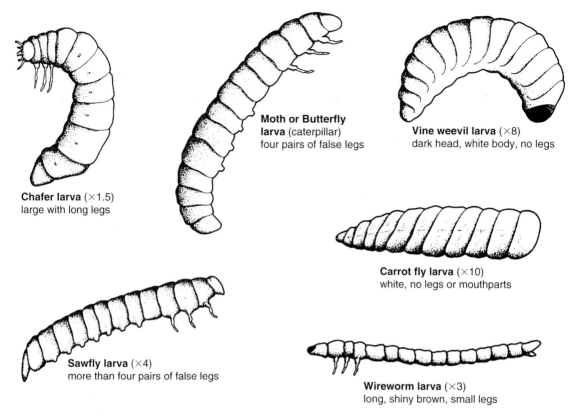

Chafer larva (×1.5)
large with long legs

**Moth or Butterfly
larva** (caterpillar)
four pairs of false legs

Vine weevil larva (×8)
dark head, white body, no legs

Carrot fly larva (×10)
white, no legs or mouthparts

Sawfly larva (×4)
more than four pairs of false legs

Wireworm larva (×3)
long, shiny brown, small legs

Figure 10.5 *Insect larva that damage crops. Identification into the groups above can be achieved by observing the features of colour, shape, legs and mouthparts.*

appearance and life cycle stages. There follows a selection of insect pests in which each species has particular features of its life cycle that warrant description. Whilst comments on **control** are mentioned, the reader should refer to Chapter 12 for details of specific types of control (cultivations, chemicals, etc.) and for explanations of terms used.

Aphids and their relatives (order Hemiptera)

This important group of insects has the egg–nymph–adult life cycle, and sucking mouthparts.

Peach-potato aphid (*Myzus persicae*).   This is often referred to by the name 'greenfly', is common in market gardens and greenhouses. It varies in colour from light green to orange, measures 3 mm

in length (Figure 10.6), and has a complex life cycle, shown in Figure 10.7, alternating between the winter host (peach) and the summer hosts, e.g. potato and bedding plants. In spring and summer, the females produce nymphs directly without any egg stage (a process called **vivipary**), and without fertilization by a male (a process called **parthenogenesis**). Only in autumn, in response to decreasing daylight length and outdoor temperatures, are both sexes produced, which, having wings, fly to the winter host, the peach. After the female is fertilized, she lays thick-walled eggs. In glasshouses, the aphid may survive the winter as the nymph and adult female on plants such as begonias and chrysanthemums, or on weeds such as fat hen.

The nymph and adult of this aphid may cause three types of damage. Using its sucking stylet,

Table 10.1 Arthropod groups found in horticulture

Group	Key features of group	Habitat	Damage
Woodlice (*Crustacea*)	Grey, seven pairs of legs, up to 12 mm in length	Damp organic soils	Eat roots and lower leaves
Millipedes (*Diplopoda*)	Brown, many pairs of legs, slow moving	Most soils	Occasionally eat under-ground tubers and seed
Centipedes (*Chilopoda*)	Brown, many pairs of legs, very active, with strong jaws	Most soils	Beneficial
Symphilids (*Symphyla*)	White, 12 pairs of legs, up to 8 mm in length	Glasshouse soils	Eat fine roots
Mites (*Acarina*)	Variable colour, usually have four pairs of legs (e.g. red spider mites)	Soils and plant tissues	Mottle or distort leaves, buds, flowers and bulbs; soil species are beneficial
Insects (*Insecta*)	Usually six pairs of legs, two pairs of wings		
Springtails (*Collembola*)	White to brown, 3–10 mm in length	Soils and decaying humus	Eat fine roots; some beneficial
Aphid group (*Hemiptera*)	Variable colour, sucking mouthparts, produce honeydew (e.g. greenfly)	All habitats	Discolour leaves and stems; prevent flower pollination; transmit viruses
Moths and butterflies (*Lepidoptera*)	Large wings; larva with three pairs of legs, and four pairs of false legs and biting mouthparts (e.g. cabbage-white butterfly)	Mainly leaves and flowers	Defoliate leaves (stems and roots)
Flies (*Diptera*)	One pair of wings, larvae legless (e.g. leatherjacket)	All habitats	Leaf mining, eat roots
Beetles (*Coleoptera*)	Horny front pair of wings which meet down centre; well-developed mouthparts in adult and larva (e.g. wireworm)	Mainly in the soil	Eat roots and succulent tubers (and fruit)
Sawflies (*Hymenoptera*)	Adult like a queen ant; larvae have three parts of legs, and more than four pairs of false legs (e.g. rose-leaf curling sawfly)	Mainly leaves and flowers	Defoliation
Thrips (*Thysanoptera*)	Yellow and brown, very small, wriggle their bodies (e.g. onion thrips)	Leaves and flowers	Cause spotting of leaves and petals
Earwigs (*Dermaptera*)	Brown, with pincers at rear of body	Flowers and soil	Eat flowers

it may inject a digestive juice into the plant phloem, which in young organs may cause severe **distortion**. Having sucked up sugary phloem contents, the aphid excretes a sticky substance called **honeydew**, which may block up leaf stomata and reduce photosynthesis, particularly when dark-coloured fungi (**sooty moulds**) grow over the honeydew. Thirdly, the aphid stylets may transmit viruses such as virus Y on potatoes and tomato aspermy virus on chrysanthemums.

The peach-potato aphid is controlled in three main ways. In outdoor crops, several organisms,

Figure 10.6 *Peach-potato aphid: note the sucking stylet (actual size of this aphid is about 3 mm long).*

e.g. ladybirds, lacewings, hoverflies and parasitic fungi (*see* **biological control**, Chapter 12), naturally found in the environment, may reduce the pest's importance in favourable seasons. In the greenhouse, a parasitic wasp, *Aphidius matricariae*, commonly controls the aphid. **Contact** chemicals, e.g. malathion, are able to penetrate the thin cuticle of the insect, while other chemicals, e.g. dimethoate, moving through the internal tissues of the plant (called **systemic** chemicals) are sucked up by the aphid stylet and reach the insect's digestive system. **Fumigant** chemicals, e.g. nicotine, enter the insect through the spiracles.

There are many other horticulturally important aphid species. The **black bean aphid** (*Aphis fabae*), which overwinters on *Euonymus* bushes, may seriously damage broad beans, runner beans and red beet. **The rose aphid** (*Macrosiphum rosae*) attacks young shoots of rose.

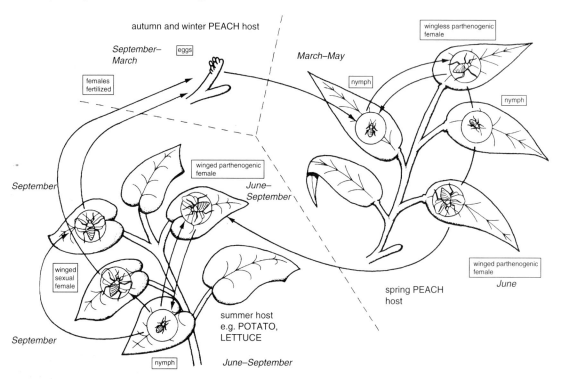

Figure 10.7 *Peach-potato aphid life cycle throughout the year. Female aphids produce nymphs on both the peach and summer host. Winged females develop from June to September. Males are produced only in autumn. Eggs survive the winter. In greenhouses the life cycle may continue throughout the year.*

Spruce-larch adelgid (*Adelges viridis*). This relative of the aphid may cause serious damage on spruce grown for Christmas trees.

The green adult develops from overwintering nymphs on **spruce**, and in May (year 1) lays about 50 eggs on the dwarf shoots. The emerging nymphs, injecting poisons into the shoots, cause abnormal growth into green **pineapple galls**, which spoil the tree's appearance. Although nursery trees of less than 4 years of age are rarely badly damaged, early infestation in the young plant may result in serious damage as it gets older. In June–September the adults move to **larch**, acquire woolly white hairs and may cause defoliation of the leaves. After a further year (year 2) on this host, the adelges returns to the **spruce**, where it lives for another year (year 3) before the gall-inducing stages are produced.

In Christmas trees, the adelges may be controlled by sprays of deltamethrin in May, when the gall-inducing nymphs are developing.

Glasshouse whitefly (*Trialeurodes vaporariorum*). This small, moth-like pest was originally introduced from the tropics, and now causes serious problems on a range of glasshouse food and flower crops. It should not be confused with the slightly larger cabbage whitefly, a less important pest on brassicas.

The adult glasshouse whitefly (Figure 10.8) is about 1 mm long. The fertilized female lays about 200 minute, white, elongated oval eggs in a circular pattern on the lower leaf surface. After turning black, the eggs hatch to produce nymphs (**crawlers**), which soon become flat immobile **scales**, the last instar being a thick-walled '**pupa**' from which the adult emerges, and 3 days later lays eggs again. All stages after the egg have sucking stylets, which may cause large amounts of honeydew and sooty moulds on the leaf surface. The whole life cycle takes 32 days in spring, and 23 days in the summer.

Plants that are seriously attacked include fuchsias, cucumbers, chrysanthemums and pelargoniums. Chickweed, a common greenhouse weed, may harbour the pest over winter in all stages of the life cycle.

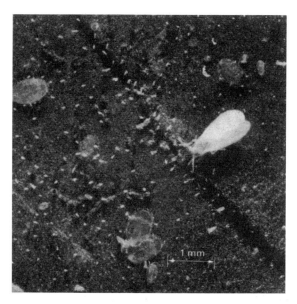

Figure 10.8 *Adult whitefly – actual size is about 1 mm long (courtesy: Shell Chemicals).*

Control of glasshouse whitefly is achieved in two main ways. A minute wasp (*Encarsia formosa*) lays an egg inside the scale of the whitefly which, being eaten away internally, turns black to release a wasp. **Chemical** control methods include soil-applied **systemic granular** compounds, e.g. oxamyl, where the chemical enters the whitefly stylet via the plant phloem. **Fumigant** chemicals, e.g. deltamethrin, quickly kill the scale and adult stages, but the eggs and 'pupae' are little affected. It is therefore suggested that serious infestations of this pest receive a regular chemical spray or fog at 3 days intervals for a month to control emergent crawlers and adults. An especially pure fatty acid detergent (surfactant) is also used to control whitefly, and its relatively low toxicity to humans and most other organisms justify its use by organic gardeners and growers.

Greenhouse mealy bug (*Planococcus citri*). This pest, a distant relative of the aphid, spoils the appearance of some glasshouse crops, particularly orchids, *Coleus* species, cacti and *Solanum* species. Being a tropical species, it develops most quickly in high temperatures and humidities, and at 30°C completes a life cycle within about 22 days. The adult measures about 3 mm in length and produces fine waxy threads. All of the stages except the egg suck phloem juices by means of a tubular mouth-part (**stylet**), and when this pest is present in dense masses it produces **honeydew** and causes leaf drop on most plant species.

Mealy bugs are difficult pests to control, as the thick cuticle resists chemical sprays, and the droplets fall off the waxy threads. A **contact** chemical, e.g. malathion, may be sprayed if the plant species is not damaged by the chemical. **Systemic** chemicals, e.g. aldicarb, may be applied to the compost and reach the pest through the plant vascular tissues and stylet of the pest. An introduced tropical lady-bird, *Cryptolaemus montrouzieri,* is effective in controlling the pest above 20°C.

Brown scale (*Parthenolecanium corni*). The female scale, measuring up to 6 mm, is tortoise shaped (*see* Figure 10.9), and has a very thick cut-icle. On fruit trees, e.g. apple, it is rarely seen now because of regular insecticide sprays, but in pri-vate gardens it may be a serious pest on vines, cur-rants and cotoneasters, and in greenhouses attacks peaches and *Amaryllis*, causing stunted growth and leaf defoliation. As with mealy-bug, control is difficult because of the thick cuticle.

Leaf hoppers (*Graphocephala fennahi*). These slender, light green insects, about 3 mm long, well known in their nymph stage as 'cuckoo spit', are found on a wide variety of crops, e.g. potato, rose, *Primula and Calceolaria*. They live on the under-surface of leaves, causing a mottling of the upper surface. In strawberries, they are vectors of the green-petal disease, while in rhododendron they carry the serious bud blast disease that kills off the flower buds.

August and September sprays of nicotine, prevent egg laying inside buds of rhododendron, and thus reduce the entry points for the fungus disease.

Common green capsid (*Lygocoris pabulinus*). This very active, light green pest, measuring 5 mm in length, and resembling a large aphid, occurs on fruit trees and flower crops, most commonly out-doors. Owing to the poisonous nature of its sali-vary juices, young foliage shows distorted growth

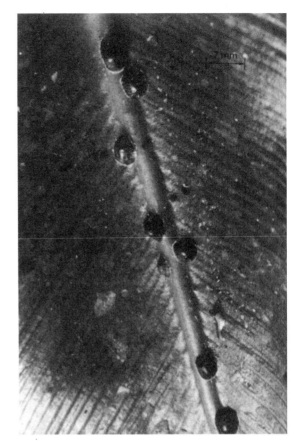

Figure 10.9 *Brown scale on a pot plant – actual size is about 5 mm long.*

with small holes, even when relatively low insect numbers are present and fruit is scarred.

The chemicals used against aphids may control this pest.

Thrips (order Thysanoptera)

Onion thrips (*Thrips tabaci*). This 1 mm long, narrow-bodied insect has feather-like wings. Due to its great activity during warm, humid weather, it is sometimes called 'thunder fly'. Its mouthparts are modified for piercing and sucking, and the toxic salivary juices cause silvering in onion leaves, straw-brown spots on cucumber leaves and white streaks in carnation blooms. The last instar of the life cycle, called the **pupa**, occurs in the soil, and it is this stage which overwinters. In greenhouses there may be seven generations per year, while at outdoors one life cycle is common. The occurrence in Britain of Western flower thrip (*Frankliniella occidentalis*) on both greenhouse and outdoor flower and vegetable crops has created serious problems for the industry, particularly because it carries the serious tomato spotted wilt virus.

Thrips are sensitive to a wide range of insecticides, e.g. abamectin applied as a spray or fog. In greenhouse crops employing biological control, a drench of a **residual** insecticide, e.g. permethrin incorporated into a sticky solution, reduces insecticide contact with the predator or parasite.

Western flower thrip, however, has shown greater resistance and a careful rotation of chemical groups are usually necessary.

Earwigs (*Forficula auricularia*)

These pests belong to the order Dermaptera, and bear characteristic pincers (cerci) at the rear of the 15 mm long body (*see* Figure 10.10). They gnaw away at leaves and petals of crops such as beans, beet, chrysanthemums and dahlias, usually from July to September, when the nymphs emerge from the parental underground nest. Upturned flower pots containing straw are sometimes used in glasshouses for trapping these shy nocturnal insects. Chemicals, e.g. pirimiphos methyl, are applied in the form of sprays or smokes, but flower scorch must be avoided.

Moths and butterflies

This order (Lepidoptera) characteristically contains adults with four large wings and curled feeding tubes. The larva (**caterpillar**), with six small legs and eight false legs, is modified for a leaf-eating habit (*see* Figures 10.3–10.5). Some species, however, are specialized for feeding inside fruit (codling moth on apple), underground (cutworms), inside

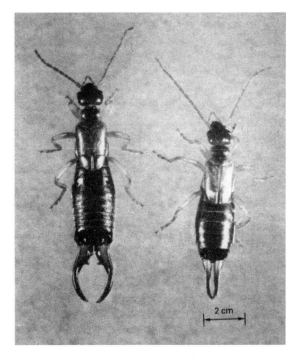

Figure 10.10 *Larger earwig is male, smaller is female (courtesy: Shell Chemicals).*

leaves (oak leaf miner) or inside stems (leopard moth). The gardener may find large caterpillar colonies of the lackey moth (*Malacosoma neustria*) on fruit trees and hawthorns. The larva is the only damaging stage of this insect group.

Large cabbage-white butterfly (*Pieris brassicae*). This well-known pest on cruciferous plants emerges from the overwintering pupa (chrysalis) in April and May and, after mating, the females lay batches of 20 to a 100 yellow eggs on the underside of leaves. Within a fortnight, groups of first instar larvae emerge and soon moult to produce the later instars, which are 25 mm long, yellow or green in colour, with clear black markings, and have well-developed mandibles. Pupation occurs usually in June, in a crevice or woody stem, the pupa (chrysalis) being held to its host by silk threads. A second generation of the adult commences in July, causing more damage than the first. The second pupa stage overwinters. The defoliating damage of

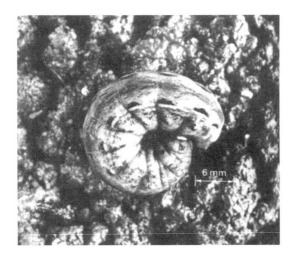

Figure 10.11 *Cutworm larva of the turnip moth – actual size is about 30 mm long (courtesy of Ministry of Agriculture, Fisheries and Food, MAFF).*

the larva may result in skeletonized leaves of cabbage, cauliflower, brussels sprouts and other hosts such as wallflowers and the shepherd's purse weed.

Care should be taken not to confuse the cabbage-white larva with the large smooth green or brown larva of the **cabbage moth**, or the smaller light green larva of the **diamond-backed moth**, both of which may enter the hearts of cabbages and cauliflowers, presenting greater problems for control.

There are several forms of control against the cabbage-white butterfly. A small wasp (*Apantales glomeratus*) lays its eggs inside the pest larva (*see* parasites). A virus disease may infect the pest, causing the larva to go grey and die. Birds such as starlings eat the plump larvae. When damage becomes severe, the larvae may be controlled with sprays of insecticides, e.g. diflubenzuron, containing extra **wetter/spreader**, to maintain the spray droplets on the waxy brassica leaves.

Winter moths (*Operophthera brumata*). These are pests, which may be serious on top fruit and ornamental members of the Rosaceae family. They emerge as the adult form from their soil-borne pupa in November and December. The male is a greyish-brown moth, 2.5 cm across its wings, while the female is **wingless**. The female crawls up the tree to lay 100–200 light green eggs in the bud clusters, which hatch at bud burst to produce green larvae with faint white stripes. These larvae, which move in a looping fashion, eat the leaf and form other leaves into loose webs, reducing the plant's photosynthesis. They occasionally scar young apple fruit before descending on a silk thread at the end of May to pupate in the soil until winter.

Grease bands wound around the main trunk of the tree in October prove very effective in preventing the female moth's progress. In large orchards, springtime sprays of an insecticide, e.g. deltamethrin, kill the young instars of the larva.

Cutworms (*e.g. Agrotis segetum*). The larvae of the **turnip moth**, unlike most other moth larvae, live in the soil, nipping off the stems of young plants and eating holes in succulent crops, e.g. bedding plants, lawns, potatoes, celery, turnips and conifer seedlings. The damage resembles that caused by slugs. The adult moth, 2 cm across, with brown forewings and white hindwings, emerges from the shiny soil-borne chestnut brown pupa from June to July, and lays about 1000 eggs on the stems of a wide variety of weeds.

The first instar larvae, having fed on the weeds, descend to the soil and eventually reach 3.5 cm in length They are grey to grey-brown in colour, with black spots along **the sides** (*see* Figure 10.11). Several other cutworm **species**, e.g. heart and dart moth (*Agrotis exclamationis*) and yellow underwing moth (*Noctua pronuba*), may cause damage similar to that of the turnip moth. This typically caterpillar-like larva should not be confused with the legless **leatherjacket** (*see* Figure 10.14). There are normally two life cycles per year, but in hot summers this may increase to three.

Good weed control reduces cutworm damage. Soil drenches of **residual** insecticides, e.g. chlorpyrifos, have proved successful against the larva stage of this pest.

Leopard moth (*Zeuzera pyrina*). It has an unusual life cycle. The adult female moth, 5–6 cm across, is white with black spots, and in early summer lays dark-yellow eggs on the bark of apples, ash, birch, lilac and many other tree species. The

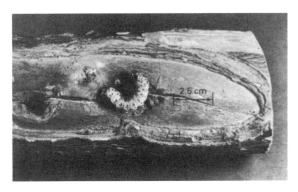

Figure 10.12 *Leopard moth larva emerging from an apple stem – actual size is about 50 mm long.*

emerging larva enters the stem by a bud, and then tunnels for 2–3 years in the **heartwood** before reaching 5 cm in length (*see* Figure 10.12), pupating in the tunnel, and completing the life cycle as the adult. The tunnelling may weaken the branches of trees which, in high winds, commonly break. Where tunnels are observed, a piece of wire may be pushed along the tunnel to kill the larva, or a fumigant chemical, e.g. paradichlor-benzene crystals, may be placed in the tunnel before sealing it off with moist soil.

Flies

This order (Diptera) is characterized by the single pair of clear forewings, the hindwings being adapted as balancing organs (halteres). The larvae are legless, elongated, and their mouthparts, where present, are simple hooks. The larvae cause crop damage.

Carrot fly (*Psila rosae*). This is a widespread and serious pest on umbelliferous crops (carrots, celery and parsnips). The adult fly, shiny black with a red head, and 8 mm long, emerges from the soil-overwintering pupa from late May to early June. The small eggs laid on the soil near the host soon hatch to give white larvae (*see* Figure 10.5) that eat fine roots and then enter the mature root using fine hooks in their mouths. When a month old, the mature larva leaves the host to turn into the cylindrical pale yellow pupa. A second generation of

adults emerges in late July, while in October a third emergence is seen in some areas.

Damage is similar in all crops. In carrots, seedlings may be killed, while in older plants the foliage may become red, and wilt in dry weather. Stunting is often seen, and affected roots, when lifted, are riddled with small tunnels that make the carrots unsaleable. Damage should not be confused with **cavity spot**, a condition associated with *Pythium* species of fungi, which produces elongated sunken spots around the root.

Damaging levels of carrot fly can be avoided by keeping hedges and nettle beds trimmed to reduce sheltering sites for the flies; by planting carrots after the May emergence has occurred. Control has been achieved by a seed treatment containing tefluthrin.

Chrysanthemum leaf miner (*Phytomyza syngenesiae*). The leaf miners are a group of small flies, the larvae of which can do serious damage to horticultural crops. This species is found on members of the plant family Asteraceae, and the hosts attacked include chrysanthemum, cineraria and lettuce. Weed hosts, e.g. groundsel and sowthistle, may harbour the pest.

The flies emerge at any time of the year in greenhouses, but normally only between July and October outdoors. These adults, which measure about 2 mm in length and are grey-black with yellow underparts, fly around with short hopping movements. The female lays about 75 minute eggs singly inside the leaves, causing white spot symptoms to appear on the upper leaf surface. The **larva** stage is greenish white in colour, and tunnels into the palisade mesophyll of the leaf, leaving behind the characteristic mines seen in Figure 10.13. On reaching its final instar, the 3.5 mm long larva develops within the mine into a brown pupa, from which the adult emerges. The total life cycle period takes about 3 weeks during the summer months.

Certain chrysanthemum cultivars, e.g. Tuneful, may be badly attacked; others, e.g. Yellow Iceberg, often resist the attack by the pest. While chemical sprays used against other pests, e.g. aphids and whitefly, may help in control of the adult, the larva stage is commonly controlled by **systemic** insecticide, e.g. aldicarb, which, after application as

Figure 10.13 *Chrysanthemum leaf miner damage: note the light-coloured tunnels caused by the larva of this species (courtesy: Glasshouse Crops Research Institute).*

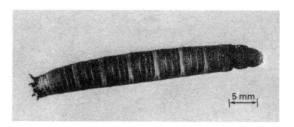

Figure 10.14 *Leatherjacket larva – actual size is about 40 mm (courtesy: Plant Pathology Laboratory, Ministry of Agriculture, Fisheries and Food, MAFF).*

granules to the soil, then moves up to the leaf. A spray containing abamectin is also effective.

The occurrence of South American leaf miner (*Liriomyza huidobrensis*) and American serpentine leaf miner (*Liriomyza trifolii*) on a wide variety of greenhouse plants has created problems for the industry.

Leatherjacket (*Tipula paludosa*). This is an underground pest, which is a natural inhabitant of grassland and causes problems on fine turf. The ploughing up of grassland may, however, result in the pest damaging following crops such as potatoes, cabbages, lettuce and strawberries.

The adult of this species is the **crane fly**, or 'daddy-long-legs', commonly seen in late August. The females lay up to 300 small eggs on the surface of the soil at this period, and the emerging larvae feeding on plant roots during the autumn, winter and spring months reach lengths of 4 cm by June. They are cylindrical, grey-brown in colour, legless and possess hooks in their mouths for feeding (*see* Figure 10.14). During the summer months, they survive as a thick-walled pupa.

This pest is particularly damaging in prolonged wet periods when the roots of young or succulent crops may be killed off. Occasionally lower leaves may be eaten.

Groundsmen sometimes control this pest by placing tarpaulins over water-soaked ground. The following morning the emerging leatherjackets may be brushed up. **Residual** chemicals, e.g. chlorpyrifos, may be drenched into soil to reduce the larval numbers. Crops sown in autumn are rarely affected, as the larva is very small at this time.

Sciarid fly (*Bradysia* sp.). The larvae of this pest (sometimes called **fungus gnat**) feed on fine roots of greenhouse pot plants, e.g. cyclamen, orchid and freesia, causing the plants to wilt. Fungus strands of mushrooms may be attacked in the compost. The slender black **females**, which are about 3 mm long, fly to a suitable site (freshly steamed compost, moss on sand benches and well-fertilized compost containing growing plants), where 100 minute eggs are laid. The emerging legless larvae are white with a **black** head, and during the next month grow to a length of 3 mm before briefly pupating and starting the next life cycle.

The larva may be controlled by diflubenzuron incorporated into the compost. Biological control by the tiny nematode *Steinernema feltiae* and mite *Hypoaspis miles* is now available. The adults are excluded from mushroom houses by means of fine mesh screens placed next to ventilator fans.

Beetles

This order of insects (Coleoptera) is characterized in the adult by hard, horny forewings which, when folded, cover the delicate hindwings used for flight. The meeting point of these hard wing cases produces the characteristic straight line down the beetles back over its abdomen. Most beetles are beneficial, helping in breakdown of humus, e.g. dung beetles, or feeding on pest species (*see* ground beetle). A few, e.g. wireworm, raspberry beetle, and vine weevil, may cause crop damage.

Wireworm (*Agriotes lineatus*). This beetle species is commonly found in grassland, but will attack most crops. The 1 cm long adult (click beetle) is brown-black and has the unusual habit of flicking itself in the air when placed on its back. The female lays eggs in weedy ground in May and June and these, after hatching, develop over a 4 years period into slender 2.5 cm long, wireworm larvae (Figure 10.5), shiny golden-brown in colour, and possessing short legs. After a 3 weeks pupation period in the soil, usually in summer, the adult emerges, and in this stage survives the winter.

Turf grass may be eaten away by wireworms to show dry areas of grass. The pest also bores through potatoes to produce a characteristic tunnel, while in onions, brassicas and strawberries the roots are eaten away. In tomatoes, the larvae bore into the hollow stem.

Serious damage to young crops may be prevented by **seed dressings** containing tefluthrin.

Raspberry beetle (*Byturus tomentosus*). The developing fruit of raspberry, loganberry and blackberry may be eaten away by the 8 mm long, golden-brown larvae of this pest. Only one life cycle per year occurs, the larva descending to the soil in July and August, pupating in a cell in which the golden-brown adult emerges and spends the winter before laying eggs in the host flower the next June.

Since the destructive **larval** stage may enter the host fruit and thus escape insecticidal control, the timing of the spray is vital. In raspberries, a **contact** chemical, e.g. malathion, applied when the fruit is pink, will achieve good control.

Vine weevils (*Otiorhyncus sulcatus*) belong to the beetle group, but possess a longer snout on their heads than other beetles. This species is 9 mm long, black in colour, with a rough textured cuticle. The forewings are fused together, making the pest incapable of flight. No males are known. The females lay eggs in August and September in the

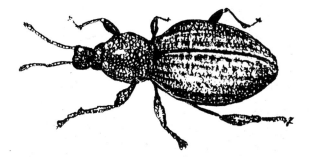

Figure 10.15 *Vine weevil adult – actual size is 9 mm long. Note the characteristic straight line between the wing cases down the back of this order of insects (Coleptera the beetles).*

soil or compost. The emerging larvae are white, legless, and with a characteristic chestnut-brown head (Figure 10.5). They reach 1 cm in length in December when they **pupate** in the soil before developing into the adult (Figure 10.15).

The larva stage is the most damaging, eating away roots of crops such as cyclamen and begonias in greenhouses, primulas, strawberries, young conifers and vines outdoors. The adults may eat out neat holes in the foliage of hosts, e.g. rhododendron and raspberry. Several related species, e.g. the clay-coloured weevil (*Otiorhyncus singularis*) cause similar damage to that of the vine weevil.

Traps of corrugated paper placed near infested crops have achieved successful control in outdoor crops, while a **residual** chemical, e.g. chlorpyrifos, may be drenched into the soil or incorporated in potting compost for control in greenhouse crops. Commercial growers now quite commonly use biological control by the nematode *Steinemena carpocapsae* incorporated into compost.

Flea beetles on leaves of cruciferous plants (e.g. stocks and cabbages) and **chafer larvae** on roots of turf in sandy areas are two other important beetle pests.

Sawflies

This group that, together with bees, wasps and ants classified in the order Hymenoptera, is characterized

Figure 10.16 *Rose leaf-rolling sawfly damage (courtesy: Plant Pathology Laboratory, Ministry of Agriculture, Fisheries and Food, MAFF).*

by adults with two pairs of translucent wings and with the fore- and hindwings being locked together by fine hooks. The slender first segments of the abdomen give these insects a characteristic appearance.

Bees are described alongside details of the process of pollination in Chapter 7.

Rose leaf-rolling sawfly (*Blennocampa pusilla*). The black shiny adults, resembling winged queen ants, emerge from the soil-borne pupa in May and early June. Eggs are inserted into the leaf lamina, which, in responding to the pest, rolls up tightly (*see* Figure 10.16).

The emerging larva (*see* Figure 10.5), which is pale green with a white or brown head, feeds on the rolled foliage and reaches a length of 1 cm by August, when it descends to the ground and forms an underground cocoon to survive the winter and pupate in March. All types of roses are affected, although climbing roses are preferred. Damage caused by leaf-rolling tortrix caterpillars, e.g. *Cacoecia oparana*, may be confused with the sawfly, although the leaves are less curled.

Control is achieved, where necessary, by an application of nicotine dust which, on hot days in May and June, has a good **fumigant** action.

Figure 10.17 *The springtail – about 2 mm in size – can jump by means of spring at the end of its body.*

Springtails (order *Collembola***)**

This group of primitive wingless insects, about 2 mm in length (Figure 10.17), has a spring-like appendage at the base of the abdomen. They are very common in soils, and normally aid in the breakdown of **soil organic** matter. Two genera, *Bourletiella* and *Collembola*, however, may do serious damage to conifer seedlings and cucumber roots respectively.

MITES

The **mites** (Acarina) are classified with spiders and scorpions in the Arachnida. Although similar to insects in many respects they are distinguished from them by the **possession of four pairs of legs, a fused body structure and by the absence of wings** (Figure 10.18). Many of the tiny soil-inhabiting mites serve a useful purpose in breaking down plant debris. Several above-ground species are serious pests on plants. The life cycle is composed of egg, larva, nymph and adult stages.

Glasshouse red spider mite (*Tetranychus urticae and T. cinnabarinus*). These pests are of tropical origin, and thrive best in high greenhouse temperatures. The first species is 1 mm long, yellowish in colour, with two black spots (*see* Figure 10.18). The female lays about 100 tiny spherical eggs on the underside of the leaf, and after a period of 3 days the tiny six-legged larva moults to produce the nymph stage that resembles the adult. The life cycle length varies markedly from 62 days at 10°C, to 6 days at 35°C. The pest's multiplication potential is

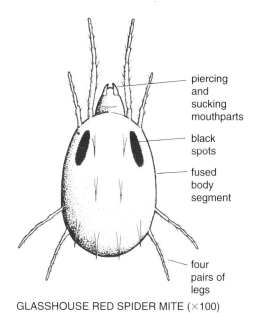

piercing
and
sucking
mouthparts

black
spots

fused
body
segment

four
pairs of
legs

GLASSHOUSE RED SPIDER MITE (×100)

Figure 10.18 *Glasshouse red spider mite. Note that the red spider mite may be light green or red in colour. Its extremely small size (0.8 mm) enables it to escape a grower's attention.*

extremely high. In autumn, when the daylight period decreases to 14 h and temperatures fall, egg production ceases and the fertilized females, which are now red in colour, move into the greenhouse structures to hibernate (diapause), representing foci for next spring's infestation. The **second** species, which is dark reddish-brown, has a similar life cycle to the first, but does not hibernate. The first species is common on annual crops such as tomatoes, cucumbers and chrysanthemums, while the second species is more common on the perennial crops such as carnations, arums and hothouse pot plants. The two species often occur together on summer hosts.

As the piercing mouthparts inject poisonous secretions, the mites cause localized death of leaf mesophyll cells. This results in a fine mottling on the leaf, not to be confused with the larger spots caused by **thrips**. In large numbers the mites can kill off leaves and eventually whole plants. Fine silk strands are produced in severe infestations,

appearing as 'ropes' on which the mites move down the plant. On chrysanthemums, these ropes make the plant unsaleable.

Control may be achieved in three ways. A predatory mite, *Phytoseiulus persimilis*, is commonly introduced into cucumber, chrysanthemum and tomato crops in spring. Winter **fumigation** of greenhouse structures with chemicals such as formalin or burning sulphur kills off some of the hibernating females. A **chemical control** uses abamectin. Care must be taken not to cause chemical scorch in plants, not to use chemicals to which the pest has become resistant, and not to kill predators by unthinking use of these chemicals (*see* integrated control).

Gall mite of blackcurrant (*Cecidophyopsis ribis*). Unlike red spider mite, this species, sometimes called **big-bud mite**, is elongated in shape and is minute (0.25 mm) in size. It spends most of the year living inside the buds of blackcurrants and, to a lesser extent, other *Ribes* species. Breeding takes place inside the buds from June to September, and January to April. In May the mites emerge and disperse on silk threads and on the bodies of aphids. The damaged bud meristem produces many scale leaves, which gives the bud its unusual appearance (*see* Figure 10.19). These buds often fail to open, or produce distorted leaves.

The mite carries the virus-like agent responsible for the damaging **reversion disease**, which stunts the plant and reduces fruit production.

The mite is controlled in three ways. **Clean planting material** is essential for the establishment of a healthy crop. **Pruning** out of stems with big bud and destruction of reversion-infected plants slow down the progress of the pest. Since no chemicals can control the mite in the bud, sprays of sulphur are applied in the May–June period when the mites are migrating.

Tarsonemid mite (*Tarsonemus pallidus*). This spherical mite, only 0.25 mm in length, lives in the unexpanded buds of a wide variety of pot plants, e.g. *Amaranthus*, Fuchsia, pelargonium and cyclamen, and is often called the 'cyclamen mite'. A closely related but distinct strain is found on strawberries. In greenhouses, the adults may lay

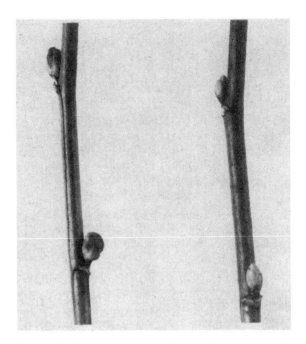

Figure 10.19 *Blackcurrant gall mite damage: note the 'big-bud' symptoms on the left compared with the normal buds on the right (courtesy: Plant Pathology Laboratory, Ministry of Agriculture, Fisheries and Food, MAFF).*

eggs all the year round, and the **2 weeks** life cycle period can cause a rapid increase in its numbers.

The small feeding holes and injected poisons from the mite mouthparts combine to distort the developing leaf and flower buds of the affected crop to such an extent that leaves and petals are stunted and misshapen, and flowers may not open properly.

Care should be taken to prevent introduction of infested plants and propagative material into greenhouses. The contact acaricide, e.g. abamectin, is effective against the mite. Addition of a **wetter/spreader** may help the spray penetrate the tight-knit scale leaves of the buds.

Four other horticulturally important mites require a mention. The fruit tree red spider mite (*Panonychus ulmi*) causes serious leaf mottling of the ornamental *Malus* and apple. Conifer spinning mite (*Oligonychus ununguis*) causes spruce to yellow, and spins a web of silk threads. Bulb-scale mite (*Steneotarsonemus laticeps*) causes internal discoloration of forced narcissus bulbs. Bryobia mite (e.g. *Bryobia rubrioculus*) attacks fruit trees, and may cause damage to greenhouse crops, e.g. cucumbers, if blown in from neighbouring trees.

OTHER ARTHROPODS

In addition to insects and mites, the phylum Arthropoda contains three horticulturally relevant classes, the Crustacea (woodlice), Symphyla (symphilids) and Diplopoda (millipedes).

Woodlouse (*Armadillidium nasutum*).   A relative of the marine crabs and lobsters, has adapted for terrestrial life, but still requires damp conditions to survive. In damp soils it may number over a million per hectare, and greatly helps the breakdown of plant debris, as do earthworms. In greenhouses, where plants are grown in hot, humid conditions, this species may multiply rapidly, producing two batches of 50 eggs per year. The adults roll into a ball when disturbed.

The damage is confined mainly to stems and lower leaves of cucumbers, but occasionally young transplants may be nipped. Partial soil sterilization by steam effectively controls woodlice. Rotting brickwork provides refuge for them and should be replaced.

Symphilids (*Scutigerella immaculata*).   These delicate white creatures, with 12 pairs of legs, resemble small millipedes. The adult female, 6 mm long, lays eggs in the soil all the year round, and the development through larvae to the adult takes about 3 months. Symphilids may migrate 2 m down into soil during hot, dry weather.

In greenhouse crops the **root hairs** are removed, and may cause lettuce to mature without a heart. Infectious fungi, e.g. *Botrytis*, may enter the roots after symphilid damage. The recognition of this pest is made easier by dipping a suspect root and surrounding soil into a bucket of water and searching for organisms floating on the water surface.

Millipedes.   These elongated, slow-moving creatures are characterized by a thick cuticle and the possession of many legs, two pairs to each body segment (Figure 10.20). Many species are

Figure 10.20 *Millipedes: this group of animals has two pairs of legs to each segment.*

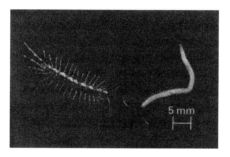

Figure 10.21 *Centipedes: two dissimilar species are shown.*

useful in breaking down soil organic matter, but two pest species, the flat millipede (*Brachydesmus superus*) and a tropical species (*Oxidus gracilus*), cause damage to roots of strawberries and cucumbers respectively.

Centipedes (Figure 10.21). These resemble millipedes, but are much more active. They help control soil pests by searching for insects and worms in the soil.

NEMATODES

This group of organisms, also called **eelworms**, is found in almost every part of the terrestrial environment, ranging in size from the large animal parasites, e.g. *Ascaris* (about 20 cm long) in livestock, to the tiny soil-inhabiting species (about 0.5 mm long). Non-parasitic species may be beneficial, feeding on plant remains and soil bacteria, and helping in the formation of **humus**. The general structure of the nematode body is shown in Figure 10.22. A feature of the plant parasitic species is the **spear** in the mouth region, which is thrust into plant cells. Salivary enzymes are then injected into the plant and the plant juices sucked into the nematode (*see* Figure 10.23). Nematodes are very active animals, moving in a wriggling fashion in soil moisture films, most actively when the soil is at **field capacity**, and more slowly as the soil either waterlogs or dries out. Five horticulturally important types are described below.

Potato cyst nematode (*Globodera rostochiensis and G. pallida*). This serious pest is found in most soils that have grown potatoes. A proportion of the eggs in the soil hatch in spring, stimulated by chemicals produced in potato roots. The larvae invade the roots, disturbing **translocation** in xylem and phloem tissues, and sucking up plant cell contents. When the adult male and female nematodes have developed, they migrate to the outside of the root, and the now swollen female leaves only her head inserted in the plant tissues. After fertilization, the white female becomes almost spherical, about 0.5 mm in size, and contains 200–600 eggs (*see* Figure 10.22). As the potato crop reaches harvest, the female changes colour. In *G. rostochiensis* (the golden nematode), the change is from white to **yellow**, and then to dark brown, while in the other species, *G. pallida*, no yellow phase is seen. The significance of the species' differences is seen later. Eventually the dark-brown female dies and falls into the soil. This stage, which looks like a minute onion, is called the **cyst**, and the eggs inside this protective shell may survive for 10 years or more.

The pest may be diagnosed in the field by the mature white or yellow females seen on the potato roots. Leaves show a yellowing symptom, plants are often severely stunted, and occasionally killed. The distribution of damage in a field is characteristically in patches. Tomatoes grown in greenhouses and outdoors may be similarly affected.

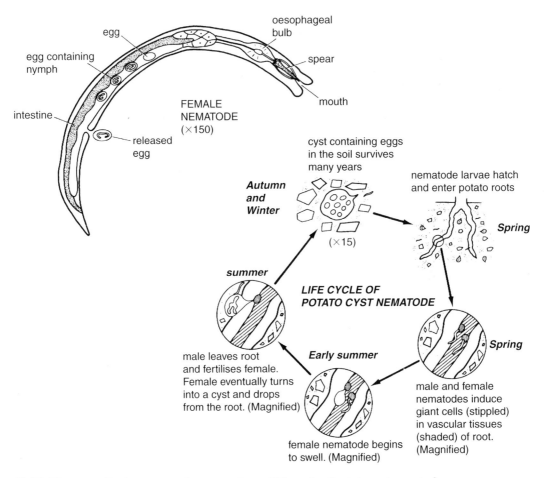

Figure 10.22 *The generalized structure of a nematode, and life cycle of potato cyst nematode.*

Several forms of control are available against this pest. Since it attacks only potatoes and tomatoes, **rotation** is a reliable if sometimes inconvenient way of overcoming the problem. Since it is known that an average soil population of 10 cysts per 100 gm of soil results in a 3 t/ha decline in yield, a soil count for cysts can indicate to a grower whether a field should be used for a potato crop. Early potatoes are lifted before most nematodes have reached the cyst stage, and thus escape serious damage.

Some potato cultivars, e.g. 'Pentland Javelin' and 'Maris Piper', are **resistant** to golden nematode strains found in Great Britain, but not to *G. pallida*.

Since the golden nematode is dominant in the south of England, use of resistant cultivars has proved effective in this region.

Residual chemicals (e.g. aldicarb), incorporated into the soil at planting time, provide economical control when the nematode levels are moderate to fairly high, but are not recommended at low levels because they are not economic, or at high levels because the chemical kills insufficient nematodes.

Stem and bulb eelworm (*Ditylenchus dipsaci*). This attacks many plants, e.g. narcissus, onions, beans and strawberries. Several strains are known, but their host ranges are not fully defined. The 1 mm long nematodes enter plant material and breed

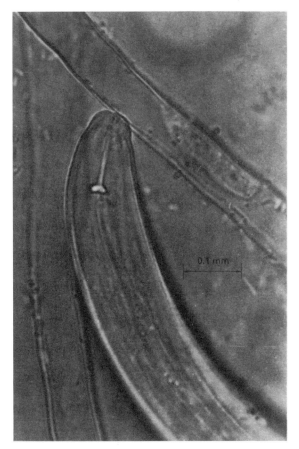

Figure 10.23 *Nematode feeding: note the spear inside the mouth, used to penetrate plant tissues (courtesy: J. Bridge).*

continuously, often with thousands of individuals in one plant. When an infected plant matures, the nematodes dry out in large numbers, appearing as white fluffy **eelworm wool** that may survive for several years in the soil. **Weeds**, such as bindweed, chickweed and speedwells, act as alternate hosts to the pest.

The damage caused by this species varies with the crop attacked. Onions show a loose puffy appearance (called bloat); carrots have a dry mealy rot; the stems of beans are swollen and distorted. Narcissus bulb scales show brown rings when cut across. Their leaves show raised yellow streaks and the crop flowers late.

Control is achieved in several ways. Control of weeds (*see* chickweed); **rotation** with resistant crops, e.g. lettuce and brassicas; use of clean, nematode-free **seed** in onions; **hot water** treatment of onions and narcissus at precisely controlled temperatures; all these methods help reduce this serious pest.

Chrysanthemum eelworm (*Aphelenchoides ritzemabosi*). It has been seen that some nematodes live in soil (e.g. cyst eelworms), others move into stems (e.g. stem eelworms). This 1 mm long nematode spends most of its life cycle in young leaves of crops, e.g. chrysanthemum, *Saintpaulia* and strawberries. The adults move along films of water on the surface of the plant, and enter the leaf through the stomata. They breed rapidly, the females laying about 30 eggs, which complete a life cycle in 14 days. During the winter they live as adults in stem tissues, but very few overwinter in the soil.

The first symptom is blotching and purpling of the leaves, which spreads to become a dead brown area between the veins. The lower leaves are worst affected. When buds are infested, the resulting leaves may be misshapen. Greenhouse grown chrysanthemums are rarely affected, as they are raised from pest-free cuttings. Warm-water treatment of dormant chrysanthemum stools, e.g. at 46°C for 5 min, is very effective for outdoor grown plants.

Root knot eelworm (*Meloidogyne* spp.). Found mainly in greenhouses, is of tropical origin, and thrives in high temperature conditions, causing typical galls, up to 4 cm in size (*see* Figure 10.24), on the roots of plants such as chrysanthemum, Begonia, cucumber and tomato. The swollen female lays 300–1000 eggs inside the root and on the root surface. These eggs can survive in root debris for over a year, and are an important source of subsequent infestations. The larvae hatch from the eggs and search for roots, reaching soil depths of 40 cm, surviving in damp soil for several months. On entering the plant, the nematode larva stimulates the adjoining root cells to enlarge. These cells block movement of water to the root stele (*see* root structure), which results in the wilting symptoms so commonly seen with this pest.

Care should be taken not to transfer infested soil with transplants from one greenhouse to another.

Figure 10.24 *Root knot nematode damage on cucumber. Note the enlarged roots (courtesy: C.C. Doncaster).*

Steam sterilization effectively controls the nematode only if the soil temperature reaches 99°C to a depth of 45 cm. Less stringent sterilization often results in a severe infestation in the next crop.

Chemical sterilization of soil with fumigant chemicals, e.g. dichloropropene and methyl bromide, is effective if a damp seedbed tilth is first prepared. **Resistant** tomato rootstocks, e.g. KVNF, have been used on grafted plants. A 2.5 cm layer of peat placed around roots of infested plants allows new root growth.

Nutrient film and soil-less methods of growing reduce the pest's likely importance in a crop.

Migratory plant nematodes. The four species of nematodes previously described spend most of their life cycle inside plant tissues (endoparasites). Some species, however, feed from the outside of the root (ectoparasites). The **dagger** nematodes (e.g. *Xiphinema diversicaudatum*) and **needle** nematodes (e.g. *Longidorus elongatus*), which reach lengths of 0.4 and 1.0 cm respectively, attack the young roots of crops such as rose, raspberry and strawberry, and cause stunted growth. In addition,

these species transmit the important **viruses**, arabis mosaic on strawberry and tomato black ring on ornamental cherries. The nematodes may survive on the roots of a wide variety of weeds.

Control is achieved in fallow soils by the injection of a fumigant chemical, e.g. dichloropropene or incorporation of dazomet.

FURTHER READING

Alford, D.V. *A Colour Atlas of Fruit Pests* (Wolfe Science, 1984).

Alford, D.V. *Pests of Ornamental trees, Shrubs and Flowers* (Wolfe Publishing, 1991).

British Crop Protection Council. *The UK Pesticide Guide* (2003).

Brown, L.V. *Applied Principles of Horticulture*, 2nd edition (Butterworth–Heinemann, 2002).

Buckle, A.P. and Smith, R.H. *Rodent Pests and Their Control* (C.A.B. International, 1984).

Buczacki, S. and Harris, K. *Guide to Pests, Diseases and Disorders of Garden Plants* (Collins, 1992).

Dent, P. *Integrated Pest Management* (Chapman & Hall, 1995).

Gratwick, M. *Crop Pests in the UK* (Chapman & Hall, 1992).

Greenwood, P. and Halstead, A. *Pests and Diseases* (Dorling Kindersley, 1997).

Hope, F. *Turf Culture: A Manual for Groundsmen* (Cassell, 1990).

Ingram, D.S. *et al.* (Editors). *Science and the Garden* (Blackwell Science Ltd, 2002).

Lloyd, J. *Plant Health Care for Woody Ornamentals* (1997).

MAAF Leaflets: No. 165 *The Woodpigeon* (1978); No. 234 *The Bullfinch* (1973); No. 318 *The Mole* (1975); No. 534 *The Rabbit* (1988); No. 608 *Control of Rats on Farms* (1987).

Malais, M. and Ravensburg, W.J. *Biology of Glasshouse Pests and Their Natural Enemies* (Koppert, 1992).

Morgan, W.M. and Ledieu, M.S. *Pests and Disease Control in Glasshouse Crops* (British Crop Protection Council, 1979).

Murton, R.K. *The Wood-pigeon* (Collins, 1982).

Pirone, P.P. *Diseases and Pests of Ornamental Plants* (Wiley, 1985).

Savigear, E. *Garden Pests and Predators* (Blandford, 1992).

Scopes, N. and Stables, L. *Pests and Disease Control Handbook* (British Crop Protection Council, 1992).

11

Fungi, Bacteria and Viruses

In this chapter the three groups of organisms are described, and emphasis is placed on the damage they cause, the important aspects of their life cycles and the control measures that are available to reduce their infection and spread. Within each group, the diseases are classified according to the part of the plant attacked. Owing to the microscopic size of the fungal spore, bacterial cell or virus particle, it may be difficult for the grower to relate the causitive **organism** *to the disease as he sees it.*

For example, Phytophthora infestans, *a fungal organism, travels through the air as a spore to infect* **potato** *leaves. When the leaves start to turn black, the plant is said to show signs or symptoms of the potato blight disease. Only when the plant's growth and tuber production are decreased by the organism is* **yield loss** *said to occur. This chapter emphasizes the fact that symptoms of a disease are the horticulturist's main guide to the presence of fungi, bacteria and viruses. A more general description of control measures is given in Chapter 12.*

FUNGI

Structure and biology

These organisms, commonly called moulds, cause serious losses in all areas of horticulture. They are thought to have common ancestors with the filamentous algae, a group including the present-day green slime in ponds. Some details of their classification are given in Chapter 3.

The fungus is composed, in most species, of microscopic strands (**hyphae**), which may occur together in a loose structure (**mycelium**), form dense resting bodies (sclerotia, *see* Figure 11.1) or produce complex underground strands (*see* rhizomorphs).

The hyphae in most fungi are capable of producing spores. Wind-borne spores are generally very small (about 0.01 mm), not sticky and often borne by hyphae protruding above the leaf surface, e.g. **grey mould**, so that they catch turbulent wind currents. Water or rain-borne spores are often sticky, e.g. **damping off**. **Asexual** spores produced without fusion of two hyphae commonly occur in seasons favourable for disease increase, e.g. humid weather for downy mildews and dry, hot weather for powdery mildews. **Sexual** spores, produced after hyphal fusion, commonly develop in unfavourable conditions, e.g. a cold, damp autumn, and they may be produced singly as in the downy mildews, or in groups within a protective hyphal **spore case**, often observable to the naked eye, as in the powdery mildews. Different genera and species are identified by microscopic measurement of the shape and size of the spores.

Horticulturists without microscopes must use the symptoms as a guide to the cause of the disease. While disease-causing or parasitic fungi are the main concern of this chapter, in many parts of the environment there are **saprophytic** fungi that

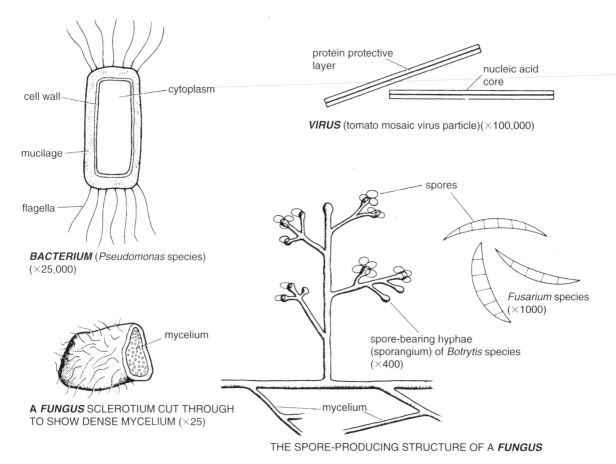

Figure 11.1 *Microscopic details of a virus, bacterium and three fungi. Note the relative sizes of the organisms.*

break down organic matter (*see* Chapter 15) and **symbiotic** fungi that may live in close association with the plant, e.g. mycorrhiza fungi in fine roots of conifers (*see* Chapter 1).

The spore of a leaf-infecting fungal parasite, after landing on the leaf, produces a germination tube, which being delicate and easily dried out, must enter through the **cuticle** or **stomata** within a few hours before dry, unfavourable conditions recur. Within the leaf, the hyphae grow, absorbing food until, within a period of a few weeks, they produce a further crop of spores (*see* Figure 11.2). Leaf diseases such as potato blight often increase very rapidly when conditions are favourable. Roots may be infected by spores, e.g. in damping off; hyphae, e.g.

wilt diseases; sclerotia, e.g. *Sclerotinia* rot; or rhizomorphs, e.g. honey fungus. Root diseases are generally less affected by short periods of unfavourable conditions and often increase at a constant rate.

Flower and leaf diseases

Downy mildew of cabbage and related plants (*Perenospora brassicae*)

This serious disease causes a white bloom mainly on the **under surface** of leaves of ornamental cruciferous plants such as stocks and wallflowers, on brassicas, and occasionally on weeds such as shepherd's purse. The disease is most damaging when seedlings

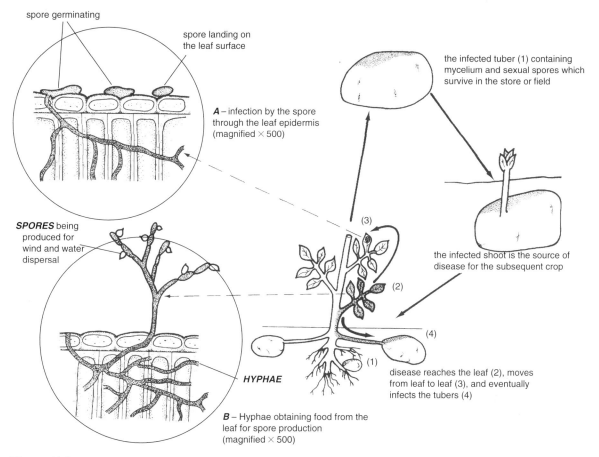

spore germinating

spore landing on the leaf surface

A – infection by the spore through the leaf epidermis (magnified × 500)

the infected tuber (1) containing mycelium and sexual spores which survive in the store or field

SPORES being produced for wind and water dispersal

the infected shoot is the source of disease for the subsequent crop

HYPHAE

disease reaches the leaf (2), moves from leaf to leaf (3), and eventually infects the tubers (4)

B – Hyphae obtaining food from the leaf for spore production (magnified × 500)

Figure 11.2 *Infection and life cycle of potato blight fungus. The left side illustrates microscopic infection of the leaf. The right side shows how the disease survives and spreads.*

are germinating, particularly in spring when the young infectable tissues of the host plant and favourable damp conditions may combine to kill off a large proportion of the developing plants. Other crops such as lettuce and onions are attacked by different downy mildews, *Bremia lactucae* and *Perenospora destructor* respectively, and no cross-infection is seen between different unrelated crops.

Asexual spores (zoospores) are produced mainly in spring and summer, and a spray of a protective chemical (e.g. dichlofluanid) is commonly used at the seedling stage to kill off spores on the leaf.

Thick-walled sexual spores (oospores) produced within the leaf tissues fall to the ground with the death of the leaf, survive the winter and initiate the spring infections. It is thus not advisable to grow successive brassicas in the same field, and particularly not to sow in spring next to overwintered crops.

Potato blight (*Phytophthora infestans*)

This important disease is a constant threat to potato production, and caused the Irish potato famine in the nineteenth century. The first symptoms seen in the field are yellowing of the foliage, which quickly goes **black** and then produces a white bloom on the under surface of the leaf in damp weather. The stems may then go black, killing off the whole plant. The tubers may show dark surface spots that, internally, appear as a **deep dry red-brown** rot. This fungus may attack tomatoes, the most notable symptom being the **dark brown blisters** on the fruit. The fungus survives the winter as mycelium and sexual spores in the tubers (*see* Figure 11.2). The spring emergence of infected shoots results in the production of asexual spores which, when carried by wind, land on potato leaves or stems and can, after infection, result in a further crop of spores within a few days under warm, wet weather conditions. Thus the disease can spread very quickly. Later in the crop, badly infected plants cause tuber infection as rainfall may wash down spores into the soil.

Several **preventative** control measures are used. Clean 'seed' lowers infection within neighbouring crops. Removal and herbicidal destruction (e.g. dichlobenil) of diseased tubers from stores or 'clamps' similarly prevent disease spread. Knowledge of the disease's moisture requirement leads to better control. By measuring both the duration of atmospheric relative humidity greater than 92 per cent, and the mean daily temperatures greater than 10°C (together known as **critical periods**), forecasts of potato blight outbreaks may be made and protectant sprays of chemicals such as **mancozeb** applied before infection take place. Resistant potato cultivars prevent rapid buildup of disease, although resistance may be overcome by newly occurring fungal strains. Early potato cultivars usually complete tuber production before serious blight attacks, while maincrop top growth may deliberately be killed off with foliage-acting herbicides such as **diquat** to prevent disease spread to tubers.

A curative control measure employs a systemic fungicide, e.g. **ofurace**, which penetrates the leaf and kills the infecting mycelium. Such chemicals must be mixed with a protectant ingredient by the manufacturer to reduce the development of fungus resistance to fungicides.

Powdery mildew of ornamental *Malus* and apple (*Podosphaera leucotricha*)

Powdery mildews should not be confused with downy mildews. This disease is distinguished by its dry powdery appearance, most commonly found on the **upper** surface of the leaf, and by its preference for **hot, dry** weather conditions (*see* examples of powdery mildew in Plates 11 and 12).

The disease survives the winter as mycelium within the buds, which often appear small, and the infected twigs have a dried, **silvery** appearance. The emergence of the mycelium with the germinating buds in spring results in a white bloom over the young leaves (**primary** mildew), which may be reduced by a **winter** application of a selective detergent-like fungicide sprayed before bud burst or by winter pruning. As the spring progresses, chains of asexual spores produced on the outside of the leaf are carried by wind and cause the destructive *secondary* mildew which, growing **externally** over the leaf surface, sucks out the leaf's moisture and may cause premature leaf drop. Flowering normally occurs before the secondary infection stage, but infection in young fruit may produce a rough skin (**russeting**). This organism may affect other species of fruit such as pears, quinces, medlars and ornamental Malus. Other species of powdery mildew commonly occur in horticulture: *Sphaerotheca pannosa* on rose (Plate 12), *S. fuliginea* on cucumber and chrysanthemum powdery mildew (Plate 11). Cross-infection between these crops does not occur.

Sexual spores may be produced inside a dark coloured **spore case** (cleistothecia), about 1 mm in size in autumn. Although not important in horticulture as an overwintering stage, it may assume a vital role in powdery mildew of cereals.

Control is achieved by preventative measures mentioned above, and by curative spring and summer sprays, using a wide choice of active ingredients which may act in a contact manner on the external mycelium, e.g. dinocap (*see* protectant), or in a systemic manner on the internal feeding hyphae (haustoria), e.g. carbendazim (*see* systemic).

Black spot of roses (*Diplocarpon rosae*)

This common disease in gardens and greenhouse-produced roses is first seen as dark leaf spots, which may be followed by general leaf yellowing and then leaf drop (*see* Plate 6). The infection of young shoots has a slow weakening effect on the whole plant.

Asexual spores produced within the leaves are released in wet and mainly warm weather conditions, and are then carried a limited distance by rain drops or irrigation water before beginning the cycle of infection again. No overwintering sexual stage is seen in Britain, and it is probable that asexual spores surviving in autumn-produced wood or in fallen leaves begin the infection process the following spring. Control is difficult, as resistance in rose cultivars is not common, and vigorous growth in late spring and summer prevents continuous protective control by chemicals, e.g. **captan**. The addition of a **wetter/spreader** may improve control by spreading the active ingredient more effectively over the leaf surface. In industrial areas the sulphur dioxide in the air may be at sufficient concentration to reduce black spot.

Carnation rust (*Uromyces dianthi*)

The rust fungi are a distinct group, which may produce five spore forms within the same species. When the spore forms occur on more than one host, e.g. blackcurrant rust (*Cronartium ribicola*), which attacks both blackcurrants and five-needle pines, the close association of the two crops may give rise to high rust levels. Most horticultural rust species are found on only **one** host species.

Carnation rust first appears as an indistinct **yellowing** of the leaf and stem, soon turning to an **elongated raised brown** spot which yields brown dust (spores) when rubbed (*see* Figure 11.3). The more common thin-walled spores (uredospores) are spread by wind currents, and infect the leaf by way of the stomata in damp conditions. The less common thick-walled spores (teleutospores) may survive and overwinter in the soil. The resistance of carnation cultivars varies, while

Figure 11.3 *Carnation rust: note the dark rusty lesions on both leaf and stem (courtesy: Glasshouse Crops Research Institute).*

related species, e.g. pinks or sweet williams, are rarely affected.

Preventative control includes the use of rust-free cuttings, sterilization of border soils and careful maintenance of greenhouse ventilators to prevent damp patches occurring in the crop. **Chemical** control is achieved by a **protectant** (e.g. mancozeb) spray. The occurrence of white rust (*Puccinia horiana*) on chrysanthemums has created serious problems for the industry and for gardeners, because of the ease with which the disease is carried in cuttings, and because of its speed of increase and spread.

Stem diseases

Grey mould (*Botrytis cinerea*)

This disease is most commonly recognized by the dense, light grey fungal mass which follows its infection. In lettuce, the whole plant rots off at the base and the plant goes yellow and dies. In tomatoes, infection in damaged side shoots, and yellow spots (ghost spots) on the unripe and ripe fruit are found. In many flower crops, e.g. chrysanthemums, infected petals show purple spots which, in very damp conditions, lead to a mummified flower head. This disease may affect many crops.

Grey mould requires **wounded tissue** for infection, which explains its importance in crops which are de-leafed, e.g. tomatoes, or disbudded, e.g. chrysanthemums. Damp conditions are essential for its infection and spore production. The millions of spores are carried by wind to the next wounded surface. Black **sclerotia**, about 2 mm across, produced in badly infected plants, often act as the overwintering stage of the disease after falling to the ground, and are particularly infective in unsterilized soils on young seedlings and delicate plants, e.g. lettuce.

Preventative control may involve soil sterilization, or a fumigant, e.g. **dicloran** used against the sclerotia. Strict attention to greenhouse humidity control, particularly overnight, limits the dew formation so important in the organism's infection. Removal of infected tissue is possible in sturdy plants, e.g. tomatoes, and a protective fungicide paste, e.g. **iprodione**, is often then applied to the cut surface. Protective sprays, e.g. **iprodione**, are often applied to greenhouse grown crops to prevent the spores germinating, and to reduce spore production.

Apple canker (*Nectria galligena*)

This fungus causes sunken areas in bark of both young and old branches of ornamental *Malus*, apples or pears (*see* Plate 13h), and occasionally on fruit. Poor shoot growth is seen, and the wood may fracture in high winds. The cankers may bear red spore cases (**perithecia**), resembling red spider mite eggs in autumn.

The fungus enters through leaf scars in autumn or through pruning wounds during winter. Care is therefore necessary to prevent infection, particularly in susceptible apple cultivars, e.g. 'Cox's Orange Pippin', by avoiding pruning in damp conditions.

Removal of cankered shoots may be necessary to prevent further infection, while in cankers of large branches, cutting out of brown infected tissue may allow the branch to be used. Removed tissue should be burnt. Some growers apply a spray of **copper** (Bordeaux) at bud burst (spring) and leaf fall (autumn) to prevent entry of germinating spores.

Dutch elm disease (*Ceratocystis ulmi*)

The first symptom of this disease is a **yellowing** of foliage in one part of the tree in early summer. The foliage then dies off progressively from this area of the tree, often resulting in death within 3 months. Trees that survive 1 year's infection may fully recover in the following year. All common species and hybrids of elm growing in Great Britain are susceptible to the disease.

The causative fungus lives in the **xylem** tissues of the stem, and produces a poison that results in a blockage of the water-conducting vessels, causing the wilt that is observed. Two black and red wood-boring species of beetle, *Scolytus scolytus* (5 mm long) and *Scolytus multistriatus* (3 mm long), enter the stems, leaving characteristic 'shot holes'. Eggs are laid, and a **fan-shaped** pattern of galleries is produced under the bark by the larvae that later, as adults, emerge from the wood, carrying sticky asexual and sexual spores to continue the spread of the disease to other uninfected elms. Graft transmission from tree to tree by roots commonly occurs in hedge grown elms.

The cost of preventative control on a large number of uninfected trees is uneconomic, although high pressure injection of a **systemic** fungicide (e.g. benomyl salts), which travels upwards through the xylem tissues, has proved successful in some cases. Selections of **disease-tolerant** hybrids, e.g. *Ulmus × vegeta* 'Groenveld', may replace the common species and hybrids.

Root diseases

Club root (*Plasmodiophora brassicae*)

This disease causes serious damage to most members of the Cruciferae family, which includes cabbage, cauliflowers, brussels sprouts, stocks and *Alyssum*. Infected plants show signs of **wilting** and yellowing of older leaves, and often severe stunting. On examination, the roots appear **stubby** and **swollen** (*see* Figure 11.4), and may show a wet rot. The club root organism survives in the **soil** for more than 5 years as minute spores which germinate to infect the **root hairs** of susceptible plants. The fungus is unusual in forming a jelly-like mass (**plasmodium**), not hyphae, within the tissue. The plasmodium stimulates root cell division and causes cell enlargement, which produces swollen roots. The flow of food and nutrients in **phloem** and **xylem** is disturbed, with consequent poor growth of the plant. With plant maturity, the spores produced by the plasmodium within the root are released as the root rots.

The disease is favoured by high soil moisture, high soil temperatures and acid soils. Several **preventative** control measures may be used. **Rotation** helps by keeping cruciferous crops away from high spore levels. Autumn-sown plants establish in soil temperatures unfavourable to the disease, and are normally less infected. In transplanted crops, the use of a seed bed previously treated with a sterilant, e.g. **dazomet**, ensures healthy transplants. Liming of soil inhibits spore activity (*see* soil fertility). Compost made from infected brassica plants should be avoided.

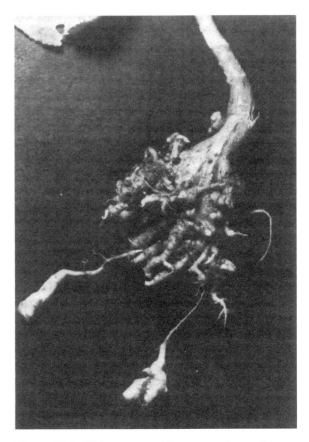

Figure 11.4 *Club root on cabbage: note the swollen tap and side roots.*

Damping off (*Pythium and Phytophthora species*)

These two fungi cause considerable losses to the delicate **seedling** stage. The infection may occur below the soil surface, but most commonly the emerging seedling plumule is infected at the soil surface, causing it to topple. Occasionally the roots of mature plants, e.g. cucumbers, are infected, turn brown and soggy, and the plants die. Both *Pythium* and *Phytophthora* occur naturally in soils as **saprophytes**, and under damp conditions produce asexual spores that cause infection. Sexual spores (oospores) are produced in infected roots, and may survive several months of dry or cold soil conditions.

Prevention control is best achieved against these diseases by sterilization of soil by heat, by chemicals, e.g. methyl bromide which kills off all stages of these fungi, or by coating the crop seed with a protective chemical (*see* seed dressing), e.g. captan, to prevent early infection. Water tanks with open tops, harbouring rotting leaves, are a common source of infected water and should be cleaned out regularly. Sand and capillary matting on benches in greenhouses should be regularly washed in hot water, and the use of door mats soaked in a fungicide, e.g. formalin, may prevent foot spread of the organisms from one greenhouse to another. Water-logged soils should be avoided, as the fungi increase most rapidly under these conditions.

Chemical prevention is achieved in some crops by the incorporation of a fungicide, e.g. **etridiazole** into compost, or by drenching with a fungicide not toxic to roots, e.g. **copper sulphate** and **ammonium carbonate** (Cheshunt) mixture.

Conifer root rot (*Phytophthora cinnamomi*)

This soil-inhibiting fungus causes the foliage of plants to turn **grey green**, then brown, and eventually to die off completely. Sliced roots show a chestnut **brown rot**, with a clear line between infected and non-infected tissues. Two hundred plant species, including *Chaemaecyparis, Erica* and *Rhododendron* species may be badly attacked. The disease is commonly introduced on infected stock plants, or contaminated footwear. It multiplies most rapidly under wet conditions, and within a temperature range of 20°C and 30°C, infecting the root tissues and producing numerous **asexual** spores, which may be carried by **water** currents to adjacent plants. Sexual **oospores** produced further inside the root are released on decay and allow the fungus to survive in the soil several months without a host.

Preventative control (*see* hygienic growing) is important. Reliable **stock** plants should be used. **Water** supply should be checked to avoid contamination. The stock plant area should be slightly **higher** than the production area to prevent infection by drainage water. Rooting trays, compost and equipment, e.g. knives and spades, should be **sterilized** (e.g. with formalin) before use. Placing container plants on **gravel** reduces infection through the base of the pot. Some chemicals, e.g. **etridiazole**, incorporated in compost protect the roots, but do not kill the fungus. Some species, e.g. *Juniperus horizontalis*, have some tolerance to this disease.

Honey fungus (*Armillaria mellea*)

This fungus primarily attacks trees and shrubs, e.g. apple, lilac and privet. In spring the foliage wilts and turns yellow. Death of the plant may take a few weeks or several years in large trees. The roots are infected by **rhizomorphs**, sometimes referred to as 'bootlaces', which radiate out underground from infected trees or **stumps** (*see* Plate 13i) for a distance of 7 m, and to a depth of 0.7 m. The nutrients they are able to conduct provide the considerable energy required for the infection of the tough, woody roots. **Mycelium**, moving up the stem to a height of several metres, is visible under the bark as white **sheets**, smelling of mushrooms. In autumn, clumps of light brown **toadstools** may be produced, often at the base of the stem. The millions of spores produced by the toadstools are not considered to be important in the infection process.

Honey fungus often establishes itself in newly planted trees and shrubs that have been planted too deeply. A less vigorous plant that is more vulnerable to infection results from this because most of its feeding roots should be very close to the surface (*see* Figure 5.4).

Control is difficult. Removal of the disease source, the infected stump, is recommended. In large stumps, a surrounding trench is sometimes dug to a depth of 0.7 m to prevent the progress of rhizomorphs. Loosening with a fork and then applying a diluted sterilant, e.g. formalin, may sterilize infected soil containing no crops.

Fusarium patch on turf (*Fusarium nivale*)

This disease appears as irregular circular patches of yellow then dead brown grass up to 30 cm in diameter on fine turf. Under extreme damp conditions, dead leaves become slimy and then are covered with a light pink bloom, most evident between May and September.

Infection of the leaves by spores and hyphae occurs most seriously between 0°C and 8°C, conditions that are present under a layer of snow (hence the name **snow mould**). However, conditions of high humidity at temperatures up to 18°C may result in typical patch symptoms. Spread is by means of wind-borne asexual spores, while the fungus survives in frosty or dry summer conditions as dormant mycelium in dead leaf matter or newly infected leaves.

Preventative control measures are most important. Avoid high soil nitrogen levels in autumn, as this promotes lush, susceptible growth in autumn and winter. Avoid thatchy growth of the turf, as this encourages high humidity and thus favours the disease organism. Drenches of preventative fungicides, e.g. **iprodione**, applied in autumn may slow down infection of the fungus, while a summer-applied systemic fungicide, e.g. **thiophanate methyl**, moves within the plants to achieve curative control.

Vascular wilt diseases (*Fusarium oxysporum and Verticillium dahliae*)

These two organisms infect the **xylem** tissues of horticultural plants, causing the leaves to 'flag' or wilt in hot conditions, a symptom which can also be caused by other factors, e.g. lack of soil moisture (*see* wilt), and nematode infestation (*see* root knot nematode page 119). The wilt diseases can be recognized by yellowing and eventual browning of the lower leaves, and by brown staining of the xylem tissue when it is exposed with a knife. Both organisms may live as **saprophytes** in the soil. *Fusarium* survives unfavourable conditions as thick-walled asexual spores, while *Verticillium* forms small **sclerotia**. Infection by both genera occurs through young roots or after nematode attack in older roots. The fungal hyphae enter the root **xylem** tissue and then move up the stem, sometimes reaching the flowers and seeds. The diseases spread by **water-borne** asexual spores.

Verticillium may attack a wide range of plants, e.g. dahlia, strawberry, lilac, tomato and potato, so that rotation is not a feasible control measure. *Fusarium oxysporum*, however, exists in many distinct forms, each specializing in a different crop, e.g. tomato, broad bean or carnation. *Verticillium* more commonly attacks in springtime, having an optimum infection temperature of 20°C, while *Fusarium* is more common in summer, with an optimum temperature of 28°C.

Control is often necessary in greenhouse crops. Infected crop **residues** should be removed from the soil at the end of the growing season, as soil sterilization by **steam** or chemicals, e.g. **metham sodium**, may not penetrate to the centre of stems and roots. Peat bags may be used as a disease-free growing medium. In unsterilized soils, growers may use resistant rootstocks, e.g. in tomatoes, which are grafted onto scions of commercial cultivars. Rotation may be employed against *Fusarium oxysporum*, as different forms attack different crops. Careful removal of infected and surrounding plants, e.g. in carnations, may slow down the progress of the diseases, especially if the soil area is drenched with a systemic chemical, e.g. **thiabendazole**, which reduces the infection in adjacent plants.

BACTERIA

These minute organisms (*see* Figure 11.1) measure about 0.001 mm and occur as single cells that divide rapidly to build up their numbers. They are important in the conversion of soil organic matter (*see* Chapter 15), but may, in a few parasitic species, cause serious losses to horticultural plants. Some details of their classification are given in Chapter 3.

Fireblight (*Erwinia amylovora*)

This disease, which first appeared in the British Isles in 1957, can cause serious damage on members of the Rosaceae family. Individual branches wilt, the leaves rapidly turning a 'burnt' chestnut brown, and when the disease reaches the main trunk, it spreads to other branches and may cause death of the tree within 6 weeks of first infection, the general appearance resembling a burnt tree, hence the name of the disease. On slicing through an infected stem, a brown stain will often be seen. Pears, hawthorn and *Cotoneaster* are commonly attacked, while apples and *Pyracantha* suffer less commonly.

The bacterium is carried by pollinating and harmful insects (e.g. aphids), and by small droplets of rain. Humid conditions and temperatures in excess of 18°C, which occur from June to September, favour the spread. Natural plant openings such as **stomata** and **lenticels** are common sites for infection. Flowers are the main entry point in pears. Badly infected plants produce a **bacterial slime** on the outside of the branches in humid weather. This slime is a major source of further infections. Fireblight, once notifiable, must now be reported only in fruit-growing areas. The compulsory removal of the susceptible 'Laxton's Superb' pear cultivar has eliminated a serious source of infection. Preventative measures such as removal of badly infected plants to prevent further infection, and replacement of hawthorn hedges close to pear orchards, help in control. Careful pruning, 60 cm below the stained wood of early infection, may save a tree from the disease. Wounds should be sealed with protective paint, and pruning implements should be sterilized with 3 per cent lysol.

Bacterial canker (*Pseudomonas morsprunorum*)

This disease affects the plant genus *Prunus* that includes ornamental species, plum, cherry and apricot. Symptoms typically appear on the **stem** (*see* Figure 11.5) as a swollen area exuding a light brown gum. The angle between branches is the most common site for the disease. Severe infections girdling the stems cause death of tissues above the infection, and the resulting brown foliage resembles the damage caused by **fireblight**. In May and June, leaves may become infected; dark brown leaf spots 2 mm across develop and may be blown out, giving a 'shot-hole' effect. The bacteria present in the cankers are mainly carried by wind-blown rain droplets, infecting leaf scars and pruning wounds in **autumn**, and young developing leaves in **summer**.

Preventative control involves the use of resistant **rootstocks** and **scions**, e.g. in plums. The careful cutting out of infected tissue followed by application of a paint, and the use of autumn sprays of Bordeaux mixture, help reduce this disease.

Soft rot (*Erwinia carotovora*)

This bacterium affects stored potatoes, carrots, bulbs and iris, where the bacterium's ability to dissolve the cell walls of the plant results in a mushy

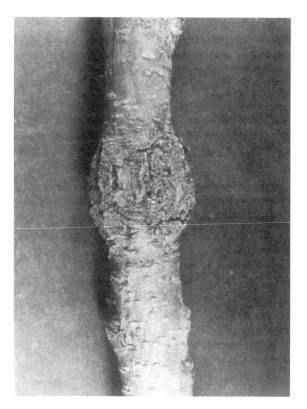

Figure 11.5 *Bacterial canker on flowering cherry: note the swollen and cracked stem (courtesy: Plant Pathology Laboratory, Ministry of Agriculture, Fisheries and Food, MAFF).*

soft rot. High temperatures and humidity caused by poor ventilation promote infection through lenticels, and major losses may occur. A related strain of this bacterium causes **black leg** on potatoes in the field.

Preventative control measures are important. Crops should be damaged as little as possible when harvesting, and diseased or damaged specimens should be removed before storage. Hot, humid conditions should be avoided in store. No curative measures are available.

Crown gall (*Agrobacterium tumifasciens*)

This bacterium affects apples, grapes, peaches, roses, and many other herbaceous plants. The disease is first seen just above ground level as a swollen, cancer-like structure growing out of the stem. It may occasionally cause serious damage, but usually is not a very important problem. The bacterium is able to survive well in soils, and infects the plant through small wounds in the roots. It is of special scientific interest in the area of plant breeding, having the unusual ability to add its genetic information into that of the plant cell. It does this by means of a small unit of DNA called a 'plasmid'. This plasmid ability of *A. tumifasciens* has been harnessed by plant breeders to transfer genetic information between unrelated plant species. And so, it is the properties of this bacterium that have led, in our language, to the new term 'genetically modified crops' or more simply 'GM' (*see* Chapter 8).

Control of crown gall depends on cultural control methods such as disease-free propagating material, avoiding wounds at planting time and budding scions to rootstocks (rather than grafting) to avoid injuries near the soil level.

VIRUSES

Structure and biology

Viruses are extremely small, very much smaller even than bacteria (*see* Figure 11.1). They appear as rods or spheres when seen under an electron microscope. The virus particle is composed of a nucleic acid core surrounded by a protective protein coat. The virus, on entering a plant cell, takes over the organization of the cell nucleus in order to produce many more virus particles. Since the virus itself lacks any cytoplasm cell contents, it is usually considered to be a non-living unit. Some details of its classification are given in Chapter 3. **The virus's close association with the plant cell nucleus presents difficulties in the production of a curative virus control chemical that does not also kill the plant.** No such commercial 'viricide' has yet been produced against plant viruses.

In recent years the broad area called 'virus diseases' has been closely investigated. Virus particles have, in most cases, been isolated as the cause of disease, e.g. cucumber mosaic. Other agents of disease to be discovered are viroids (e.g. in chrysanthemum stunt disease), and these are much smaller than viruses. **Mycoplasmas** (e.g. aster yellows disease) are larger than and unrelated to viruses. In some diseases, e.g. 'reversion disease' on blackcurrant, a causitive agent has yet to be isolated. All agents are placed together in this section.

A number of organisms (**vectors**) transmit viruses from plant to plant. **Peach-potato aphid** is capable of transmitting over 200 strains of virus (e.g. cucumber mosaic) to different plant species; the aphid stylet injects salivary juices containing virus into the **parenchyma** and **phloem** tissues, and, along the phloem, the virus may travel to other parts of the plant. Other vector/virus combinations include blackcurrant big bud mite and reversion virus; bean weevils and broad bean stain virus; migratory soil nematodes, *Xiphinema* and arabis mosaic; and *Olpidium* soil fungus and big vein agent on lettuce. Other important methods of transmission involve **vegetative** material (e.g. chrysanthemum stunt viroid and plum pox), infected **seed** (e.g. bean common mosaic virus), **seed testa** (e.g. tomato mosaic virus) and **mechanical transmission** by hand (e.g. tomato mosaic virus).

General symptoms

The presence of a damaging virus in a plant is recognized by horticulturists only by the symptoms, although they may consult the virologist, whose identification techniques include electron microscopy, transmission tests on sensitive plants, e.g. *Chenopodium* spp., and serological reactions against specific antisera. **Leaf mosaic**, a yellow mottling, is the most common symptom (e.g. tomato mosaic virus). Other symptoms include leaf **distortion** into feathery shapes (cucumber mosaic virus), flower **colour** streaks (e.g. tulip break virus), fruit **blemishing** (tomato mosaic and plum pox), internal **discoloration** of tubers (tobacco rattle virus-causing 'spraing' in potatoes) and **stunting** of plants (chrysanthemum stunt viroid). Symptoms similar to those described above may be caused by misused herbicide sprays, genetic '**sports**', poor soil fertility and structure (*see* deficiency symptoms) and mite damage. In the following descriptions of major viruses, Latin names of genus and species are omitted, since no consistent classification is yet accepted.

Cucumber mosaic

Several strains of virus cause this disease, and many families of plants are attacked. On cucumbers, a mottling of young leaves occurs, followed by a twisting and curling of the whole foliage, and fruit may show yellow sunken areas. On the shrub *Daphne oderata*, a yellowing and slight mottle is commonly seen on infected foliage, while *Euonymus* foliage produces bright yellow leaf spots. Infected tomato leaves are reduced in size (**fern-leaf** symptom).

The virus may be transmitted by infected hands, but more commonly an aphid (e.g. peach-potato aphid) is involved. Many crops (e.g. lettuce, maize, *Pelargonium* and privet) and weeds (e.g. fat hen and teasel) may act as a reservoir for the virus.

Since there are no curative methods for control, care must be taken to carry out **preventative** methods. Choice of **uninfected stock** is vital in vegetatively propagated plants, e.g. *Pelargonium*. Careful control of **aphid vectors** may be important where susceptible crops (e.g. lettuce and cucumbers) are grown in succession. Removal of infected **weeds**, particularly from greenhouses, may prevent widespread infection.

Tulip break

The petals of infected tulips produce irregular coloured streaks and may appear distorted. Leaves may become light green, and the plants stunted after several years infection. The virus is transmitted mechanically by knives, while three aphid vectors are known: the bulb aphid in stores, the melon aphid in greenhouses, and the peach-potato aphid outdoors and in greenhouses. Preventative control must be used against this disease. Removal of **infected** plants in the field prevents a source of virus for aphid transmission. **Aphid** control in field, store and greenhouse further reduces the virus's spread.

Tomato mosaic

This disease may cause serious losses in tomatoes. Infected seedlings have a stunted, spiky appearance. On more mature plants leaves have a pale green **mottled** appearance, or sometimes a bright yellow (aucuba) symptom. The stem may show brown **streaks** in summer when growing conditions are poor, a condition often resulting in death of the plant. Fruit yield and quality may be lowered, the green fruit appearing **bronze**, and the ripe fruit hard, making the crop unsaleable.

The virus may survive within the **seed coat** (testa) or endosperm. **Heat** treatment of **dry** seed at 70°C for 4 days by seed merchants helps remove initial infection. Infected **debris**, particularly roots, in the soil enables the virus to survive from crop to crop, and soil temperatures of 90°C for 10 min are normally required to kill the organism. Peat-growing bag and nutrient-film methods enable the grower to avoid this source of infection. The virus is spread very easily by sap. Hands and tools should be washed in soapy water after working with infected plants. Clothing may harbour the virus. The period from plant infection to symptom expression is about 15 days.

Cultivars and rootstocks containing several factors for **resistance** are commonly grown, but changing virus strains may overcome this resistance. A **mild strain** spray inoculation method has been used at the seedling stage to protect non-resistant cultivars from infection with severe strains. Extreme care is required to avoid mosaic-contaminated equipment when using this method.

Plum pox

This disease, sometimes called 'Sharka', has increased in importance in the British Isles since 1970, after its introduction from mainland Europe. Plums, damsons, peaches, blackthorn and ornamental plum are affected, while cherries and

Figure 11.6 *Plum pox: note the patches on the fruit (courtesy: Plant Pathology Laboratory, Ministry of Agriculture, Fisheries and Food, MAFF) (see notifiable diseases).*

flowering cherries are immune. Leaf symptoms of **feint interveinal yellow blotches** can best be seen on leaves from the centre of the infected tree. The most **reliable** symptoms, however, are found on fruit (*see* Figure 11.6), where sunken **dark blotches** are seen. Ripening of infected fruit may be several weeks premature, yield losses may reach 25 per cent, and the fruit is often **sour**.

The virus enters a nursery or orchard through infected **planting stock**. Spread of the virus during the early summer and autumn by **aphids** (e.g. leaf curling plum aphid) is **slow** in widely spaced orchards, but more rapid in closely planted nurseries, e.g. nursery stock areas.

Preventative control is the only option open to growers. Clean ministry-certified stock should be used. Routine aphid-controlling **insecticides** should be applied in late spring, summer and autumn. Suspected infected trees must be reported and the infected trees must be **removed** and **burnt**.

Chrysanthemum stunt viroid

This disease, found only on plants of the Asteraceae family and mainly on the *Chrysanthemum* genus,

produces a stunted plant, often only half the normal size but **without** any distortion. Flowers often open 1 week earlier than normal, and may be small and lacking in colour. The virus enters gardens and nurseries through infected **cuttings**, and is readily transmitted by leaf contact and by **handling**. Symptoms may take several months to appear, thus seriously reducing the chance of early removal of the disease source.

The grower must use **preventative control**. Certified planting material derived from **heat-treated meristem** stock (*see* tissue culture) reduces the risk of this disease.

Arabis mosaic

This virus infects a **wide** range of horticultural crops. On strawberries, yellow spots or mottling are produced on the leaves, and certain cultivars become **severely stunted**. On ornamental plants, e.g. *Daphne odorata*, yellow rings and lines are seen on infected leaves, and the plants may slowly die back, particularly when this virus is associated with cucumber mosaic inside the plant. Several weeds, e.g. chickweed and grass spp., may harbour this disease, and in soft fruit severe attacks of the disease may occur when planted into ploughed-up grassland. The virus is transmitted by a common soil-inhabiting nematode, *Xiphinema diversicaudatum*, which may retain the virus in its body for several months.

Control of this disease may be achieved only by **preventative** methods. Virus-free soft fruit **planting material** is available through the Nuclear Stock Scheme. **Fumigation** of soil with chemicals such as **dichloropropene**, applied well before planting time, eliminates many of the eelworm vectors. No curative chemical is available to eliminate the virus inside the plant.

Reversion disease on blackcurrants

This virus disease seriously reduces blackcurrant yields. Flower buds on infected bushes are almost hairless on close inspection, and appear brighter in colour than healthy buds. Infected leaves may have fewer main veins than healthy ones. After several years of infection, the bush may cease to produce fruit, the effect of different virus strains producing different levels of sterility. The virus is transmitted by the **blackcurrant gall mite**, and reversion infected plants are particularly susceptible to attack by this pest. Removal and burning of infected plants is an important form of control.

Use of **certified plant material**, raised in areas away from infection and vectors, is strongly recommended. Control of the mite **vector** in spring and early summer has already been described.

FURTHER READING

Agrios, E.N. *Plant Pathology* (Academic Press, 1997).

Brown, L.V. *Applied Principles of Horticulture*, 2nd edition (Butterworth-Heinemann, 2002).

Buczacki, S. and Harris, K. *Guide to Pests, Diseases and Disorders of Garden Plants* (Collins, 1998).

Cooper, J.I. *Virus Diseases of Trees and Shrubs* (Institute of Terrestrial Ecology, 1979).

Fletcher, J.T. *Diseases of Greenhouse Plants* (Longman, 1984).

Forsberg, J.L. *Diseases of Ornamental Plants* (University of Illinois, 1975).

Greenwood, P. and Halstead, A. *Pests and Diseases* (Dorling Kindersley, 1997).

Hope, F. *Turf Culture: A Manual for Groundsmen* (Cassell, 1990).

Ingram, D.S. *et al.* (editors). *Science and the Garden* (Blackwell Science Ltd, 2002).

Lloyd, J. *Plant Health Care for Woody Ornamentals* (1997).

Morgan, W.M. and Ledieu, M.S. *Pest and Disease Control in Glasshouse Crops* (British Crop Protection Council, 1979).

Scopes, N. and Stables, L. *Pest and Disease Control Handbook* (British Crop Protection Council, 1989).

Snowdon, A.L. *Post-harvest Diseases and Disorders of Fruits and Vegetables* (Wolfe Scientific, 1991).

Welcome to the World of Environmental Products. (Rhone-Poulenc, 1992).

Whitehead, R. (editor) *UK Pesticide Guide* (CABI Publishing, 2003).

12

Control Measures

In the three preceding chapters, important weeds, pests and diseases have been described with an emphasis on symptoms and damage, life cycles, and brief comments on control relevant to the particular causative organism. In this chapter, the main types of control measures are described in some detail to include legal aspects, crop management methods, use of beneficial organisms and the rather complex area of chemical control. The horticulturist should aim to use as many appropriate methods as possible within a crop cycle to bring about precise and efficient control. Distinction is drawn between preventative and curative control methods. The concept of economic damage is discussed in relation to supervised control.

LEGISLATION AND CONTROL

Before 1877, no legal measures were available in the UK to prevent importation of plants infested with pests such as Colorado beetle. Measures taken at ports from that year onwards were brought together in the 1927 Destructive Insects and Pests Acts, empowering government officials to inspect and, if necessary, refuse plant imports. Within this Act, the 'Sale of Diseased Plants Order' placed on the grower the responsibility for recognition and

reporting of serious pests and diseases, e.g. blackcurrant gall mite and silver leaf of plums. Lack of education and enforcement led to the need for specific orders relevant to particular current problems, e.g. in 1958 the fireblight-susceptible pear cultivar, 'Laxton's Superb', was declared **notifiable** and prohibited under the Fireblight Disease Order. Recent orders have helped prevent outbreaks of white rust on chrysanthemums, plum pox virus and two American leaf miner species; less success has been achieved with the Western flower thrip organism. Further importation legislation under the '1967 Plant Health Act' prohibits the landing of any non-indigenous pest or disease by aircraft or post, and the 'Importation of Plants, Produce and Potatoes Order 1971' specifically names prohibited crops, e.g. plum rootstocks from eastern Europe; crops subject to a healthy plant (**phytosanitary**) certificate, e.g. potato tubers from Europe; and crops to be examined, e.g. *Acacia* shrubs and apricot seeds. The operation of these orders is supervised by the Plant Health Branch of the Department for Environment, Food and Rural Affairs (DEFRA). Complete success in preventing the introduction of damaging organisms may be limited by dishonest importations and by the difficulty of detection of some diseases, especially viruses. European Council directives, e.g. 77/93/EEC, are moving member nations towards a unified approach in reducing the transfer of infected plant material across national boundaries. The Weeds Act 1959 places a legal obligation on each grower to prevent the spread of creeping thistle, spear thistle, curled dock, broad-leaved dock and ragwort.

CULTURAL CONTROL

Horticulturists, in their everyday activities, may remove or reduce damaging organisms, and thus **protect** the crop. Below are described some of the more important methods used.

Cultivation

Ploughing and **rotavating** of soils enable a physical improvement in soil structure as a preparation for the growing of crops. The improved drainage and tilth may reduce damping-off diseases, disturb annual and perennial weeds, e.g. chickweed and couch grass, and expose soil pests, e.g. leather jackets and cutworms, to the eager beaks of birds. Repeated rotavation may be necessary to deplete the reserves of perennial weeds, e.g. couch grass. **Hoeing** annual weeds is an effective method, provided the roots are fully exposed, and the soil dry enough to prevent their re-establishment.

Partial soil sterilization

Greenhouse soils are commonly sterilized by high pressure steam released to penetrate downwards into the soil, which is covered by heat resistant plastic sheeting (**sheet steaming**). The steam condenses on contact with soil particles, and moves deeper only when that layer of soil has reached steam temperature. Some active soil pests, e.g. symphilids, may move downwards ahead of the steam 'front'. The temperatures required to kill most nematodes, insects, weed seeds and fungi are 45°C, 55°C, 55°C and 60°C respectively. Beneficial bacteria are not killed below 82°C, and therefore growers attempt to reach but not exceed this soil temperature. In this way, organisms difficult to sterilize, such as fungal sclerotia, and *Meloidogyne* and *Verticillium* in root debris may be killed. Sheet steaming is effective only to depths of about 15 cm, and its effect is reduced when soil aggregates are large and hard to penetrate, or when soils are wet and hard to heat up. When soil pests and diseases occur deep in the soil, heating pipes may be placed below the soil surface, as grids or spikes, to achieve a more thorough effect. The 'steam-plough' achieves a similar result, as it is winched along the greenhouse. If soil is to be used in composts it should be sterilized (*see* sterilizing equipment). The clear advantage of soil sterilization may occasionally be lost if a serious soil fungus (e.g. *Pythium*) is accidentally introduced into a crop where it may quickly spread in the absence of fungal competition.

Chemical sterilization

This involves the use of substances toxic to most living organisms, thus necessitating application during the fallow, or intercrop, period. **Soil applied** chemicals include methyl bromide (applied as a gas), metham sodium (commonly applied through a nutrient diluter), dazomet (applied as a granule) and dichloropropene (applied by an injection apparatus against nematodes). The fumigant action of these substances is prolonged by rolling the soil, or covering it with plastic sheeting (in the case of the methyl bromide). Care should be taken that no chemical residues are allowed to remain, and thus kill off early stages of the succeeding crop. **Greenhouse structures** may be sterilized by toxic gases and liquids such as formaldehyde, formic acid and burning sulphur. Common pests and diseases such as whitefly, red spider mite and grey mould may be greatly reduced by this intercrop method of control.

European legislation is causing the withdrawal of methyl bromide use by 2005 on the grounds of environmental safety. Whilst being very effective as a sterilant of growing media, methyl bromide has three serious drawbacks. It is very poisonous to man and animals. It is a gas and therefore finds its way into the atmosphere. It is also chemically related to the chlorinated hydrocarbons, such as the refrigerator coolants, that have been held responsible for much of the 'global warming' phenomenon. These three factors combine to rule out its continued use in horticulture.

Soil fertility

While the correct content and balance of major and minor nutrients (*see* Chapter 16) in the soil are recognized as vitally important for optimum crop yield and quality, excessive nitrogen levels may encourage the increase of insects such as peach-potato aphid, fungi, e.g. grey mould, and bacteria, e.g. fireblight. Adequate levels of potassium help control fungal diseases, e.g. *Fusarium* wilt on carnation, and tomato mosaic virus. Club root disease of brassicas is less damaging in soil with a pH greater than 6, and lime may be incorporated before planting these crops to achieve this aim. Amenity horticulturists apply mulches, e.g. composted bark, grass cuttings or straw, to bare soil in order to control annual weeds by excluding the source of light. Black polythene sheeting is used in soft fruit production to achieve a similar objective.

Crop rotation

Some important soil-borne pests and diseases attack specific crops, e.g. potato cyst nematode on potato and clubroot on cruciferous plants. As they are soil-borne, they are slow in their dispersal and can be difficult to control. By the simple method of planting a given crop in a different plot each season, such pests or diseases are excluded from their preferred host crop for several seasons. This method does not work well against unspecific problems, e.g. grey mould, or rapidly spreading organisms such as aphids.

Planting and harvesting times

Some pests emerge from their overwintering stage at about the same time each year, e.g. cabbage root fly in late April. By planting early to establish tolerant brassica plants before the pest emerges, a useful supplement to chemical control is achieved. The deliberate planting of early potato cultivars enables harvesting before the maturation of potato cyst nematode cysts, so that damage to the crop and the release of the nematode eggs is avoided. Annual weeds may be induced to germinate in a prepared seedbed by irrigation. After they have been controlled with a contact herbicide, e.g. paraquat, a crop may then be sown into the undisturbed bed or **stale seedbed**, with less chance of further weed germination.

Clean seed and planting material

Seed producers take stringent precautions to exclude weed seed contaminants and pests and diseases from their seed stocks. While weed seeds are, in the main, removed by mechanical separators, and insects can be killed by seed dressings, systemic fungal seed infections, e.g. celery leaf spot disease, are best controlled by immersion of dry seed in a 0.2 per cent thiram solution at 30°C for 24 h (**thiram soak treatment**). The seed is then re-dried. Equal care is taken to monitor seed crops likely to carry virus disease (e.g. tomato mosaic). Curative control by **dry heat** at 70°C for 4 days is usually effective, although it may reduce subsequent seed germination rates.

Vegetative propagation material is used in all areas of horticulture, as bulbs (e.g. tulips and onions), tubers (e.g. dahlias and potatoes), runners (e.g. strawberries), cuttings (e.g. chrysanthemums and many trees and shrubs) and graft scions in trees. The increase of nematodes, viruses, fungi and bacteria by vegetative propagation is a particular problem, since the organisms are inside the plant tissues, and since the plant tissues are sensitive to any drastic control measures. **Inspection** of introduced material may greatly reduce the risk of this problem. Soft narcissus bulbs, chrysanthemum cuttings with an internal rot, whitefly or red spider mite on stock plants, virus on nursery stock, are all symptoms that would suggest either careful sorting, or rejection of the stocks. Accurate and rapid methods of **virus testing** (using test plants, electron microscopy and staining by ELISA technique) now enable growers quickly to learn the quality of their planting stocks. Fungal levels in cuttings (e.g. *Fusarium* wilt of carnations) can be routinely checked by placing plant segments in sterile nutrient culture.

Warm water treatment is used for pests such as stem and bulb nematodes in narcissus bulbs. Immersion of bulbs for 2 h at 44°C controls the pest without seriously affecting bulb tissues. Chrysanthemum stools and strawberry runners may similarly be treated, using temperature/time combinations favourable to each crop. **Viruses** (e.g. aspermy virus on chrysanthemum) are more difficult to control, since they are more intimately associated with the plant cells. Virus concentrations may be greatly reduced in meristems of stock plants grown at temperatures of 40°C for about a month. This has enabled the production of **tissue-cultured** disease-free stock material of both edible and non-edible crops.

Hygienic growing

During the crop, the grower should aim to provide optimum conditions for growth. Water content of soil should be adequate for growth (*see* field capacity), but not be so excessive that root diseases (e.g. damping off in pot plants, club root of cabbage and brown root rot of conifers) are actively encouraged. Water sources should be analysed for *Pythium* and *Phytophthora* species if damping-off diseases are a constant problem. Covering, and regular cleaning, of water tanks to prevent the breeding of these fungi in rotting organic matter may be important in their control. Conifer nursery stock grown on raised gravel beds are less likely to suffer the water-borne spread of conifer brown rot. Carnations are grown in **isolated beds** or **peat modules** to reduce spread of wilt-inducing organisms (e.g. *Fusarium* spp.).

High humidity encourages many diseases. In greenhouses, the careful timing of daily overhead irrigation, and of ventilation (to reduce overnight condensation on leaves or flowers), may greatly reduce levels of diseases such as grey mould on pot plants or downy mildew on lettuce. **Transmission** of pests and diseases from plant to plant or field to field can be slowed down. Virus diseases such as tomato mosaic virus may be confined by delaying till the end of the de-leafing or harvesting of infected plants. Washing knives and hands regularly in warm, soapy water will reduce subsequent viral spread. Soil-borne problems, e.g. club root, eelworms and damping-off diseases, are easily carried by boots and tractor wheels. Foot and wheel **dips**, containing a general chemical sterilant, e.g. formaldehyde, have successfully been used, especially in preventing damping-off problems in greenhouses.

Traps and repellants

Measures described in this section aim to prevent the pest or disease from arriving at the crop. A **grease band** wrapped around an apple trunk prevents the wingless female winter moth's attempted crawl up the tree to lay eggs in winter. A fine mesh screen placed in front of the ventilator fan prevents the entry of many mushrooms and glasshouse pests, e.g. sciarid flies. A **trench** dug around a large stump infected with honey fungus may prevent the **rhizomorphs** ('bootlaces') from radiating out to infect other plants. Interplanting of onions amongst carrots may deter the carrot fly from attacking its host crop. **Pheremone traps** containing a specific synthetic attractant are used in apple orchards to lure male codling and tortrix moths onto a sticky surface, thus enabling an accurate assessment of their numbers, and a more effective control.

Alternate hosts

Alternate hosts harbouring pests and diseases should be removed where possible. Soil-borne problems, e.g. club root of cabbage and free-living eelworms on strawberries, are harboured by shepherd's purse (*Capsella bursapastoris*) and chickweed (*Stellaria media*) respectively. Groundsel (*Senecio vulgaris*) is an alternate host of the air-borne powdery mildew of cucumber, while docks (*Rumex* spp.) act as a reservoir of dock sawfly, which damages young apple trees.

Removal of infected plant material

With **rapid-increase** problems, e.g. peach-potato aphid and white rust of chrysanthemum fungus in greenhouses, removal is practicable in the early stages of the crop, but becomes unmanageable after the pest or disease has increased in number and dispersed throughout the plants. **Slow-increase** problems, e.g. *Fusarium* wilt disease on carnations and vine weevil larvae, may be removed throughout the crop cycle, but the infected roots and soil must be carefully placed in a bag to prevent dispersal of the problem. In outdoor production, labour costs often prevent removal during the growing season.

However, chemical destruction of blight-infected potato foliage with a herbicide, e.g. diquat, reduces infection of the tubers. **Burning** of post-harvest leaf material and lifting of root debris after harvest (against grey mould on strawberries and club root on brassicas respectively) may help prevent problems in the next crop. In tree species, routine **pruning** operations may remove serious pests, such as fruit tree red spider mite, and diseases, such as powdery mildew. Tree stumps harbouring serious underground diseases, e.g. honey fungus, should be removed where practicable.

RESISTANCE

Wild plants show high levels of resistance to most pests and diseases. In the search for high yields and extremes of flower shape and colour, plant breeders have often failed to include this wild plant resistance. However, in crops such as antirrhinum, lettuce and tomatoes, one or more resistance **genes** have been deliberately incorporated to give protection against rust, downy mildew and tomato mosaic virus respectively. The disease organisms may **overcome** these genetic barriers,

and the crop thus again becomes infected. Growers may sow a sequence of cultivars (e.g. lettuce), each with different resistance genes, in order that the disease organism (e.g. downy mildew) is constantly exposed to a new resistance barrier, and thus limit the disease.

Vegetatively propagated species (e.g. potatoes) and **tree** crops (e.g. apple) which remain genetically unaltered for many years are now being bred with high levels of 'wild plant' resistance (to blight and powdery mildew respectively on potato and apple) so that the crops may more permanently resist these serious problems. Crop resistance to **insects** is now being more seriously considered by plant breeders. Some lettuce cultivars are resistant to lettuce root aphid (*Pemphigus bursarius*).

BIOLOGICAL CONTROL

Many pests of outdoor horticultural crops, e.g. peach-potato aphid, are **indigenous** (i.e. they originally evolved, and are still present, in wild plant communities of this country). Pest populations are often reduced in nature by other organisms which, as **predators**, eat the pest, or as **parasites**, lay eggs within the pest. These beneficial organisms, found also on horticultural crops, are to be encouraged, and in some cases deliberately introduced.

The **black-kneed capsid** (*Blapharidopterus angulatus*) found on fruit trees alongside its pestilent relative, the **common green capsid**, eats more than 1000 fruit tree red spider mites per year. Its eggs are laid in August and survive the winter. Winter washes used against apple pests and diseases often kill off this useful insect. The closely related **anthocorid** bugs, e.g. *Anthocoris nemorum*, are predators on a wide range of pests, e.g. aphids, thrips, caterpillars and mites, and have recently been used for biological control in greenhouses.

Some species of **lacewings**, e.g. *Chrysopa carnea*, lay several hundred eggs per year on the end of fine stalks, located on leaves. The resulting hairy larvae predate on aphids and fruit tree red spider mite, reaching their prey in leaf folds which ladybirds cannot reach.

The 40 species of **ladybird** beetle are a welcome sight to the professional horticulturist and lay-man alike. Almost all are predatory. The red two-spot ladybird (*Adalia bipunctata*) emerges from the soil in spring, mates and lays about 1000 elongated yellow eggs on the leaves of a range of weeds and crops, e.g. nettles and beans, throughout the growing season. The emerging slate-grey and yellow larvae and the adults feed on a range of aphid species. The ground beetle (e.g. *Bembidion lampros*) actively predates on soil pests, e.g. cabbage root fly eggs, greatly reducing their numbers.

Hoverflies superficially resembling wasps are commonly seen darting above flowers in summer. Several of the 250 British species, e.g. *Syrphus ribesii*, lay eggs in the midst of aphid colonies, and the legless larva consumes large numbers of aphids.

Predatory mites, e.g. *Typhlodromus pyri* on fruit tree red spider mite, may contribute importantly to pest control. The numerous species of web-forming and hunting **spiders** help in a largely unspecific way in the reduction of all forms of insects.

About 3000 **wasp** species of the families Ichneumonidae, Braconidae and Chalcidae are parasitic on insects in Britain. The red ichneumon (*Opion* spp.) lays eggs in many moth caterpillars. The cabbage white caterpillar may bear 150 parasitic larvae of the braconid wasp (*Apanteles glomeratus*) which pupate outside the pest's body as yellow cocoon masses. The woolly aphid on apples may be reduced by the chalcid *Aphelinus mali*.

The spiracles of insects provide access to specialized parasitic fungi, particularly under damp conditions. Aphid numbers may be quickly reduced by the infection of the fungus *Entomophthora aphidis*, while codling moth caterpillars on apple may be enveloped by *Beauveria bassiana*. Cabbage white caterpillar populations are occasionally much reduced by a virus, which causes them to burst.

The predators and parasites previously described may be irregular in their distribution and time of

Table 12.1 Biological control organisms used in horticulture

Disease or pest	Crop	Name of controlling organism	Type of controlling organism
Thrips	C, F, P	*Amblyseius cucumeris*	Mite
	C, F, P	*Orius laevigatus*	Anthocorid bug
Aphids	G	*Aphidoletes aphidimyza*	Midge
	G	*Aphidius* spp.	Wasp
	Ch	*Verticillium lecanii*	Fungus
Glasshouse whitefly	T	*Macrolophus caliginosus*	Anthocorid bug
	G	*Encarsia formosa*	Wasp
Red spider mite	G	*Phytoseiulus persimilis*	Mite
	T, C, F	*Therodiplosis persicae*	Midge
Leaf miner	T, C, F	*Dacnusa sibirica*	Wasp
	T, C, F	*Diglyphus isaea*	Wasp
Caterpillar	G	*Trichogramma* spp.	Wasp
	G	*Bacillus thuringiensis*	Bacterium extract
Leaf hopper	T	*Anagrus atomus*	Wasp
Mealy bug	G	*Cryptolaemus montrouzieri*	Ladybird
	G	*Leptomastix dactylopii*	Wasp
Vine weevil	G	*Steinernema capsicarpae*	Nematode
Sciarid fly	G	*Steinernema feltiae*	Nematode
	G	*Hypoaspis miles*	Mite
Silver leaf fungus	Tf	*Trichoderma viride*	Fungus
Tomato mosaic virus	T	–	Mild strain of virus

T: tomato; C: cucumber; P: sweet peppers; F: flowers; Tf: top fruit; Ch: chrysanthemum; G: general use.

emergence. For reliable results, deliberate intro-duction may be necessary. The culturing and meas-ured application of certain predators and parasites are now common features of greenhouse plant pro-tection, particularly where pests have developed **resistance** to chemicals. The greenhouse represents a controlled environment where pest–predator interactions can be accurately predicted. Develop-ments in outdoor plant production may yield similarly successful results in future. Some of the more effective species being used are described below and the wider selection of species is given in Table 12.1.

Phytoseiulus persimilis (*see* Figure 12.1)

This is a globular, deep orange, predatory tropical mite used in greenhouse production to control glasshouse red spider mite (*see* page 114). It is raised on spider mite-infected beans, and then evenly distributed throughout the crop, e.g. cucum-bers at the rate of one predator per plant. Some growers who suffer repeatedly from the pest first introduce the red spider mite throughout the crop at the rate of about five mites per plant a week before predator application, thus maintaining even levels of pest–predator interaction. The predator's

short egg–adult development period (7 days), laying potential (50 eggs per life cycle) and appe-tite (five pest adults eaten per day), explain its extremely efficient action.

Encarsia formosa (*see* Figure 12.2)

This is a small (2 mm) wasp, which lays an egg into the glasshouse **whitefly** (*see* page 107) scale, caus-ing it to turn black and eventually release another wasp. This parasite is raised on whitefly-infested tobacco plants. It is introduced to the crop, e.g. tomato, at a rate of 100 blackened scales per 100 plants. The parasite's introduction to the crop is successful only when there is less than one white-fly per 10 plants, and its mobility (about 5 m) and successful parasitism are effective only at tempera-tures greater than 22°C when its egg-laying ability exceeds that of the whitefly. The wasp lays most of

Figure 12.2 *Encarsia parasite of glasshouse whitefly (courtesy: Glasshouse Crops Research Institute).*

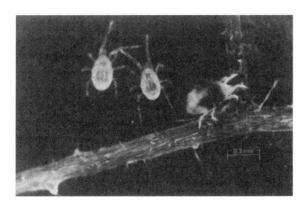

Figure 12.1 *Phytoseiulus predator: note the difference in appearance between the round, long-legged preda-tors (left) and the glasshouse red spider mite (right) (courtesy: Glasshouse Crops Research Institute).*

its 60 or more eggs within a few days of emergence from the black scale. Thus a series of weekly or fortnightly applications from late February onwards ensures that parasite egg laying covers the susceptible whitefly scale stage.

A combination of biological methods may be used on some crops, e.g. chrysanthemums, tomatoes and cucumbers, in order to control a range of organisms (*see* integrated control). Biological control programmes enable pollution-free reduction of some major pests without the development of **resistant** pest organisms. An understanding of the pests' and biological control organisms' life cycles is, however, necessary to ensure success. Several specialist firms now have contracts to apply biological control organisms to greenhouse units.

The careful selection of pesticides (*see* pirimicarb) enables simultaneous biological and chemical control, to the grower's advantage.

CHEMICAL CONTROL

This method of control aims ideally to use a selected chemical for reduction of weed, pest or disease without harming man, crop or wildlife. This aim is not always achieved, although increasingly stringent demands are placed on the chemical manufacturer, both in terms of the chemical's efficiency and its safety. In past centuries, pests, e.g. apple woolly aphid, were sprayed with natural products, e.g. turpentine and soap, while weeds were removed by hand. In the nineteenth century, the chance development of **Bordeaux mixture** from inorganic copper sulphate and slaked lime, and in the early twentieth century the expansion of the organic chemical industry, enabled a change of emphasis in crop protection from cultural to chemical control. **The word 'pesticide' is used in this book to cover all crop protection chemicals, which include herbicides (for weeds), insecticides (for insects), acaricides (for mites), nematicides (for nematodes) and fungicides (for fungi).** About 3 million tonnes of crop protection chemicals are used worldwide each year, two fifths being herbicides, two fifths insecticides and one fifth fungicides.

Active ingredient.   Each container of commercial pesticide contains several ingredients. The active ingredient's role is to kill the weed, pest or disease. More detailed lists of the range of active ingredients can be found in government literature. The other constituents of pesticides are described under **formulation**.

Herbicides

Herbicides that are applied to the seedbed or growing crop must have a **selective action**, i.e. kill the weed but leave the crop undamaged.

This selective action may succeed for one of several reasons. Chemicals often affect different plant families in different ways. The broad-leaved turf weed, daisy (*Bellis perennis*, a member of the Asteraceae) is controlled by 2,4-D, leaving the turf grasses (Graminae) unaffected.

Sometimes plant species are affected by different concentrations of the chemical to a degree that can be exploited. The correct **concentration** of selective chemicals may be vital if the crop is to remain unharmed. The following relative values (parts per million, ppm) for the amount of propyzamide herbicide required to kill different plant species illustrate this point:

- *Crops*
  - carrot   0.8;
  - cabbage   1.0;
  - lettuce   78.0;
- *Weeds*
  - knotgrass   0.08;
  - black nightshade   0.2;
  - fat hen   0.2;
  - pennycress   0.6;
  - groundsel   78.0.

It can thus be seen that a concentration of 25 ppm of propyzamide applied to lettuce would leave the crop unaffected, but control all the weeds except groundsel. A low concentration of simazine is used to control annual weeds around raspberry plants, while a high concentration gives total control on paths and other uncultivated areas.

A third form of selectivity operates by **correct timing** of herbicide application. A seedbed with crop seeds below and weed seeds germinating at the surface may receive a **contact** chemical, e.g. paraquat, which permits germination of the crop without weed competition. A similar effect is achieved when a **residual** herbicide, e.g. propachlor, is sprayed onto the soil surface to await weed seed germination. The situations for weed control are summarized in Figure 12.3.

Herbicides may conveniently be divided into two main groups: the **foliage-acting**, and the **soil-acting (residual)** chemicals.

Foliage-acting herbicides. These enter the leaf through fine pores in the cuticle, or the stomata. The herbicide may move through the **vascular** system (**translocated** chemicals) to all parts of the plant before killing plant cells, or it may kill on contact with the leaf. Four active ingredients are described, each belonging to a different chemical group, and each having a different effect on weeds:

1 **Paraquat** is commonly used to scorch and kill top growth of a wide spectrum of weeds in stale seedbeds, after harvest, in perennial crops, or in waste land. Although translocated when in dilute concentrations, its rapid, light-induced unselective contact action is most commonly utilized. It is quickly absorbed, in damp soils, by clay particles, thus allowing planting soon after its application. Its absorption prevents any problem of residual action except in extremely dry summers. It should never be used on foliage of growing plants, although carefully directed sprays between the rows of growing soft fruit are recommended.

2 **Amitrole** is used in similar situations to paraquat, but is more residual, surviving in the soil for several weeks. It stops photosynthesis, scorching both grass and broad-leaved weeds (**unselective**). It is especially useful on uncropped land and, when applied in autumn, it is translocated to underground rhizomes of **couch** that are then killed. It should not be sprayed onto the foliage of growing plants.

3 **2,4-D** is an **auxin** and causes uncontrolled abnormal growth on leaves, stems and roots of **broad-leaved** weeds, which eventually die. It is a useful selective herbicide on turf because the protected meristems of grasses can survive unaffected. It must be kept well away from nearby border plants and from some crops, e.g. tomatoes, which are extremely sensitive to minute quantities.

4 **Glyphosate** enters the foliage of actively growing annual and perennial weeds (**unselective**) and is **translocated** (*see* page 58) to underground organs, subsequently killing them. It is commonly used several weeks before drilling or planting of crops, around perennial plants such as apples or in established nursery stock trees. Glyphosate is inactivated in soils (particularly **peats**), thus preventing damage to newly sown crops. It may cause damage if spray-drift to adjoining plants or fields occurs.

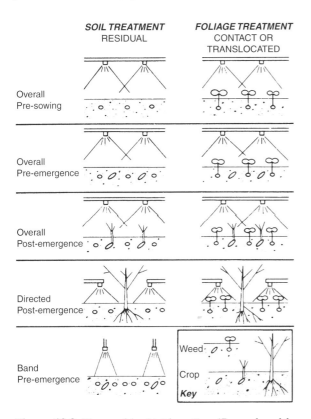

Figure 12.3 *Types of herbicide action (Reproduced by permission of Blackwell Scientific Publications).*

Soil-acting herbicides.   These are either sprayed onto the soil surface (*see* Figure 12.3) or soil incorporated. They must be persistent (**residual**) for several weeks or months to kill the seedling before or after it emerges. Root hairs are the main point of entry. Increased rates may be necessary for **peat soils** that inactivate some herbicides. The chemical may be applied as a spray or granule before the crop is sown (**pre-sowing** stage), before the crop emerges (**pre-emergence**) or, with more selective chemicals, after the crop emerges (**post-emergence**). Three active ingredients are described, each belonging to a different chemical group, and each having a different effect on weeds:

1 **Chlorpropham**, a relatively insoluble compound, is applied as a pre-emergent spray to control many germinating weeds species, e.g. chickweed, in crops such as bulbs, onions, carrots and lettuce. It usually persists for less than 3 months in the soil. In light, porous soils with low organic matter, its rapid penetration to underlying seeds make it an unsuitable chemical. Earthworm numbers may be reduced by its presence.
2 **Propachlor**, a relatively insoluble compound, is applied as a pre-sowing or pre-emergent spray to control a wide variety of annual weeds in brassicas, strawberries, onions and leeks. For weeds in established herbaceous borders (e.g. rose), the granular formulation gives a residual protection against most germinating broad-leaved and grass weeds.
3 **Dichlobenil** gives **total** control against germinating weeds, couch grass and some perennial weeds in waste ground, soft fruit, top fruit and established ornamental shrub and tree areas. The compound remains in the soil for more than 6 months, and young crops should not be planted within a year of its application.

Mixtures.   The horticulturist must deal with a wide range of annual and perennial weeds. The somewhat specialized action of some of the herbicide active ingredients previously described may be inadequate for the control of a broad weed spectrum. For example, in the case of **chlorpropham**, the addition of **diuron** enables an improved control of charlock and groundsel, while a different formulation containing **chlorpropham** plus **linuron** is designed to have greater contact action and thus control both established and germinating weeds in bulb crops. Careful **selection** of the most suitable mixture of active ingredients is therefore necessary for a particular crop/weed situation.

Insecticides and acaricides

The insects and mites have three main points of weakness for attack by pesticides which are as follows: their waxy exoskeletons (*see* Figure 10.2) may be penetrated by wax-dissolving **contact** chemicals; their abdominal spiracles allow **fumigant** chemicals to enter tracheae; and their digestive systems, in coping with the large food quantities required for growth, may take in **stomach** poisons. Four main groups of insecticides are described (Details of associated hazards to spraying operators and the general public are discussed later in this chapter:

1 **Dormant-season** control of pests may be achieved on trees such as apple by the use of toxic contact insecticides, e.g. **tar oil**. It kills eggs (**ovicide**) of aphids, red spider mite and capsids, but useful predators are also eliminated (*see* integrated control). Most other insecticides are active on a more limited number of pests.
2 **Malathion** belongs to the organophosphorus group. It enters through the cuticle and, on reaching the nervous system, interferes with 'messages' crossing the nerve endings of pests such as aphids, mealy bug, flies and red spider mites. The related chemical **dimethoate** is slightly soluble in water, and may **systemically** move through the xylem and phloem tissues of the plant before being sucked up by the aphid stylet. The long-lasting (**residual**) property of another ingredient, **chlorpyriphos**, enables its use as a soil insecticide against emerging root fly larvae.
3 **Pirimicarb** belongs to the third (carbamate) group, is slightly systemic, and controls many

aphid species without affecting beneficial lady-birds. **Aldicarb** combines a soil action against nematodes with a systemic, broad-spectrum activity against foliar pests, e.g. aphids, whitefly, leaf miners, mites and nematodes of ornamental plants. This group of chemicals acts on the insect **nervous** system in a similar manner to the organophosphorus group.

4 **Chemicals derived from plants**. **Nicotine**, a natural extract from tobacco, is used as a spray or smoke, and enters the spiracles of aphids, capsids, leaf miner adults and thrips to reach their nervous system. It persists only briefly on the plant. **Pyrethrum**, a natural extract from a chrysanthemum species, has been largely superseded by a range of related synthetic products (called pyrethroids). **Cypermethrin** is one such chemical which has stomach and contact action against aphids, caterpillars and thrips. **Derris**, an extract from a tropical legume (and originally a fish-pond poison), interferes with the **respiration** of a wide range of insects and mites. The insecticide **diflubenzuron** acts selectively on caterpillars and sciarid fly larvae by disturbing the insect's moulting.

Nematicides

No active ingredients are, at present, available exclusively for nematode control. Soil-inhabiting stages of cyst nematodes, stem and bulb eelworm, and some ectoparasitic root eelworms are effectively reduced by soil incorporation of granular pesticides, e.g. **aldicarb** at planting time of crops such as potatoes and onions. This group of chemicals acts systemically on leaf nematodes of plants such as chrysanthemum and dahlia.

Fungicides

Fungicides must act against the disease but not seriously interfere with plant activity. **Protectant** chemicals prevent the entry of hyphae into roots, and the germination of spores into leaves and other aerial organs (*see* Figure 11.2). **Systemic** chemicals enter roots, stems and leaves, and are translocated to sites where they may affect hyphal growth and prevent spore production. Although there are many fungicidal chemical groups, three are chosen here as examples:

1 **Inorganic chemicals** (i.e. containing no carbon) have long been used to protect horticultural crops. **Copper** salts, when mixed with slaked lime (**Bordeaux mixture**) form a barrier on the leaf to fungi, e.g. potato blight. Fine-grained (colloidal) **sulphur** controls powdery mildews, and may be heated gently in greenhouse 'sulphur lamps' to control this disease by vapour action on plants such as roses.

2 **Organic chemicals** contain carbon. **Mancozeb** (dithiocarbamate group) and related synthetic compounds act protectively on a wide range of quite different foliar diseases, e.g. downy mildews, celery leaf spot and rusts, by preventing spore germination.

3 **Carbendazim** (benzimidazole group) is an example of a **systemic** ingredient, which moves upwards through the plant's xylem tissues, slowing hyphal growth and spore production of fungal wilts, powdery mildews and many leaf spot organisms. Damping off, potato blight and downy mildews are unaffected by this chemical group. Many different systemic groups are now used in horticulture.

About 200 active ingredients for weed, pest and disease control are available. Some are withdrawn and some introduced every year. The DEFRA and commercial literature are constantly updated to keep growers informed.

Resistance to pesticides

The development of resistant individuals from the millions of susceptible weeds, pests and diseases occurs most rapidly when exposure to a particular chemical is continuous, or when a pesticide acts against only one body process of the organism. Resistance, e.g. in aphids, to one member, e.g. malathion, of a chemical group confers resistance to other chemicals in the same (e.g. organophosphorus) group. Horticulturists should therefore follow the strategy of alternating between different **groups** and not simply changing active ingredients. Particular care should be taken with **systemic** chemicals that present to the organism inside the plant a relatively weak concentration against which the resistant organism can develop. Increase in **dosage** of the chemical will not, in general, provide a better control against resistant strains. Biological control, unlike chemical control, does not create resistant pests.

Formulations

Active ingredients are mixed with other ingredients to increase the efficiency and ease of application, prolong the period of effectiveness or reduce the damaging effects on plants and man. The whole product (**formulation**) in its bottle or packet is given a **trade name**, which often differs from the name of the active ingredient. The main formulations are as follows:

- **Liquids** (emulsifiable concentrates) contain a light oil or paraffin base in which the active ingredient is dissolved. Detergent-like substances (**emulsifiers**) present in the concentrate enable a stable emulsion to be produced when the formulation is diluted with water. In this way, the correct concentration is achieved throughout the spraying operation. Long chain molecular compounds (**wetter/spreaders**) in the formulation help to stick the active ingredients onto the leaf after spraying, particularly on smooth, waxy leaves such as cabbage.
- **Wettable powders** containing extremely small particles of active ingredient and wetting agents form a stable suspension for only a short period of time when diluted in the spray tank. Continuous stirring or shaking of the diluted formulation is thus required. An inert **filler** of clay-like material is usually present in the formulation to ease the original grinding of particles, and also

to help increase the shelf life of the product. It is suggested that this formulation is mixed into a thin **paste** before pouring through the filter of the sprayer. This prevents the formation of lumps that may block the nozzles.

- **Dusts** are applied dry to leaves or soil, and thus require less precision in grinding of the constituent particles, and less wetting agent.
- **Seed dressings** protect the seed and seedling against pests and diseases. A low percentage of active ingredient, e.g. **iprodione** applied in an inert clay-like filler or liquid reduces the risk of chemical damage to the delicate germinating seed.
- **Baits** contain attractant ingredients, e.g. bran and sugar mixed with the active ingredient, e.g. **methiocarb**, both of which are eaten by the pest, e.g. slugs.
- **Granules** formulated to a size of about 1.0 mm contain an inert filler, e.g. pumice or charcoal, onto which is coated the active ingredient. Granules may act as soil sterilants (e.g. **dazomet**), residual soil herbicide (e.g. **dichlobenil**), residual insecticide (e.g. **chlorpyrifos**), or broad-spectrum soil nematicide and insecticide (e.g. **aldicarb**). Granular formulations normally present fewer hazards to the operator and fewer spray-drift problems.
- **Smokes** containing **sodium chlorate**, a sugar and heat resistant active ingredient, e.g. **dicloran**, produce, on ignition, a vapour that reaches all parts of a greenhouse to fumigate against diseases, e.g. *Botrytis*.

Labels on commercial formulations give details of the active ingredient contained in the product. Application rates for different crops are included. The DEFRA approves pesticide products for effectiveness..

Application of herbicides and pesticides

This subject is described in detail in machinery texts. However, certain basic principles related to the covering of the leaf and soil by sprays will be mentioned. The application of liquids and wettable powders by means of **sprayers** may be adjusted in terms of pressure and nozzle type to provide the required spray rate. **Cone** nozzles produce a turbulent spray pattern suitable for fungicide and insecticide use, while **fan** nozzles produce a flat spray pattern for herbicide application. In periods of active plant growth, fortnightly sprays may be necessary to control pests and diseases on newly expanding foliage. **High volume** sprayers apply the diluted chemical at rates of 600–1000 l/ha in order to cover the whole leaf surface with droplets of 0.04–0.10 mm diameter. Cover of the under-leaf surface with pesticides may be poor if nozzles are not directed horizontally or upwards. Soil applied chemicals, e.g. herbicides or drenches, may be sprayed at a larger droplet size, 0.25–0.5 mm in diameter, through a selected **fan** nozzle. The correct height of the sprayer boom above the plant is essential for downward-directed nozzles if the spray pattern is to be evenly distributed. Savings can be achieved by **band spraying** herbicides in narrow strips over the crop to leave the inter-row for mechanical cultivation.

Medium volume (200–600 l/ha) and **low volume** (50–200 l/ha) equipment, such as knapsack sprayers, apply herbicides and pesticides onto the leaf at a lower droplet density, and in tree crops, mist blower equipment creates turbulence, and therefore increased spray travel, by means of a power driven fan. **Ultra-low volume** sprays (up to 50 l/ha) are dispersed on leaving the sprayer by a rapidly rotating disc which then throws regular-sized droplets into the air. Larger droplets (about 0.2 mm) are created by herbicide sprayers to prevent spray-drift problems, while smaller droplets (about 0.1 mm) allow good penetration and leaf cover for insecticide and fungicide use.

Fogging machines used in greenhouses and stores produce very fine droplets (about 0.015 mm diameter) by thermal and mechanical methods, and use small volumes of concentrated formulation (less than 1 l in 400 cm^3) which act as fumigants in the air, and as contact pesticides when deposited on the leaf surface. **Dust** and **granule applicators** spread the formulations evenly over the foliage, or ground surface. When mounted on seed drills and/or fertilizer applicators, granules may be incorporated into the soil. Care must be taken to ensure good distribution to prevent pesticide damage to germinating seeds or planting material.

Integrated control

Integrated control increasingly termed **Integrated Pest Management** requires the grower to understand all types of control measure, particularly biological and chemical, in order that they complement each other. In greenhouse production of cucumbers, the *Encarsia formosa* parasite and *Phytoseiulus persimilis* predator are used for whitefly and red spider mite control respectively. However, the other harmful pest and disease species must be controlled, often by chemical means, but without killing the parasites and predators. Drenches of systemic insecticide, e.g. **pirimicarb** against aphids, soil insecticides, e.g. **deltamethrin** against thrips pupae, and systemic fungicide drenches, e.g. **carbendazim** against wilt diseases and powdery mildew, are all applied away from the sensitive biological control organisms. Similarly, high volume sprays of selective chemicals, e.g. **dichlofluanid** against grey mould, *Bacillus thuringiensis* extracts against caterpillars, have little or no effect on the parasite and predator. Similar considerations may be given in control of apple pests and diseases. Reduced usage of extremely toxic winter washes, and increased use of **selective** caterpillar and powdery mildew control by chemicals, e.g. **diflubenzuron** and **fenarimol** respectively, allow the almost unhindered build-up of beneficial organisms, e.g. predatory capsids and mites.

The methods of **organic growers** emphasize the non-chemical practices in plant protection (as well as in soil fertility). Hedges are developed within 100 m of production areas and are clipped only 1 year in 4 to maintain natural predators and parasites. Rotations are closely followed to enable soil-borne pest or disease decline, while encouraging soil fertility. Resistant cultivars of plant are chosen, and judicious use of mechanical cultivations and flame weeding enables pests, diseases and weeds to be exposed or buried. A restricted choice of pesticide products such as **pyrethrins**, derris, **metaldehyde** (with repellant), **sulphur**, **copper salts** and **soft soap** are allowed to be applied, should the need arise. *Bacillus thuringiensis* extract, and also pheremone attractants, are similarly used. Table 12.2 gives a list of permitted substances.

Supervised control

Most plants can tolerate low levels of pest and disease damage without yield reduction unless the damage is to parts of the plant that become unacceptable (e.g. fruits for the supermarket trade). Thus, cucumbers require more than 30 per cent leaf area affected by red spider mite before

Table 12.2 Permitted products for plant pest and disease control in organic crop production

Preparations on basis of metaldehyde containing a repellent to higher animal species and as far as possible applied within traps
Preparations on basis of pyrethrins extracted from *Chrysanthemum* cinerariaefolium, containing possibly a synergist
Preparations from *Derris elliptica*
Preparations from *Quassia amara*
Preparations from *Ryania speciosa*
Propolis
Diatomacious Earth
Stone meal
Sulphur
Bordeaux mixture
Burgundy mixture
Sodium silicate
Sodium bicarbonate
Potassium soap (soft soap)
Pheremone preparations
Bacillus thuringiensis preparations
Granulose virus preparations
Plant and animal oils
Paraffin oil

economic damage occurs in terms of yield loss. This enables methods of control that depend on some damage being done to ensure continued success such as the use of predators. Damage assessments are used in apple orchards to decide whether control measures are necessary. Thus, at green-cluster stage (before flowers emerge) chemical sprays are considered only when an average of half the observed buds have five aphids/bud. Similarly, three winter moth larvae per bud-cluster merit control at late blossom time.

Pheremone traps enable the precise time of maximum codling moth emergence to be determined in early June. Catches of less than 10 moths per trap per week do not warrant control. The DEFRA issue **spray warning** information to growers when serious pests, e.g. carrot root fly, and diseases, e.g. potato blight, are likely to occur. Supervised control may greatly reduce pesticide costs.

Safety with herbicides and pesticides

The basic biochemical similarities between all groups of plants and animals demand careful examination of active ingredients before their commercial release; otherwise serious damage or death to non-target organisms, particularly humans, may result.

Regulations under the **Food and Environmental Protection Act 1985 (FEPA)** control the approval of pesticide products in terms of their safety to humans and wildlife. The lethal dose figure (LD_{50}), expressing the amount of active ingredient in milligrams which kills 1 kg of animal tissue, dictates to a large extent the precautions needed for a grower to safely mix and apply a product. The lower the LD_{50} figure for a chemical, the more toxic it is. The label present on each packet or bottle of pesticide must provide detailed instructions with regard to precautions and protective clothing required for a chemical's safe usage. The amount of protection stated on the label commonly reflects the LD_{50} status of the toxic ingredient. Highly toxic chemicals, e.g. the soil-sterilant methyl bromide ($LD_{50} = 1$), must be applied only by specially trained personnel.

The Control of Substances Hazardous to Health Regulations 1988 (COSHH) requires the horticulturist to assess whether each pesticide application is necessary. They also require the use of the safest ingredients, equipment and protective clothing to reduce the risk to humans.

Health and Safety Regulations 1975, summarized in the government 'Poisonous Chemicals on the Farm' leaflet, specify the correct procedures for pesticide use. A detailed register must be kept of spraying operations and any dizziness or illness reported. Correct washing facilities must be provided. A lockable dry store is necessary to keep chemicals safe. Warnings of spraying operations should be prominently displayed. Suitable first aid measures should be available. Used pesticide containers should be burnt or buried in a safe place.

Protective clothing appropriate to the pesticide should be worn. A one-piece fabric coverall suit with a hood protects most of the body from diluted pesticide. Rubberized suits may be used in conditions of greater danger, e.g. in an enclosed greenhouse environment when dealing with ultra-low volume spray, or when applying upward-directed sprays into orchards. Rubber boots should be worn inside the legs of the suit. Thick gauge gauntlets are worn outside the suit when dealing with concentrates, but inside when spraying. Face shields should be worn when mixing toxic concentrates. A face mask covering the mouth and/or nose is capable of filtering out less toxic active ingredients from sprays, but a **respirator** with its large filter is required for toxic products, particularly when used in greenhouses where toxic fume levels build up.

Wildlife. Pesticides should not be sprayed near ponds and streams unless designed for aquatic weed control. Crops frequented by **bees**, e.g. apples and beans, should be sprayed with insecticides only in the evening when most of the insects' foraging has ceased. Beekeepers should be informed of spraying operations. Very long-lasting insecticides, e.g. gamma-HCH and DDT, are no longer used because they were shown to accumulate in concentration along the food chains (*see* page 10). The levels of pesticide present in predators such as hawks rose to such high levels that legislative action became a necessity. Public and government awareness of pesticide dangers have resulted in more wide-ranging legislation under Section III of the **FEPA**. This requires that chemical manufacturers, distributors and professional horticulturists show demonstrable skills in the choice and application of pesticides. The Act also seeks to make information about pesticides available to the public.

Phytotoxicity

Phytotoxicity (or plant damage) may occur when pesticides are unthinkingly applied to plants. Soil applied insecticides, e.g. aldicarb, cause pot plants, e.g. begonias, to go yellow if used at more than the recommended rate. Plants growing in greenhouses are more susceptible because their leaf cuticle is thinner than plants growing at cooler temperatures. Careful examination of the pesticide (particularly **herbicide**) packet labels often prevents this form of damage.

FURTHER READING

Alford, D. (editor) *Pest and Disease Management Handbook* (Blackwell Science Ltd, 2000).

Brown, L.V. *Applied Principles of Horticulture*, 2nd edition (Butterworth-Heinemann, 2002).

Cremlyn, R.J. *Agrochemicals, Preparation and Mode of Action* (Wiley, 1991).

Debach, P. *Biological Control by Natural Enemies* (Cambridge University Press, 1991).

Dent, D. *Integrated Pest Management* (Chapman & Hall, 1995).

Hance, R.J. and Holly, K. *Weed Control Handbook*, Vol. 1 (Blackwell Scientific Publications, 1990).

Helyer, N. *et al. A Colour Handbook of Biological Control in Plant Protection* (Manson Publishing, 2003).

Hussey, N.W. and Scopes, N. *Biological Pest Control* (Blandford Press, 1985).

Ingram, D.S. *et al.* (editors) *Science and the Garden* (Blackwell Science Ltd, 2002).

Ivens, G.W. *Plant Protection in the Garden* (British Crop Protection Council, 1989).

Lever, B.E. *Crop Protection Chemicals* (Ellis Horwood, 1990).

Lloyd, J. *Plant Health Care for Woody Ornamentals* (1997).

Van Emden, H.F. and Peahall, D. *Beyond Silent Spring – Integrated Pest Control and Chemical Safety* (Chapman & Hall, 1996).

Whitehead, R. (editor) *UK Pesticide Guide* (CABI Publishing, 2003).

13

Soil as a Growing Medium

The plant takes up water and nutrients from the growing medium through its roots, which also provide anchorage (see root structure). The root also requires a supply of oxygen and produces carbon dioxide, which is harmful if it builds up in the root zone (see respiration).

In order to secure water throughout the season the roots penetrate deep into the soil. The plant nutrients are extracted from a very dilute soil solution and so the roots must explore thoroughly in the top layers to maintain nutrient supplies. Consequently, the roots are normally very extensive and with a shape that brings the maximum absorptive surface into contact with soil particle surfaces around which is the water and nutrients. Within one growing season a single plant growing in open ground develops some 700 km of root, which has a surface area of 250m^2; and 700 m^2 if the surface area includes the root hairs. The vast root system that develops is usually more than is required to supply the plant in times of plenty but the extent of the root system is indicative of what the plant needs to protect itself against unfavourable conditions. It also serves to remind horticulturists of what has to be provided when growth is restricted accidentally or deliberately. When growing in containers, there is the opportunity to provide an ideal growing medium but the continued supply of water and nutrients becomes more critical (see Chapter 17).

In this chapter, the formation and development of different soils is explained and the characteristics of the main soil types found in the British Isles are outlined. The nature of soil is detailed and its qualities as a root environment are explored. The basis of managing soils as a growing medium for horticultural plants is established.

ROOT REQUIREMENTS

The growing tip of the root wriggles through the growing medium following the line of least resistance. Roots are able to enter cracks that are, or can be readily opened up to, about 0.2 mm in diameter, which is about the thickness of a pencil line. Compacted soils severely restrict **root exploration** but once into these narrow channels the root is able to overcome great resistance to increase its diameter. Anything, which reduces root exploration and activity, can limit plant growth. When this happens action must be taken to remove the obstruction to root growth or to supply adequate **air**, **water** and **nutrients** through the restricted root volume.

The root normally provides the **anchorage** needed to secure the plant in the soil. Plants, notably trees with a full leaf canopy, become vulnerable if their roots are in loose material, in soil made fluid by high water content or are restricted, e.g. shallow roots over rock strata close to the surface. Until their roots have penetrated extensively into the surrounding soil, transplants are very susceptible to **wind rocking**: water uptake remains limited as roots become detached from the soil and delicate root growth is broken off. The plant may be left less upright.

In order to grow and take up water and nutrients, the root must have an **energy** supply. A constant supply of energy is only possible so long as oxygen is brought to the site of uptake (*see* respiration). Consequently the soil spaces around the root must contain air as well as water. There must be good gaseous exchange between the atmosphere around the root and the soil surface. This may sometimes be achieved by the selection of plants that have modifications of their structure that enables this to occur throughout the plant tissues (*see* adaptations), but is normally a result of maintaining a suitable soil structure. A lack of oxygen or a build-up of carbon dioxide will reduce the root's activity. Furthermore, in these conditions anaerobic bacteria will proliferate and many produce toxins such as ethylene. In warm summer conditions roots can be killed back after 1 or 2 days in waterlogged soils.

COMPOSITION OF SOILS

Mineral soils form in layers of rock fragments over the Earth's surface. They are made up of mineral matter comprising **sand**, **silt** and **clay** particles. There is also a small quantity of organic matter which is the part derived from living organisms. This framework of solid material retains water and gases in the gaps or **pore space**. The water contains dissolved materials including plant nutrients and oxygen, and is known as the **soil solution**. The **soil atmosphere** normally comprises nitrogen, rather less oxygen and rather more carbon dioxide than in normal air and traces of other gases. Finally, a soil capable of sustaining plants is alive with **micro-organisms** (organisms, such as bacteria, fungi and nematodes, too small to be seen with the naked eye). Larger organisms such as earthworms and insects are also normally present (*see* page 35).

The composition of a typical mineral soil is given in Figure 13.1, which also illustrates the variation

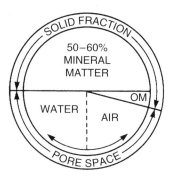

Figure 13.1 *Composition of a typical cultivated soil. The solid fraction of the soil is made up of mineral (50–60 per cent) and organic matter (OM), (1–5 per cent). This leaves a total pore space of 35–50 per cent that is filled by air and water, the proportions of which vary constantly.*

that can occur. The content of the pore space varies continually as the soil dries out and is re-wetted. The spaces can be altered by the compaction or 'opening up' of the soil which in turn has a significant effect on the proportions of air and water being held.

Over a longer period the organic matter level can vary. The composition of the soil can be influenced by many factors and, under cultivation, these have to be managed to provide a suitable root environment. Organic soils have a considerably higher organic matter content and are dealt with in Chapter 15.

SOIL FORMATION

The Earth is formed from a ball of molten rock minerals. The least dense rocks floated on the top and as they cooled the surface layer of granite, with basalt just below, solidified to form the Earth's crust. The Earth's surface has had a long and turbulent history during which it has frequently fractured, crumpled, lifted and fallen, with more molten material being pushed up from below through the breaks in the crust and in volcanoes.

Weathering and erosion

From the moment rocks are formed and exposed to the elements they are subjected to **weathering**, the breakdown of rocks, and **erosion**, the movement of rock fragments and soil.

Chemical weathering is mainly brought about by the action of **carbonic acid** that is produced wherever carbon dioxide and water mix, as in rainfall. Some rock minerals dissolve and are washed away. Others are altered by various chemical reactions, most of which occur when the rock surface is exposed to the atmosphere. All but the inert parts of rock are eventually decomposed and the rock crumbles as new minerals are formed and soluble material is released. **Oxidation** is particularly important in the formation of iron oxides, which give soils their red and yellow (when aerobic), or blue and grey colours (in anaerobic conditions).

Physical or mechanical weathering processes break the rock into smaller and smaller particles without any change in the chemical character of the minerals. This occurs on exposed rock surfaces along with chemical weathering but, in contrast, has little effect on rocks protected by layers of soil. The main agents of physical weathering are frost, heat, water, wind and ice. In temperate zones, frost is a major weathering agent. Water percolates into cracks in the rock and expands on freezing. The pressures created shatter the rock and, as the water melts, a new surface is exposed to weathering. In hot climates the rock surface can become very much hotter than the underlying layers. The strains created by the different amounts of expansion and the alternate expansion and contraction cause fragments of rock to flake off the surface; this is sometimes known as the 'onion skin' effect. Moving water or wind carries fragments of rock that rub against other rocks and rock fragments, wearing them down. Where there are glaciers the rock is worn away by the 'scrubbing brush' effect of a huge mass of ice loaded with stones and boulders bearing down on the underlying rock.

Biological weathering is attributable to organisms such as mosses, ferns and flowering plants which fragment rock by both chemical and physical means, e.g. they produce carbon dioxide which, in conjunction with water, forms carbonic acid; roots penetrate cracks in the rock and, as they grow

thicker, they exert pressure which further opens up the cracks.

Igneous rocks

Igneous rocks are those formed from the molten material of the Earth's crust. All other rock types, as well as soil, are ultimately derived from them. When examined closely, most igneous rocks can be seen to be a mixture of crystals. For example, **granite** contains crystals of quartz, white and shiny, felspars that are grey or pink, and micas, which are shiny black (*see* Plate 19). Many of these crystalline materials have a limited use in landscaping as formal structures rather than in the construction of rock gardens.

As granite is weathered ('rotted') the felspars are converted to kaolinite (one of the many forms of clay) and soluble potassium, sodium and calcium, which are the basis of plant nutrition. Similarly, the mica present is chemically changed. Whilst the clays retain much of the potassium, the other soluble material is carried by water to the sea making the sea 'salty'. The inert quartz grains are released and form sand grains.

Sedimentary rocks

Sedimentary rock is derived from accumulated fragments of rock. Most have been formed in the sea or lakes to which agents of erosion carry weathered rock. Organisms in the seas with shells die and accumulate on the bottom of the sea. Layers of sediment build up and, under pressure and slow chemical change, eventually become rock strata such as shale, chalk or limestone. In subsequent earth movements much of it has been raised up above sea level and weathered again. Similarly, the sand grains that accumulate to great depths in desert areas eventually become sandstones.

Moving water and winds are able to carry rock particles and are thus important agents of erosion. As their velocity increases, the '**load**' they are able to carry increases substantially. The fast-moving water in streams is able to carry large particles but in the slower-moving rivers some of the load is dropped. The particles settle out in order of size (*see* settling velocities). This leads to the **sorting** of rock fragments, i.e. material is moved and deposited according to particle size. By the time the rivers have reached the sea or lakes only the finest sands, silts and clays are in the water. As the river slows on meeting the sea or lake all but clay is dropped. The clay eventually settles slowly in the still water of the sea or lake. Moving ice is also an agent of erosion but the load dropped on melting consists of unsorted particles known as **boulder clay** or till.

The type of sedimentary rock formed depends on the nature of its ingredients. Sandstones, silt-stones and mudstones are examples of sedimentary rocks derived from sorted particles in which characteristic layering is readily seen (*see* Plate 19). Limestones are formed from the accumulation of shells or the precipitation of materials from solution mixed with varying amounts of deposited mud. Chalk is a particularly pure form derived from the calcium carbonate remains of minute organisms that lived in seas in former times. Many of these are attractive materials for use in hard landscaping, where care should be taken to align the strata (layers) for a natural effect.

Metamorphic rocks

Metamorphic rock is formed from igneous or sedimentary rocks. The extreme pressures and temperatures associated with movements and fracturing in the Earth's crust or the effect of huge depths of rock on underlying strata over very long periods of time has altered them. Slate is formed from shale, quartzite from sandstone, and marble from limestone. Metamorphic rock tends to be more resistant to weathering than the original rock.

SOIL DEVELOPMENT

Soil development occurs in the loose rock fragments overlying the Earth's crust. This is the parent material that has an important effect on the nature of the soil formed. However, the soil formed is also influenced by climate, vegetation, topography, drainage as well as animals including man and time. Young soils (regosols) are those that have just formed, but over time they take on characteristics that depend on the influence of the other factors to give rise to the main soil types.

Topography is the detailed description of land features that are the result of the interaction between the underlying rocks, the agents of weathering and erosion, and time. The landscape may look as though it is quite stable but even dramatic mountain ranges are worn down to flat plains, a process that has occurred several times in the history of the Earth following the numerous crustal disturbances.

On rocks and rock debris plant growth begins with mosses and lichens that help to stabilize the loose material by binding the surface and reducing wind speed over the surface. The dead plants become incorporated in the young soils and their breakdown products also help hold it together. The released nutrients are held in the top surface and recycled by a complex colony of soil organisms instead of being washed away (*see* nutrient cycles). As the young soil deepens, larger plants are able to develop. Their roots help stabilize the soil further and, along with the carbonic acid they produce, extend the depth of weathering. The process of soil formation, which takes thousands of years, speeds up as the particles become more finely divided (*see* surface area) and the living organisms become established.

The physical characteristics of soil in the field are normally described with reference to the layers, or horizons, revealed by digging a soil pit (*see* Figure 13.2). In the **soil profile** so exposed, the organic litter on the surface that has not been incorporated in the soil is usually referred to as the 'L' layer. The upper layer of the soil from which components are normally washed downward is the 'A' horizon, usually recognized by its darker colouring, which is a result of the significant levels of humus present. The lighter layer below it, where finer materials tend to accumulate, is the 'B' or illuvial horizon. Under cultivation, the 'A' horizon

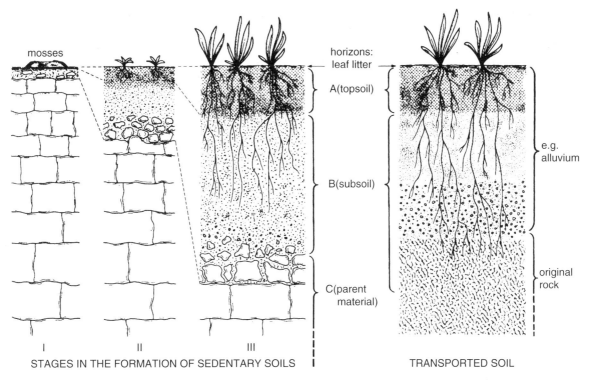

Figure 13.2 *The development from a young soil consisting of a few fragments of rock particles to a deep sedentary soil is shown alongside a transported soil. A subsoil, topsoil and leaf litter layer can be identified in each soil.*

broadly aligns with the 'topsoil' and the 'B' with the 'subsoil'. The parent material below these is the 'C' horizon and where there is an underlying unweathered rock layer it is often known as bedrock.

Sedentary soils

Sedentary soils develop in the material gradually weathered from the underlying rock. True sedentary soils are uncommon because most loose rock is eroded, but the same process can be seen where great depths of transported material have formed the parent material, as in the boulder clays left behind after the Ice Ages. A hole dug in such a soil shows the gradual transition from unweathered rock to an organic matter rich topsoil (Figure 13.2). Under cultivation a distinct topsoil develops in the plough zone.

Transported soils

Transported soils are those that form in eroded material that has been carried from sites of weathering sometimes many hundreds of miles away from where deposition has occurred, e.g. by glaciers. They can be recognized by the definite boundary between the eroded material and the underlying rock and its associated rock fragments.

Where more than one soil material has been transported to the site, as in many river valleys, several distinct layers can be seen. The right-hand part of Figure 13.2 shows an example.

Raindrops striking soil dislodge loose particles that tend to move downhill. As a result, surface soil is slowly removed from higher ground and accumulates at the bottom of slopes. This means that soils on slopes tend to be shallow, whereas at the bottom of the slopes deep, transported soils develop, known as **colluvial** soils. Material washed away in running water eventually settles out according to particle size. The river valley bottoms become covered with material, called alluvium, in which **alluvial** soils develop. Wind removes dry sands and silts that are not 'bound in' to the soil and large areas have become covered with wind-blown deposits known as 'loess' or 'brick earth'. Many of these transported soils provide ideal rooting conditions for horticultural crops because they tend to be deep, loose and open. Most are easily cultivated. However, those that have a high silt or fine sand content, notably the brick earths, may be prone to compaction.

SOIL TYPES

Soils continue to undergo changes under the influence of **climate**, **vegetation**, **topography** and **drainage** which interact over **time** to give rise, in the British Isles, to four main types of mineral soil: **brown earths**, **gleys**, **rendzinas** and **podsols** (*see* Plate 22). **Peats** develop in waterlogged conditions (*see* organic soils, page 190).

Brown earth soils develop in the well-drained medium to heavy soils in the lowlands of the British Isles. They are associated with a climax vegetation of broadleaved woodland especially oak, ash and sycamore, the roots of which have ensured that nutrients moving down the soil profile are captured and returned to the soil via the leaf fall. Surplus water does not accumulate and the soil remains aerobic for most of the year. The plentiful earthworms incorporate the deep litter layers. The resultant dark A horizon ('topsoil') rich in organic matter (a 'mull') mergers gradually into a bright brown and deep B horizon ('subsoil'). The soil structures that develop in the surface layers are granular and rounded fine blocky in which there is an excellent balance of air and water and into which roots can readily penetrate.

These soils are usually mildly acid (pH 5.5–6.5), but **acid brown earths** (pH 5.5–4.5) can develop on lighter-textured soils in wetter areas (800–1000 mm per year) especially under beech or birch woodland.

There is less earthworm activity with a resultant reduced incorporation of organic matter down the profile. The soil structure is usually less satisfactory and clay particles that work their way down can form clay pans (*see* page 165) in the B horizon. These can be productive soils if ameliorated with lime and fertilizer (*see* Chapter 16).

Gleys occur in poorly drained soils (*see* page 176). **Surface water gleys** occur where the percolation of water is restricted by the poor structure in the A or B horizon to produce a perched water table (*see* page 173). This is typically where the subsoil is heavy and impervious especially in wetter regions. Oxygen in the waterlogged soil is depleted and, in these anaerobic conditions below the water table, the iron oxides that colour the soil become dull grey or bluey (in aerobic conditions the iron oxides are rust coloured). The extent of the waterlogging that the soil has been subjected to as the water table fluctuates can be judged from the degree to which it has become completely grey; usually there is a rusty mottle present indicating that aerobic conditions exist in the soil for part of the year (*see* Plate 23). Plants growing in them are often shallow rooted and suffer from drought in dry periods. These soils are only productive after they have been drained, limed and fertilized.

Ground water gleys develop where there is a permanent water table that is very near the surface of the soil so that to lower the water table the drainage has to be undertaken on a regional basis, e.g. Romney Marsh. Drainage pipes can only be used when the water can run to a ditch with a water level below that desired in the field; for some areas this can only be achieved by maintaining an artificially low level by the use of pumps (powered in former times by windmills).

Podsols (from the Russian meaning 'ash like') are strongly leached, very acid soils that develop on freely draining soils such as coarse sands and gravels commonly under heather or pine or spruce forest in high rainfall areas. Because of the high acidity levels, earthworms are absent so there is a build-up of the litter layer. Poorly decomposed organic matter that is not incorporated (a 'mor' humus) is characteristic of this soil type. Some of the organic matter combines with the iron in the top layers to form soluble compounds, which are leached ('podsolization') to leave a grey ('ash like') A horizon (all that remains are bleached sand grains). These compound become insoluble again in the conditions that prevail in the B horizon where organic matter accumulates to create a dark or black horizon below which is an iron-rich red layer. The iron compounds that accumulate can form a strongly cemented 'iron pan'. As a continuous pan that water (and roots) cannot penetrate is formed, a waterlogged area develops and peat can form at the surface.

Podsols are droughty and 'hungry' soils that require considerable ongoing inputs of lime and manures to make them productive. They are of little use in horticulture except for the growing of acid-loving trees and shrubs.

Rendzinas are very thin dark-brown, sometimes black, soils with a strong granular structure sitting directly onto chalk or limestone. They are typical of the soils on the steeper slopes of chalk or limestone hills under grass. Shallow soils develop because the continued erosion on the slopes, which also keeps these soils heavily charged with lime. Where the soils become deeper on the less severe slopes it is common for the A horizons to become acid as the lime is leached downwards. They are well drained because of the slope and because of the porous nature of the underlying rock. Rendzinas are not suitable for most horticultural purposes because the high lime content causes induced nutrient deficiencies (*see* page 205). Roots are severely restricted by the shallow soils and vulnerable to drought.

SOIL COMPONENTS

The solid parts of soils consist of mineral matter derived from rocks and organic matter derived from living organisms. Levels of organic matter are dealt with in Chapter 15. **Most soils have predominantly mineral particles that vary enormously in size from boulders, stones and gravels down to the soil particles, sand, silt and clay.**

Particle size classes

There is a continuous range of particle sizes but it is convenient to divide them into classes. Three major classification systems in use today are those of the International Society of Soil Science (ISSS), United States Department of Agriculture (USDA) and the Soil Survey of England and Wales (SSEW). These are illustrated in Figures 13.3 and 13.4. In the text the SSEW scale used by the Agricultural Development and Advisory Service of England and Wales (ADAS) is adopted. In each case, **soil is considered to consist of those particles that are less than 2 mm in diameter.** The silt and clay particles are sometimes referred to as 'fines'.

Sand

Sand grains are particles between 0.06 and 2.0 mm in diameter. They are gritty to the touch; even fine

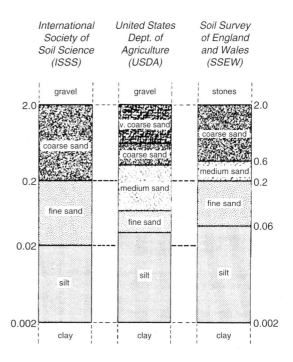

Figure 13.3 *Particle size classes (diameters in mm).*

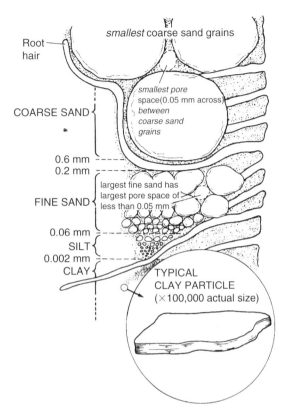

Figure 13.4 *The relative sizes of coarse sand, fine sand, silt and clay particles (based on SSEW classification) with root hairs drawn alongside for comparison. Note that even the smallest pore spaces between unaggregated spherical coarse sand grains still allow water to be drawn out by gravity and allow some air in at field capacity, whereas most pores between unaggregated fine sand grains remain water filled (pores less than 0.05 mm diameter).*

sand has an abrasive feel. Sand is mainly composed of quartz. (Although any particle of this size is a sand grain, it is most often quartz because, unlike other minerals, it resists weathering.)

The shape of the particles varies from the rough and angular sand to more weathered, rounded grains. They are frequently coated with iron oxides, giving sand colours from very pale yellow to rich, rusty brown. Silver sand has no iron oxide covering. Chemically most of the sand grains are **inert**;

they neither release nor hold on to plant nutrients and they are not cohesive.

The influence of sand on the soil is mainly physical and as such the size of the particles is the important factor. As the particles become smaller and the volume of individual grains decreases, the **surface area** of the same quantity of sand becomes greater. Taking a cube and then cutting it up into smaller cubes readily demonstrates this (Figure 13.5). While the total volume is the same in all the small cubes compared with the original large cube, the sides of each are smaller but the total surface area is much greater because new surfaces have been exposed. Many soil particle characteristics are directly related to particle size and in particular to surface area. Sand grains are non-porous so their water-holding properties are directly related to their surface areas. It can be readily seen that, since water will not flow through gaps less than about 0.05 mm in diameter, there are very big differences in the drainage characteristics of coarse and fine sands (Figure 13.4). Consequently, soils dominated by coarse sand are usually free draining but have poor water retention, whereas those composed mainly of unaggregated fine sand hold large quantities of water against gravity. The water held on all sand particles is readily removed by roots (*see* water, available).

Clay

Clay particles are those less than 0.002 mm in diameter. There are many different clay minerals, e.g. kaolinite, montmorillinite, vermiculite, and mica, all of which are derived from rock minerals by chemical weathering. Most clay minerals have a layered crystalline structure and are plate like in appearance (Figure 13.4). The clay particles have surface charges that give clay its very important and characteristic property of **cation exchange**. The charges are predominantly negative which means that the clay platelets attract positively charged **cations** in the soil solution. These include the nutrients potassium, as K^+; ammonia, as NH_4^+; magnesium, as Mg^{++}; and calcium, as Ca^{++}, as well as

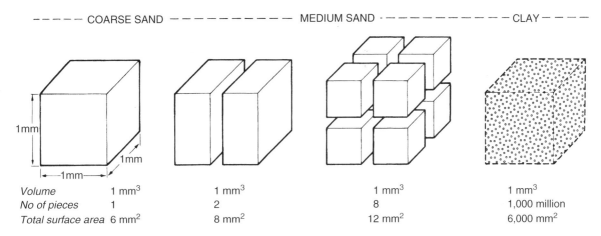

Figure 13.5 *Surface area of soil particles. The effect of subdividing a cube corresponding in size to a grain of coarse sand. The same volume of medium sand is made up of over eight times more pieces that have a total surface area more than double that of coarse sand. It requires over a 1000 million of the largest clay particles to make up the volume of one grain of coarse sand and their total surface area is approximately 1000 times greater.*

hydrogen and aluminium ions. These ions are held in an **exchangeable** way so that they remain available to plants but are prevented from being leached unless displaced by other cations. The greater the **cation exchange capacity**, the greater the reserves of cations held this way.

Hydrogen and aluminium cations make the soil acid. The other cations Ca^{++}, Mg^{++}, K^+ and Na^+ are called **bases** and make soils more alkaline (*see* soil pH). The proportion of the cation exchange capacity occupied by bases is known as its **percentage base saturation**. A soil's **buffering capacity**, i.e. its ability to resist changes in soil pH, also depends on these surface reactions. The presence of high levels of exchangeable aluminium and hydrogen means that very large quantities of calcium, in the form of lime, are required to raise the pH of acid clays. In contrast only small quantities of lime are needed to raise the pH of a sand by the same amount (*see* liming).

The clay particles are so small that the minute electrical forces on the surface become dominant (Figure 13.5); thus clay and water mixtures behave as colloids. Note that as a particle is subdivided the total surface area increases; the surface area doubles each time the sides of the individual

pieces are reduced by half. In particles that are less than 0.001 mm in diameter, which includes most clay, colloidal properties are observed; most notably the properties of their surface dominate their chemical behaviour. **Colloids** are mixtures that are in permanent suspension (*see* Table 13.1). Water-based colloids, such as clay, are 'runny' when mixed with plenty of water (a 'sol') but with less water they are stiff and jelly like (a 'gel'), e.g. paste. As they dry, these mixtures become sticky and eventually hard. Many natural materials such as gelatin, starch, gums and protoplasm (mainly protein and water) are colloidal. This gives clay soil properties of cohesion, plasticity, shrinkage and swelling. The small particles can pack and stick together very closely and in a continuous mass they restrict water movement.

The water-holding capacity of clay-dominated soils is very high because of the large surface areas and because many of the particles are porous. However, a high proportion of the water is held too tightly for roots to extract (*see* water, available). Moist balls of clay are plastic, i.e. can be moulded. On drying, they harden and some may shrink. In the soil, the cracks that form on shrinking become an important network of drainage channels. The

Table 13.1 Colloidal systems

Mixture	Colloidal system	Examples
Solid dispersed in gas	Solid aerosol	Smoke, dusts
Solid dispersed in liquid	Sol or gel	Paste, clay, humus, protoplasm
Liquid dispersed in gas	Liquid aerosol	Mist, fog
Liquid dispersed in liquid	Emulsion	Milk
Gas dispersed in gas		Atmosphere
Gas dispersed in liquid	Foam	Fire extinguishers, soap

cracks remain open until the soils are re-wetted and the clay swells. Humus and calcium appear to combine with clay in such a way that when the combination dries, extensive cracking occurs and favourable growing conditions result. Some clays are non-shrinking and are consequently more difficult to manage, although they present less problems with regard to building foundations.

Silt

Silt particles are those between 0.002 and 0.06 mm in diameter. Most in this size range are inert and non-porous like sands but many particles, including felspar fragments, have the properties of clay. Soils dominated by silt do have a small cation exchange capacity but in the main they behave more like a very fine sand. They have very good water-holding capacity and plants can take up a high proportion of this water. When wetted they have a distinctly soapy or silky feel. Silt soils are made up of particles that readily pack closely together but have little ability to form stable crumbs (*see* soil aggregates). This makes them particularly difficult to manage.

Stones and gravel

Particles larger than 2 mm in diameter are known variously as grit, gravel, stones and boulders, according to size. The effect of stones on cultivated areas depends on the type of stone, size and the proportion in the soil. The presence of even a few stones larger than 20 cm prevents cultivation. Stones in general have detrimental effects on mechanized work; ploughshares, tines and tyres are worn more quickly, especially if the stones are hard and sharp such as broken flint. Stones interfere with drilling of seeds and the harvesting of roots. Close cutting of grasses is more hazardous where there are protruding stones. Mole draining becomes less effective in stony soils and large stones make it impossible.

Stones can accumulate in layers and become interlocked to form **stone pans**. In very gravelly soils the water-holding capacity is much reduced and the increased leaching leads to acid patches. Nutrient reserves are also reduced by the dilution of the soil with inert material. However, stones can help water infiltration, protect the surface from capping and check erosion by wind or water.

SOIL TEXTURE

Soil texture describes the composition of a soil. In most cultivated soils the mineral content forms the framework and exerts a major influence on its characteristics.

Although there is no universally accepted definition of **soil texture**, it can usefully be defined as **the relative proportions of the sand, silt and clay particles in the soil**. Examples of different textures are given in Figure 13.6. Texture can be considered to be a fixed characteristic and provides a useful guide to a soil's potential. Fine-textured soils such as clays, clay loam, silts and fine sands have good

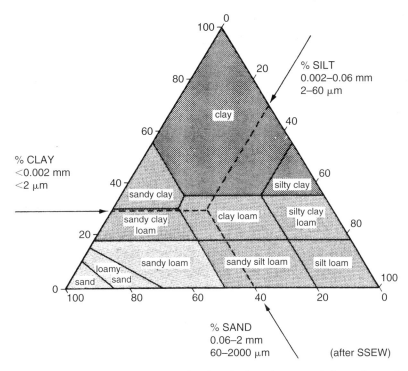

Figure 13.6 *Soil textural triangle. The soil texture can be identified on this type of chart when at least two of the major size of fractions are known, e.g. 40 per cent sand, 30 per cent silt and 30 per cent clay is a clay loam (SSEW Soil-Particle Size Classification).*

water-holding properties; whereas coarse-textured soils have low water-holding capacity but good drainage. This also means that **soil temperatures** are closely related to soil texture because water has a very much higher specific heat value than soil minerals. Consequently freely draining, coarse sand warms up more quickly in the spring but is also more vulnerable to frosts than wetter soils.

Soils with high clay contents have good general nutrient retention, whereas nutrients are readily lost from sandy soils, especially those with a high coarse sand fraction. The application rate of pesticides and herbicides is often related to soil texture. The power requirement to cultivate a clay soil is very much greater than that for a sandy soil. The expression 'heavy' for clay and 'light' for sandy soils is derived from this difference in working properties rather than the actual weight of the soil. The texture of a soil also influences the soil structure and soil cultivations. In general the texture of a

soil can be considered to be a fixed character. The addition of a calcareous clay to a sandy topsoil, a practice known as **marling**, can improve its water-holding capacity as well as reducing wind erosion, but it requires the incorporation of 500 t of dry clay per hectare to convert it to a sandy loam. The practice of adding clay is now largely confined to the building of cricket squares. To 'lighten' a clay loam topsoil to a sandy loam, more than 2000 t of dry sand is needed on each hectare. The addition of smaller quantities of sand is often an expensive exercise to no effect; at worst it can make the resultant soil more difficult to manage.

Mechanical analysis of soils

Soil texture can be determined by finding the particle size distribution. There are several methods but all depend on the complete separation of the particles, the destruction of organic matter and the removal of particles greater than 2 mm in diameter. Sieving can separate the stones, coarse sand, medium sand and fine sand fractions.

Finer particles are usually separated by taking advantage of their different **settling velocities** when in suspension. The settling velocity of a particle depends on its density and radius, the viscosity and density of the liquid and the acceleration due to gravity, the method is simplified by assuming that soil particles are spherical and have the same density and the investigations are conducted in water at 20°C.

Particles that are less than 0.001 mm in diameter are kept permanently in suspension by the bombardment of vibrating water molecules and are referred to as **colloids**, e.g. most clay particles. All sand particles will have fallen more than 10 cm after 50 seconds: so a sample taken at that depth can be used to calculate the clay plus silt left in the suspension. A sample taken at this depth after 8 hours will only contain particles less than 0.002 mm in diameter, i.e. clay alone. The soil texture can be deduced from this information using a **textural triangle** (Figure 13.6), which is the basis of identifying soil types.

Texturing by feel

A more practical method of determining soil texture, especially in the field, is by feel. This can, with experience, be a very accurate means of distinguishing between over 30 categories.

A ball of soil about the size of a walnut is moistened and worked between the fingers to remove particles greater than 2 mm and to break down the soil crumbs. It is essential that this preparation is thorough or the effect of the silt and clay particles will be masked.

Sands are soils that have little cohesion. **Sand** has little tendency to bind even when wetted and it cannot be rolled out into a 'worm'. **A loamy sand** has sufficient cohesiveness to be rolled into a 'worm' but it readily falls apart. What is generally known as **loam**, moulds readily into a cohesive ball

and it has no dominant feel of grittiness, silkiness or stickiness. If grittiness is detected and the ball is readily deformed it is a **sandy loam**. If it is readily deformed but has a silky feel it is **silty loam**. **Clay loams** bind together strongly, do not readily deform, and take a polish when rubbed with the finger. **Clays** bind together and are very difficult to deform. A **clay** soil readily takes a very marked polish. If there is also a feeling of silkiness it is a **silty clay**, but if grittiness, it is a **sandy clay**. Wherever grittiness is detected, the designation sand can be further qualified by stating whether it is coarse, medium or fine sand, e.g. coarse sandy loam. Table 13.2 shows the range of textural groupings commonly used.

Determining texture by feel has the limitation that the influence of organic matter and chalk cannot be eliminated. Chalk tends to give a soil a silky or gritty feel but the fact that a soil is known to be chalky should not influence the texturing. Its textural class may be prefixed 'calcareous', e.g. calcareous silty clay. **Organic matter** tends to increase the cohesiveness of light soils, reduce the cohesiveness of heavy soils and large quantities can impart a silky or greasy feel. The prefix 'organic' can be used for describing mineral soils with 6–20 per cent organic matter. Soils with 20–35 per cent organic matter are **peaty loams**, 35–50 per cent organic matter **loamy peats** and soils with greater than 50 per cent organic matter are termed **peat** (*see* organic soils).

SOIL STRUCTURE

Soil structure **is the arrangement of particles in the soil**. In order to provide a suitable root environment for cultivated plants the soil must be constructed in such a way as to allow good gaseous exchange whilst holding adequate reserves of available water. There should be a high water infiltration rate, free drainage and an interconnected network of spaces allowing roots to find water and nutrients without hindrance. There should be no large cavities that prevent thorough contact between soil and roots, and allow roots to dry out in the seedbed. The soil should be managed so that

Table 13.2 Soil texture classification based on hand texturing

Textural class	Symbol	Textural group*	'Sands' 'Other'†	
Coarse sand	CS			
Sand	S			
Fine sand	FS	Sands		
Very fine sand	VFS			
Loamy coarse sand	LCS			
			'Sands'	
Loamy sand	LS			
Loamy fine sand	LFS	Very light soils		
Coarse sandy loam	CSL			
Loamy very fine sand	LVFS			
Sandy loam	SL	Light soils		
Fine sandy loam	FSL			
Very fine sandy loam	VFSL			
Silty loam	ZyL	Medium soils		
Loam	L			
Sandy clay loam	SCL			
Clay loam	CL		'Other'	
Silt loam	ZL	Heavy soils		
Silty clay loam	ZyCL			
Sandy clay	SC			
Clay	C	Very heavy soils		
Silty clay	ZyC			

*Commonly used for determining soil-acting herbicide application rates.
†Commonly used for determining fertilizer application or flooding levels.

erosion is minimized. Good structural stability should be maintained so that the structure does not deteriorate and limit crop growth.

Porosity

The plant roots and soil organisms live in the pores between the solid components of the growing medium. In the same way that a house is mainly judged by the living accommodation created by the bricks, wood, plaster, cement, etc., so a soil is evaluated by examining the spaces created. In general the smallest pores, **micropores**, contain only water that rarely dries out and is unavailable to plants (*see* permanent wilting point). The middle-sized pores, **mesopores**, contain water available to plants and the air moves in as it is removed by plant roots. Pores greater than about 0.05 mm in diameter, called **macropores**, can drain easily to allow in air within hours of being saturated, i.e. fully wetted. Ideally there should be sufficient mesopores to ensure good retention of available water, but sufficient macropores to allow free drainage, gaseous exchange and thorough root exploration as shown in Figure 13.7.

The key to managing most growing media is in maintaining a high proportion of air-filled pores without restricting water supply. An important indicator of a satisfactory growing medium is its air-filled porosity or air capacity, i.e. the percentage volume filled with air when it has completed draining, having been saturated with water.

Bulk density is the mass of soil per unit volume and it can be measured by taking a core of soil of known volume and weighing it after thorough

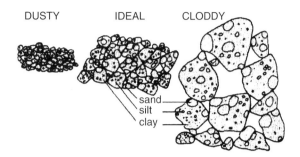

DUSTY   IDEAL   CLODDY

sand
silt
clay

Figure 13.7 *Tilth. The ideal tilth for most seedbeds is made up of soil aggregates between 0.5 and 5mm diameter. Within these crumbs are predominantly small pores (less than 0.05 mm) that hold water and between the crumbs are large pores (greater than 0.05 mm) that allow easy water movement and contain air when soil is at field capacity (actual size).*

drying. In normal mineral soils results are usually between 1.0 and 1.6 g/ml. The difference is largely attributable to variation in total pore space. Finer-textured soils tend to have more pore space and therefore lower bulk density than sands, but for all soils higher values indicate greater packing or **compaction**.

This information is not only useful to diagnose compaction problems but can also be used to calculate the weight of soil in a given volume. Assuming a cultivated soil to have a bulk density of 1.0 g/ml, the weight of dry soil in 1 ha to a plough depth of 15 cm is 1500 tonnes; when compacted, the same volume weighs 2400 tonnes. Similarly, 1 m³ of a typical topsoil with a bulk density of 1.0 will weigh 1 tonne (1000 kg) when dry and up to half as much again when moist.

Soil structures

The pore space does not depend solely upon the size of the soil particles as shown in Figure 13.4 because they are normally grouped together. These **aggregates**, or peds, are groups of particles held together by the adhesive properties of clay and humus. The ideal arrangement of small and

large pores is illustrated in Figure 13.7 alongside a dusty tilth with too few large pores and a cloddy tilth that has too many large pores.

A soil with a **simple structure** is one in which there is no observable aggregation. If this is because none of the soil particles are joined together, as in sands or loamy sands with low organic matter levels, it is described as **single grain** structure. Where all the particles are joined with no natural lines of weakness the structure is said to be **massive**. A **weakly developed** structure is one in which aggregation is indistinct and the soil, when disturbed, breaks into very few whole aggregates but a lot of unaggregated material. This tends to occur in loamy sands and sandy loams. Soils with a high clay content form **strongly developed** structures in which there are obvious lines of weakness and, when disturbed, aggregates fall away undamaged. The prismatic, angular blocky, round blocky, crumbs and platy structures which are found in soils are illustrated in Figure 13.8.

Development of soil structures

Soil structure develops as the result of the action on the soil components of natural structure-forming **agents**: wetting and drying, freezing and thawing, root growth, soil organisms and cultivations. The wetting and drying cycle can affect the whole rooting depth. Cracks open up in heavier soils as the clay shrinks. As well as being a major factor in the drying of deeper soil layers, the **roots** play an important part in soil structure by growing into the cracks and keeping them open. They help establish the natural fracture lines. In strong structures, a close-fitting arrangement of **prismatic** (*see* Plate 23) or **angular blocky** aggregates is readily seen. In soils with low clay content the roots are vital in maintaining an open structure. The exploring roots probe the soil, opening up channels where the soil is loose enough and producing sideways pressure as they grow. On death, the root leaves behind channels stabilized by its decomposed tissue for other roots to follow. Fine **granular** structures are developed under pastures by the action of the

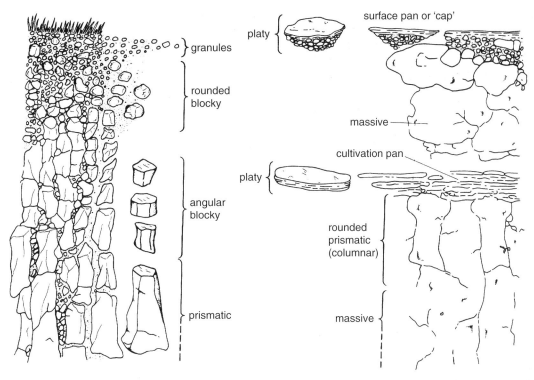

Figure 13.8 *Soil structures. The soil profile on the left is composed of soil particles aggregated into structures that produce good growing conditions. Examples of structures that create a poor rooting environment are shown in the profile on the right.*

fibrous rooting over many years. The soil structure is greatly improved by the root ball. Its physical influence is most easily appreciated by shaking out the soil crumbs from around the root of a tuft of well-established grass and comparing them with the structure of soil taken from a nearby bare patch. The shattering of clods by **frost action**, producing a frost mould, is largely confined to the surface layers and is vital in the management of clays. Freshly exposed land is often referred to as **raw**; when weathered it becomes mellow. Once **mellow**, a seedbed is more easily prepared. The weathering process and influence of cultivation tend to produce rounded blocky **structures** and **rounded granules** in the cultivated zone (Figure 13.8).

Earthworms and other soil organisms play an important part in loosening the soil, maintaining the network of drainage channels and stabilizing the soil structure. **Cultivation** of soil by hand or mechanized implements is undertaken to produce a suitable rooting environment for plants, to destroy pests and weeds, and to mix in plant residues, manures and fertilizers. However, the use of cultivators can lead to the formation of platy layers or **pans**, which are characterized by the lack of vertical cracks and form an obstruction to root and water movement. **Natural pans** develop in some soils as a result of fine material cementing a layer of soil together. In some sandy soils rich in iron oxide, these oxides cement together a layer of sand where there has been a fluctuating water table, to produce an **iron pan**. The collapse of surface crumb structure can lead to the formation of a surface pan, crust or 'cap' (*see* Plate 21).

Structural stability

The structural stability of soil refers to its ability to resist deformation when wet. Soil aggregates with little or no stability collapse spontaneously as they soak up water, i.e. they slake. Those high in fine sand or silt are particularly vulnerable to slaking. Aggregates with better stability maintain their shape when wetted for a short time but gradually pieces fall off if left immersed in water. Aggregates with **good structural stability** are able to resist damage when wet unless vigorously disturbed. Soils with a high clay content have better stability than those with low levels. Stability is also increased by the presence of calcium carbonate (chalk), iron oxides and, most importantly, **humus**.

Tilth

The soil surface or seedbed should be carefully managed to produce the required tilth: the structure of the top 50 mm of the soil. Sandy soils are easily broken down to the right size with cultivation equipment. Heavier soils are less easy to cultivate and benefit from weathering to produce a frost 'mould'.

The fineness of a seedbed should be related to the size of seeds but ideally consists of aggregate or crumbs between 0.5 and 5 mm in diameter (Figure 13.7). Cloddy surfaces lead to poor germination as well as poor results from soil herbicide treatments. The rain on the soil surface breaks down tilth. As soil crumbs break up, the particles fill in the gaps; this reduces infiltration rates. As the surface dries, a **cap** or **pan** is formed. Thus fine 'dusty' tilths should be avoided and the soil crumbs should be stable so that they can withstand the effect of rain until plants are established. This is particularly important on fine sandy and silty soils, which tend to have poor structural stability. In general, fine tilths should be avoided outdoors until well into spring when conditions are becoming more favourable and growth through any developing cap is rapid.

CULTIVATIONS

In temperate areas the conventional preparation of land for planting is a thorough disturbance of the top 20–30 cm of soil. Digging or ploughing buries residues of previous plantings and weeds, and with repeated passes of rakes or harrows a suitable **tilth** is created. This procedure is very demanding on energy, labour and time. Many of the cultivations tend to override the natural structure-forming agents and when undertaken at the wrong time they create pans or leave a bare, loose soil vulnerable to erosion. Some of the compaction problems are overcome by cultivating in **beds** which confines traffic to well-defined paths between the growing areas. The advent of effective herbicides has, in certain cases, enabled the inversion of soil to be eliminated. The use of powered implements has speeded up work and reduced the number of tillage passes. In some areas of horticulture the adoption of **minimum** or **zero tillage** has preserved natural structure while beneficially concentrating organic matter levels in the surface layers and reducing wind and water erosion.

Ploughing and digging

Ploughing and digging are used to loosen and invert the soil. The land is broken up into clods and an increased area is exposed to weathering. As the soil is inverted, weeds, plant residues and bulky manures are incorporated. The depth of ploughing or digging should be related to the depth of topsoil because bringing up the subsoil reduces fertility in the vital top layers, seriously affecting germination of seeds and establishment of plants. If deeper layers are to be loosened, a **subsoiler** should be used. In plastic soil conditions the plough can smear the soils, particularly when the wheels of the tractor spin in the furrow bottom. These **plough pans** tend to develop with successive ploughing to the same depth. Ploughing at different depths or attaching a subsoil tine can reduce their incidence. Digging with a spade does not produce a cultivation pan and is still used on small areas. **Spading machines** or **rotary diggers** imitate the digging action without the disadvantages of ploughing, but tend to be very slow.

Rotary cultivators

Rotary cultivators are used to create a tilth on uncultivated or on roughly prepared ground. The type of tilth produced depends on suitable adjustment of forward speed, rotor speed, blade design and layout, shield angle and depth of working. The 'hoe' blade is normally used for seedbed production but does have the disadvantage of smearing plastic soils at the cultivation depth, producing a **rotovation pan**. 'Pick' tines produce a rougher tilth but less readily cause a pan. Subsoil tines can be fitted to prevent these pans developing.

Harrowing and raking

Harrowing and raking are methods of levelling soils, incorporating fertilizers and producing a suitable tilth on the roughly prepared ground. The soil must be in a **friable** condition for this operation and it is made easier if the top layers have been suitably weathered. The impact of the tines breaks the clods.

'**Progressive**'-**type cultivators** were introduced essentially to loosen coarse structured clays by drawing through the soil banks of tines, increasing in depth from the front, to cultivate the soil from the top down in one pass. Although this requires powerful tractors to pull, especially if subsoiling tines are attached, it is a time-saving operation and the re-compaction inherent in multiple pass methods is reduced. These cultivators should not be used on well-structured soils where full depth loosening is unnecessary.

'**Under-loosening**' **cultivators** have been designed to loosen compact topsoils without disturbing the surface, which ensures a level, clod free and organic-matter-rich tilth. Used under the right conditions these implements improve water movement and plant growth. However, loosened soils are more susceptible to compaction and consequently the equipment should only be used when compaction is known to be present.

Subsoiling

Subsoiling is used to improve soil structure below plough depth by drawing a heavy cultivation tine through the soil to establish a system of deep cracks in compacted zones. This helps the downward movement of water, circulation of air and penetration of roots (*see* Figure 13.9). The operation is most effective when the subsoil is friable and the surface dry enough to be able to withstand the heavy tractor that is needed (*see* load bearing).

Effective subsoiling is made easier if the top surface is loosened by prior cultivation. Although the draught is higher, subsoil disturbance is increased substantially by attaching inclined blades or wings. Successful subsoiling is accompanied by a lift in the soil surface (soil heave) which usually makes it unsuitable for improving conditions in playing fields.

Subsoiling should only be used when the cause of any waterlogging is related to a soil structure fault (*see* also drainage). Slow subsoil permeability caused by high clay content is usually rectified with **mole drainage**. If the soil is too sandy or stony, a subsoiler can be used so long as the cracks created lead the water into a natural or artificial drainage system. Subsoilers used in the right conditions readily burst massive structures and soil pans created by machinery but some natural pans are too strong for normal equipment. The problem of cultivation pans can be dealt with by using conventional subsoilers or by attaching small subsoil tines to the cultivation equipment. This tends to increase the power requirement but eliminates the pan as it is created.

MANAGEMENT OF MAIN SOIL TYPES

Sandy soils

Sandy soils are usually considered to be easily cultivated but serious problems can occur because

1 Conventional

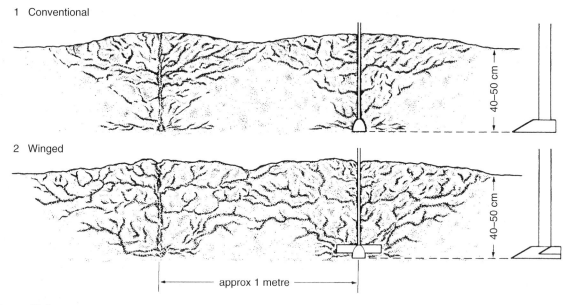

2 Winged

40–50 cm

40–50 cm

approx 1 metre

Figure 13.9 *Subsoiling. The subsoiler is drawn through the soil to burst open compacted zones. It leaves cracks which remain open to improve aeration, drainage and root penetration. The cracks created should link up with artificial drainage systems unless the lower layers are naturally free draining.*

the particles readily pack together, especially when organic matter levels are low. Consequently many sandy soils are difficult to firm adequately without causing over-compaction. Pans near the surface caused by traffic and deeper cultivation pans frequently occur on sandy soils, resulting in reduced rooting and water movement. **Subsoiling** is frequently undertaken on a routine basis every 4–6 years, although the need can be reduced by keeping machinery off land while it has low **load-bearing** strength and by encouraging natural structure-forming agents.

Coarse sands have low water-holding capacity, which makes them vulnerable to drought, particularly in drier areas. This is not such a disadvantage if irrigation equipment is installed and water is readily obtainable. In many categories of horticulture there is a demand for soils with **good workability**. Coarse sands, loamy sands and sandy loams have the advantage of good porosity and can be cultivated at field capacity. Sands tend to go acid

rapidly and are vulnerable to overliming because of their **low buffering capacity** (*see* page 159).

Silts and fine sands

These can be very productive soils because of their good water-holding capacity and, while organic matter levels are kept above 4 per cent, their ease of working. However silts and fine sands present soil management problems, especially when used for intensive plantings, because they have **weak structure**, are vulnerable to **surface capping**, and are easily compacted to form **massive structures**. To achieve their high potential, efficient drainage is vital to maximize the rooting depth. Fine tilths in the open should be avoided, especially in autumn and early spring, because frosts and heavy rainfall reduce the size of surface crumbs. For the same reason, care should be taken with irrigation droplet size that, if too large, can damage the surface structure.

Improving soil structure is not easy after winter root crop harvesting or orchard spraying on wet soils because low clay content results in very little cracking during subsequent wetting and drying cycles. Improvement therefore depends on other natural structure-forming agents or on subsoiling.

Clay soils

Clay soils tend to be **slow draining, slow to warm** up in Spring, and have **poor working properties** (*see* workability). A serious limitation is that the soil is still plastic **at field capacity**, which delays soil preparation until it has dried by evaporation. Permanent plantings are established to avoid the need to rework the soil. Playing surfaces created over clays have severe limitations, particularly when required for use in all-weather conditions. Where high standards have to be maintained, as in golf greens, fine turf is established in a suitable growing medium overlying the original soil. However, a high clay content is an advantage for the preparation of cricket squares where a hard, even surface is required but is played on only in drier weather. Increasingly, heavily used areas are replaced by artificial surfaces.

Horticultural cropping of clays is limited to summer cabbage, Brussels sprouts and to some top fruit in areas where the water table does not restrict rooting depth. Under-drainage is normally necessary. In wetter areas most clays are put down to grass. Timeliness, encouraging the annual drying cycle of the soil profile and maximizing the effect of weathering to help cultivations are essential for successful management of clay soils.

Peat soils

Peat soils have very many advantages over mineral soils for intensive vegetable and outdoor flower production. Fenland soils and Lancashire Moss of England; peatlands of the midland counties of Ireland; the 'muck' soils of North America; and similar soils in the Netherlands, Germany, Poland and Russia have proved valuable when their limitations to commercial cropping have been overcome.

Well-drained peat at the correct pH is an **excellent root environment**. It has a very much higher water-holding capacity than the same volume of soil and yet gaseous exchange is good. Root development is uninhibited because friable peat offers hardly any mechanical resistance to root penetration. This leads to high quality root crops that are easily cleaned. These cultivated peat lands **warm up quickly** at the surface because the Sun's energy is efficiently absorbed by their dark colour, with consequent rapid crop growth. These soils have a very **low power requirement** for cultivation, are free of stones, and can be worked over a wide moisture range.

Plant nutrition is complicated by natural **trace element deficiencies** and the effect of pH on plant **nutrient availability**. Peat has **poor load-bearing** characteristics and specialized equipment is often needed to harvest in wet conditions. Whilst peat warms up quickly on sunny days, its dark surface makes it vulnerable to air frost because it acts as an efficient radiator. Firming the surface and keeping it moist combat this. Weeds grow well and their control is made more difficult by the ability of peat to absorb and **neutralize soil-acting herbicides**. The high organic matter levels also make the peats and sandy peats **vulnerable to wind erosion** in spring when the surface dries out and there is no crop canopy to protect it.

FURTHER READING

Brown, L.V. *Applied Principles of Horticultural Science*, 2nd edition (Butterworth-Heinemann, 2002).
Coker, E.G. *Horticultural Science and Soils* (Macmillan, 1970).
Curtis, L.F., Courtney, F.M. and Tredgill, S. *Soils in the British Isles* (Longman, 1976).
Davies, D.G., Eagle, D.T. and Finley, J.B. *Soil Management*, 5th edition (Farming Press Books and Videos, 1993).
Handreck, K. and Black, N. *Growing Media for Ornamental Plants and Turf* (New South Wales University Press, 1989).

Ingram, D.S. *et al* (editors) *Science and the Garden*, (Blackwell Science Ltd., 2002).

Mackney, D. (editor) *Soil Type and Land Capability*, Soil Survey Technical Monograph No. 4 (HMSO, 1974).

MAFF. *Code of Good Agricultural Practice for the Protection of Soil*, (DEFRA, formerly MAFF Publications, 1998) http://www.defra.gov.uk/environ/cogap/soilcode.pdf.

Simpson, K. *Soil* (Longmans Handbooks in Agriculture, 1983).

White, R.E. *Introduction to the Principles and Practice of Soil Sciences*, 3rd edition (Blackwell Scientific Publications, 1997).

14

Soil Water

Plants require a constant supply of water to maintain growth. Water is taken up by the plant with minerals by the roots and is lost by **transpiration**. *Approximately 500 kg of water is needed to replace the water lost from the leaves over a period when the plant grows by 1 kg of dry weight. A mature tree can take up about 1000 l a day. A single hectare of full canopy crop grown under glass can use over 1000 m^3 (1 million litres) of water over a year.*

In this chapter the characteristics of soil water are established whilst following the process of wetting a dry growing medium, then the drying out of a fully wetted one. The concept of available water is related to the ability of the plant root to extract water from different growing media with different moisture contents. Irrigation and drainage are explained as the means of maintaining optimum water levels in the soil. The chapter is concluded by an examination of the nature of water quality and water conservation.

WETTING OF A DRY SOIL

Rainfall is recorded with a rain gauge (*see* Figure 2.10) and is measured in millimetres of water. Thus '1 mm of rain' is the amount of water covering any area to a depth of 1 mm. Therefore '1 mm of rain'

on 1 hectare of land is equivalent to $10 \, m^3$ or 10 000 litres of water per hectare (area $10\,000\,m^2 \times$ depth 0.001 m).

As rain falls on a dry surface the water either soaks in (**infiltration**) or runs off over the surface as **surface run-off**. **Ponding** is the accumulation of water on the surface as a result of infiltration rates slower than rainfall. Ponding leads to capping, which further reduces infiltration rates. Soil surfaces can be protected with mulches and care should be taken with water application rates during irrigation.

Saturated soils

As water soaks into the dry soil the surface layers become saturated or waterlogged, i.e. water fills all the pore spaces. As water continues to enter the soil it moves steadily downwards, with a sharp boundary between the saturated zone and dry, air-filled layers, as shown in Figure 14.1. So long as water continues to soak into the soil, this **wetting front** moves to greater depths. When rainfall ceases the water in the larger soil pores continues to move downwards. The water that is removed from wet soil by gravity is known as **gravitational water**.

Water is held in the soil in the form of water films around all the soil particles and aggregates. Forces in the surface of the water films, surface tension, hold water to the soil particles against the forces of gravity and the suction force of roots. As the volume of water decreases, its surface area and

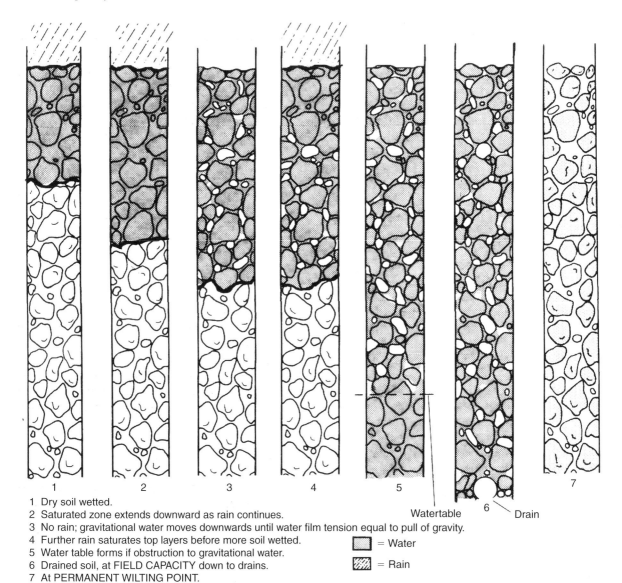

1 Dry soil wetted.
2 Saturated zone extends downward as rain continues.
3 No rain; gravitational water moves downwards until water film tension equal to pull of gravity.
4 Further rain saturates top layers before more soil wetted.
5 Water table forms if obstruction to gravitational water.
6 Drained soil, at FIELD CAPACITY down to drains.
7 At PERMANENT WILTING POINT.

Watertable   Drain

☐ = Water
▨ = Rain

Figure 14.1 *Water in the soil.*

hence its **surface tension** becomes proportionally greater until, in very thin films of water, it prevents the reduced volume of water from being removed by gravity. A useful comparison can be seen when one's hands are lifted from a bowl of water. They drip until the forces in the surface of the thin film become equal to the forces of gravity acting on the remaining small volume of water over the hands.

Field capacity (FC)

A soil that has been saturated, then allowed to drain freely without evaporation until drainage effectively ceases, is said to be at field capacity (FC). This may take 2 days or less on sandy soils, but far longer on clay where the process of drainage may continue indefinitely.

Table 14.1 Soil water. The amount of water in a given depth of soil at FC or PWP can be calculated by simple proportion

Soil texture	Water held in 300 mm soil depth (mm)		
	at FC, i.e. WHC	at PWP	available water (AWC)
Coarse sand	26	1	25
Fine sand	65	5	60
Coarse sandy loam	42	2	40
Fine sandy loam	65	5	60
Silty loam	65	5	60
Clay loam	65	10	55
Clay	65	15	50
Peat	120	30	90

At FC the soil pores less than about 0.05 mm remain full of water, whereas in the **macropores** air replaces the gravitational water as illustrated in Figure 14.1 (*see* porosity).

The amount of water held at FC is known as the **water-holding capacity** (WHC) or **moisture-holding capacity** (MHC). Examples are given in Table 14.1. The WHC is expressed in millimetres of water for a given depth of soil. Thus a silty loam soil 300 mm deep holds 65 mm of water when at FC. Conversely, if a silty loam had become completely dry to 300 mm depth, it would require 65 mm of rain or irrigation water to return it to FC. Since 1 mm of water is equivalent to $10 \, m^3/ha$, a hectare of silty loam would hold $650 \, m^3$ water in the top 300 mm when at FC (*see* rainfall). The principle described enables WHC or irrigation requirement to be determined for any soil depth. The amount of water required to return a soil to FC is called the **soil moisture deficit** (SMD).

Watertables

Groundwater occurs where the soil and underlying parent material are saturated (*see* Figure 14.1); the **watertable** marks the top of this saturated zone, which fluctuates over the seasons, normally being much higher in winter. In wetlands the watertable is very near the soil surface and the land is not suitable for horticulture until the watertable of the whole area is lowered (*see* drainage).

Where water flows down the soil profile and is impeded by an impermeable layer such as saturated clay or silty clay, a **perched watertable** is formed. Water from above cannot drain through the impermeable barrier and so a saturated zone builds up over it. **Springs** appear at a point on the landscape where an overlying porous material meets an impermeable layer at the soil surface, e.g. where chalk slopes or gravel mounds overlie clay.

Capillary rise

Capillary rise occurs only from saturated soils. Water is drawn upwards from the watertable in a continuous network of pores. The height to which water will rise depends on the continuity of pores, and on their diameter. In practice the rise from the watertable is rarely more than 20 mm for coarse sands, typically 150 mm in finer textured soils but can be substantially greater in silty soils and in chalk.

The upward movement of water in these very fine pores is very slow. The principle of capillary rise is used in watering plants grown in containers (*see* capillary benches). Several 'self-watering' containers also depend on capillary rise from a water store in their base (*see* aggregate culture).

DRYING OF A WET SOIL

Soil water is lost from the soil surface by evaporation and from the rooting zone by plant transpiration.

Evaporation

The rate of water loss from the soil by **evaporation** depends on the drying capacity of the atmosphere just above the ground and the water content in the surface layers. The evaporation rate is directly related to the **net radiation** (*see* page 13) from the sun which can be measured with a solarimeter (*see* page 27). Evaporation rates increase with higher air temperatures and wind speed or lower humidity levels. As water evaporates from the surface, the water films on the soil particles become thinner. The surface tension forces in the film surface become proportionally greater as the water volume of the film decreases. This leaves water films on the particles at the surface with a high surface tension compared with those in the films on particles lower down in the soil. Water moves slowly upwards to restore the equilibrium.

Whilst the surface layers are kept moist by water moving slowly up from below, the losses by evaporation in contrast are quite rapid. Consequently the surface layers can become dry and the evaporation rate drops significantly after '5 mm of water' is lost. Evaporation virtually ceases after the removal of '20 mm of water' from the soil. A dry layer on the soil surface helps conserve moisture in the lower layers.

Mulches (*see* page 193) can also reduce water loss from the soil surface. The evaporation from the soil surface is almost eliminated by a leaf canopy that shades the surface, thus reducing airflow and maintaining a humid atmosphere over the soil (*see* Humidity, page 25).

Evapotranspiration

As a leaf canopy covers a soil the rate of water loss becomes more closely related to transpiration rates. **The potential transpiration rate represents the estimated loss of water from plants grown in moist soil with a full leaf canopy. It can be calculated from weather data** (*see* Table 14.2).

As roots remove water it is slowly replaced by the water film equilibrium, but rapid water uptake by plants necessitates root growth towards a water supply in order to maintain uptake rates. At any point when water loss exceeds uptake, the plant loses turgor and may wilt. This tends to happen in very drying conditions even when the growing medium is moist. Wilting is accompanied by a reduction in carbon dioxide movement into the leaf, which in turn reduces the plant's growth rate (*see* photosynthesis). The plant recovers from this **temporary wilt** as the rate of water loss falls below that of the uptake, which usually occurs in the cool of the evening onwards. **Continued loss of water causes the soil to reach the permanent wilting point (PWP) which is when plants wilt but do not regain turgor overnight because their roots can extract no more water within the rooting zone.** When the soil has reached the PWP there is still water in the smallest of the soil pores, within clay particles, and in combination with other soil constituents, but it is too tightly held to be removed by

Table 14.2 Potential transpiration rates. The calculated water loss (mm) from a crop grown in moist soil with a full leaf canopy, over different periods of time and based on weather data collected in nine areas in the British Isles

Area	April	May	June	July	August	September	Summer	Winter	Annual
Ayr	46	81	90	83	65	38	405	70	475
Bedford	50	78	89	91	80	43	430	70	500
Cheshire	53	75	83	88	76	44	420	80	500
Channel Isles	51	86	91	99	84	46	457	103	560
Essex (NE)	50	79	98	98	83	45	450	80	530
Hertford	49	79	91	94	80	43	435	75	510
Kent (Central)	50	79	93	96	83	44	445	65	510
Northumberland	44	64	81	76	60	34	360	70	430
Dyfed	46	75	84	81	74	44	405	105	510

roots. Typical water contents of different types of soil at their PWP are given in Table 14.1.

Available water

Roots are able to remove water held at tensions up to 15 atmospheres within the rooting zone, and gravitational water drains away. **Consequently the available water for plants is the moisture in the rooting depth between FC and the PWP.** The available water content (AWC) of different soil textures is given in Table 14.1. Fine sands have very high available water reserves because they hold large quantities of water at FC and there is very little water left in the soil at PWP (*see* sands, page 158). Clays have lower available water reserves because a large proportion of the water they hold is held too tightly for roots to extract (*see* clay, page 159).

Roots remove the water from films at FC very easily. Even so, plants can wilt temporarily and any restriction of rooting makes wilting more likely. Water uptake is also reduced by high soluble salt concentrations (*see* osmosis) and by the effect of some pests and diseases (*see* vascular wilt diseases). As the soil dries out, the water films become thinner and the water becomes more difficult for the roots to extract. After about half the AWC has been removed, temporary wilting becomes significantly more frequent. Irrigating when available water levels fall below this point minimizes slowing of growth rates. Plants grown under glass are often irrigated more frequently to maintain a suitably formulated growing medium near to FC. This ensures maximum growth rates since the roots have access to 'easy' water, i.e. water removed by low suction force.

Workability of soils

The number of days each year that are available for soil cultivation depends on the weather but more specifically on soil consistency. This describes the effect of water on those physical properties of the soil influencing the timing and effect of cultivations. It is assessed in the field by prodding and handling the soil. A very wet soil can lose its structure and flow like a thick **fluid**. In this state it has no **load-bearing strength** to support machinery. As the soil dries out the soil becomes **plastic**; the particles adhere and are readily moulded. In general, the soil is difficult to work in this condition because it sticks to the cultivation equipment, has insufficient load-bearing strength, is readily compacted and is easily smeared by cultivating equipment. As the soil dries further it becomes **friable**. At this stage the soil is in the ideal state for cultivation because it has adequate load-bearing strength but the soil aggregates readily crumble. If the soil dries out further to a **harsh consistency** the load-bearing strength improves considerably, but whilst coarse sands and loams still readily crumble in this condition, soils with high clay, silt or fine sand content form hard-resistant clods. The **friable range** can be extended by adding organic matter (*see* humus). At a time when bulky organic matter is more difficult to obtain it is important to note that a fall in soil humus content narrows the friable range. This allows less latitude in the timing of cultivations and increases the chances of cultivations being undertaken when they damage the soil structure. **Timeliness is the cultivation of the soil when it is at the right consistency. Whereas many sands and silts can be cultivated at FC, clays and clay loams do not become friable until they have dried out to well below FC.**

DRAINAGE

Drainage is the removal of gravitational water from the soil profile. As this water leaves the macropores, air that takes its place enables gaseous exchange to continue. Horticultural soils should return to at least 10 per cent air capacity in the top half metre within 1 day of being saturated (*see* porosity). Some soils, notably those over chalk or gravel, are naturally free draining but many have underlying materials which are impermeable or only slowly permeable to water. In such cases artificial drainage, sometimes referred to as field drainage or under drainage, is put into carry away the gravitational

(a) Simple Interceptor Drainage System:

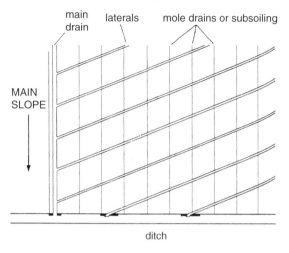

(b) Outfalls

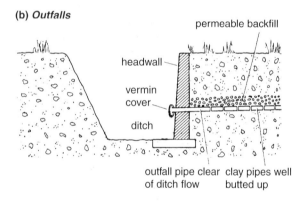

(c) Silt trap/Inspection Chamber

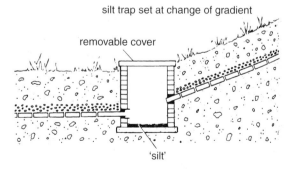

Figure 14.2 *Drainage.*

water (*see* Figure 14.2). This helps the soil to reach its FC rapidly but does not reduce its WHC.

Well-drained soils are those that are rarely saturated within the upper 900 mm except during or immediately after heavy rain. Uniform brown, red or yellow colours indicate an **aerobic** soil, i.e. a soil in which oxygen is available (*see* Plate 22). **Imperfectly drained soils** are those that are saturated in the top 600 mm for several months each year. These soils tend to have less bright colours than well-drained soil. Greyish or ochreous colours are distinct at 450 mm, giving a characteristic rusty mottled appearance (*see* Plate 23). **Poorly drained soils** are saturated within the upper 600 mm for at least half the year and are predominantly grey (*see* Plate 22).

Symptoms of poor drainage

These include restricted rooting; reduced working days for cultivation; weed, pest and disease problems, and excess fertilizer requirements. Soil pits dug in appropriate places reveal the extent of the drainage problem and help pinpoint the cause, which is the basis of finding the solution. The level of water that develops in the pit indicates the current watertable. Further indications of poor drainage are the presence of high organic matter levels (*see* organic soils) and small black nodules of manganese dioxide. Topsoils waterlogged for long periods in warm conditions have a smell of bad eggs (*see* sulphur cycle). The presence of compacted zones should be looked for as they indicate obstructions to the flow of gravitational water (*see* bulk density).

Soil colours show the history of waterlogging in the soil. Whereas free drainage is indicated by uniform red, brown or yellow soil throughout the subsoil, the iron oxide which gives soils these colours in the presence of oxygen is reduced to grey or blue forms in **anaerobic** conditions, i.e. when no oxygen is present. Zones of soil that are saturated for prolonged periods have a dull grey appearance, referred to as **gleying**. Reliance on colour alone as an indication of drainage conditions is not recommended because it persists for a long time after efficient drainage is established.

Structural damage whether caused by water (*see* stability), machinery (see cultivation) or by accumulations of iron (*see* natural pans) is an obstruction to water flow in the soil profile. Platy structures near the surface can be broken with cultivating equipment on arable land or spiking on grassland; but subsoiling should burst those deeper in the soil. If water cannot soak away from well-structured rooting zones, artificial drainage is required.

Low permeability soils

Low permeability of subsoils is the major reason for under-drainage in horticultural soils (*see* porosity). Clay, clay loam and silty clays when wetted become almost impermeable as the clay swells and the cracks close.

Pipe drainage. Lines of pipes are placed in the subsoil to intercept the trapped water. An even **gradient** from their highest point to the outfall in a ditch should be established to prevent silting up and **silt traps** should be placed at regular intervals to help to service the system at points where there is a change of gradient or direction (*see* Figure 14.2).

The spacing between the lines of pipes depends on the permeability of the soil, a maximum of 5 m intervals being necessary in clay subsoils. Soil permeability and the land use dictate the **depth of the drains** which is normally more than 60 cm. Drains should be set deeply in cultivated land where heavy equipment and deep cultivation might disturb the pipes. Shallow drains can be used where rapid drainage is a high priority and the pipes are not likely to be crushed by heavy vehicles or severed by cultivating equipment, e.g. sports grounds. **The diameter of the pipe** depends on the gradient available and the amount of water to be carried when wet conditions prevail. Most frequently used are 75 and 100 mm diameter pipes, usually leading into larger drains.

Pipes are made of clay or plastic. **Tiles** (clayware) are usually 300 mm sections of pipe butted tightly together to allow entry of water but not soil particles. It is recommended that they are covered with permeable fill, usually stones or clinker, to improve water movement into the drains. **Plastic**

pipes usually consist of very long lengths of pipe perforated by many small holes.

Water has to be discharged into a ditch above the wet season water level to allow water out of the pipes. The outlet of the drains is very vulnerable to damage and so it should consist of a strong, long pipe set flush in a concrete or brick **headwall** so that it is not dislodged by erosion in the ditch nor by people using it as a foothold. Pipes not set flush should be glazed to prevent frost damage. **Vermin traps** should be fitted to prevent pipes being blocked by nests or dead animals.

Mole drainage is very much cheaper than pipe drainage. A mole plough draws a 75 mm 'bullet' followed by a 100 mm plug through the soil at a depth of 500–750 mm from a ditch up the slope of a field or across a pipe drain system with permeable backfill (*see* Figure 14.2). The soil should be plastic at the working depth so that a tunnel to carry water is created. The soil above should be drier so that some cracks are produced as the implement is drawn slowly along. These cracks improve the soil structure and conduct water to the mole drain. Sandy and stony areas are unsuitable because tunnels are not properly formed or collapse as water flows. Tunnels drawn in clay soils can remain useful for 10–15 years but in wetter areas their useful life may be nearer 5 or even as little as 2 years. Pipe drainage is usually combined with secondary treatments such as mole drainage or subsoiling to achieve effective drainage at reasonable costs. Deep subsoiling improves soil permeability and the pipes carry the water away. Installation costs can be reduced because pipes can be laid further apart. Similarly mole drainage over and at right angles to the pipes enables them to be spaced 50–100 m apart.

Sandslitting is used on sports grounds to remove water from the surface as quickly as possible. It involves cutting trenches at frequent intervals in the soil and infilling with carefully graded sand that conducts water from surface to a free draining zone under the playing surface.

Water that spills out onto lower ground from springs can be intercepted with **ditches** placed at the junction of the permeable and impermeable layers. **French drains** can be placed around impermeable surfaces such as concrete hard standings and stone patios to intercept the run-off.

Maintenance of drainage systems

Under-drainage is very expensive to install and must be serviced to ensure that the investment is not wasted. **Ditches** need regular attention because they are open to the elements. Weed growth should be controlled, rubbish cleared out and collapsed banks repaired, because obstructions lead to silting up or the undercutting of the bank. The design of the ditches depends on the soil type and should be maintained when being repaired. **Drain outlets** are a particularly vulnerable part of the drainage system, especially if not set into a headwall. They should be marked with a stake (holly trees were traditionally used in some areas) and inspected regularly after the soil returns to FC. Blockages should be cleared with rods and vermin traps refitted where appropriate. Wet patches in the field indicate where a blockage in a pipe has occurred. The pipe should be exposed and the cause of the obstruction remedied. Silted-up pipes can be rodded, broken sections replaced or dislodged pipes realigned. **Silt traps** need to be cleaned out regularly to prevent accumulated soil being carried into the pipes.

At all times it should be remembered that the drains only carry away water that reaches the pipes. Every effort must be made to maintain good soil permeability and to avoid compaction problems. **Subsoilers** (*see* page 167) should be used to remedy subsoil structural problems. Once drainage has been installed the soil dries more quickly, leading to better soil structure because cracks appear more extensively and for longer periods. Deeper layers of the soil are dried out as roots explore the improved root environment, which gives another turn in the improving cycle.

IRRIGATION

Irrigation is used to prevent plant growth being limited by water shortage. Irrigation should be seen as a husbandry aid in addition to otherwise sound

practice. It is assumed in the following that water is being added to a well-drained soil unaffected by capillary rise. The need for irrigation depends on available water in the rooting zone and the effect of water stress on the plant's stage of growth. **Response periods** are the growth stages when the use of irrigation during periods of rainfall deficiency is likely to show economic benefits. In general all plants benefit from moist seedbeds, and eliminating water stress maximizes vegetative growth. Initiation of flowering and fruiting is favoured by drier conditions. The response periods of a range of plants grown in the UK is given in Table 14.3.

The very large quantities of water required for commercial production are illustrated clearly in the estimates for growing in protected culture where all the requirements have to be delivered to the crop by irrigation. In the British Isles, the daily consumption of water from a full cover crop such as tomatoes or cucumbers about 20 000 l/ha in March rising to double that in June. This amounts to about $9000\,m^3$ per year (approximately 750 000 gallons/acre). A more exact estimate can be obtained by measuring the light levels outside the greenhouse; 2200 l/ha are required for each megajoule per square metre (*see* page 27). This can be compared with the $6000\,m^3$ of rainfall that could be collected, on average, from the roof of a hectare of glass in the south-east of England (*see* page 171). To take advantage of this contribution there would need to be substantial storage facilities and the water quality issues would need to be addressed.

Irrigation plan

In general terms water is added to a soil when moisture levels fall to 50 per cent of AWC in the rooting zone. Outdoors 25 mm of water is the minimum that should be added at any one time in order to reduce the frequency of irrigation, to reduce water loss by evaporation and to prevent the development of shallow rooting. On most soils the amount of water added should be such as to return the soil to FC. Addition of water to clays and clay loams should be minimized so as not to reduce the vital

Table 14.3 Irrigation guide

Plants	Response periods: growth stages at which to irrigate and time of year when they occur		Irrigation plan (mm of water at mm SMD)		
			A Low* AWC	B Medium AWC	C High** AWC
Beans, runner	Early flowering onwards	June to August	25 at 25+	50 at 50+	50 at 75
Brussels sprouts	When lower buttons 15 to 18 mm diameter	August to October	40 at 40	40 at 40	40 at 40
Carrots	Throughout life	June to September	25 at 25	40 at 50	
Cauliflowers early summer	Throughout life	April to June	5 at 25	25 at 25	
Flowers annuals and biennials	Throughout life	April to early September	25 at 25	25 at 25	25 at 25
Perennial	Throughout life	April to September	25 at 25	50 at 75	50 at 75
Lettuce summer	Throughout life	April to August	25 at 25	25 at 25	25 at 50
Nursery stock trees and shrubs	(a) To establish newly planted stock	April to June	25 at 25	25 at 50	25 at 50+
	(b) Established stock	May to July	25 at 25	25 at 50	25 at 50+
	(c) To aid early lifting	September	25 at 25+	25 at 50+	25 at 50+
Potatoes, first early	After tuberization reaches 10 mm diameter	May to June	25 at 25	25 at 50	25 at 50
Maincrop and second earlies	From time tubers reach marble stage onwards	June to August	25 at 25	25 at 50	25 at 50
Rhubarb	When pulling has stopped	May to September	40 at 50+	40 at 50+	50 at 75+
Strawberries fruit		September to October	50 at 50	50 at 75	50 at 75
Top fruit Apples Pears		July to September July to August	When SMD is more than 50 mm apply 50 mm of water to suffice for 2 weeks. Then continue irrigation to make the total water supply (rain + irrigation) equal to 50 mm/ fortnight for the remainder of July, 40 mm/fortnight in August and 25 mm/fortnight in September.		

*Less than 40 mm available water per 300 mm soil, e.g. gravels, coarse sands.
**More than 65 mm available water per 300 mm soil, e.g. silts, peats.

drying and wetting cycles, and if they have to be irrigated they should not be returned to FC in case rain follows (*see* ponding). Irrigation should never result in fertilizers being leached from the rooting depth unless it is the specific objective, as in flooding of greenhouse soils (*see* conductivity).

Most recommendations are given in a simplified form taking the above points into account. The recommended plan is usually expressed in terms of how much water to apply, at a given SMD, for a named crop on a soil of stated AWC. Thus for outdoor-grown summer lettuce crop grown on soils of a medium AWC, 25 mm of water should be added when a 25 mm SMD occurs. This would require the application of 250 000 l/ha or 25 l/m^2. Further examples are given in Table 14.3.

SMD

SMD is the amount of water required to return the growing medium to FC. SMD can be calculated by keeping a **soil water balance sheet**. The account is conveniently started after rain returns the soil to FC, i.e. when SMD is zero. In Britain it is assumed that, unless it has been a dry winter, the soil is at FC until the end of March. From the first day of April a day-by-day check can be made of water gains and losses.

Rainfall varies greatly from year to year from one locality to the next and so it should be determined on site (*see* rain-gauge) or obtained from a local weather station. Water loss for each month does not vary very much over the years and so **potential transpiration rates** based on past records can be used in the calculation. There are potential transpiration rate figures available for all localities having weather stations. Examples are given in Table 14.2. These figures can be used when calculating water loss but until there is 20 per cent leaf canopy, a maximum SMD of 20 mm is not exceeded, because in the early stages water loss is predominantly from the soil surface by **evaporation**.

A worked example of a weekly water balance sheet is given in Table 14.4; a daily water balance sheet may be more appropriate in some situations.

In protected cropping all the water that plants require has to be supplied by the grower, who must therefore have complete control over irrigation. With experience the grower can determine

Table 14.4 A weekly soil balance sheet for established nursery stock grown on sandy loam (AWC 55 mm per 300 mm) in Essex. The irrigation plan is to apply 25 mm water if a 50 mm SMD is reached (*see* Table 14.3). Water loss estimated from Table 14.2

Week beginning	Water loss (mm)	Water gains in mm Rainfall (irrigation)	SMD at end of week (mm)
March 31			0
April 7	11	10 (0)	0 + 11 − (10 + 0) = 1
14	11	8 (0)	1 + 11 − (8 + 0) = 4
21	12	16 (0)	4 + 12 − (16 + 0) = 0
28	12	5 (0)	0 + 12 − (5 + 0) = 7
May 4	16	28 (0)	7 + 16 − (28 + 0) = 0*
11	17	10 (0)	0 + 17 − (10 + 0) = 7
18	18	14 (0)	7 + 18 − (14 + 0) = 11
25	18	4 (0)	11 + 18 − (4 + 0) = 25
June 1	18	10 (0)	25 + 18 − (10 + 0) = 33
8	23	14 (0)	33 + 23 − (14 + 0) = 42
15	23	18 (0)	42 + 23 − (18 + 0) = 47
22	23	20 (0)	47 + 23 − (20 + 0) = 50**
29	23	10 (25)	50 + 23 − (10 + 25) = 38
July 6	22	8 (0)	38 + 22 − (8 + 0) = 52**
13	22	18 (25)	52 + 22 − (18 + 25) = 31
20	22	24 (0)	31 + 22 − (24 + 0) = 29
27	22	5 (0)	29 + 22 − (5 + 0) = 46

*SMD cannot be less than zero because water above FC drains away.
**Irrigation might have been delayed if prolonged heavy rain forecast.

water requirements by examining plants, soil, root balls or by tapping pots. A **tensiometer** can be used to indicate the soil water tension but, while this is useful to indicate when to water, it does not show directly how much water is needed. **Evaporimeters** distributed through the planting can give the water requirement by showing how much water has been evaporated. A **solarimeter** measures the total radiation received from the sun and the readings obtained can be used to calculate the water losses, often expressed in litres per square metre for convenience.

Methods of applying water

These should be carefully related to plant requirements, climate and soil type. On a small scale, **watering cans** or **hoses** fitted with trigger lances can be used, but care should be taken to avoid damaging the structure of the growing medium. Water can be sprayed from fixed or mobile equipment but it is essential that the rate of application is related to soil infiltration rate. The droplet size in the spray should not be large enough to damage the surface structure (*see* tilth). Indoors, **spray lines** can be fitted with nozzles to control the direction and quantity of water. Overhead lines can lead to very high humidity levels and wet foliage, predisposing some plants to disease (*see* grey mould). Consequently, it should be restricted to watering low level crops, e.g. lettuce, deliberately increasing humidity ('damping down' or 'spraying over') or winter flooding (*see* conductivity). **Trickle** lines deliver water very slowly to the soil, leaving plant foliage and the soil surface dry, which ensures a drier atmosphere and reduced water loss. However, care is needed because there is very little sideways spread of water into coarse sand, loose soil or a growing medium that has completely dried out. **Drip** irrigation is a variation on the trickle method but the water is applied through pegged down thin, flexible 'spaghetti' tubes to exactly where it is needed, e.g. in each pot or base of each plant.

Simple **flooded benches** are sometimes used to water pot plants, the shallow tray of the benched area is filled with water from which the pots take up water after which the water is drained off ('ebb and flow'). This tends to produce a high humidity around the plants and **capillary benches** have come to be preferred. The pots stand on, and the contents make contact with, a level 50 mm bed of sand kept saturated at the base by an automatic water supply. Water lost by evaporation at the surface and from the plant is replaced by **capillary rise**. The sand must be fine enough to lift the water but coarse enough to ensure that the flow rate is sufficient. **Capillary matting** made of fibre woven to a thickness and pore size to hold, distribute and/or lift water has many uses in watering containerized crops indoors or outside. Containers with built-in water reserves and easy watering systems utilize capillarity to keep the rooting zone moist. Sub-irrigated sand beds are used for standing out container plants in nursery production and are less wasteful of water that the more usual overhead spray lines.

WATER QUALITY

Water used in horticulture is taken from different sources and has different dissolved impurities. Soft water has very few impurities, whereas **hard water** contains large quantities of calcium and/or magnesium salts which raise the pH of the growing medium, especially where the impurities accumulate (*see* liming). Even small quantities of **micro-elements** such as boron or zinc have to be allowed for when making up nutrient solutions which are to be recirculated (*see* hydroponics). Water taken from boreholes in coastal areas can have high concentrations of salt that can lead to **salt concentration problems**. The quantity of dissolved salt in water can be measured by its conductivity; the higher the salt concentration the greater its electrical conductivity. Providing the levels of useful salts are not too high, the water can be used as long as the additional nutrient levels (fertilizers) are suitably adjusted (*see* conductivity).

In the recirculation systems that are becoming more prevalent in protected culture, the salts not used by plants become concentrated in the water. These dissolved salts can interfere with the uptake of useful salts such as potassium, make it difficult to create a balanced feed within the safe conductivity limits and reduce the plant growth rates as they become too concentrated.

Rainwater is increasingly being used as a major source of water. It is usually of high quality, i.e. low conductivity but there can be contamination related to the location or the method of collection or storage, e.g. high levels of zinc when collected through galvanized gullies.

Good quality rainwater can be used to dilute otherwise unsuitable water to bring it into use. Alternatively, poor quality water can be treated using reverse osmosis; water under pressure is forced through a membrane which holds back most of the dissolved salts. Alternatively, deionization can be used, which involves passing the water over resins to remove the unwanted salts. In both cases, an environmentally sound method for disposal of the concentrated solution produced remains a problem. The high-energy distillation and electro-dialysis methods are generally too expensive for cleaning water for growing.

Water drawn from rivers, lakes or even on-site reservoirs may contain algal, bacterial or fungal pollution, which can lead to blocked irrigation lines or plant disease (*see* hygienic growing).

To avoid disease problems, water supplies can be sterilized. On a commercial scale this is usually done by heat sterilization. Ultraviolet light or ozone treatments are usually more expensive and the use of hydrogen peroxide tends to be less effective.

WATER CONSERVATION

The need to manage water efficiently is a major concern in the use of scarce resources. Responsible action is increasingly supported by legislation and the higher price of using water. Clearly the major factors that determine the level of water use are related to the choice of plant species to be grown and the reasons for growing. **The selection of drought tolerant rather than water intensive plantings is fundamental.** Likewise the recycling of water and the capture of rainwater are important considerations in the choice of water source. Some growing systems are inherently less water intensive, but in most of them there are many ways in which water use can be reduced if certain principles are kept in mind and acted upon appropriately.

Whenever possible water should not be used; alternative strategies should be considered. If it has to be applied, recycled water should be considered. Water must be used efficiently.

Water is lost primarily through drainage or evaporation. Where application is partially controlled, the correct relationship between water applied and water holding (*see* WHC) helps to prevent leaching, which leads to nutrient loss (*see* nitrogen). Thus returning an outdoor soil to less than FC helps avoid losses to drainage and losses by run off in the event of unexpected rainfall.

Reducing the action of the drying atmosphere can minimize evaporation losses. Overhead application of water in the open can be limited by increasing the growing medium's water reservoir. Soils have different available WHC but most can be improved by the addition of suitable organic matter. Most importantly, maintaining good soil structure can increase the rooting depth. Plants should be encouraged to establish as quickly as possible but, after the initial watering-in, infrequent applications will encourage the plant to put down deep roots by searching for water. When water does have to be applied overhead, this should be undertaken in cool periods. However, care should be taken to avoid creating conditions that encourage diseases such as *Botrytis*.

Water is lost more rapidly from a moist than a dry soil surface. After just 5 mm of water has been lost from the surface, the rate of evaporation falls significantly. Infrequent application thus helps, but even more effective is the delivery of water to specific spots next to plants (*see* trickle lines) or from below through pipes to the rooting zone. Avoid bringing moist soil to the surface. If hoeing is undertaken it should be confined to the very top layers, this also reduces the risk of root damage. Losses from the surface can be reduced considerably by plant cover and almost eliminated by the use of mulches. Loss of water from the plants themselves is reduced when they are grouped together rather than spaced out.

Unless maximum growth rates are the main consideration, **reduced application** saves water, money and staff time without detriment to most plantings. In production horticulture, the introduction of sophisticated moisture-sensing equipment and computer control has enabled water to be delivered more precisely when and where it is needed. This has led to considerable reductions in water use.

Nutrient loss and run off from **overhead watering** used in container nursery stock production can be minimized by matching application to each of the following: rainfall, growing medium container size, plant species, stage of growth and the time of year. Nozzles should be maintained to ensure even water application. There tends to be less loss from sub-irrigated capillary sand beds. Recirculation (closed) systems should be considered in new developments.

The quantity of water required for **flooding** soils in protected culture (e.g. to remove excess nutrients when a crop sensitive to high salt levels, such as lettuce, is to be grown after a tolerant one, such as tomatoes) can be reduced by discontinuing the liquid feeding of the first crop as soon as possible.

In non-recirculating (open) **hydroponics systems** excessive water waste should be avoided by using flow meters to measure the quantity of run-off and comparing it with standard figures for the growing system used. A run-off of over 30 per cent is usually considered to be excessive and the amount and frequency of nutrient applications delivered by the nozzles or drippers should be reviewed. Closed systems (*see* NFT, page 218) recirculate the nutrient solution but this is not always practical. Where they are, the system must not be emptied illegally into watercourses or soakaways. It is recommended that the volume in the system be run down before discharge and the waste nutrient solution be sprayed onto crops during growing season. Permission to empty into public sewers might be granted but is usually subject to a charge depending on volume and contamination level.

FURTHER READING

Baily, R. *Irrigated Crops and Their Management* (Farming Press, 1990).

Brown, L.V. *Applied Principles of Horticulture*, 2nd edition, (Butterworth-Heinemann, 2002).

Castle, D.A., McCunnell, J. and Tring, I.M. *Field Drainage: Principles and Practice* (Batsford Academic, 1984).

Farr, E. and Henderson, W.C. *Land Drainage*, Longman Handbooks in Agriculture, (Longman, 1986).

Hope, F. *Turf Culture: A Manual for the Groundsman* (Cassell, 1990).

Ingram, D.S. *et al.* (Editors) *Science and the Garden* (Blackwell Science Ltd., 2002).

MAFF Advisory Booklets:
No. 2067 *Irrigation Guide* (1979).
No. 2140 *Watering Equipment for Glasshouse Crops* (1980).

MAFF Advisory Leaflets:
Nos 721–740 *Getting Down to Drainage* (various dates).
No. 776 *Water Quality for Crop Irrigation* (1981).

MAFF Advisory Reference Book No. 138 *Irrigation* (1976).

MAFF Technical Bulletin No. 34 *Climate and Drainage* (1970).

MAFF *Code of Good Agricultural Practice for the Protection of Water* (1991).

15

Soil Organic Matter

Organic matter exerts a profound influence on crop nutrition, soil structure, and cultivations. In this chapter the three main categories of organic matter are described; the living organisms, dead but identifiable organic matter and humus. The nutrient cycles describe how minerals are released from plant tissue and made available in the soil as plant nutrients. The interlocked nature of the different nutrient cycles is illustrated by considering the effect of the carbon:nitrogen ratio. The organic matter levels in different soils and the factors that cause the variations are examined. The beneficial effects of organic matter are established and the characteristics of different sources of bulky organic matter are considered.

LIVING ORGANISMS IN THE SOIL

As in any other plant and animal community the organisms that live in the soil form part of the **food webs** (*see* page 6). The main types present in any soil are the **primary producers** which are those capable of utilizing the sun's energy directly, synthesizing their own food by photosynthesis, such as green plants (*see* photosynthesis), the **primary consumers** which are those organisms which feed directly on plant material and **secondary consumers** which feed only on animal material. In practice, there are some organisms that feed on both plants and animals and also parasites living on organisms in all categories.

Decomposers are an important group, which have the special function within a community of breaking down dead or decaying matter into simpler substances with the release of inorganic salts, making them available once more to the primary producers. Primary decomposers are those organisms that attack the freshly dead organic matter. These include insects, earthworms and fungi. Fungi are particularly important in the initial decomposition of fibrous and woody material. **Secondary decomposers** are those organisms that live on the waste products of other decomposers and include bacteria and many species of fungi.

Plant roots

These are important as contributors to the organic matter levels in the soil. They shift and move soil particles as they penetrate the soil and grow in size. This rearrangement changes the sizes and shapes of soil aggregates and when these roots die and decompose, a channel is left which provides drainage and aeration. Root channels are formed over and over again unless the soil becomes too dense for roots to penetrate. Roots absorb water from soils and dry it, causing those with a high clay content to shrink and crack. This helps develop and improve structures on heavier soils (*see* page 164).

Earthworms

There are 10 common species of earthworm in Britain that vary in size from *Lumbricus terrestris*, which can be in excess of 25 cm, to the many small species less than 3 cm long. The main food of earthworms is dead plant remains. Casting species of earthworms are those that eat soil as well as organic matter and their excreta consist of intimately mixed, partially digested, finely divided organic matter and soil. Many species never produce casts and only two species regularly cast on the surface giving the **worm casts** that are a problem on fine grass areas, particularly in the autumn. It has been estimated that in English pastures the production of casts each year is 20–40 t/ha, the equivalent of 5 mm of soil deposited annually. This surface casting also leads to the incorporation of the leaf litter and the burying of stones. However, *L. terrestris* is the organism mainly responsible for the **burying** of large quantities of litter by dragging plant material down its burrows.

The **network of burrows**, which develops as a result of worm activity, is an important factor in maintaining a good structure, particularly in uncultivated areas and in soils of low clay content. Some species live entirely in the surface layers of the soils, others move vertically establishing almost permanent burrows down to 2 m.

Earthworm activity and distribution is largely governed by moisture levels, soil pH, temperature, organic matter and soil type. Most species tend to be more abundant in soils where there are good reserves of calcium. Earthworm populations are usually lower on the more acid soils, but most thrive in those near neutral. Worm numbers decrease in dry conditions, but they can take avoiding action by burrowing to more moist soil or by hibernating. Each species has its optimum temperature range; for *L. terrestris* this is about 10°C, which is typical of soil temperatures in the spring and autumn in the UK. Soils with low organic matter levels support only small populations of worms. In contrast, compost heaps and stacks of farmyard manure (FYM) have high populations. In oak and beech woods where the fallen leaves are palatable to worms, their populations are large and they can remove a high proportion of the annual leaf-fall. This also happens in orchards unless harmful chemicals such as copper have reduced earthworm populations. Light and medium loams support a higher total population than clays, peat and gravelly soils.

Slugs and **snails**, **arthropods** such as millipedes, springtails and mites, and **nematodes** are also found in high numbers and play an important part in the decomposition of organic matter. Several species are also horticultural pests (*see* Chapter 10).

Bacteria

Bacteria are present in soils in vast numbers. About 1000 million or more occur in each gram of fertile soil. Consequently, despite their microscopic size, the top 150 mm of fertile topsoil carries about 1 t of bacteria per hectare. There are many different species of bacteria to be found in the soil and most play a part in the decomposition of organic matter. Many bacteria attack minerals; this leads to the weathering of rock debris and the release of plant nutrients. **Detoxification** of pesticides and herbicides is an important activity of the bacterial population of cultivated soils.

Soil bacteria are inactive at temperatures below 6°C but their activities increase with rising temperature up to a maximum of 35°C. Actively growing bacteria are killed at temperatures above 82°C, but several species can form thick-walled resting spores under adverse conditions. These spores are very resistant to heat and they survive temperatures up to 120°C. **Partial sterilization** of soil can kill the actively growing bacteria but not the bacterial spores. The growth rate and multiplication depend also upon the **food supply**. High organic matter levels support high bacterial populations so long as a balanced range of nutrients is present. Bacteria thrive in a range of **pH 5.5–7.5**; fungi tend to dominate the more acid soils. Aerobic conditions should be maintained because the beneficial organisms as well as plant roots require oxygen, whereas many of the bacteria that thrive under anaerobic conditions are detrimental.

Fungi

The majority of fungi live saprophytically on soil organic matter. Some species are capable only of utilizing simple and easily decomposable organic matter whereas others attack cellulose as well. There are some important fungi that can decompose **lignin**; making them one of the few primary decomposers of wood and fibrous plant material. Several fungi in the soil are parasites and examples of these are discussed in Chapter 11. Fungi appear to be able to tolerate acid conditions and low calcium better than other micro-organisms and are abundant in both neutral and acid soils. Most are well adapted to survive in dry soils but few thrive in very wet conditions. Their numbers are high in soils rich in plant residues but decline rapidly as the readily decomposable material disappears. The bacteria persist longer, where present, and eventually consume the fungal remains.

The rhizosphere

The rhizosphere (*see* also page 8) is a zone in the soil that is influenced by roots. Living roots change the atmosphere around them by using up oxygen and producing carbon dioxide (*see* respiration). Roots exude a variety of organic compounds that hold water and form a coating that bridges the gap between root and nearby soil particles. Micro-organisms occur in greatly increased numbers and are more active when in proximity to roots. Some actually invade the root cells where they live as **symbionts**. The *Rhizobium* spp. of bacteria lives symbiotically with many legumes.

Symbiotic associations involving plant roots and fungi are known as mycorrhizae. There is considerable interest in exploiting the potential of **mycorrhizae**, which appear to be associated with a high proportion of plants especially in less fertile soils. In this symbiotic relationship the fungus obtains its carbohydrate requirements from the plant. In turn, the plant gains greater access to nutrients in the soil, especially phosphates, through the increased surface area for absorption and because the fungus appears to utilize sources not available to higher plants. Most woodland trees have fungi covering their roots and penetrating the epidermis. Orchids and heathers have an even closer association in which the fungi invade the root and coil up within the cells. The association appears to be necessary for the successful development of the seedlings. Mycorrhizal plants generally appear to be more tolerant of transplanting and this is thought to be an important factor for orchard and container-grown ornamentals.

NUTRIENT CYCLES

All the plant nutrients are in continuous circulation between plants, animals, the soil and the air. The processes contributing to the production of simpler inorganic substances such as ammonia, nitrites, nitrates, sulphates and phosphates are sometimes referred to as **mineralization**. Mineralization yields chemicals that are readily taken up by plants from the soil solution. The formation of humus, organic residues of a resistant nature, is known as **humification**. Both mineralization and humification are intimately tied up in the same decomposition process but the terms help identify the end product being studied. Likewise it is possible to follow the circulation of carbon in the carbon cycle and nitrogen in the nitrogen cycle, although these nutrient cycles along with all the others are interrelated.

Carbon cycle

Green plants obtain their carbon from the carbon dioxide in the atmosphere and during the process of photosynthesis are able to fix the carbon, converting it into sugar. Some carbon is returned to the atmosphere by the green plants themselves during respiration, but most is incorporated into plant tissue as carbohydrates, proteins, fats, etc. The carbon incorporated into the plant structure is eventually released as carbon dioxide, as illustrated in Figure 15.1.

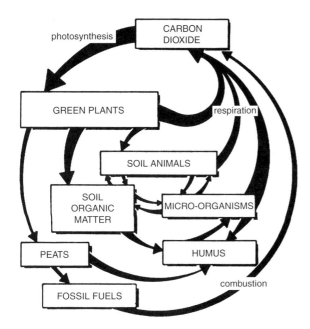

Figure 15.1 *Carbon cycle. The recycling of the element carbon by organisms is illustrated. Note how all the carbon in organic matter is eventually released as carbon dioxide by respiration or combustion. Green plants convert the carbon dioxide by photosynthesis into sugars which form the basis of all the organic substances required by plants, animals and micro-organisms.*

All living organisms in this food web release carbon dioxide as they respire. The sugars, cellulose, starch and proteins of **succulent** plant tissue, as found in young plants, are rapidly decomposed to yield plant nutrients and have only a short-term effect. In contrast, the **lignified tissue** of older plants rots more slowly. Besides the release of nutrients, **humus** is formed from this fibrous and woody material, which has a long-term effect on the soil. Plants grown in the vicinity of vigorously decomposing vegetation, e.g. cucumbers in straw bales, live in a carbon dioxide enriched atmosphere. Carbon dioxide is also released on combustion of all organic matter, including the fossil fuels such as coal and oil. Organic materials such as paraffin or propane, which do not produce harmful gases when burned cleanly, are used in protected culture for **carbon dioxide enrichment**.

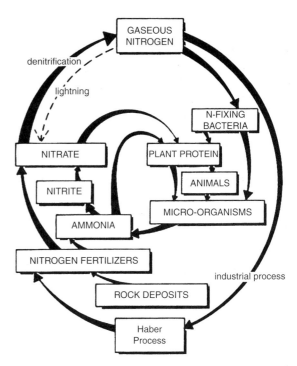

Figure 15.2 *Nitrogen cycle. The recycling of the element nitrogen by organisms is illustrated. Note the importance of nitrates that can be taken up and used by plants to manufacture protein. Micro-organisms also have this ability but animals require nitrogen supplies in protein form. Gaseous nitrogen only becomes available to organisms after being captured by nitrogen-fixing organisms or via nitrogen fertilizers manufactured by man. In aerobic soil conditions, bacteria convert ammonia to nitrates (nitrification), whereas in anaerobic conditions nitrates are reduced to nitrogen gases (denitrification).*

Nitrogen cycle

Plants require nitrogen to form proteins. Although plants live in an atmosphere largely made up of nitrogen they cannot utilize gaseous nitrogen. Plants take up nitrogen in the form of nitrates and, to a lesser extent, as ammonia. Both are released from proteins by a chain of bacterial reactions as shown in Figure 15.2.

Ammonifying bacteria convert the proteins they attack to ammonia. **Ammonia** from the breakdown of protein in organic matter or from **inorganic**

nitrogen fertilizers is converted to **nitrates** by **nitrifying bacteria**. This is accomplished in two stages. Ammonia is first converted to **nitrites** by *Nitrosomonas* spp. **Nitrites** are toxic to plants in small quantities but they are normally converted to nitrates by *Nitrobacter* spp. before they reach harmful levels. Ammonifying and nitrifying bacteria thrive in aerobic conditions.

Where there is no oxygen, anaerobic organisms dominate. Many anaerobic bacteria utilize nitrates and in doing so convert them to **gaseous nitrogen**. This **denitrification** represents an important loss of nitrate from the soil, which is at its most serious in well-fertilized, warm and waterlogged land.

Nitrogen fixation.   Although plants cannot utilize gaseous nitrogen it can be converted to plant nutrients by some micro-organisms. *Azotobacter* are free-living bacteria that obtain their nitrogen requirements from the air. As they die and decompose, the nitrogen trapped as protein is converted to ammonia and then nitrates by other soil bacteria. The *Rhizobia* spp. which live in root nodules on some legumes, also trap nitrogen to the benefit of the host plant. Finally, nitrogen gas can be converted to ammonia industrially in the **Haber process**, which is the basis of the artificial nitrogen fertilizer industry.

Sulphur cycle

Sulphur is an essential constituent of plants which accumulates in the soil in organic forms. This sulphur does not become available to plants until aerobic micro-organisms, which yield soluble **sulphates**, mineralize the organic form. Under anaerobic conditions there are micro-organisms which utilize organic sulphur and produce hydrogen sulphide which has a characteristic smell of bad eggs.

Carbon to nitrogen ratio

All nutrients play a part in all nutrient cycles simply because all organisms need the same range of nutrients to be active. Normally there are adequate quantities of nutrients, with the exception of carbon or nitrogen, which are needed in relatively large quantities. **A shortage of nitrogenous material would lead to a hold-up in the nitrogen cycle but would also slow down the carbon cycle, i.e. the decomposition of organic matter is slowed because the micro-organisms concerned suffer a shortage of *one* of their essential nutrients. A useful way of expressing the relative amounts of the two important plant foods is in the carbon to nitrogen (C:N) ratio.**

Plant material has relatively wide C:N ratios, but those of micro-organisms are much narrower. This is because micro-organisms utilize about three-quarters of the carbon in plants during decomposition as an energy source. The carbon utilized this way is released as carbon dioxide, whereas, usually, all the nitrogen is incorporated in the microbial body protein. This concentrates the nitrogen in the new organism that is living on the plant material.

Sometimes the C:N ratio is so wide that some nitrogen is drawn from the soil and 'locked up' in the microbial tissue. This is what happens when **straw** (and similar fibrous or woody material such as wood chips and bark) with a ratio of 60:1 is dug into the soil. For example, if a thousand 12 kg bales of straw are dug into 1 ha of land then the addition to the soil will be 12 000 kg of straw containing 4800 kg of carbon and 80 kg of nitrogen. Three-quarters of the carbon (3600 kg) is utilized for energy and lost as carbon dioxide and a quarter (1200 kg) is incorporated over several months into microbial tissue. Microbial tissue has a C:N ratio of about 8:1 which means that by the time the straw is used up some 150 kg of nitrogen is locked up with the 1200 kg of carbon in the micro-organisms. Since there was only 80 kg of nitrogen in the straw put on the land, the other 70 kg has been '**robbed**' from the soil. This nitrogen is rendered unavailable to plants ('locked up') until the micro-organisms die and decompose. To ensure rapid decomposition or to prevent a detrimental effect on crops the addition of straw must be accompanied by the addition of nitrogen.

Nitrogen is released during decomposition if the organic material has a C:N ratio narrower than

30:1, such as young plant material, or with nitrogen-supplemented plant material such as FYM.

In general, fresh organic matter decomposes very rapidly so long as conditions are right, but the older residues tend to decompose very slowly.

HUMUS

Active micro-organisms gradually decompose the dead organic matter of the soil until it consists of finely divided plant and micro-organism remains. **It is a black colloidal material which coats soil particles and gives topsoil its characteristic dark colour.** This process of humification leads to the formation of **humus**, a collection of humic acids, which is the slowly decomposing residue of soil organic matter. It is mainly derived from the decomposition of fibrous vegetation that is rich in **lignin** such as straw. This colloidal material has a high **cation exchange capacity** and therefore can make a major contribution to the retention of exchangeable cations, especially on soils low in clay (*see* sands, page 157). It also adheres strongly to mineral particles, which makes it a valuable agent in soil **aggregation**. In sandy soils it provides a means of sticking particles together whereas in clays it forms a clay–humus complex that makes the heavier soils more likely to crumble. Its presence in the soil crumbs makes them more stable, i.e. more able to resist collapse when wetted and it increases the range of soil **workability** (*see* page 175). Bacteria eventually decompose humus so the amount in the soil is very much dependent on the continued addition of appropriate bulky organic matter.

ORGANIC MATTER LEVELS

The routine laboratory method for estimating **organic matter** levels depends upon finding the total carbon content of the soil. A simpler method is to dry a sample of soil and burn off the organic matter. After cooling, the soil can be re-weighed and the loss in weight represents destroyed organic matter. These methods give an overall total of soil organic matter excluding the larger soil animals.

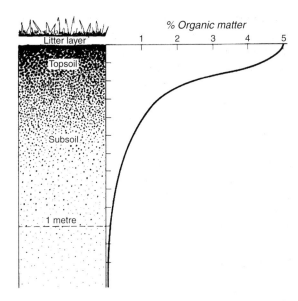

Figure 15.3 *Distribution of organic matter in an uncultivated soil. Organic matter content of soil decreases from the soil surface downwards. Note that the topsoil is significantly richer in humus, which gives it a characteristically darker colour.*

Most topsoil contains between 1 and 6 per cent of organic matter, whereas subsoil usually contains less than 2 per cent. The distribution of organic matter under grass in normal temperate areas is shown in Figure 15.3. Soil organic matter is concentrated in the topsoil because most of the roots occur in this zone and the plant residues tend to be added to the surface forming the leaf litter layer. **The organic matter level in any part of the soil depends upon how much fresh material is added compared with the rate of decomposition. It is stable when these two processes are balanced and the equilibrium reached is determined mainly by climate, soil type and treatment under cultivation.**

Climate

Climate affects both the amount of organic matter added and the rate of decomposition. Below 6°C there is no microbial activity, but it increases with increasing temperature so long as conditions are otherwise favourable. In dry areas there is not only less plant growth, resulting in less organic matter being added to the soil, but also less microbial action. In **warm climates**, where there is adequate moisture, low organic matter results from very much increased decomposition. In **cooler areas** there tends to be an accumulation of organic matter because the decreased plant growth is more than offset by the reduced micro-organism activity that occurs over the long winter periods. Organic matter also tends to accumulate in **wetter conditions**. Where waterlogging is prevalent, 10–20 per cent organic matter levels develop; where waterlogging is permanent, organic matter accumulates to give rise to **peat**.

Soil type

Generally, soils with lower clay contents have lower organic matter levels. Coarse sands and sandy loams tend to be warmer than finer-textured soils and have better aeration, which results in higher microbial activity. Such soils often support less plant growth because of poor fertility and poor water-holding capacity. These factors combine to give soils with low organic matter levels. In cultivation these same soils become a problem unless large quantities of organic matter are applied at frequent intervals to maintain adequate humus levels. Such soils are often referred to as 'hungry soils' because of their high demand for manure. On finer-textured soils the higher fine sand, silt or clay content increases the water-holding capacity. This reduces soil temperature, resulting in less microbial activity. The presence of clay directly reduces the rate of decomposition because it combines with humus and protects it from microbial attack.

Cultivation

On first cultivation the increased aeration and nutrients stimulate micro-organisms and a new equilibrium with lower soil organic matter levels prevails. Once under cultivation, grasses and high-producing legumes tend to increase levels but most crops, particularly those in which complete plant removal occurs, lead to decreased organic matter levels. Only large, regular dressings of bulky organic matter such as straw, FYM, leaf mould and compost can improve or maintain the level of soil organic matter on cultivated soils.

Organic matter can accumulate under grass and form a mat on the surface where the carbon cycle is slowed because of nutrient deficiency usually induced by surface soil acidity or excess phosphate levels. This is part of the reason for the development of '**thatch**' in turf.

Organic soils

While all soils contain some organic matter, most are classified as mineral soils. Organic soils are those that have enough organic matter present to dominate the soil properties and they develop where decomposition is slow because the activity of micro-organisms is reduced by cold or waterlogged conditions. **Peat** is formed of partially decomposed plant material. This occurs in waterlogged conditions, usually low in nutrients, where decomposition rates are low. There are great differences between peats because of the variations in conditions where they occur and the species of plants from which they are formed. Some peat is formed in shallow water, as found in poorly drained depressions or infilling lakes. In such circumstances the water drains from surrounding mineral soils and consequently has sufficient nutrients to support vegetation often dominated by sedges, giving rise to **sedge peat**. As the waterlogged area, pond or lake becomes full of humified organic matter it forms a bog, moor or fen. In the drier conditions of eastern England some of these areas have been drained to form the productive **fenland**. In the wetter west, **sphagnum moss**, which is able to live on very low nutrient levels that prevail, grows on top of the infilled wet land. The dead vegetation becomes very acid and decomposes slowly. It builds up to form a high moor.

Some of the peatlands, which are enriched with minerals, prove very valuable when drained. Many of these soils are used to produce vegetables and other high value crops. Unfortunately the increased aeration allows the organic matter to be decomposed at a rate faster than it can be replenished. Furthermore, when the surface dries out the light particles are vulnerable to wind erosion. Consequently, the soil level of these areas is falling at the rate of 3 m every 100 years. Keeping the watertable as high as possible and providing protection against wind erosion can minimize subsidence.

BENEFITS OF ORGANIC MATTER

There are three main types of organic matter in the soil; the living organisms, the dead ones in varying degrees of decomposition and the humus.

The presence of partially decomposed organic matter creates an **open soil structure** and, on many soils, increases the water-holding capacity. As it decomposes it can act as a dilute **slow release** source of nutrients.

The **humus** coats the soil particles and modifies their characteristics. On sandy and silty soils the humus enables stable crumbs to be formed. Stable, well-structured fine sands and silts are only possible under intensive cultivation if high humus levels are maintained by the addition of large quantities of bulky organic matter. The surface charges on humus are capable of combining with the clay particles, thereby making heavy soils less sticky and more friable. These surface charges also enable humus to hold cations against leaching, which is very important in soils low in clay. Humus also improves **water-holding properties** of the soil. Its darkening effect increases heat absorption.

The **living organisms** in the soil play their part in the conversion of plant and animal debris to minerals and humus. The *Rhizobia* and *Azotobacter* spp. fix gaseous nitrogen while other bacteria play an important role in the detoxification of harmful organic materials such as pesticides and herbicides.

Soil structure is modified by the influence of plant roots and earthworms.

ADDITION OF ORGANIC MATTER

It is normal in horticulture to return **residues** to cultivated areas where possible. Whether or not the plant remains are worked into the soil in which they have been grown depends upon their nature. The residue of some crops such as tomatoes in the greenhouse are removed to reduce the disease carryover and because it cannot easily be incorporated into the soil. Other crops such as hops are removed for harvesting and some of the processed remains, spent hops, can be returned or used elsewhere. Wherever organic matter is removed, whether it is just the marketed part such as top fruit from the orchard or virtually the whole crop such as cucumbers from a greenhouse, the nutrients removed must be replaced to maintain fertility (*see* fertilizers).

Although some forms do not return nutrients to the soil, **bulky organic matter** such as compost, straw, FYM and peat is an important means of maintaining organic matter and humus levels. The main problem is obtaining cheap enough sources because their bulk makes transport and handling a major part of the cost. They can be evaluated on the basis of their small nutrient value and their effect on the physical properties of soil as appropriate.

Composting

Composting refers to the rotting down of plant residues before they are applied to soils. Many gardeners depend on composting as a means of using garden refuse to maintain organic matter levels in their soils. On a larger scale there is interest in the use of composted **town refuse** for horticultural purposes. Many councils are now supplying composting equipment to encourage householders to recycle organic matter as well as glass and metals. Horticulturists are increasingly concerned with the recycling of wastes and attention is being given to modern composting methods. For successful composting, conditions must be favourable for the decomposing micro-organisms. The material must be moist and well aerated throughout. As the heap is built, separate layers of lime and nitrogen are added as necessary to ensure the correct pH and C:N ratio. Organic waste brought together in large enough quantities under ideal conditions can generate enough heat to take the temperature to over 70°C within 7 days. If all the material is brought to this temperature it has the advantage of killing harmful organisms and weed seeds.

Straw

Straw is an agricultural crop residue readily available in many parts of the country, but care should be taken to avoid straw with harmful **herbicide residues**. It is ploughed in or composted and then worked in. There appears to be no advantage in composting if allowance is made for the demand on nitrogen by soil bacteria. About 6 kg of nitrogen fertilizer needs to be added for each tonne of straw for composting or preventing soil robbing (*see* page 188). Chopping the straw facilitates its incorporation and while under-composed it can open up soils. On decomposition, it yields very little nutrient for plant use but makes an important contribution to maintaining soil humus levels. Straw bales suitably composted on site are the basis of producing an open growing medium for cucumbers.

FYM

This is the traditional material used to maintain and improve soil fertility. It consists of straw, or other bedding, mixed with animal faeces and urine. The exact value of this material depends upon the proportions of the ingredients, the degree of decomposition and the method of storage. Samples vary considerably. Much of the FYM is rotted down in the first growing season but almost half survives for another year, and half of that goes onto a third season and so on. A full range of nutrients is released into the soil and the addition of the major nutrients should be allowed for when calculating **fertilizer requirements**. The continued release of large quantities of nitrogen can be a problem, especially on unplanted ground in the autumn, when the nitrates formed are leached deep into the soil over the winter.

FYM is most valued for its ability to provide the organic matter and humus for maintaining or improving soil structure. As with any other bulky organic matter, FYM must be worked into soils where conditions are favourable for its continued decomposition. Where fresh organic matter is worked into wet and compacted soils the need for oxygen outstrips supply and anaerobic conditions develop to the detriment of any plants present. Where this occurs a foul smell (*see* sulphur) and grey colourings occur. FYM should not be worked in deep, especially on heavy soil.

Horticultural peats

Sphagnum moss peats have a fibrous texture, high porosity, high water retention and a low pH. They are used extensively in horticulture as a source of bulky organic matter and are particularly valued as an ingredient of potting composts because, with their stability, excellent porosity and high water retention, they can be used to create an almost ideal root environment.

Sedge peats tend to contain more plant nutrients than sphagnum moss. They are darker, more decomposed, and have a higher pH level but a slightly lower water-holding capacity. They tend to be used for making peat blocks.

Considerable efforts are being made to find alternative materials to replace peat in order to avoid destroying valued wetland habitats from which they are harvested.

Leaves

Leaf mould is made of rotted leaves of deciduous trees. It is low in nutrients because nitrogen and phosphate are withdrawn from the leaves before they fall and potassium is readily leached from the ageing leaf. They are often composted separately from other organic matter and much valued in ornamental horticulture for a variety of uses such as an attractive mulch or, when well rotted down, as a compost ingredient. They are commonly composted in mesh cages, but many achieve success by putting them in polythene bags well punched with holes. The leaves alone have a high C:N ratio so decomposition is slow and it is not usually until the second year that the dark brown crumbly material is produced although the process can be speeded up by shredding the leaves first.

Unless they are from trees growing in very acid conditions, the leaves are rich in calcium and the leaf mould made from them should not be used with calcifuge plants.

Pine needles are covered with a protective layer that slows down decomposition. They are low in calcium and the resins present are converted to acids. This extremely acid litter is almost resistant to decomposition. It is valued in the propagation and growing of calcifuge plants such as rhododendrons and heathers, and as a material for constructing decorative pathways.

Air-dried digested sludge

This consists of sewage sludge that has been fermented in sealed tanks, drained and stacked to dry. The harmful organisms and the objectionable smells of raw sewage are eliminated in this process.

It provides a useful source of organic matter but is low in potash. Advice should be taken before using sewage sludges because in some regions they contain large quantities of heavy metals such as zinc, nickel and cadmium that can accumulate in the soil to levels toxic to plants.

Leys

The practice of **ley** farming involves grassing down areas and is common where arable crop production can be closely integrated with livestock. At the end of the ley period the grass or grass and clover sward is ploughed in. The root action of the grasses and the increased organic matter levels can improve the structure and workability of problem soils. There are some pest problems peculiar to cropping after grass that should be borne in mind (*see* wireworms), and generally the ley enterprise has to be profitable in its own right to justify its place in a horticultural rotation. It is practised in some vegetable production and nursery stock areas.

Mulching

Mulches are materials applied to the surface of the soil to suppress weeds, modify soil temperatures, reduce water loss, protect the soil surface and reduce erosion. Many organic materials are used for this purpose, including straw, leaf mould, peat, compost, lawn mowings and spent mushroom compost. The organic mulches increase earthworm activity at the surface, which promotes better and more stable soil structure in the top layers. Soil compaction by water droplets is reduced and, as the organic mulches are incorporated, the soil structure can be improved. If thick enough, mulches can suppress weed growth but it is counterproductive to introduce a material that contains weeds. Likewise, care should be taken not to introduce pests and disease or use a material such as compost where slugs can be a problem.

When organic matter is added as a mulch it is acting, in effect, as an extra layer of loose soil. Thus, water loss from the soil surface is reduced because it is covered with a dry layer (*see* evaporation). Soil temperatures lag behind the surface temperatures because of its insulatory properties with the greater lag at greater depth. They tend to reduce soil temperatures in the Summer but retain warmth later in the Autumn.

Manufactured materials such as paper, metal foil or, most commonly, polythene are also used but these have very little insulatory effect. However, these materials are particularly effective in reducing water loss by evaporation at the surface (*see* water conservation). The colour of the mulch

Table 15.1 Sources of nutrients for use in organic growing

Farmyard and poultry manure
Slurry or urine
Composts from spent mushroom and vermiculture substrates
Composts from organic household refuse
Composts from plant residues
Processed animal products from slaughterhouses and fish industries
Organic by-products of foodstuffs and textile industries
Seaweeds and seaweed products
Sawdust, bark and wood waste
Wood ash
Natural phosphate rock
Calcinated aluminium phosphate rock
Basic slag
Rock potash
Sulphate of potash*
Limestone
Chalk
Magnesium rock
Calcareous magnesium rock
Epsom salt (magnesium sulphate)
Gypsum (Calcium sulphate)
Trace elements (boron, copper, iron, manganese, molybdenum and zinc)*
Sulphur*
Stone meal
Clay (bentonite and perlite)

*Need recognized by control body.

is important because light-coloured material will reflect radiation, whereas dark material can lead to earlier cropping by warming up the soil earlier.

ORGANIC PRODUCTION

Organic production in the European Union is subject to regulations laid down in 1991. These require that the fertility and the biological activity of the soil must be maintained or increased by the cultivation of legumes, green manures or deep-rooting crops in an appropriate multi-annual rotation and by the incorporation of organic matter including FYM, composted or not, from holdings producing according to the same regulations. If adequate nutrition or soil conditioning cannot be achieved by these means then other, specified, organic or mineral fertilizers, as listed in Table 15.1, may be applied. For compost activation, appropriate micro-organisms or plant-based preparations may be used. These organic or mineral fertilizers may be applied only to the extent that the adequate nutrition of the crop being rotated, or soil conditioning, is not possible by the preferred methods.

FURTHER READING

Advisory Reference Book 210 *Organic Manures* (MAFF, 1976).
Bragg, N. *Peatland: Its Alternatives* (Horticultural Development Council, 1991).
Brown, L.V. *Applied Principles of Horticulture*, 2nd edition (Butterworth-Heinemann, 2002).
Edwards, C.A. and Lofty, J.R. *Biology of Earthworms*, 2nd edition (Halsted Press, 1977).
Hills, L.D. *Organic Gardening* (Penguin Books Ltd., 1977).
Jackson, R.M. and Raw, F. *Life in the Soil*. (Edward Arnold).
Postgate, J. *Nitrogen Fixation – Studies in Biology No. 92*, 3rd edition (Ed Arnold, 1998).
Robinson, D.W. and Lamb, J.G.D. (Editors). *Peat in Horticulture* (HEA/Academic Press, 1975).
Russell, E.J. *The World of the Soil* (Collins New Naturalist, 1957).

16

Plant Nutrition

Green plants require 15 elements in order to grow normally including carbon, oxygen and hydrogen (see Chapter 5). The 12 essential minerals enter the plant tissue in the form of ions from the growing media or to a lesser extent through the leaves. In established plant communities such as forest or grassland the minerals are recycled through the complex food webs and the community develops according to the many factors that affect plant growth, including the net gain or loss of minerals.

Removing a plant or part of it breaks the natural cycle and prevents minerals contained in the plant from returning to the growing medium for re-use. These minerals can be replaced in many different ways. Where only a small quantity of nutrient is needed it can be supplied through suitable types of bulky organic matter which release sufficient nutrient when mineralized. It is often impracticable to supply large quantities of nutrients by the addition of vast quantities of bulky organic matter; organic or inorganic fertilizers, which are more concentrated sources of major plant nutrients, resolve this dilemma. Many growing media, especially those used in composts, are very deficient in minerals and therefore supplementation with plant nutrients is essential. Ensuring mineral uptake is a major

concern. The roots must be able to find the nutrients (see soil structure), and soil pH and mineral balance should be adjusted to provide optimum availability of nutrients.

This chapter describes the nature of soil pH, its effect on nutrient uptake and the methods of changing it to maintain optimum growing conditions. The methods of applying nutrients are examined and the characteristics of major and minor ('trace') elements in growing media are outlined. Considering how to apply the correct quantities of nutrient to different plants concludes the chapter.

CONTROL OF SOIL pH

Life in the soil is greatly influenced by the soil pH, either directly or indirectly. The pH scale is a means of expressing the degree of acidity or alkalinity. pH values less than 7 are acid and the lower the figure, the greater the acidity. Values greater than 7 indicate increasing alkalinity and pH 7 is neutral. Temperate area soils usually lie between pH 4 and 8; the vast majority are between 5.5 and 7.5.

For ideal growing conditions most plants require a soil of about pH 6.5, which is slightly acid. At this point most of the plant nutrients are available for uptake by the roots. Alkaline conditions are usually created by the presence of large quantities of calcium ('lime'), which interferes with the uptake and utilization of several of the plant nutrients.

Calcicoles, or 'lime-loving' plants, have evolved a different metabolism and are tolerant of high soil pH. In contrast, the **calcifuge** or 'lime-hating' plants, such as rhododendrons and some heathers, do not even tolerate the level of calcium in soils at pH 5.5. Consequently, they must be grown in more acid conditions. At very low pH some substances such as aluminium become soluble at levels that are toxic to plants.

Acidity and alkalinity

Pure water is neutral, i.e. neither acid nor alkaline. It is made up of two hydrogen atoms and one oxygen atom, expressed as the familiar formula H_2O. Most of the water is made up of water molecules in which the atoms stay together, but a tiny proportion disassociates, i.e. they form ions. Equal numbers of positive ions, called cations, and negative ions, called anions, are formed. In the case of water, an equal number of hydrogen cations, H^+, and hydroxyl anions, OH^-, exist within the clusters of water molecules (H_2O). When, as in water, the concentration of hydrogen ions is the same as that of hydroxyl ions, there is neutrality. As the concentration of hydrogen ions is increased, the concentration of hydroxyl ions decreases and acidity increases. Likewise, addition of hydroxyl ions and a decrease in hydrogen ions lead to increased alkalinity.

Many compounds form ions as they dissolve and mix intimately with water to produce a solution. All acids release hydrogen ions when dissolved in water. Whereas a strong acid (such as hydrochloric acid) dissociates when dissolved, only a part of a weak acid (such as carbonic or acetic acid) breaks up into ions. Bases, such as caustic soda, dissolve in water and increase the concentration of hydroxyl ions.

The pH scale expresses the amount of acidity or alkalinity in terms of hydrogen ion concentration. In order to present the scale simply, negative logarithms are used: **'pH' is the negative logarithm**, the mathematical symbol for which is 'p', **of the hydrogen ion concentration**, abbreviated as 'H'. It is important to note that, as the scale is logarithmic, a one-unit change represents a 10-fold increase or decrease in hydrogen ion concentration, and two units a 100-fold change. Thus a solution of pH 3 is 10 times more acid than one of pH 4, 100 times more acid than pH 5, and a 1000 times more than pH 6.

The **buffering capacity** of a substance is its ability to resist change in pH. Pure water has no buffering capacity: the addition of minute quantities of acid or alkali has an immediate effect on its pH. In contrast, the cation exchange capacity of clays reduces the effect because the hydrogen ions exchange with calcium ions on the clay's colloid surface. Since the number of hydrogen ions being released or absorbed is small compared with the clay's reserve, the pH changes very little. High humus soils similarly have the advantage of a high buffering capacity. A related buffer effect is seen when acids, such as the carbonic acid of rain, are incorporated into soils with 'free' lime present: the acid dissolves some of the carbonate with no accompanying change in pH.

Soil acidity

The balance of hydrogen ions and basic ions determines soil acidity. A clay particle with abundant hydrogen ions acts as a weak acid, whereas if fully charged with bases (such as calcium, Ca) it has a neutral or alkaline reaction (*see* base saturation). Consequently, soil pH is usually regulated by the presence of calcium cations; soils become more acid as calcium is leached from the soil faster than it is replaced, e.g. by mineral weathering. This is the tendency in temperate areas where rainfall, which is a weak acid (*see* carbonic acid), exceeds evaporation over the year. Thus hydrogen and aluminium ions take over the soil's cation exchange sites and the pH falls. Soils with large reserves of calcium, such as those derived from chalky boulder clay, do not become acid because they are kept base saturated. In contrast, calcium ions are readily leached from free-draining sands in high rainfall areas and these soils tend to go acid rapidly.

In addition to the carbonic acid in rainfall, there are several other sources of acid that affect the soil. **Acid rain** (polluted rain and snow) is directly harmful to vegetation but also contributes to the fall in soil pH.

Organic acids derived from the microbial breakdown of organic matter, e.g. humic acids, also lead to an increase in soil acidity. The bacterial nitrification of **ammonia** to nitrate yields acid hydrogen ions. Consequently fertilizers containing ammonium salts prevent calcium from attaching to soil colloids and cause calcium loss in the **drainage water**. Other fertilizers have much less effect. Calcium and magnesium are plant nutrients and

the soil's lime reserves are therefore gradually reduced by **crop removal**.

Effects of liming

When lime is added to an acid soil, the calcium or magnesium replaces the exchangeable hydrogen on the soil colloid surface and neutralizes the soluble acids (*see* cation exchange). Eventually hydrogen ions are completely replaced by bases and **base saturation** is achieved, producing a soil pH of about 7. The influence of soil pH on plant **nutrient availability** is demonstrated in Figure 16.1. It can be seen that for mineral soils the most favourable level for ensuring the availability of all

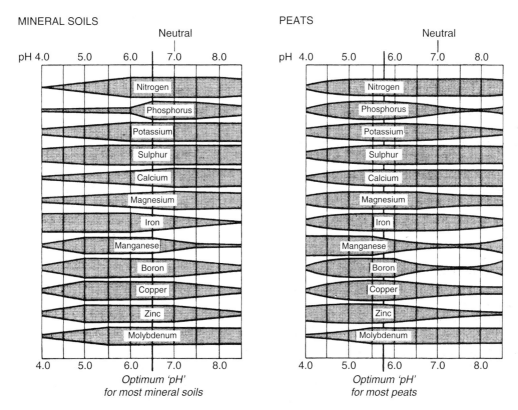

Figure 16.1 *Effect of soil pH on nutrient availability. The availability of a given amount of nutrient is indicated by the width of the band. The growing media should be kept at a pH at which all essential nutrients are available. For most plants the optimum pH is 6.5 in mineral soils and 5.8 in peats.*

nutrients is pH 6.5, while peat soils should be limed to pH 5.8 in order to maximize overall nutrient availability. In acid conditions some nutrients such as manganese and other soil minerals such as aluminium may become toxic.

Beneficial **soil organisms** are affected by soil acidity and liming. A few soil-borne disease-causing organisms tend to occur more frequently on lime-deficient soils (*see* clubroot), whereas others are more prevalent in well-limed soils. Calcium sometimes improves soil structure and soil stability. It is probable that this is mainly because it creates conditions favourable for decomposition of organic matter, yielding **humus**, and encourages **root activity**. Free lime in clay soils sometimes, but not always, leads to better crumb formation on drying and shrinking.

Plant tolerance

Tolerance to soil pH and calcium levels varies considerably, but all plants are adversely affected when the soil becomes too acid. Table 16.1 shows

Table 16.1 Soil acidity and plant tolerance

Plants	pH below which plant growth may be restricted on mineral soils
Beans	6.0
Cabbage	5.4
Carrots	5.7
Celery	6.3
Lettuce	6.1
Potato	4.9
Tomato	5.1
Apple	5.0
Blackcurrant	6.0
Raspberry	5.5
Strawberry	5.1
Carnation	6.0
Chrysanthemum	5.7
Daffodil	6.1
Hydrangea (pink)	5.9
Hydrangea (blue)	4.1
Rose	5.6

the point below which the growth of common horticultural plants is significantly reduced. In the case of calcifuges (i.e. 'lime-hating' plants), the highest point before growth is affected by the presence of calcium should be noted, e.g. for *Rhododendrons* and some *Ericas* this is at pH 5.5.

Lime requirement

The lime requirement of soil depends on the required rise in pH and the soil texture (*see* buffering capacity). Lime requirement is expressed as the **amount of calcium carbonate in tonnes per hectare required to raise the pH of the top 150 mm to the desired pH. A pH of 6.5 is recommended for temperate plants on mineral soils, pH 5.8 on peats.** The amount of a liming material needed to meet the lime requirement will depend on its **neutralizing value (NV)** and sometimes fineness.

Liming materials

Liming materials can be compared by considering their ability to neutralize soil acidity, fineness and cost to deliver and spread. **The NV of a lime indicates its potency. It is determined in the laboratory by comparing its ability to neutralize soil acidity with that of the standard, pure calcium oxide. A NV of 50 signifies that 100 kg of that material has the same effect on soil acidity as 50 kg of calcium oxide.** The **fineness** of the lime is important because it indicates the rate at which it affects the soil acidity (*see* surface area). It is expressed, where relevant, in terms of the percentage of the sample that will pass through a 100 mesh sieve. Liming materials commonly used in horticulture are listed below with some of their properties.

Calcium carbonate is the most common liming material. Natural soft chalk or limestone that is high in calcium carbonate is quarried and ground. It is a cheap liming material, easy to store and safe to handle. A sample in which 40 per cent will pass through a 100 mesh sieve can be used at the standard rate to meet the lime requirement. Coarser samples, although cheaper to produce, easier to spread and longer lasting in the soil, require heavier dressings. Shell sands have NV from 25 to 45. Whilst the purest samples can be used at nearly the same rate as calcium carbonate, twice as much of the poorer samples is required to have the same effect.

Calcium oxide, also known as quicklime, burnt lime, cob lime or caustic lime, is produced when chalk and limestone are very strongly heated in a limekiln. Calcium oxide has a higher calcium content than calcium carbonate and consequently a higher NV. Pure calcium oxide is used as the standard to express NV (100) and the impure forms have lower values (usually 85–90). If used instead of ground limestone, only half the quantity should be applied. In contact with moisture, lumps of calcium oxide slake, i.e. react spontaneously with water to produce a fine white powder, calcium hydroxide, with release of considerable heat. Although rarely used now calcium oxide should be used with care because it is a fire risk, burns flesh and scorches plant tissue.

Calcium hydroxide, hydrated or slaked lime is derived from calcium oxide by the addition of water. The fine white powder formed is popular in horticulture. It has a higher NV than calcium carbonate and its fineness ensures a rapid effect on the growing medium. Once exposed to the atmosphere it reacts with carbon dioxide to form calcium carbonate.

It should be noted that all forms of processed lime quickly revert to calcium carbonate when added to the soil. Calcium carbonate, which is insoluble in pure water, gradually dissolves in the weak carbonic acid of the soil solution around the roots.

Magnesian limestone, also known as Dolomitic limestone, is especially useful in the preparation of composts because it both neutralizes acidity and introduces magnesium as a nutrient. Magnesium limestone has a slightly higher NV (50–55) than calcium limestone, but tends to act more slowly.

Lime application

Unless very coarse grades are used, lime raises the soil pH over a 1–2 year period, although the full effect may take as long as 4 years; thereafter pH falls again. Consequently lime application should

be planned in the planting programme. It is normally worked into the top 150 mm of soil. If deeper incorporation is required, the quantity used should be increased proportionally. The lime should be evenly spread and regular moderate dressings are preferable to large infrequent applications. Very large applications needed in land restoration work should be divided for application over several years.

Care should be taken that the surface layers of the soil do not become too acid even when the lower topsoil has sufficient lime. Top layers are the first to become depleted with consequent effect on plant establishment. This tendency has to be carefully watched out for in turf management.

Applications of organic manures or ammonium fertilizers should be delayed until lime has been incorporated. If mixed they react to release **ammonia** which can be wasteful and sometimes harmful.

Decreasing soil pH

This is sometimes necessary for particular plants, e.g. *Ericas* requiring acid soils. In some circumstances it is appropriate to grow plants in a raised bed of **acid peat** or to work large quantities of peat into the topsoil. Adding acids can reduce either in conjunction with this approach or as an alternative, the base saturation of the mineral soil. Some acid industrial by-products can be used but the most usual method is to apply agricultural **sulphur**, which is converted to sulphuric acid by soil micro-organisms. The sulphur requirement depends on the pH change required and the soil's buffering capacity. The application of large quantities of **organic matter** gradually makes soils more acid. Nitrogen fertilizers releasing **ammonia** considerably reduce soil pH over a period of years in outdoor soils (*see* soil acidity) and can be used in liquid feeding to offset the tendency of hard water to raise pH levels in composts.

FERTILIZERS

Fertilizers are concentrated sources of plant nutrients that are added to growing media. **Straight**

Table 16.2 Nutrient analysis of fertilizers

	N %	$P_2O_5(P)$ %	K_2O (K) %	Mg %	Ca %	S %	Na %
Ammonium nitrate	33–35						
Ammonium sulphate	20–21					24	
Bone meal	3	20 (9)					
Calcium nitrate	15.5				20		
Calcium sulphate					23	18	
Chilean potassium nitrate	15		10 (8)				20
Dried blood	12–14						
Hoof and horn	12–14						
Kieserite				15		21	
Magnesium sulphate				10		13	
Meat and bone meal	5–10	18 (8)					
Monoammonium phosphate	12	37 (15)					
Phosphoric acid		54 (24)					
Potassium chloride			59 (49)				
Potassium nitrate	14		46 (38)				
Potassium sulphate			50 (42)			17	
Shoddy (wool waste)	2–15						
Superphosphate		18–20 (8–9)			20	12–14	
Triple superphosphate		47 (20)			14		
Urea	46						

fertilizers are those that supply only one of the major nutrients: nitrogen, phosphorus, potassium or magnesium (*see* Table 16.2). The amount of nutrient in the fertilizer is expressed as a percentage. Nitrogen fertilizers are described in terms of percentage of the element nitrogen in the fertilizer, i.e. per cent N. Phosphate fertilizers have been described in terms of the equivalent amount of phosphoric oxide, i.e. per cent P_2O_5, or increasingly as percentage phosphorus, per cent P. Likewise potash fertilizers, i.e. per cent K_2O, or percentage potassium, per cent K. Magnesium fertilizers are described in terms of per cent of Mg. The percentage figures clearly show the quantities, in kg, of nutrient in each 100 kg of fertilizer.

Compound fertilizers are those that supply two or more of the nutrients nitrogen, phosphorus and potassium. The nutrient content expressed as for straight fertilizers is, by convention, written on the bag in the order nitrogen, phosphorus and potassium. For example, 20–10–10 denotes 20 per cent N, 10 per cent P_2O_5 and 10 per cent K_2O.

Fertilizer regulations require that further details of trace elements, pesticide content and phosphorus solubility should appear where applicable on the invoice. Fertilizers and manures are available in many different forms. Generally the term **organic** implies that the fertilizer is derived from living organisms, whereas **inorganic** fertilizers are those derived from non-living material. However, in the context of organic growing it is necessary to look at specific requirements of the regulations (Table 15.1).

Application methods

Fertilizers are applied in several different ways. **Base dressings** are those that are incorporated in the growing medium. **Combine drilling** with seeds and fertilizer running into the same drill can achieve this. In horticulture, however, **band placement** of fertilizers is far more common, involving equipment that drills the seeds in rows and places a band of fertilizer in parallel a few centimetres below and to one side. The risk of retarded germination or scorch of young plants due to highly soluble fertilizers placed near seeds is thus avoided (*see* salt concentration). There is much less risk if fertilizer is **surface broadcast**, i.e. scattered on prepared soil surface, or broadcast on the surface to be cultivated-in during the final stages of seedbed preparation. **Top-dressings** are fertilizers added to the soil surface but not incorporated. Such fertilizers must be soluble and not fixed by soil because the nutrient is carried to the roots by soil water. Nitrogen is the material most frequently applied by this method mainly because the large applications to crops require a base dressing and one or more topdressings to minimize the risk of scorch and loss by leaching. Fertilizers are carefully incorporated in composts during the mixing of the ingredients (*see* compost mixing). **Liquid feeding** is the application of fertilizer diluted in water to the root zone. **Foliar feeding** is the application of a liquid fertilizer in suitably diluted form to be taken up through leaves. This technique is usually restricted to the application of trace elements.

Formulations

Quick-acting fertilizers contain nutrients in a form which plant roots can take up, and dissolve as soon as they come in contact with water, e.g. ammonium nitrate and potassium chloride. Many are obtainable as powders or crystals. These are difficult to spread or place evenly but several are formulated this way to help in the preparation of liquid feeds. For this purpose they must be readily soluble and free of impurities that might lead to blockages in the feed lines. Some of the less soluble fertilizers, as well as lime, are spread in a finely divided form for maximum effect on soil. One of the major problems with many of the fertilizers is their **hygroscopic** nature, i.e. they pick up water from the atmosphere and create storage and distribution problems. Powdered forms in particular go sticky as they take up water then 'cake' (form hard lumps) as they dry. Fertilizers formulated as **granules** are more

satisfactory for accurate placement or broadcasting. They flow better, can be metred, and are thrown more accurately. **Prilled** fertilizers represent an improvement on granules because of their uniform spherical shape.

Slow-release fertilizers are those in which a large proportion of the nutrient is released slowly. Several of these fertilizers, such as rock phosphate, are insoluble or only slightly soluble and the nutrients are released only after many months, even years. Micro-organisms break down organic products and the rate at which nutrients become available depends on their activity (*see* bacteria). Some slow-release artificial fertilizers, such as those based on urea formaldehyde, dissolve slowly in the soil solution whilst others are formulated in such a way that the soluble fertilizer they contain diffuses slowly through a resin coat, e.g. Osmocote, or sulphur coating, e.g. Gold-N. Some of these slow-release fertilizers have been formulated in such a way as to release nutrients at a rate that matches a plant's uptake and as such are sometimes referred to as **controlled-release** fertilizer. **Frits**, made from fine glass powders containing nutrient elements, are used either to release soluble materials slowly or to overcome the trace element problem caused by the narrow limits between deficiency and toxicity (*see* trace elements). Frits ease the difficulties experienced in mixing tiny amounts evenly through large volumes of compost. **Ion-exchange resins** release their nutrients by exchange with cations in the surrounding water. These resins help to overcome the problems of high salt concentration and leaching of nutrients from growing media based on inert materials (*see* aggregate culture).

Some plant nutrients are formed as **chelates** to maintain availability in extreme conditions where the mineral salt is 'locked up'. There are many different chelating or sequestrating agents selected for each element to be protected, and for each unavailability problem. Iron is chelated with EDDHA to form the product Chel 138 or Sequestrine 138 which releases the element in all soils including those with a high pH (*see* iron deficiency). Ethylenediaminetetraacetic acid (EDTA), effective where there are high levels of copper, zinc and manganese, is used to chelate iron to be applied in foliar sprays.

PLANT NUTRIENTS

Nitrogen

Nitrogen is taken up by plants as the nitrate and to a lesser extent, the ammonium ion. Nitrate is converted to ammonium in the plant where it is utilized to form protein. Plants use large quantities and it is associated with vegetative growth. Consequently large dressings of nitrogen are given to leafy crops, whereas fruit, flower or root crops require limited nitrogen balanced by other nutrients to prevent undesirable characteristics occurring.

Excess nitrogen produces soft, lush growth making the plant vulnerable to pest attack and more likely to be damaged by cold. Very large quantities of nitrogen are undesirable since they can harm the plant by producing high salt concentrations at the roots (*see* **conductivity**) and are lost by leaching. Large quantities are usually applied as a split dressing, e.g. some in base dressing and the rest in one or more top-dressings.

Nitrates are mobile in the soil, which makes them vulnerable to leaching. In the British Isles it is assumed that all nitrates are removed by the winter rains so that virtually none is present until the soils warm up and nitrification begins or artificial nitrogen is applied (*see* nitrogen cycle). Nitrates leached through the root zone may find their way into the groundwater that is the basis of the water supply in some areas. Nitrification also leads to the **loss of bases**; for every 1 kg N in the ammonia form that is oxidized to nitrate and leached, up to 7 kg of calcium carbonate or its equivalent is lost. Nitrogen is also lost from the root zone by denitrification, especially in warm, waterlogged soil conditions. When in contact with calcareous material, ammonium fertilizers are readily converted to ammonia gas which is lost to the soil unless it dissolves in surrounding water. For this reason urea or ammonia-based fertilizers should not be applied to such soils as a top dressing or used in contact with lime.

Nitrogen fertilizers used in horticulture and their nutrient content are given in Table 16.2. **Ammonium nitrate** is now commonly used in horticulture. In pure form it rapidly absorbs moisture to become wet; on drying it 'cakes' and can be a fire risk. Pure ammonium nitrate can be safely handled in polythene sacks and as prills. **Ammonium sulphate** has a very acid reaction in the growing medium. **Urea** has a very high nitrogen content and in contact with water it quickly releases ammonia. Its use as a solid fertilizer is limited but it is utilized in liquid fertilizer or in foliar sprays. The addition of a sulphur coating to urea not only creates a controlled-release action, but also a fertilizer with an acid reaction. Other manufactured organic fertilizers include urea formaldehydes (nitroform, ureaform, etc.) which release nitrogen as they are decomposed by micro-organisms, isobutylidene urea (IBDU) which is slightly soluble in water and releases urea and crotonylidene (CDU, e.g. Crotodur). The latter breaks down very slowly and evenly, which makes it ideal for applying to turf.

Natural organic sources of nitrogen, including dried blood, hoof and horn and, shoddy, amongst others, are generally considered to provide slow-release nitrogen, but in warm greenhouse conditions decomposition is quite rapid.

Phosphorus

Phosphorus is taken up by plants in the form of the phosphate anion $H_2PO_4^-$. Phosphorus is mobile in the plant and is constantly being recycled from the older parts to the newer growing areas. In practice this means that, although seeds have rich stores of phosphorus, phosphate is needed in the seedbed to help establishment. Older plants have a very low phosphate requirement compared with quick growing plants harvested young.

Most soils contain very large quantities of phosphorus but only a small proportion is available to plants. The concentration of available phosphate ions in the soil water and on soil colloids is at its highest between pH 6 and 7. Phosphorus is released from soil organic matter by micro-organisms (*see* mineralization), but most of it and any other soluble phosphorus, including that from fertilizers, is quickly converted to insoluble forms by a process known as **phosphate fixation**. Insoluble aluminium, iron and manganese phosphates are formed at low pH and insoluble calcium phosphate at high pH. The carbonic acid in the vicinity of respiring roots and organisms (*see* respiration) in the rhizosphere such as **mycorrhizae** (*see* page 9) facilitate phosphorus uptake. The low solubility of phosphorus in the soil makes it virtually immobile, with the result that roots have to explore for it. Soils should be cultivated to allow roots to explore effectively; compacted or waterlogged areas deny plants phosphorus supplies. Phosphate added to the soil should be placed near developing roots (*see* band placement) in order to reduce phosphorus fixation and ensure that it is quickly found. If applied to the surface, phosphate fertilizers should be cultivated into the root zone.

Unlike soils, most artificial growing media have no reserves of phosphorus and when added in soluble form it remains mobile and subject to leaching. Incorporating phosphorus in liquid feeds in hard water is complicated by the precipitation of insoluble calcium phosphates that lead to blocked nozzles. Slow-release phosphates are often selected in these situations to reduce losses and to eliminate the need for phosphorus in the liquid feeds.

Phosphorus nutrition used to be based on organic sources such as bones, but now phosphate fertilizers are mainly derived from rock phosphate ore. **Slow-acting forms** such as rock phosphate, bone meal and basic slag can be analysed in terms of their 'citric soluble' phosphate content, this being a good guide to their usefulness in the first season. Such materials should be finely ground to enhance their effectiveness. These phosphates are applied mainly to grassland, tree plantings and in the preparation of herbaceous borders, to act as long-term reserves, particularly on phosphate-deficient soils. Magnesium ammonium phosphate (MagAmp, Enmag), calcium metaphosphate and potassium metaphosphate contain other nutrients but are slow-release phosphates for use in soilless growing media. Treating rock phosphates with acids produces **water-soluble phosphates**. Superphosphate, derived from rock phosphate by treating with sulphuric acid, is composed of a water-soluble phosphate and calcium sulphate (gypsum), whereas triple superphosphate, derived from a phosphoric acid treatment, is a more concentrated source of phosphorus with less impurity. Both superphosphate and triple superphosphate are widely used in horticulture and are available in granular or powder form. Whilst they have a neutral effect on soil pH they tend to reduce the pH of composts. High-grade monoammonium phosphate is used as a phosphorus source in liquid feeds because it is low in iron and aluminium impurities that lead to blockage in pipes and nozzles.

Potassium

Potassium is taken up by the roots as the potassium cation and is distributed throughout the plant in inorganic form where it plays an important role in plant metabolism. For balanced growth the nitrogen to potassium ratio should be 1:1 for most crops, but 2:3 for roots and legumes. Leafy crops take up large amounts of potassium, especially when given large amounts of nitrogen. Where potassium supplies are abundant some plants, especially grasses, take up 'luxury' levels, i.e. more than needed for their growth requirements. Consequently, if large proportions of the plant are taken off the land, e.g. as grass clippings, there is a rapid depletion of potassium reserves.

Potassium forms part of clay minerals and is released by chemical weathering. The potassium in soil organic matter is very rapidly recycled and exchangeable potassium cations held on the soil colloids and in the soil solutions are readily available to plant roots. Potassium is easily leached from sands low in organic matter and from most soilless-growing media.

Potassium and magnesium ions mutually interfere with the uptake of each other. This ion antagonism is avoided when the correct ratio between 3:1 and 4:1 (available potassium to magnesium) is present in the growing medium. Availability of potassium is also reduced by the presence of calcium (*see* induced deficiency).

The main potassium fertilizers used in horticulture are detailed in Table 16.2. Although cheaper and widely used in agriculture, potassium chloride causes scorch in trees and can lead to salt concentration problems because the chloride ion accumulates as the potassium is taken up. Commercial potassium sulphate can be used in base dressings for composts but only the more expensive refined grades should be used in liquid feeding. More usually potassium nitrate is used to add both potassium and nitrate to liquid feeds, but is hygroscopic. Most potassium compounds are very soluble so that the range of slow-release formulations is limited to resin-coated compounds.

Magnesium

Magnesium is an essential plant nutrient in leaves and roots and taken up as a cation. There are large reserves in most soils, especially clays, and those soils receiving large dressings of farmyard manure. Deficiencies are only likely on intensively cropped sandy soils if little organic manure is used. Magnesium ion uptake is also interfered with by large quantities of potassium ions or calcium ions because of **ion antagonism**. Chalky and over-limed soils are less likely to yield adequate magnesium for plants.

Magnesium fertilizers include magnesian limestones containing a mixture of magnesium and calcium carbonate that raises soil pH (*see* liming). Magnesium sulphate as kieserite provides magnesium ions without affecting pH levels and in a purer form, Epsom salts, is used for liquid feeding and foliar sprays.

Calcium

Calcium is an essential plant nutrient taken up by the plant as calcium cations. Generally a satisfactory pH level of a growing medium indicates suitable calcium levels (*see* liming). Gypsum (calcium sulphate) can be used where it is desirable to increase calcium levels in the soil without affecting soil pH. Deficiencies are infrequent and usually caused by lime being omitted from composts. Inadequate calcium in fruits is a more complex problem involving the distribution of calcium within the plant. Calcium nitrate or chloride solutions can be applied to apples to ensure adequate levels for safe storage (*see* plant tissue analysis).

Sulphur

Sulphur taken up as sulphate ions is a nutrient required in large quantities for satisfactory plant growth. It is not normally added specifically as a fertilizer because the soil reserves are replenished by re-circulated organic matter and air pollution. Furthermore, several fertilizers used to add other nutrients are in sulphate form, e.g. ammonium sulphate, superphosphate and potassium sulphate, and as such supply sulphur as well. As air pollution is reduced and fewer sulphate fertilizers are used, it is becoming necessary for growers to take positive steps to include sulphur in their fertilizer programme.

TRACE ELEMENTS

Trace elements, also known as micro-elements or minor elements, are present in plants in very small quantities but are just as essential for healthy growth as major elements. Furthermore, they can be toxic to plants if too abundant. This means that rectifying deficiencies with soluble salts has to be undertaken carefully.

Deficiencies

Simple deficiencies are those in which too little of the nutrient is present in the growing medium. Most soils have adequate reserves of trace elements and so simple deficiencies in them are uncommon, especially if replenished with bulky organic matter. Sandy soils tend to have low reserves and so too have several organic soils from which trace elements have been leached. In horticulture simple deficiencies of trace elements are mainly associated with growing in soilless composts which require careful supplementation.

Induced deficiencies are those in which sufficient nutrient is present but other factors such as soil pH or **ion antagonism** interfere with plant **nutrient availability**. On mineral soils boron, copper, zinc, iron and manganese become less available in alkaline soils, whereas molybdenum availability is reduced severely in soils with pH levels below 5.5 as shown in Figure 16.1. Trace element problems are aggravated in dry soils or where waterlogging, root pathogens or poor soil structure reduces root activity.

Iron deficiency is induced by the presence of large quantities of calcium and this **'lime-induced' chlorosis** (yellowing) occurs on overlimed soils and calcareous soils. The natural flora of chalk and limestone areas is calcicoles. Other plants grown in such conditions usually have a typically yellow appearance. Deficiencies can also be induced by high levels of copper, manganese, zinc and phosphorus. Top fruit and soft fruit are particularly susceptible, as well as crops grown in complete nutrient solutions. The problem is overcome by using iron chelates.

Boron deficiency tends to occur when pH is above 6.8. It is readily leached from peat. Crops grown in peat are particularly susceptible when pH levels rise (Figure 16.1)..Boron can be applied to soils before seed sowing in the form of borax or 'Solubor'.

Manganese deficiency is more frequent on organic and sandy soils of high pH. Plant uptake can be reduced by high potassium, iron, copper and zinc levels. Manganese availability is greatly increased at low pH and can reach toxic levels which most commonly occur after steam sterilization of acid, manganese-rich soils. High phosphorus levels can be used to reduce the uptake of manganese in these circumstances.

Copper deficiency usually occurs on peat and sands, notably reclaimed heathland, and in thin organic soils over chalk. High rates of nitrogen can accentuate the problem. Soils can be treated with copper sulphate or plants can be sprayed with copper oxychloride.

Zinc deficiencies are not common and are usually associated with high pH.

Molybdenum deficiency occurs on most soil types at a low pH. Availability becomes much reduced below pH 5.5 especially in the presence of high manganese levels. Cauliflowers are particularly susceptible and soils are limed to solve the problem. Sodium or ammonium molybdate can be added to growing media or liquid feeds where molybdenum supplies are inadequate.

FERTILIZER PROGRAMME

The fertilizer applications required to produce the desired plant growth vary according to the type of plant, climate, season of growth and the nutrient status of the soil. General advice is available in many publications including those of the national advisory services and horticultural industries. Examples are given in Table 16.3.

Growing medium analysis

The nutrient status of growing media varies greatly between the different materials and within the same materials as time passes. The nutrient levels change because they are being lost by plant uptake, leaching and fixation and gained by the weathering of clay, mineralization of organic matter and the addition of lime and, fertilizers.

There are many visual symptoms which indicate a deficiency of one or more essential nutrients (*see* minerals) but unfortunately by the time they appear the plant has probably already suffered a check in growth or change in the desired type of growth. The concentration of minerals in the plant and the nature of growth are linked so that **plant tissue analysis**, usually on selected leaves, can provide useful information, particularly in the diagnosis of some nutrient deficiencies, e.g. it is used to identify the calcium levels in apples in order to check

Table 16.3 Examples of fertilizer requirements

Carrots

N, P or K index			0	1	2	3	4	over 4
					(kg/ha)			
Carrots, early bunching		N	60	25	Nil	–	–	–
		P_2O_5	400	300	250	150	125	Nil
		K_2O	200	125	100	Nil	Nil	Nil
Carrots,	fen peats	N	Nil	Nil	Nil	–	–	–
(maincrop)	other soils	N	60	25	Nil	–	–	–
	all soils	P_2O_5	300	250	200	125	60	Nil
		K_2O	200	125	100	Nil	Nil	Nil

Carrots on sandy soils respond to salt: 150 kg/ha Na (400 kg/ha salt) should be applied and potash reduced by 60 kg/ha K_2O. Salt must be worked deeply into the soil before drilling or be ploughed in.

Dessert apples: mature trees

	Summer rainfall	Cultivated or overall herbicide	Grass/ herbicide strip	Grass
		(kg/ha per year)		
Nitrogen (N)	more than 350 mm	30	40	90
	less than 350 mm	40	60	120

P, K or Mg index	0	1	2	3	over 3
		(kg/ha per year)			
P_2O_5	80	40	20	20	Nil
K_2O	220	150	80	Nil	–
Mg	60	40	30	Nil	–

For the first 3 years, fertilizer is not required by *young trees* grown in herbicide strips, provided that deficiencies of phosphate, potash and magnesium are corrected before planting by thorough incorporation of fertilizer.

Lettuce: base dressings for border soils under glass

Nitrate P, K or Mg index	Ammonium nitrate	Triple superphosphate	Sulphate of potash	Kieserite
		g/m^2		
0	30	150	160	110
1	15	140	110	80
2	Nil	130	50	30
3	Nil	110	Nil	Nil
4	Nil	80	Nil	Nil
5	Nil	45	Nil	Nil
Over 5	Nil	Nil	Nil	Nil

Increase the nitrogen application by 50 per cent for summer grown crops. Lettuce is sensitive to low soil pH and the optimum pH is the range 6.5–7.0. It is also sensitive to salinity, and growth may be retarded on mineral soils when the soil conductivity index is greater than 2.

their storage qualities. However, nutrient supply is usually assessed by analysis of the growing medium. There is general agreement about the methodology for **analysing soils**. However, there needs to be some care where analysis of other growing media is undertaken because there are considerable differences between the methods particularly with regard to dilution of the nutrient extractant.

A **representative sample** of the growing medium is taken and its nutrient status determined. This involves extracting the **available nutrients** and measuring the quantities present. The **pH level** is determined and, where appropriate, the **lime requirement**. The **conductivity** of growing media from protected culture is also measured. The **nitrogen status** of soils is usually determined from previous cropping because, outdoors, nitrates are washed out over winter and their release from organic matter reserves is very variable. In protected planting, nitrate and ammonia levels are usually determined.

Results are often given in the form of an index number in order to simplify their presentation and interpretation. The ADAS soil analysis index is based on a 10 point scale from 0 (indicating levels corresponding to probable failure of plants if nutrient is not supplied) to 9 (indicating excessively high levels of nutrient present).

Fertilizer recommendations

The results of the **growing medium analysis** are interpreted with the appropriate **nutrient requirement tables** to determine the actual amount of fertilizer to apply. These tables usually have growing medium nutrient status indices to aid interpretation and results are normally given in kg of nutrient per hectare or grams of nutrient per square metre (Table 16.3). In some cases the amount of named fertilizer required is stated; if another fertilizer is to be used to supply the nutrient the quantity needed must be calculated using the nutrient content figures (Table 16.3). It is important that throughout the fertilizer planning process the same units are used, i.e. per cent P_2O_5 *or* P per cent; K_2O

or per cent K. Conversion figures are:

$$\% \ P_2O_5 = \% \ P \times 2.29$$

$$\% \ P = \% \ P_2O_5 \times 0.44$$

$$\% \ K_2O = \% \ K \times 1.20$$

$$\% \ K = \% \ K_2O \times 0.83$$

Sampling

Normally only a small proportion of the whole growing medium is submitted for analysis and therefore it must be a **representative sample** of the whole. This is not easy because of the variability of growing media, particularly soils. It is recommended that each sample submitted for testing should be taken from an area no greater than 4 ha (*see* Figure 16.2). The material sampled must itself be uniform and so only areas with the same characteristics and past history should be put in the same sample. Irrespective of the area involved, from small plot to 4 ha field, at least 25 sub-samples should be taken by walking a zig-zag path avoiding the atypical areas such as headlands, wet spots, old paths, hedge lines, old manure heaps, etc. The same amount of soil should be taken from each layer to a depth of 150 mm. This is most easily achieved with a soil auger or tubular corer.

Peat bags should be sampled with a cheese-type corer by taking a core at an angle through the planting hole on the opposite side of the plant to the drip nozzle from each of 30 bags chosen from an area up to a maximum of 0.5 ha. Discard the top 20 mm of each core and if necessary take more than 30 cores to make up a 1 l sample for analysis.

Samples should be submitted to analytical laboratories in clean containers capable of completely retaining the contents. They should be accompanied by name and address of supplier, the date of sampling and any useful background information. All samples must be clearly identified. Further details of sampling methods in greenhouses or orchards, bags, pots, straw bales, water, etc. are obtainable from the advisory services used. Remember, the result of the analysis can be no

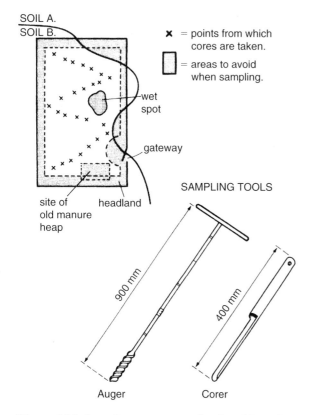

SOIL A.
SOIL B.

✗ = points from which cores are taken.

▢ = areas to avoid when sampling.

wet spot

gateway

SAMPLING TOOLS

site of old manure heap

headland

900 mm

400 mm

Auger   Corer

Figure 16.2 *Sampling growing media. Suitable tools to remove small quantities of growing media are corers or augers which have the advantage of removing equal quantities from the top and bottom of the sampled zone. The material to be sampled must be clearly identified, then 25 cores should be removed in a zig-zag that avoids anything abnormal.*

better than the extent to which the sample is representative of the whole.

SOIL CONDUCTIVITY

The **soil solution** is normally a weaker solution than the plant cell contents. In these circumstances plants readily take up water through their roots by osmosis. As more salt, such as soluble fertilizer, is added to the soil solution, **salt concentrations** are increased and less water, on balance, is taken up by roots. When salt concentrations are balanced as much water passes out of the roots as into them. When salt concentrations are greater in the soil the roots are plasmolysed. The root hairs, then the roots, are 'scorched', i.e. irreversibly damaged, and the plant dries up.

Symptoms of high salt concentration above ground are related to the water stress created. Plants wilt more often and go brown at the leaf margin. Prolonged exposure to these conditions produces hard, brittle plants, often with a bluey tinge. Eventually severe cases become desiccated.

Salt concentration levels are measured indirectly using the fact that the solution becomes a better conductor of electricity as salt concentration is increased. The conductivity of soil solution is measured with a **conductivity meter**.

Salt concentration problems are most common where fertilizer salts accumulate, as in climates with no rainfall period to leach the soil; and in protected culture. Periods when rainfall exceeds evaporation, as in the British Isles during winter, ensure that salts are washed out of the ground. Any plant can be damaged by applications of excess fertilizer. Some plants such as tomatoes and celery are more tolerant than others but seedlings are very sensitive. Young roots can be scorched by the close proximity of fertilizer granules in the seedbed (*see* band placement).

In **protected culture** large quantities of fertilizer are used and residues can accumulate, particularly if application is not well adjusted to plant use. Sensitive plants such as lettuce are particularly at risk when following heavily fed, more tolerant plants such as tomatoes or celery. Salt concentration levels should be carefully monitored and feeding adjusted accordingly, applying water alone if necessary. Soils can be **flooded** with water between plantings to leach excess salts. Large quantities of water are needed, but should be applied so that the soil surface is not damaged. Every effort should be made to minimize the effect on the environment and quantities of water needed to flush out the excess salts by reducing the nutrient levels as the crop comes to an end.

FURTHER READING

ADAS/ARC. *The Diagnosis of Mineral Disorders in Plants*, Vol. 1 *Introduction*, General editor Robinson, JBD. (HMSO, 1982).

ADAS/ARC. *Vegetable Crops*, Vol. 2 General editor Robinson, JBD. (HMSO, 1987).

ADAS/ARC. Winsor, G. and Adams, P. (Editors). *Glasshouse Crops*, Vol. 3 (HMSO, 1987).

Archer, J. *Crop Nutrition and Fertilizer Uses*, 2nd edition (Farming Press, 1988).

Brown, L.V. *Applied Principles of Horticulture*, 2nd edition (Butterworth-Heinemann, 2002).

Hay, R.K.M. *Chemistry for Agriculture and Ecology* (Blackwell Scientific Publications, 1981).

Ingram, D.S. *et al.* (Editors) *Science and the Garden* (Blackwell Science Ltd., 2002).

MAFF Reference Book No. 209 *Fertilizer Recommendations* (1988).

Roorda von Eysinga, J.P.N.L. and Smilde, K.W. *Nutritional Disorders in Chrysanthemums* (Centre for Agricultural Publishing and Documentation, Wageningen, 1980).

Roorda von Eysinga, J.P.N.L. and Smilde, K.W. *Nutritional Disorders in Glasshouse Tomatoes, Cucumbers and Lettuce* (Centre for Agricultural Publishing and Documentation, Wageningen, 1981).

Simpson, K. *Fertilizers and Manures* (Longman Handbooks in Agriculture, 1986).

17

Alternatives to Growing in the Soil

The soil has many advantages over alternative growing media, not least because it is usually the most available, and plants normally grow in it. Furthermore, it tends to be expensive to modify a soil or use an alternative growing medium. However, soil does have serious limitations for use in many aspects of horticulture and consequently the plants are frequently grown in suitable material put over the soil or, more commonly, in containers such as pots, liners, troughs, modules, cells, etc. In this chapter the principles underlying the use of containers and the mixes used in them are established, the nature of alternative materials and systems including hydroculture is examined and the advantages and disadvantages of the different approaches are discussed.

GROWING IN CONTAINERS

The importance of supplying water to plants in a restricted root volume is usually understood, but the difficulties associated with achieving it whilst maintaining adequate **air-filled porosity** (**AFP**) are less well appreciated (*see* page 163).

Roots require oxygen to maintain growth and activity. As temperatures rise, the plant requires more but the amount of oxygen that can be dissolved in water decreases. Even in cool conditions, the oxygen that can be extracted from the water provides only a fraction of the root requirements. So, unless the plants have special modifications to transport oxygen through their tissues, as in aquatics, there has to be good gaseous movement through the growing medium. Many large interconnected pores allow rapid entry of oxygen (*see* soil structures).

It is generally agreed that 10–15 per cent AFP is needed for a wide range of plants. Azaleas and epiphytic orchids require 20 per cent or more, whereas others, including chrysanthemums, lilies and poinsettia, tolerate 5–10 per cent AFP and carnations, conifers, geraniums, ivies and roses can be grown at levels as low as 2 per cent.

Creating successful physical conditions depends on the use of components, which provide a high proportion of macropores. Even in mixes which retain a good reservoir of water, very large quantities of water have to be applied over the course of a season so that the materials chosen must have very good **stability**; fine sand and silt soils collapse too quickly and reduce the size of the pore spaces. The sizes of the components used must be selected carefully to ensure that they create macropores, but also so that the gaps between the larger particles are not subsequently filled in by smaller particles ('fines'). This is most easily achieved by using closely graded coarse particles. The reverse is achieved when combining many different-sized particles, as one would in mixing concrete where

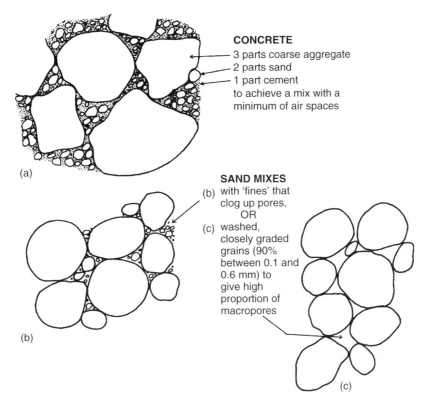

Figure 17.1 *Pore spaces in (a) concrete mix (b) and (c) sand mixes.*

the object is to minimize the airspaces as shown in Figure 17.1.

In addition to open ground or greenhouse borders, plants may be grown in pots, troughs, bags and other containers where restricted rooting makes more critical demands on the growing medium for air, water and nutrients.

Ensuring that a growing medium in a container has adequate AFP is made difficult because water does not readily leave the container unless it is in good contact through its holes with similar-sized pore spaces. This is the case when placed on sand or capillary matting, but when standing out on gravel or wire the water will cling to the particles in the container (*see* surface tension). This can be tested by fully watering a pot of compost, holding it until it has finished dripping then touching the compost through a hole; normally a stream of water will run down your finger. In fact the compost acts as a sponge and if it is at less than container capacity it will 'suck up' water from below. Furthermore, the lower layers remain almost saturated irrespective of the height or width of the container (You may understand this better if you fully wet a washing sponge and leave it to drain, after water has left the sponge, under the influence of gravity, the lower layers remain saturated). This makes it particularly difficult to get good aeration in shallow trays, modules and blocks.

Providing the **nutrients** for the plant through a small volume means that, if supplied in soluble form in one application, the salt concentration produced is often too high, especially for seedlings (*see* conductivity). Consequently feeding has to be modified using split dressings, slow-release fertilizers or liquid feeds.

COMPOSTS

In horticulture the growing media used in containers are usually referred to as 'composts'. These materials are also called plant substrates, plant growing media, or just 'mixes' or 'media'. Over the years growers have added a wide variety of materials such as leaf mould, pine needles, spent hops, old mortar, crushed bricks, composted animal and plant residues, peat, sand and grit to selected soils to produce a compost with suitable physical properties. To supplement the nutrient released from the materials in the compost, if any, various slow-release organic manures or small dressings of powdered soluble inorganic fertilizers have been added to the mixtures to provide the necessary nutrition.

The correct physical and nutritional conditions are vital to successful growing in a restricted rooting volume. The most significant developments were as a result of the work done in the 1930s at the John Innes (JI) Institute where the importance of 'sterile' (pest and disease free), stable and uniform ingredients was demonstrated. The range of composts that resulted from this work established the methods of achieving uniform production and reliable results with a single potting mixture suitable for a wide range of plant species.

Loam composts

Loam composts, typified by JI composts, are based on loam sterilized to eliminate the soil-borne fungi (*see* damping off) and insects that largely caused the unreliable results from traditional composts. There is a risk of ammonia toxicity developing after sterilization of soil with pH greater than 6.5 or very high in organic matter (*see* nitrogen cycle). Induced nutrient deficiencies are possible in soils with a pH greater than 6.5 or less than 5.5. Furthermore, loam should have sufficient clay and organic matter present to give good structural stability. Peat and sand are added to further improve the physical conditions, the peat giving a high water holding capacity and the coarse sand

ensuring free drainage and therefore good aeration. There are two main JI composts, one for seed sowing and cuttings, the other for potting.

JI seed compost consists of two parts loam, one part peat and one part sand by volume. Well-drained turfy clay loam low in nutrients and a pH between 5.8 and 6.5, undecomposed peat graded 3–10 mm with a pH between 3.5 and 5.0 and lime-free sand graded 1–3 mm should be used; 1200 g of superphosphate and 600 g of calcium carbonate are added to each cubic metre of compost.

JI potting (JIP) composts consist of seven parts by volume loam, three parts peat and two parts sand. To allow for the changing nutritional requirements of a growing plant, the nutrient level is adjusted by adding appropriate quantities of JI base fertilizer which consists of two parts by volume hoof and horn, two parts superphosphate and one part potassium sulphate. To prepare JIP 1, 3 kg JI base fertilizer and 600 g of calcium carbonate are added to 1 m³ of compost. To prepare JIP 2 and JIP 3, double and treble fertilizer levels, respectively, are used.

Whilst the standard JI composts are suitable for a wide range of species, some modification is required for some specialized plants. For example, calcifuge plants such as *Ericas* and *Rhododendrons* should be grown in a JI(S) mix in which sulphur is used instead of calcium carbonate.

All loam-based composts should be made up from components of known characteristics and according to the specification given. Such composts are well proven and are relatively easy to manage because of the water-absorbing and nutrient-retention properties of the clay present.

These composts are commonly used by amateurs, for valuable specimens, and for tall plants where pot stability is important; but loam-based composts have been superseded in horticulture generally by cheaper alternatives. The main disadvantage of loam-based composts has always been the difficulty in obtaining suitable quality loam as well as the high costs associated with steam sterilizing. Furthermore, the loam must be stored dry before use and the composts are heavy and difficult to handle in large quantities. Many loam-based composts currently produced have relatively low loam contents and consequently exhibit few of its advantages.

Loamless or soilless composts

Loamless composts introduced the advantages of a uniform growing medium, but with components that are lighter, cleaner to handle, cheaper to prepare and which do not need to be sterilized (unless being used more than once). Many have a low nutrient levels which enables growers to manipulate plant growth more precisely through nutrition, but the control of nutrients is more critical as many components have a low **buffering capacity**.

Peat has until recently been the basis of most loamless composts. It is used alone or in combination with materials such as sand to produce the required rooting environment. Peats are derived from partially decomposed plants and their characteristics depend on the plant species and the conditions in which they are formed (*see* Chapter 15). Peats vary and respond differently to herbicides, growth regulators and lime. All peats have a high cation exchange capacity, which gives them some buffering capacity. The less decomposed sphagnum peats have a desirable open structure for making composts and all peats have high water-holding capacities.

Considerable efforts are being made to reduce the destruction of wetland habitats by finding alternatives to peat for use in horticulture. A list of some of the materials used is given in Table 17.1. Much progress has been made by using suitably processed bark or coconut fibre in composts. Along with several other organic sources they are waste based and recycling them helps in conserving resources. All such alternatives must be free of toxins and pathogens, particularly those that may be a hazard to humans. Most of the inorganic alternatives are made from non-renewable resources (sand, loam and pumice) or consume energy in their manufacture (plastic foams and polystyrene) or both (vermiculite, perlite and rockwool). It seems unlikely that versatile peat will be replaced by a single alternative but rather different sectors will adopt substitutes best suited to their requirements.

Table 17.1 Alternatives to peat

Organic materials	Inorganic materials
Pine	Expanded aggregates
Coir	Extracted minerals
Garden compost	Hydroponics
Heather/bracken	Perlite
Leaf-mould	Polystyrene
Lignite	Rockwool
Recycled landfill	Dredgings/warp
Refuse-derived humus	Vermiculite
Seaweed	Topsoil
Sewage sludge	
Spent hops and grains	
Spent mushroom compost	
Straw	
Vermicomposts	
Wood chips/fibre	
Woodwastes	
Wood fibre	

Alternatives to peat

Sand and gravel are used in composts, frequently in combination with peat. They have no effect on the nutrient properties of composts except by diluting other materials. They are used to change physical properties. As sand or gravel is added to lightweight materials the density of the compost can be increased, which is important for ballast when tall plants are grown in plastic pots. Sand is also used as an inert medium in aggregate culture. Sand should be introduced with caution because it tends to reduce the AFP of the final mix. It is important that the sands used should have low lime levels, otherwise they may induce a high pH and associated mineral deficiencies (*see* trace elements).

Pulverized bark has been used as a mulch and soil conditioner for many years. More recently it has been tried in compost mixtures as a replacement for peat. There are many different types of bark and they have different properties. Its problems include the presence of toxins, overcome by composting, and a tendency to 'lock-up' nitrogen (*see* carbon:nitrogen ratio), which can be offset by extra nitrogen in the feed. When composted with sewage sludge, a material suitable as a plant-growing medium is produced. It is increasingly being incorporated into growing mixes in the attempt to reduce the use of peat.

However, the great variation of barks, especially when they are from a mixed source, makes it difficult to incorporate into growing mixes. Much of the conifer bark tends to be stringy. Consequently the main role of bark is in mulching. The import of bark is strictly controlled by the Forestry Commission to prevent the introduction of pests and diseases. Wood-fibres based on stabilized shredded wood are being used to increase the AFP of mixes but they tend to be dusty and not easily dispersed in compost mixes. Sawdust and off-cuts from the chipboard industry are also being tested for use in growing, but there are problems associated with their stability and fungal growth in the freshly stored material.

Coconut wastes such as **coir** (the dust particles) are proving to be useful in growing mixes. The material has good water-holding capacity, rewetting and AFP characteristics. It has a pH between 5 and 6, which makes it suitable for a wide range of plants, but cannot replace peat directly in mixes for calcifuges. It has a carbon to nitrogen ratio of 80:1 which means that allowance has to be made for its tendency to lock-up nitrogen (*see* page 188).

Rockwool is an insulation material derived from a granite-like rock crushed, melted and spun into threads. The resulting slabs of lightweight spongy, absorbent, inert and sterile rockwool provide ideal rooting conditions with high water-holding capacity and good aeration. Shredded rockwool can be used in compost mixes (*see* Plate 20). Its pH is high but easily reduced by watering with a slightly acid nutrient solution.

It is frequently used in tomato and cucumber production and film-wrapped cubes are available for plant raising and pot plants. It is necessary to use a complete nutrient feed (*see* aggregate culture). It has some buffering capacity but this is very low on a volume basis. The main problem areas lie in calcium and phosphorus supply and the control of pH and salt concentration. Some rockwool has been formulated with clay to overcome some of these problems. This increases its cation exchange properties, making it very suitable for interior landscaping. Rockwool is also available in water-absorbent and water-repelling forms. Mixtures of these enable formulators to achieve the right balance between AFP, water holding and capillary lift. Rockwool is available as granules that provide a flexible alternative for those who produce their own mixes. However, it is most usually supplied as wrapped slabs, cubes, propagation blocks and plugs that are modularized to create a complete growing system.

Perlite is a mineral that is crushed and then expanded by heat to produce a white, lightweight aggregate (*see* Plate 20). The granules are porous and the rough surface holds considerably more water than gravel or polystyrene balls. It tends to be used to improve aeration of growing media generally and the rewetting of peat. It is devoid of nutrients and has no cation exchange capacity. Graded samples may be used in aggregate culture, but tend to be used to add to mixes to improve the uptake of water.

Vermiculite is a mica-like mineral expanded to 20 times its original size by rapid conversion to steam of its water content. The finished product is available in several grades all of which produce growing media with good aeration and water-holding properties (*see* Plate 20). There is a tendency for the honeycomb structure to break down and go 'soggy'. Consequently, for long-term planting, it tends to be used in mixtures with the more stable peat or perlite. Some vermiculites are alkaline but the slightly acid samples are preferred in horticulture. Vermiculite has a high cation exchange capacity, which makes it particularly useful for propagation mixes. Most samples contain some available potassium and magnesium.

Pumice is a porous volcanic rock that is prepared for use as a growing medium by crushing, washing (to remove salt and 'fines') and grading. It is most commonly used to grow long-term crops such as carnations in troughs or polysacks.

Expanded polystyrene balls or flakes provide a very lightweight inert material, which can be added to soils or composts as a physical conditioner. It is non-porous and so reduces the water-holding capacity of the growing medium while increasing its aeration, thus making it less liable to waterlogging when over-watered. This has made it an attractive option for winter propagation mixes. However, it is less popular than it might be because it is easily blown away and sticks to most surfaces.

Plastic foams of several different types are becoming popular for propagation because of their open porous structure. They are available as flakes and balls for addition to composts or as cubes into which the cuttings can be pushed.

Chopped straw has been used with some success. Generally the main types available, wheat and barley, break down too easily and a practicable method of stabilizing them has not yet been found. Stable, friable material has been derived from bean and oil seed rape straws although care is needed in mixes because of the high potassium levels.

Lignite is very variable soft brown coal formed from compressed vegetation, often found at the base of the larger peat bogs. The dusts, 'fines', have been used as carriers for fertilizers and the more granular material can be used to replace grit in mixes often bringing an improved water retention.

Absorbent polymers have the ability to hold vast quantities of water that is available to plants. However, this is considerably reduced in practice because water absorption falls as the salt concentration of the water increases and the release patterns appear to be very similar to that of some compost ingredients such as sphagnum moss peats.

Wetters or non-phytotoxic detergents, are included in mixes to enable water to wet dry composts. They reduce the surface tension of the water, which improves its penetration of the pores. This speeds up the wetting process and maximizes the water holding capacity of the materials used. Wetters should be selected with care because the different types need to be matched with the peat in the mix and above all must not be harmful to the plants.

Compost formulations

Materials alone or in combination are prepared and mixed to achieve a rooting environment that is free from pests and disease organisms and has adequate AFP, easily available water and suitable bulk density for the plant to be grown.

While lightweight mixes are usually advantageous, 'heavier' composts are sometimes formulated to give pot stability for taller specimens. This should not be achieved by compressing the lightweight compost but by incorporating denser materials such as sand. Quick-growing plants are normally the aim and loosely filling containers with the correct compost formulation and settling it with applications of water obtain this. Firming with a rammer reduces the total pore space whilst increasing the amount of compost and nutrients in the container. The reduction in available water and increase in soluble salt concentration leads to slower growing, harder plants (*see* conductivity).

The addition of nutrients has to take into account not only the plant requirements but also the nutrient characteristics of the ingredients used. Most loamless composts require trace element supplements and many, including those based on peat, need the addition of all major nutrients and lime.

Glasshouse Crops Research Institute (GCRI) developed **general-purpose potting composts** based on a peat/sand mix (*see* Table 17.2). They contain different combinations of nutrients and consequently their storage life differs. One of the range has a slow-release phosphate, removing the need for this element in a liquid feed (*see* phosphorus).

The **GCRI seed compost** contains equal parts by volume of sphagnum peat and fine, lime-free sand. To each cubic metre of seed compost is added 0.75 kg of superphosphate, 0.4 kg potassium nitrate and 3.0 kg calcium carbonate.

Table 17.2 GCRI composts

Constituents	Seed compost	Potting composts		
		General use	*Urea formaldehyde types**	*High P type***
			Winter use / Summer use	
Peat:sand		**1**	**2**	**3**
(per cent by volume)	50:50	75:25	75:25 / 75:25	75:25
Base dressings (kg/m³)				
Ammonium nitrate	Nil	0.4	Nil / Nil	0.2
Urea formaldehyde	Nil	Nil	0.5 / 1.0	Nil
Magnesium ammonium phosphate	Nil	Nil	Nil / Nil	1.5
Potassium nitrate	0.4	0.75	0.75 / 0.75	0.4
Normal superphosphate	0.75	1.5	1.5 / 1.5	Nil
Ground chalk	3.0	2.25	2.25 / 2.25	2.25
Ground magnesian limestone	Nil	2.25	2.25 / 2.25	2.25
Fritted trace elements (WM225)	Nil	0.4	0.4 / 0.4	0.4

*Composts containing urea formaldehyde should not be stored longer than 7 days.
**For longer-term crops where there is a risk of phosphorus deficiency and liquid feeding with phosphate is not desired, use commercial magnesium ammonium phosphate. This also contains 11 per cent K_2O.

Compost mixing

It is most important when making up the desired compost formulation to achieve a uniform product and, commercially, it must be undertaken with a minimum labour input. The ingredients of the compost must be as near as possible to the specification for the chosen formulation. Materials must not be too moist when mixing because it then becomes impossible to achieve an even distribution of nutrients.

There are several designs of **compost mixer**. Continuous mixers are usually employed by specialist compost mixing firms and require careful supervision to ensure a satisfactory product. Batch mixers of the 'concrete mixer' design are produced for a wide range of capacities to cover most nursery needs. Many of the bigger mixers have attachments which aid filling. Emptying equipment is often linked to automatic tray or pot-filling machines.

Ingredients used in loamless composts or growing modules do not normally require partial sterilization unless they are being reused, but **sterilizing equipment** is certainly needed to prepare loams for inclusion in loam-based composts. Where steam is used it is injected through perforated pipes on a base plate and rises through the material being sterilized. In contrast a steam–air mixture injected from the top under an air-proof covering is forced downwards to escape through a permeable base.

Storage of prepared composts should be avoided if possible and should not exceed 3 weeks if slow-release fertilizers are incorporated. If nitrogen sources in the compost are mineralized, **ammonium ions** are produced followed by a steady increase in **nitrates** (*see* Chapter 15). These changes lead to a rise in compost pH followed by a fall. As nitrates increase, the salt concentration rises towards harmful levels (*see* conductivity). Peat-based composts can become infested during storage by sciarid flies.

PLANT CONTAINERS

The characteristics of the container affect the root environment, as does the standing-out area. **Clay pots** are porous and water is lost from the walls by evaporation. Consequently clay pots dry out quicker than plastic ones, especially in the winter and, although air does not enter through the walls, this can help improve AFP. The higher evaporation rate also keeps the clay pots slightly cooler, which can be beneficial in hot conditions. Likewise the contents of white plastic pots can be as much as 4°C lower than in other colours. Pots of white or light green plastic can transmit sufficient light to adversely affect root growth and encourage algal growth.

Biodegradable containers such as those made from paper have become popular because they can be planted directly. Some materials decompose more rapidly than others and there can be a temporary 'lock-up' of nitrogen, but most peat containers are now manufactured with added available nitrogen. It is essential that these containers are soaked and surrounding soil is kept moist after planting or the roots fail to escape from the dry wall.

The air to water characteristics of the mixture in the container depends not only on the nature of the contents but also the characteristics of the base on which the container stands. If containers are stood out on wire mesh or on stones relatively little water leaves so the oxygen content remains poor. This is because the surface water films around the finer particles in the compost hold the water against gravity. More water can be drawn out of the container if the standing out material is of a similar particle size to the contents and there is a good connection between the two. (You can demonstrate this to yourself if you fully wet a pot of compost and let it drain on a wire mesh or suspended in the air. When the water has stopped dripping from the holes, touch the compost in the pot through one of the drainage holes and be ready to have water running down your sleeve.)

Blocks

Blocks are made of a suitable compressed growing medium into which the seed is sown with no container or simply a net of polypropylene. Aeration tends to be poorer than in pots but this is a successful means of growing some vegetables on a large scale. One type of block comes in the form of a dry compressed disc that expands quickly ready to receive the seed in the shallow depression in the top surface.

Modules

Increasingly traditional seedbed, bare-rooted or block transplant techniques have become replaced by raising a wide variety of plants in modules. A module is made by adding a loose growing medium mix to a tray of cells. The cells are variously wedge or pyramid shaped, so designed to enable a highly mechanized transplanting process to be used. Fine, free-flowing mixes of peat, polystyrene or bark are used to fill the cells, which have large drainage holes and no rim to hold free water. Roots in the wedge-shaped cells are 'air-pruned' as they reach the edge of the cell, which encourages secondary root development. 'Plugs' are mini-modules in which each transplant develops in less than $10\,cm^3$ of growing medium and are used for bedding plants as well as vegetable production. The rate of establishment is largely determined by the water stress experienced by the transplant. Irrigation of the module or plug is found to be more successful than applying water to the surrounding growing medium.

Hydroponics

Hydroponics (water culture) involves the growing of plants in water. The term often includes the growing of plants in solid rooting medium watered with a complete nutrient solution, which is more accurately called **'aggregate culture'**. Plants can be grown in nutrient solutions with no solid material so long as the roots receive oxygen and suitable anchorage and support is provided.

The advantages of hydroponics compared with soil in temperate areas include accurate control of the nutrition of the plant and hence better growth and yield. There is a constant supply of available water to the roots. Evaporation is greatly reduced and loss of water and nutrients through drainage is minimal in re-circulating systems. There can be a reduction in labour and growing medium costs and a quicker 'turnround' time between crops in protected culture. The disadvantages include the high initial costs of construction and the controls of the more elaborate automated systems.

Active roots require a constant supply of oxygen, but oxygen only moves slowly through water.

This can be resolved by pumping air through the water that the plants are grown in, but it is usually achieved on a large scale by growing in thin films of water as created in the nutrient film technique (NFT) or a variation on the very much older aggregate culture methods.

NFT

This is a method of growing plants in a shallow stream of nutrient solution continuously circulated along plastic troughs or gullies. The method is commercially possible because of the development of relatively cheap non-phytotoxic plastics to form the troughs, pipes and tanks (*see* Figure 17.2). There is no solid rooting medium and a mat of

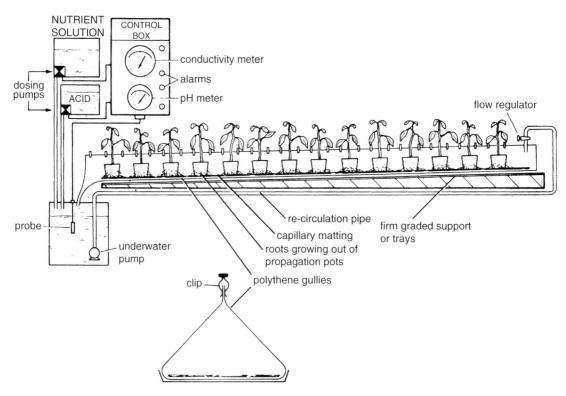

Figure 17.2 *The NFT layout. The nutrient solution is pumped up to the top of the gullies. The solution passes down the gullies in a thin film and is returned to the catchment tank. The pH and nutrient levels in the catchment tank are monitored and adjusted as appropriate.*

roots develops in the nutrient solution and in the moist atmosphere above it. Nutrient solution is lifted by a pump to feed the gullies directly or via a header tank. The ideal flow rate through the gullies appears to be 4 litres/min. The gullies have a flat bottom, often lined with capillary matting to ensure a thin film throughout the trough. They are commonly made of disposable black/white polythene set on a graded soil or on adjustable trays. There must be an even slope with a minimum gradient of 1 in 100, areas of deeper liquid stagnate and adversely affect root growth (*see* anaerobic conditions).

The nutrient solution can be prepared on site from basic ingredients or proprietary mixes. It is essential that allowance be made for the local water quality, particularly with regard to the micro-elements such as boron or zinc that can become concentrated to toxic levels in the circulating solution. The nutrient level is monitored with a conductivity meter and by careful observation of the plants. Maintenance of pH between 6 and 6.5 is also very important. Nutrient and pH control is achieved using, as appropriate, a nutrient mix, nitric acid or phosphoric acid to lower pH (*see* mineral acids) and, where water supplies are too acid, potassium hydroxide to raise pH. Great care and safety precautions are necessary when handling the concentrated acids during preparation.

The commercial NFT installations have automatic control equipment in which conductivity and pH meters are linked to dosage pumps. The high and low level points also trigger visual or audible alarms in case of dosage pump failure. Dependence on the equipment may necessitate the grower installing fail-safe devices, a second lift pump and a standby generator. A variation on this method is to grow crops such as lettuce in gullies on suitably graded greenhouse floors (*see* Plate 18a and b).

Aggregate culture

In aggregate culture the nutrient solution is broken up into water films by an essentially inert solid medium such as coarse sand or gravel. More commonly today materials such as **rockwool, perlite, polyurethane foam, duraplast foam** or **expanded clay aggregates** (*see* Plate 20) are used. These are in the form of polythene wrapped slabs or 'bolsters' of granules sitting on a polythene covered floor graded across the row. Polyurethane slabs are often placed underneath them to help create even slopes and insulate them from the cooler soil below.

These growing containers, on which the plants sit, are drip fed with a complete nutrient solution at the top with the surplus running out through slits at the bottom on the opposite side. When this method was first developed the NFT systems were copied, i.e. the water was re-circulated, but it was soon found to be difficult where the quality of water was poor and there was a risk of a build up of water-borne pathogens and trace elements. It was found that the surplus nutrient solution was most easily managed by allowing it to run to waste into the soil. However, this **open system** presents environmental problems and increasingly a **closed system** has had to be adopted. It is now becoming more usual to run the waste to a storage sump via collection gullies or pipes. Some of this can be used to irrigate outdoor crops if nearby. To re-circulate the water it is necessary to have equipment to remove the excess salts or accept a gradual deterioration of the nutrient solution then flush it out to a sump when it becomes unacceptable.

Sources of infection such as *Pythium* are minimized by isolation from soil and using clean water; the risks of re-circulating pathogens is addressed by using one of the four main methods of sterilization (*see* water quality).

Rockwool slabs are a very successful way of growing and widely used for a range of commer-cial crops such as tomatoes, cucumbers, peppers, melons, lettuce, carnations, roses, orchids and strawberries in protected culture. It is not biodegradable so the vast quantity of rockwool now produced has created a serious disposal problem. The slabs can be used successfully several times, if sterilized on each occasion, but eventually they lose their structure. Tearing them up and incorporating in composts or soils can deal with a limited amount, but far more can now be recycled in the production of new slabs.

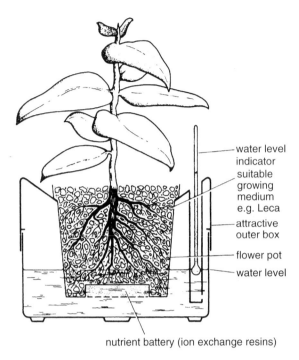

water level indicator

suitable growing medium e.g. Leca

attractive outer box

flower pot

water level

nutrient battery (ion exchange resins)

Figure 17.3 *Plant pots with water reserves. Plants grown in a variety of growing media can be fitted with reservoirs that supply water by capillarity. A water level indicator is frequently incorporated and in some systems the nutrients are supplied from ion exchange resins. While this system can be used for any pot size it is particularly attractive in large displays.*

Several types of **expanded clay aggregates** used in the building industry such as Leca or Hortag have been used particularly in interior landscaping (*see* Plate 20). Smooth but porous granules 4–8 mm in diameter, giving a capillary rise of about 100 mm, are used to create an ideal rooting environment with a dry surface which makes it an attractive method of displaying house plants (*see* Figure 17.3). All forms of aggregate culture require feeding with all essential minerals. Trace element deficiencies occur less frequently when clay aggregates are used. Ion exchange resins are an ideal fertilizer formulation in these circumstances because the nutrients are released slowly, remove harmful chlorides and fluorides from irrigation water and aid pH control.

SPORT SURFACES

The specifications for sports playing surfaces are such that turf has increasingly given way to artificial alternatives typified by the trend towards playing 'lawn' tennis on 'clay' courts. This is partly attributable to maintenance requirements, but at the higher levels of sport it is because the users or the management expect play to continue with a minimum of interference by rainfall. The usual problem is that the soil in which the turf grows does not retain its structure under the pounding it receives from players and machinery, especially when it is in the wet plastic state. Turf is still preferred by many, but to achieve the high standards required it has to be grown in a much modified soil (*see also* sand slitting) or, increasingly, in an alternative such as sand. The most extreme approach is to grow the turf in pure sand isolated from the soil, sometimes within a plastic membrane. The high cost of these methods is such that it is only used to create small areas such as golf greens.

Normally the existing topsoil is removed from the site and the subsoil is compacted to form a firm base and graded to carry water away to drains. Drainage pipes are laid, above which is placed a drainage layer usually consisting of washed, pea-sized gravel, as shown in Figure 17.4. As it is considerably coarser than the sand placed on it, this layer prevents the downward percolation of water (*see* water films) and creates a perched watertable. This helps to give the root zone a large reserve of available water whilst ensuring that gravitational water, following heavy rain or excess irrigation, is removed very rapidly.

A 25–30 cm root zone of free-draining sand is placed uniformly over the drainage layer, evenly consolidated. Allowance has to be made for continued settling over the first year. It is essential that the sand used has a suitable particle size distribution, ideally 80–95 per cent of the particles being between 0.1 and 0.6 mm diameter. A minimum of 'fines' is essential to avoid the clogging up of the pores in the root zone (*see* Figure 17.1). Sometimes a small amount of organic matter is worked into the top 5 cm to help establish the

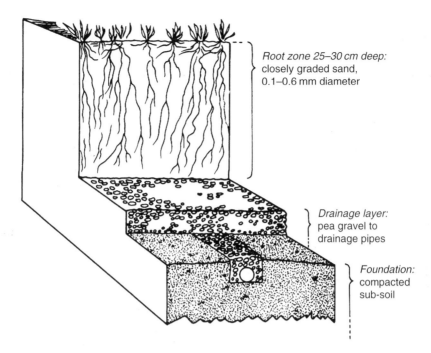

Root zone 25–30 cm deep:
closely graded sand,
0.1–0.6 mm diameter

Drainage layer:
pea gravel to
drainage pipes

Foundation:
compacted
sub-soil

Figure 17.4 *Pure sand root zone.*

grass, although success is probably as easily achieved with no more than regular light irrigation and liquid feeding.

Some very sophisticated all-sand systems, such as the **cell system**, are constructed so that the root zone is subdivided into bays with vertical plastic plates and supplied with drains that can be closed so that the water in each of them can be controlled. Tensiometers are used to activate valves that allow water back into the drainage pipes to sub-irrigate the turf.

FURTHER READING

Bragg, N. *Grower Handbook 1 – Growing Media* (Grower Books, 1998).

Bunt, A.C. *Media and Mixes for Container Grown Plants* (Unwin Hyman, 1988).

Cooper, A. *The ABC of NFT* (Grower Books, 1979).

Handreck, K.A. and Black, N.D. *Growing Media for Ornamentals and Turf*, Revised 3rd edition (New South Wales University Press, 2002).

Mason, J. *Commercial Hydroponics* (Kangaroo Press, 1990).

Pryce, S. *The Peat Alternatives Manual* (Friends of the Earth, 1991).

Smith, D. *Grower Manual 2, Growing in Rockwool* (Grower Books, 1998).

Index

(Page numbers of words that appear in **bold** in the text are **bold** in the index. Page numbers of words that appear as headings in the book are *italic* in the index)